OXFORD WORLD'S CLASSICS

ARTHUR SCHNITZLER

Round Dance
and Other Plays

Translated by
J. M. Q. DAVIES

With an Introduction and Notes by
RITCHIE ROBERTSON

OXFORD
UNIVERSITY PRESS

OXFORD
UNIVERSITY PRESS

Great Clarendon Street, Oxford OX2 6DP

Oxford University Press is a department of the University of Oxford.
It furthers the University's objective of excellence in research, scholarship,
and education by publishing worldwide in

Oxford New York

Auckland Bangkok Buenos Aires Cape Town Chennai
Dar es Salaam Delhi Hong Kong Istanbul Karachi Kolkata
Kuala Lumpur Madrid Melbourne Mexico City Mumbai Nairobi
São Paulo Shanghai Taipei Tokyo Toronto

Oxford is a registered trade mark of Oxford University Press
in the UK and in certain other countries

Published in the United States by Oxford University Press Inc., New York

Translations © J. M. Q. Davies 2004
Editorial material © Ritchie Robertson 2004

First published as an Oxford World's Classics paperback 2004

British Library Cataloguing in Publication Data

Data available

ISBN 0-19-280459-6

1

Typeset in Ehrhardt
by RefineCatch Limited, Bungay, Suffolk
Printed in Great Britain by
Clays Ltd, St Ives plc

OXFORD WORLD'S CLASSICS

ROUND DANCE
AND OTHER PLAYS

ARTHUR SCHNITZLER was born in 1862 into the Jewish professional bourgeoisie of Vienna and somewhat reluctantly followed his father, a distinguished laryngologist, into a medical career. After his father's death in 1893, however, Schnitzler devoted himself largely to literature. Thanks to his love-tragedy *Flirtations* and his series of one-act plays about a Viennese man-about-town, *Anatol*, he acquired a reputation as the chronicler of Viennese decadence which, to his annoyance, stayed with him all his life, despite the variety and originality of his later works. *Round Dance*, written in the late 1890s, exposes sexual life in Vienna with such witty frankness that it could not be staged till after the First World War, when it provoked a riot in the theatre and a prosecution for indecency. Elsewhere Schnitzler explores love, sexuality, and death, sometimes in polished one-act plays such as *The Green Cockatoo*, *The Last Masks*, and *Countess Mizzi*, sometimes in extended social comedies such as *The Vast Domain*, always with a sharp, non-judgemental awareness of the complexity and mystery of the psyche. The ironic comedy *Professor Bernhardi*, based on his and his father's medical experiences, examines the conflict between the secular state and the Church in a period increasingly poisoned by anti-Semitism. His prose fiction ranges from the early stream-of-consciousness narrative *Lieutenant Gustl* (1900), which led him to be deprived of his officer status for satirizing the army, to the enigmatic *Dream Story* (1926), recently adapted by Stanley Kubrick as *Eyes Wide Shut*, and the exploration of a consciousness sinking into madness, *Flight into Darkness* (1931). Schnitzler died in 1931, one of the most famous German-language authors of his day.

J. M. Q. DAVIES read German and Modern Greek at Oxford and spent two years teaching in Vienna, prior to pursuing an academic career in English and Comparative Literature. His publications include *Blake's Milton Designs: The Dynamics of Meaning* (1993) and several translations from German, among them Schnitzler's *Dream Story* (1999) and a selection of his shorter fiction.

RITCHIE ROBERTSON is a Professor of German at Oxford University and a Fellow of St John's College. He is the author of *Kafka: Judaism, Politics, and Literature* (OUP, 1985), *Heine* (Peter Halban, 1988), and *The 'Jewish Question' in German Literature, 1749–1939* (OUP, 1999), and editor of *The Cambridge Companion to Thomas Mann* (CUP, 2002). He has also edited *The German-Jewish Dialogue: An Anthology of Literary Texts, 1749–1993* for the O

OXFORD WORLD'S CLASSICS

For over 100 years Oxford World's Classics have brought
readers closer to the world's great literature. Now with over 700
titles—from the 4,000-year-old myths of Mesopotamia to the
twentieth century's greatest novels—the series makes available
lesser-known as well as celebrated writing.

The pocket-sized hardbacks of the early years contained
introductions by Virginia Woolf, T. S. Eliot, Graham Greene,
and other literary figures which enriched the experience of reading.
Today the series is recognized for its fine scholarship and
reliability in texts that span world literature, drama and poetry,
religion, philosophy and politics. Each edition includes perceptive
commentary and essential background information to meet the
changing needs of readers.

CONTENTS

INTRODUCTION

ALTHOUGH Schnitzler came to literature relatively late, with his first play, *Das Märchen*, performed only when he was 31, his early successes coloured his reputation for the rest of his life. He was constantly described, much to his irritation, as the author of *Anatol* (1888–91), a series of one-act plays about a young Viennese man-about-town (a sexually hyperactive Bertie Wooster figure), and of the love-tragedy *Flirtations* (*Liebelei*, written 1894). Yet his subsequent works included some so innovative in form as to place him among the pioneers of literary modernism, and so satirical in content as to call forth censorship, lawsuits, and denunciation. Foremost among them are his cyclical drama *Round Dance* (*Reigen*, written 1896–7) and the story *Lieutenant Gustl* (*Leutnant Gustl*, 1900), which not only anticipates Joyce's *Ulysses* in its use of interior monologue but also, by using this technique to satirize the idiocy of an army lieutenant and the cult of duelling, created a scandal which cost Schnitzler his rank as an officer of the reserve (that is, liable to be called up in the event of war). 'No writer has ever received so much abuse in the course of his career as I have,' he wrote (diary, 19 November 1917). Up to his death in 1931 he wrote a range of plays and prose narratives, including two full-length novels, which have given him an assured place not only among the significant writers of turn-of-the-century Vienna but among the major modernist writers in the German language.

In recent decades Schnitzler's oeuvre has been enlarged by important posthumous publications. An autobiography covering his early life, *My Youth in Vienna* (*Jugend in Wien*), appeared in 1968. But the great discovery has been his diaries. Their existence in manuscript was well known to scholars, but nobody could be found to finance their publication until the Austrian Academy of Sciences agreed to support a complete edition.[1] They run from 19 March 1879, when Schnitzler was 16, to 19 October 1931, two days before his death. An industrious person has calculated that over this period of 52 years there is an entry for 16,079 days (though 164 of these entries consist only of the date), and that from 1900 to 1931 only 92 days lack an entry.[2] Many entries

---

[1] Arthur Schnitzler, *Tagebuch*, ed. Werner Welzig and others, 10 vols. (Vienna, 1981–2000). Quoted as 'Diary' with date of entry.

[2] Bettina Riedmann, *'Ich bin Jude, Österreicher, Deutscher': Judentum in Arthur Schnitzlers Tagebüchern und Briefen* (Tübingen, 2002), 3.

are merely brief records of activities, social meetings, plays seen or books read, but others give more insight into Schnitzler's emotions and his judgements of his acquaintances, and some are sustained reflections on his psychological constitution and the (usually difficult) state of his relationships. Even when concise, the diaries have a strong personal flavour; besides being an invaluable source for cultural and literary history, they convey some sense of what it was like to be Schnitzler; and recent studies of Schnitzler draw on them with gratitude and fascination.

Schnitzler was born into a medical family of Jewish origin. His father, Johann Schnitzler, was a prominent laryngologist, and his mother, Louise Markbreiter, was a doctor's daughter. His brother Julius, three years his junior, became a surgeon, and his sister Gisela, five years younger, married the rhinologist Markus Hajek. It was taken for granted that Arthur too should study at Vienna's famous Medical School and follow his father's career. Unfortunately, as his diaries make clear, Schnitzler found medicine uncongenial. Though it sharpened his vision and cleared his mind, it did not suit his 'artistic nature' (9 May 1886), and he loathed the prospect of walking the wards and examining patients' sputum. He had many rows with his father, who was annoyed by his lack of application, his dandified elegance, his literary leanings, and his affairs with women. Although Schnitzler worked in the clinic run by his father, and helped to edit his father's medical journal, Johann Schnitzler's death in 1893 gave Arthur a welcome opportunity to leave the clinic and confine himself to private practice.

Paternal authority, however, was hard to escape. The year after his father's death, Schnitzler experienced auditory hallucinations in which voices uttered meaningless sentences, the only distinct voice being that of his father (24 October 1894). Two years later he began to suffer from tinnitus, which became a lifelong affliction, and it may not be extravagant to suspect a psychosomatic connection: having refused to listen to his father's voice during his lifetime, Schnitzler was condemned to hear it incessantly after his death.

Even while officially a full-time physician, Schnitzler was more intrigued by psychology. Like his contemporary Freud, he took an interest in the hypnotic experiments conducted by Jean-Martin Charcot in Paris. Adopting this method, he succeeded in curing some cases of aphonia (in which patients had lost their voice for no discernible organic cause), and went on to induce local anaesthesia and conduct minor operations, including once the painless extraction of a

tooth, while his patients were hypnotized. He also, more mischiev-
ously, instructed patients under hypnosis to murder him or a colleague, ensuring that they had no weapon more dangerous than a blunt
paper-knife. Not surprisingly, these tricks aroused criticism, and he
abandoned hypnosis. He retained, however, his interest in what
another Viennese contemporary, Hugo von Hofmannsthal, called the
'cavernous kingdom of the self'[3] and what his own character Friedrich
Hofreiter calls the 'vast domain' of the soul. In his fiction this interest
underlies the interior monologues of *Lieutenant Gustl* and *Fräulein
Else* (1924), the latter recording the thoughts and feelings of a young
woman in the crisis-ridden hours preceding her suicide; the exploration of the unconscious in *Dream Story* (1926); and his last story,
Flight into Darkness (*Flucht in die Finsternis*, 1931), told from inside the
mind of a man descending into paranoia.

The parallels between Schnitzler and Freud have been much discussed: most famously by Freud himself. On Schnitzler's sixtieth
birthday, Freud sent him a confessional letter, explaining that he had
refrained from seeking Schnitzler's acquaintance from an uneasy feeling that Schnitzler was a kind of double, whose beliefs corresponded
uncannily to his own: 'Your determinism as well as your scepticism—
what people call pessimism—your preoccupation with the truth of the
unconscious and of the instinctual drives in man, your dissection of
the cultural conventions of our society, the dwelling of your thoughts
on the polarity of love and death; all this moves me with an uncanny
feeling of familiarity.'[4] Schnitzler himself had followed Freud's work,
reading *The Interpretation of Dreams* as soon as it came out. Moreover,
both belonged to Vienna's extensive network of highly educated,
liberal-minded Jewish families, and had many personal links. Schnitzler's brother Julius played cards with Freud every Saturday, and it was
his brother-in-law Markus Hajek who examined the cancerous growth
on Freud's jaw (and recognized it as such, according to Ernest Jones,
so belatedly as to make the patient's condition worse).[5] Freud invited
Schnitzler to his house on 16 June 1922, and other pleasant meetings
followed, but Schnitzler shows his ambivalence by writing: 'His whole
character attracted me, and I sense a certain desire to talk with him
about all the abysses of my work (and my existence)—but I don't think

[3] Hugo von Hofmannsthal, letter to Hermann Bahr, 1904, in his *Briefe 1900–1909*
(Vienna, 1937), 155.

[4] *Letters of Sigmund Freud, 1873–1939*, ed. Ernst L. Freud, trans. Tania and James
Stern (London, 1961), 345.

[5] Ernest Jones, *Sigmund Freud: Life and Work*, 3 vols. (London, 1953–7), iii. 98–9.

I will' (diary, 16 August 1922). Psychoanalysts seemed to Schnitzler always close to monomania, especially when they talked about complexes and symbols. There is a touch of monomania, though, in the care Schnitzler takes to record his dreams. The more than 600 dreams recounted, often at some length, make the diaries invaluable as a chronicle not only of conscious but also of unconscious experience.

Schnitzler differed from Freud, however, in his involvement in the cultural life of turn-of-the-century Vienna. In the 1890s he belonged to the circle of writers known as 'Young Vienna' who met in the Café Griensteidl (demolished in 1897, thus occasioning Karl Kraus's satirical attack on Young Vienna, *The Demolition of Literature*, but restored in 1990); they also included the versatile critic, playwright, and novelist Hermann Bahr, the precocious poet and dramatist Hugo von Hofmannsthal, Felix Salten (later famous for writing both the animal tale *Bambi* and the classic pornographic novel *Josefine Mutzenbacher* which was often misattributed to Schnitzler), and numerous others. While their antagonist Kraus championed the vigorous and masculine spirit of Berlin Naturalism, Bahr, the impresario of Young Vienna, argued that Naturalism, the unsparing registration of contemporary life in minute detail, now needed to be transferred from outer to inner experience and must take a psychological turn. Hofmannsthal's lyrical dramas and reflective poems illustrated this programme, as did Schnitzler's studies of indecision and complex motivation.

The psychological insights in Schnitzler's stories and plays derive also from the erotic experience which bulks so hugely in the diaries. The phrase 'sweet maid', used in *Round Dance*, first served Schnitzler to describe Jeanette Heeger, whom he accosted one evening in 1887. It suggests a young woman from the working class or lower middle class who, while working as a shop assistant, seamstress, or possibly actress, has emotionally undemanding, erotically enjoyable relationships with upper-class young men, as Mizi does with Theodor in *Flirtations*. But the case of Jeanette indicates, as does Schnitzler's play, that such relationships were partly a male fantasy. Jeanette's sensuality so fascinated Schnitzler that he took to recording in his diary the number of orgasms (occasionally eight a night, usually about fifty a month) he enjoyed with her and other girlfriends. Not only is there something strange about this urge to turn experiences into facts, and facts into figures, but Schnitzler's diary reports that he soon got bored with Jeanette and broke off the relationship. After a brief, unsuccessful marriage, she took to prostitution; Schnitzler once passed her in the street, ignoring her desperate cry 'Arthur!' (diary, 7 September 1893).

Schnitzler's relationships always overlapped. While still enjoying Jeanette he began a relationship with a patient, Marie Glümer, which lasted intermittently for some ten years. During it, he had a stormy affair with the famous actress Adele Sandrock, known as Dilly, who played the leading lady in his drama *The Fairy-Tale* (*Das Märchen*, 1891). Dilly was an emancipated woman, like the Actress in *Round Dance*, who had no hesitation about taking the sexual initiative. She resembled the 'interesting women' who so torment Fritz in *Flirtations*. Schnitzler wrote that play during their affair, and when it was over, Dilly played what might seem the incongruous role of Christine. By then, to his relief, Schnitzler had passed her on to Felix Salten, and another patient, Marie Reinhard, had become his great (though not exclusive) love. In 1897 Schnitzler spent an afternoon arranging both care for the child Marie was going to bear him, and a lodging for secret rendezvous with Rosa Freudenthal, with whom he had begun a passionate affair that summer: he felt the situation would suit a farce (diary, 31 August 1897). But the farce turned serious. Marie's child was stillborn. Schnitzler records his unexpected emotion on seeing the dead baby and kissing its cheek (diary, 24 September 1897). Two years later Marie herself died. Schnitzler visited her grave every year. He also fictionalized the story in his novel *The Road into the Open* (*Der Weg ins Freie*, 1908). Whether doing so was therapeutic, or whether turning his experience into fiction simply continued the brooding on the past that becomes increasingly evident in the diaries, is an open question.

Not long after Marie's death, Schnitzler, perhaps on the rebound, began a relationship with Olga Gussmann, twenty years his junior, who became his wife and the mother of two children, Heinrich and Lili. Marriage gave Schnitzler some unforeseen happiness. 'Every feeling can be anticipated, except one's feeling for one's own child,' he wrote (diary, 15 February 1907). But the marriage was not easy. Schnitzler was clearly a difficult character. What he calls 'hypochondria', the self-tormenting temperament that made him bait his girlfriends with jealous remarks about their previous lovers, also soured his marriage. Olga for her part felt, rightly or wrongly, that by marrying Schnitzler she had sacrificed her own career as a singer. Eventually she began an affair with Wilhelm Gross, a pianist, closer to her own age. Her marriage to Schnitzler was officially dissolved in 1921. The prolonged marital crisis is recorded in long and painful diary entries: Schnitzler mentions that every morning for over a year he would wake up weeping with anger. It also affected the children. Heinrich ('Heini') was older and more resilient, but Lili, her father's pet, took to behaving strangely (for example, secretly cutting off her pigtail and claiming that a stranger had removed it in the street) and developed alarming fantasies about sex and violence. She fell madly in love with an Italian Fascist officer whom she met on holiday in Venice, and insisted on marrying him; after a year of unhappy marriage, she shot herself with his pistol. Here Schnitzler's diary becomes eloquent through its very concision.

By a strange irony, Schnitzler had anticipated this situation—the suicide of a beloved daughter, the despair of her surviving father— over thirty years before in *Flirtations*, a play which illustrates the pervasiveness of death in his literary work. His first major story, *Dying* (*Sterben*, written 1892), tells impassively how the slow death of an invalid degrades his character and alienates his lover. Most often, however, death in Schnitzler comes suddenly, as an accident or, surprisingly often, in a duel. In part, Schnitzler intended to deride the code of honour which required an officer (including officers of the reserve, like Fritz and Theodore in *Flirtations*) to avenge an insult unless it came from someone whose lower social standing disqualified him from giving satisfaction. The rules of duelling were codified in handbooks and regulated by courts of honour. An officer who killed his opponent in a duel could expect to be pardoned by the Emperor.

Schnitzler's preoccupation with death, however, extends far beyond social criticism. It is a prominent theme throughout modern German literature, from Thomas Mann's *Death in Venice* (*Der Tod in Venedig*, 1912) to Hermann Broch's *The Death of Virgil* (*Der Tod des Vergil*, 1945). Hofmannsthal's early play *The Fool and Death* (*Der Tor und der Tod*, 1894) presents Death both as a judge of how one has lived and as promising an experience of Dionysiac intensity; Rilke deplores the mass-produced character of death in the modern city and advocates an individualistic concentration on a death of one's own; and Heidegger urges living towards death as the condition of authentic existence. Schnitzler's secular, liberal background immunized him against the suggestions of mysticism that haunt these constructions, and his medical training helped him to look clear-sightedly at how death happens. But what fascinates him is the discrepancy between this terminal, incommensurable event and the life that goes on around it. In *Flirtations*, the messenger of death, the gentleman who challenges Fritz to a duel, interrupts a party which continues after his departure. In *Professor Bernhardi* the death of a hospital patient whom we never see instigates a series of scandals. And in *The Vast Domain* (*Das weite Land*) the suicide of Korsakow, another character who dominates the play in which he does not appear, is discussed in an atmosphere of tennis doubles and sexual pairing. Schnitzler differs from his contemporaries in facing the modern situation in which the decline of religious ritual has left death exposed as a monstrous and inadmissible fact.

Of the present selection, the play that places death most firmly in the foreground is *The Last Masks* (*Die letzten Masken*). Dying in a hospital ward, the failed writer Karl Rademacher wants to vent his bitterness against his successful rival Weihgast. To help him practise, his fellow-patient Jackwerth, an actor, plays the part of Weihgast, so that Rademacher can unload his anger, culminating in the revelation that he was the lover of Weihgast's wife. But all this is rehearsal for a première that never comes. When Weihgast does arrive, full of phoney eloquence, Rademacher has not the heart to take revenge. On Weihgast's departure, he prepares to die. But what was the last mask? Rademacher's anger or his resignation?

Death and love coexist also in *Flirtations*. Of the two young men, Theodore advocates shallow and trouble-free relationships (though even he makes obsessive allusions to Mizi's past affairs), while Fritz is drawn not only to stormy, dramatic relationships but to wanton games with danger. Conversely, the exuberant Mizi despises men and warns Christine against emotional involvement, while Christine, on a very brief acquaintance, has become fatally devoted to Fritz. She does not know of his affair with a married woman, yet this woman, who never appears in the play, dominates its events.

The time scale covers six days. On the first, Fritz went to the theatre, where Mizi and Christine, from their cheap seats in the gallery, observed him in a box with a party including a lady in black velvet. Instead of joining them and Theodore for supper after the play, he stood them up, and, we learn, had a convivial dinner with the lady (his lover) and her supposedly unsuspecting husband. Act One is set on the evening of the following day. Earlier, Fritz and Theodore have been out to the country; then, in the afternoon, his lover visited Fritz, in mortal terror in case her husband had discovered their relationship and was watching from the street. Fritz, left alone, is still recovering from this scene when Theodore arrives, soon followed by Mizi and Christine. The lady's fears were justified, for the impromptu party is interrupted by a visit from the injured husband, who returns his wife's letters and requires Fritz to fight a duel. The intruder has been seen as an 'allegorical Death figure'.[6] There is an echo of the ghostly

---

[6] Martin Swales, *Arthur Schnitzler: A Critical Study* (Oxford, 1971), 186.

Commendatore who interrupts Don Giovanni's dinner in Mozart's opera. But the real disruption comes from the fury and loathing which the injured husband can barely control and which burst out in an inarticulate shriek, revealing the elemental passions hidden under polite formulae.

On the third day (Act Two) Fritz pays a surprise visit to Christine in her humble suburban room. Childishly vulnerable in her affection, she can elicit from him only the admission that *she* loves *him*, and when she tries to find out something about his life, he tells her only that he is briefly leaving for his parents' country estate. He knows, but she does not, that a duel has been arranged for early the following morning. In Act Three, set on the sixth day, Christine, wondering why Fritz has not returned, faces a series of evasions. First Mizi cynically (but still ignorantly) warns her that Fritz and Theodore have probably abandoned them; then her father, knowing of Fritz's death, tries to prepare her for a life without him, but only makes her suspicious. Theodore reports Fritz's death but pretends not to know the reason for the duel; Christine voices suspicions about another woman which she has no doubt long nourished, and which are accurate. It would be funny, were it not for the tragedy of the situation, that Theodore commits one blunder after another. He tells Christine that Fritz 'talked about you too', offers the useless consolation 'He was certainly very fond of you', talks self-pityingly about his own emotional state, and explains that Fritz's funeral was attended only by his closest friends and relatives. Christine suffers not only grief but humiliation, realizing that her devotion to Fritz was undervalued even by him. Yet Schnitzler's double optic permits us not only to respond to her pathos and anger but to feel, as Dagmar Lorenz suggests, that she has been trying to live by theatrical conventions of unconditional love which have their place in melodrama but prove fatal in reality, or at least in a realist play.[7] In this spirit, she affirms that she will never love anyone else, darkly hinting that she wants to visit his grave only to die there.

Flirtations confirms the judgements passed by an acute critic, the novelist and psychoanalyst Lou Andreas-Salomé, after reading Schnitzler's earlier dramas. She praised his lightness of touch: 'One feels, as when dancing, that the heaviness of an object has been lifted.' She also noted how negative was Schnitzler's portrayal of men: 'Man

---

[7] Dagmar C. G. Lorenz, 'The Self as Process in an Era of Transition', in Lorenz (ed.), *A Companion to the Works of Arthur Schnitzler* (Rochester, NY, 2003), 129–47 (p. 133).

and woman, thus opposed, almost resemble sickness versus health.'[8]
Like Fedor Denner, the ostensibly enlightened but in fact hopelessly
selfish lover in *The Fairy-Tale*, which Lou read, Fritz is a morbid, self-
destructive character whose mood is lightened only when he is with
the natural, spontaneous Christine. In an echo of Goethe's *Faust*, Fritz
enjoys the simplicity of Christine's room, as Faust is enraptured by
the simple neatness of Gretchen's room. Nature is invoked when they
also spend time in a park on the edge of the city, where children play
and lilac blooms. Its antithesis is the sombre, deathly black worn by the
married lady at the theatre and shown on stage in Theodore's funereal
garb in Act Three.

Death again broods over the ten interlocked scenes of *Round Dance*.
Not only is it referred to in the first scene, where the Soldier thinks
that falling into the Danube might be the best thing, and the last,
where the Count, seeing the Prostitute asleep, is reminded of sleep's
allegorical brother Death. But for readers in the 1890s the sexual
roundabout would inevitably have suggested the danger of venereal
infection, especially since syphilis would resist medical treatment for
another decade. Reviewing a medical study of syphilis in 1891, Schnitzler stressed that, despite myths to the contrary, syphilis spread most
readily through extramarital sexual intercourse.[9] He was himself
rightly afraid of infection, though such fears did not prevent him from
picking up prostitutes (diary, 12 March 1896).

In each of the expertly composed scenes, however, we observe the
contrast between before and after the sexual act. Schnitzler owned a
copy of Hogarth's engravings 'Before' and 'After', where prior resist-
ance is contrasted with subsequent satisfaction (diary, 1 July 1917).[10]
Flattery and cajolery are used to get partners into bed. Masks are
donned: the Young Master asserts his devotion in high-flown language,
the Husband warns his wife with affected prudery against consorting
with immoral women, and confesses his own past misdemeanours in a
way that perhaps adds energy to his own love-making; when picking
up the Sweet Maid he falls into colloquial Viennese which makes his
marital language sound even more false in retrospect. We also hear
lines repeated: the Sweet Maid tells the Husband and the Poet almost
the same story about having been in a *chambre séparée* only with her
friend and the friend's fiancé; the Poet applies the term 'divine

---

[8] Unpublished letter to Schnitzler, 15 May 1894, quoted in Ulrich Weinzierl, *Arthur
Schnitzler: Lieben Träumen Sterben* (Frankfurt a.M., 1994), 92.

[9] Schnitzler, *Medizinische Schriften*, ed. Horst Thomé (Vienna, 1988), 249–50.

[10] See Jenny Uglow, *Hogarth: A Life and a World* (London, 1997), 178–81.

simplicity' to both her and the Actress. After the act, the men often turn cool and distant, rebuffing the women's emotional appeals, sometimes with the help of a post-coital cigarette. As soon as the Young Master and the Young Wife have had their delayed sex, she starts panicking about the time and about what she will tell her husband. Despite saying this must be the last time, she readily agrees to dance with him the next day and arrange another assignation (and as W. E. Yates points out, she has brought her own button-hook with her for getting dressed again).[11] And when she has gone, the Young Master says with the self-satisfied air of one recording a social triumph: 'So here I am, having an affair with a respectable married woman.' The professional vanity of the Poet and the Actress soon blurs their sexual enjoyment. The scene between the Actress and the Count brings a variation because she has to seduce him. That between the Prostitute and the Count brings another: there is no coupling on stage, and the Count likes to think that none has happened, that he has only kissed her tenderly on the eyes, but it turns out that he did have sex with her before falling asleep: the sex drive is all-powerful.

Schnitzler's erotic realism includes an unsparing portrayal of male sexuality. The husband, idealizing his wife but letting himself go with the Sweet Maid, illustrates the conflict between affection and sensuality described by Freud in 'On the Universal Tendency to Debasement in the Sphere of Love' (1912) which polarizes male images of women between madonnas and whores. Similarly, the Young Master suffers erectile failure on his first attempt to copulate with a 'respectable' woman. Small wonder that the play was initially banned and then, when performed in 1921, provoked a scandal.

While *Round Dance* follows the sexual daisy-chain or chain-gang through a wide range of society, Schnitzler elsewhere writes with particular fascination, but no great respect, about the aristocracy. *The Green Cockatoo* (*Der grüne Kakadu*) is set among the French aristocracy on the eve of the Revolution, *Countess Mizzi* (*Komtesse Mizzi*) among the contemporary Viennese upper class. Both are shown to be permeated with pretence. The restaurant 'The Green Cockatoo' attracts aristocratic clients by employing actors disguised as revolutionaries to give the diners an agreeable thrill by uttering bloodthirsty threats. Reality and illusion, however, are difficult to disentangle. Henri claims to have murdered the Duke of Cadignan for

<hr />

[11] W. E. Yates, *Schnitzler, Hofmannsthal and the Austrian Theatre* (New Haven, 1992), 134.

sleeping with his wife, and the landlord believes him. It turns out, however, that Henri was only acting. He alone did not know that his wife was unfaithful to him. On learning the truth, he stabs the Duke. But death, the touchstone of reality, is not immediately effective. The audience at first take this as part of the performance, and when real revolutionaries rush in, straight from the fall of the Bastille, they too are initially thought to be actors.

Countess Mizzi at first seems content with painting. Her father is puzzled that she has never married, and indeed she once considered becoming a nun. To the actress Lolo Langhuber, however, Mizzi hints that she has had a satisfying sex life, and we meet its product, the natural son she has had with Prince Ravenstein; we also see her calmly ending the affair with her art teacher. All this might suggest the civilized management of one's emotions, but in fact Mizzi feels bitter, with good reason, towards the Prince for refusing to leave his wife and accept responsibility for his son, whom Mizzi has never till now been allowed to know. When she talks in veiled terms to her father about the callousness with which the boy's mother has been treated, he replies even more callously, supposing the mother to have been a lower-class woman, 'These women usually die young anyway.' This brilliant play exposes selfishness and manipulation with an understated adroitness worthy of Thackeray.

With *The Vast Domain* we enter the world of industrialists and financiers who spend much of their time at the holiday resort of Baden, near Vienna, or in the Tyrolean Alps. Alongside tennis and mountaineering, their favourite sport is adultery. Friedrich Hofreiter, having ended his affair with Adele Natter, takes up with the young Erna Wahl; his wife Genia, having rejected the pianist Korsakow, starts an affair with the naval lieutenant Otto von Aigner; the officer Stanzides takes Friedrich's place with Adele Natter. Although Genia suggests that mutual indifference might be the best foundation for a marriage, and describes love affairs as an amusing game, this sexual circus is driven by emotions which prove dangerous playthings. The characters repeatedly discourse on how puzzling emotions are. We fail to feel what we officially ought to, and we are assailed by unexpected feelings that initiate fatal actions. Genia's rejection of Korsakow prompted his suicide. Although Dr Mauer is Friedrich's closest friend, Friedrich has no compunction about starting an affair with the woman to whom he knows Mauer is attracted. The banker Natter knows about his wife's infidelities yet is still hopelessly in love with her, and cares enough to avenge himself on Friedrich by planting a story that Friedrich brought about Korsakow's death by challenging him to an American duel and then cheating. (In an American duel, to remove any advantage arising from superior skill with weapons, both parties drew lots and the loser was obliged to commit suicide.) When Friedrich challenges Otto to a duel, he has no strong feelings, simply a desire not to be made a fool of, but when they face each other Friedrich knows that one or the other must die.

Not only the 'vast domain' of the soul, but the presence of death, sets the tone of the play. Tom Stoppard did well to entitle his English version *Undiscovered Country*, after Hamlet's soliloquy on suicide. The play begins just after Korsakow's funeral. Friedrich has recently had a narrow escape from death in a motor accident. Further back, he was in a mountaineering accident in which a friend was killed. In Act Three, set in the Dolomites, he and his party turn out to have climbed the Aignerturm, a notoriously dangerous pinnacle. Mountaineering is associated with sex, both by the legendary sexual conquests of Aigner, who first climbed the pinnacle, and by the embrace between Friedrich and Erna outside their mountain hut. Against this background, Friedrich seems like a grown-up version of Fritz from *Flirtations*, compulsively playing with danger.

In *Professor Bernhardi*, the off-stage death in Act One enables Schnitzler to address a crucial issue of his time, namely anti-Semitism. Though Schnitzler encountered no anti-Semitism at school, he watched as anti-Semitism entered public discourse in the rhetoric of Georg von Schönerer's German Nationalist Party, founded in 1882, and, still more, in the populist speeches of Karl Lueger, who was Mayor of Vienna from 1897 till his death in 1910. In a letter of 12 January 1899, Schnitzler wrote to the Danish critic Georg Brandes:

Do you ever read Viennese newspapers, reports on Parliament and the City Council? It is astonishing what swine we live among here; and I keep thinking even anti-Semites should notice that anti-Semitism, apart from everything else, has the strange power of drawing forth the meanest and most dishonest aspects of human nature and developing them to an extreme.[12]

In his autobiography Schnitzler quotes with particular indignation from the 'Waidhofen Resolution' drawn up by German nationalist duelling societies which declared Jews to lack honour: 'Every son of a Jewish mother, every human being in whose veins flows Jewish blood,

---

[12] Schnitzler, *Briefe 1875–1912*, ed. Therese Nickl and Heinrich Schnitzler (Frankfurt a.M., 1981), 366.

is from the day of his birth without honour and void of all the more refined emotions.'[13] According to Schnitzler, in turn-of-the-century Vienna it was impossible to forget that one was a Jew. During and after the War, things got worse. A notoriously anti-Semitic Jesuit, Father Abel, asserted in a sermon that the Jews had not done their duty during the war, were to blame for the country's misery, and should be exterminated (diary, 16 July 1918). Schnitzler and others feared pogroms. His worst direct experience of anti-Semitism came in 1922 when a public reading he gave in Teplice (in Czechoslovakia) was broken up by National Socialists, an event described at length in his diary (3 November 1922).

In *Bernhardi* Schnitzler draws on his own medical experience and that of his father. In 1872 Johann Schnitzler helped to found a private clinic, the Polyclinic, as Bernhardi does the Elisabethinum, and in 1884 he became its director, having already received a professorship for his medical achievements. He resembled Bernhardi also in having aristocratic private patients, in what his son calls his 'amiable, slightly ironic way of conversing',[14] and in the secular principles which he formulated thus:

The physician's religion is humanity, that is, the love of mankind, irrespective of wealth or poverty, with no distinction of nationality or confession. Accordingly, whenever and wherever the conflicts of classes and races, national chauvinism and religious fanaticism prevail, he should and must be an apostle of humanity, acting in support of international peace and the brotherhood of man.[15]

These principles are tested in the play. In Act One, a young woman is dying from a botched abortion. She has no emotional support; her lover has disappeared. She cannot live more than another hour, but has no idea that she is dying, for a camphor injection has put her in a state of euphoria. A nurse who belongs to a Catholic lay sisterhood fetches a priest to give the young woman the last rites. Bernhardi thinks it cruel to take her out of her euphoria and frighten her; he asserts that it is his duty as a doctor to give his patients a happy death, and he therefore explicitly forbids the priest to enter the sick-room, touching him lightly on the shoulder to deter him. What further means of

---

[13] Schnitzler, *My Youth in Vienna*, trans. Catherine Hutter (London, 1971), 128. Cf. diary, 30 Mar. 1896.

[14] *My Youth in Vienna*, 168.

[15] 'Johann Schnitzlers Bekenntnis zum Arztberuf', 10 Dec. 1884, in Hans-Ulrich Lindken, *Arthur Schnitzler: Aspekte und Akzente* (Frankfurt a.M., 1984), 3–4.

deterrence Bernhardi might have used we never learn, for at that point
the nurse reports that the young woman is dead. Neither Bernhardi
nor the priest has attained his object: the woman died in fear but
without receiving the sacraments. Nevertheless, this confrontation
between a Jewish doctor and a priest is blown up into a huge scandal,
with a question asked in Parliament, an official inquiry, and a court
case in which Bernhardi is sentenced to two months' imprisonment
and forbidden to practise medicine.

Bernhardi is neither a crusader nor a martyr: released from prison,
he wants only to return to private life, though his associates want him
to use media opportunities to promote his beliefs. Politics are seen as
inherently corrupting, the domain of the eel-like Flint, while the
staunch old liberal Pflugfelder is a forlorn and ineffectual figure. In the
Vienna that Schnitzler shows us, principles exist only in personal life
and the public world is dominated by rhetoricians without inner sub-
stance. His depiction reflects his long-felt contempt for politics as
such: 'It is the lowest thing and has the least to do with the *essence* of
humanity' (diary, 10 May 1896). Yet in supposing that he can exercise
his principles privately without wider repercussions, Bernhardi shows
a naivety which is caricatured in the cluelessness of his protégé
Wenger.

Schnitzler was stimulated to write the play in part by the
'Wahrmund affair' (diary, 18 March 1908). In January 1908 Ludwig
Wahrmund (1860–1932), professor of canon law at Innsbruck University, gave a public lecture in which he declared that Catholic dogma
was incompatible with free scholarship; there followed demonstrations
and counter-demonstrations, a question was asked in Parliament,
there was a general strike at the universities; in June, Wahrmund was
transferred to Prague. He secretly accepted 10,000 Kronen annually to
finance research leave for up to two years, and an annual pension of
2,000 Kronen if he retired thereafter. When these payments became
known, Wahrmund gave them up. In place of this discreditable com-
promise, Bernhardi stands by his principles and serves a prison sentence. The affair encouraged Schnitzler to dramatize the conflict
between humanist and Catholic principles.

Above all, professional and public life in the play are dominated by
the Jewish question. Even a disagreement between two doctors about a
patient's diagnosis turns into a Jewish–Gentile dispute. Here the
detailed stage directions which Schnitzler, like his contemporaries
Shaw and Hauptmann, provides, enable us to recognize degrees of
'Jewishness', assimilation, or 'Austrianness', from the shambling

posture of Dr Löwenstein or the 'beery German' with occasional Jewish tones uttered by the convert Dr Schreimann to the exaggerated
Austrian accent of Dr Ebenwald. In the lawyer Goldenthal, who is
baptized, ostentatiously Catholic, and sends his son to an exclusive
Jesuit-run school, we have a specimen of a type Schnitzler detested,
the Jew who lacks self-respect and at all costs curries favour with
Christians.

Bernhardi, the enlightened Jewish scientist, is given no 'Jewish'
traits, a tribute to the universalist humanism which Schnitzler shared
with his father and with Freud. Large questions stemming from the
conflict between science and religion loom over the play. Bernhardi
remarks ironically that the complicated nature of illness might make
one question Providence. His patron Prince Constantine warns him
that a few hundred years earlier he would have been burnt at the stake,
and we have several references to how the Church in the past persecuted scientists. Bernhardi's antagonist the Priest is represented as a
decent man, yet he justifies his conduct in court in a manner too
reminiscent of Flint's opportunism, by saying that his trivial truth
would have turned into a greater lie. Despite the reconciliation
between the Priest and Bernhardi on a human level in Act Four, the
play is heavily weighted in favour of Bernhardi's secular humanism.
His attempt to protect his patient is twice defended at length, once by
Cyprian and once by Pflugfelder. Bernhardi's key word is 'Glück'
(happiness). Reflecting on the young woman who is dying, Bernhardi
says sadly that such an experience—the sexual encounter with an
unfaithful, perhaps anonymous lover—was once called 'Liebesglück',
'the joys of love': that is, the young girl too wanted to be happy,
following a normal human instinct, and as a doctor he cannot save her
life, but only allow her a few moments of happiness based on an
illusion. Here the scientific search for truth reaches an aporia in which
it seems better to be happily deluded.

Bernhardi was in some ways Schnitzler's favourite among his plays:
'There are works of mine I like better, but nowhere do I like myself
better than in *Bernhardi*' (diary, 27 March 1918). It is the most open
in its assertion of Schnitzler's sceptical, humane, though not entirely
tolerant liberalism. But it shares with his other masterpieces the abil-
ity to capture the trivial day-to-day surface of human life (Schnitzler's
ear for dialogue has few rivals in German–language drama) while
drawing attention to its boundaries: the frontier represented by death,
and the search for an elusive happiness in love. Utopian hopes for
reforming human life receive no encouragement here, but nor are the

plays cynical. Their most attractive characters combine disillusion-ment and decency, like the actress Lolo Langhuber (who shows her natural good feeling by almost her first remark, expressing disgust at a schoolboy's morbid interest in murderers), and the doctor Kurt Pflugfelder, who has shed his father's liberalism, is indeed a reformed anti-Semite, but denounces and challenges the proto-fascist Hochroitzpointner.

Although Schnitzler is an important figure in Modernism, he remains difficult to classify. His oeuvre is diverse, including two sub-stantial novels of which one, *Therese*, is still undervalued, but lacking any large-scale work to stand beside such massive Modernist monu-ments as *Ulysses, Remembrance of Things Past*, or *The Magic Mountain*. Nevertheless, in 1914, when apparently Austria was due for the Nobel Prize for Literature, Schnitzler learnt that the Nobel Committee were considering dividing the prize between himself and the Viennese sketch-writer Peter Altenberg (diary, 1 August 1914); but the outbreak of war prevented the award of any prize that year. In retrospect, however, the absence of any overwhelming masterpiece fits with the lightness, variety, and constant experimentation of his work.

Schnitzler's Modernism is in any case qualified by the form of his plays, which stand between conservatism and innovation. *Bernhardi* owes much to Ibsen, particularly to his *An Enemy of the People*.[16] *Flirtations* and *The Vast Domain* are constructed with skilful crafts-manship, learned from the French comedy of manners; *Flirtations* is also indebted to the classic German domestic tragedy (Lessing's *Emilia Galotti* (1772), Schiller's *Cabals and Love* (*Kabale und Liebe*, 1784), Hebbel's *Maria Magdalena* (1844)) which usually features a cross-class love affair and a close father–daughter relationship. Else-where Schnitzler developed the potential of the one-act play. After a brief vogue in the mid-nineteenth century, this form was revived by the moderns.[17] It matched their scepticism by its brief, tentative char-acter, tending to evoke an atmosphere rather than enunciate a world-view. *The Green Cockatoo, Countess Mizzi*, and *The Last Masks* are all one-acters, the last-named from a series called *Living Hours* (*Lebendige Stunden*), while *Round Dance* is essentially an artfully linked series of one-act plays. The one-acter as a genre shows Schnitzler's especial

[16] For a comparison, see Ritchie Robertson, *The 'Jewish Question' in German Litera-ture, 1749–1939* (Oxford, 1999), 106–12.

[17] See W. E. Yates, 'The Rise and Fall of the One-Act Play', in W. E. Yates, Allyson Fiddler, and John Warren (eds.), *From Perinet to Jelinek: Viennese Theatre in its Political and Intellectual Context* (Bern, 2001), 115–26.

dramatic talents: his economy, his command of dialogue, and his focus, sharpened by his medical training, on the body as the site of the crucial experiences of life and death. This concentration on essentials has saved Schnitzler's best works from dating, even though they are set in a highly specific milieu, and helps to explain why they have been adapted in our day by Tom Stoppard (in *Undiscovered Country*) and Stanley Kubrick (whose *Eyes Wide Shut* is based on the late novella *Dream Story*).

But Schnitzler also reaches across the generations to address a widespread mood of the present day. His semi-outsider position as a Jew (felt more intensely later in his life), and the detachment inculcated by his medical training, no doubt contributed to the tolerant scepticism with which he regarded the many ideologies—Germanic nationalism, conservatism, Socialism, Zionism—that demanded allegiance from his contemporaries. In the literary world around him, he perceived the petty motives underlying exalted aims: the snobbery behind his friend Hofmannsthal's involvement in the Catholicizing Salzburg Festival, or the ruthless careerism behind the love for humanity professed by the Expressionist dramatists. Noting that Hofmannsthal had obtained permission to have a play staged in Salzburg Cathedral by making a contribution to the church restoration fund, Schnitzler denounced his opportunism and added: 'That is how most sacrifices look when you see them close up' (diary, 17 August 1922). His great theme, in his plays and still more in his prose fiction, is self-deception. He unmasks it, however, without the scathing violence of Nietzsche, or the often tiresome self-assurance of Shaw, but with scepticism about his own claims to offer any final insight. Underneath the last mask there is always another. To readers dubious about grand narratives, and worried about new fanaticisms and new crusades, Schnitzler's resigned, intelligent tolerance is bound to have a lasting appeal.

NOTE ON THE TEXT

ALL translations in this volume are based on the texts published in Arthur Schnitzler, *Die Dramatischen Werke*, 2 vols. (Frankfurt a.M.: Fischer, 1962).

SELECT BIBLIOGRAPHY

English Translations and Adaptations of Schnitzler

Anatol, trans. Frank Marcus (London, 1982).
Beatrice and her Son, trans. Shaun Whiteside (London, 1999).
Casanova's Return to Venice, trans. Ilsa Barea (London, 1998).
Dream Story, trans. J. M. Q. Davies (London, 1999).
Dr. Graesler, trans. E. C. Slade (New York, 1930).
The Final Plays, trans. G. J. Weinberger (Riverside, Calif., 1996).
Flight into Darkness, trans. William A. Drake (London, 1932).
Fräulein Else (London, 1998).
My Youth in Vienna, trans. Catherine Hutter (London, 1971).
Night Games and Other Stories and Novellas, trans. Margret Schaefer (Chicago, 2002).
Plays, trans. William Cunningham and David Palmer (Evanston, Ill., 2003): includes *Anatol*.
The Road into the Open, trans. Roger Byers (Berkeley, 1992).
The Round Dance and Other Plays, trans. Charles Osborne (Manchester, 1982).
Selected Short Fiction, trans. J. M. Q. Davies (London, 1999).
Theresa: The Chronicle of a Woman's Life (London, 1929).
Stoppard, Tom, *Dalliance* and *Undiscovered Country*, adapted from Arthur Schnitzler (London, 1986).

Critical Studies

Fliedl, Konstanze, 'Love's Labour's Lost: Translations of Schnitzler's *Reigen*', *Austrian Studies*, 4 (1993), 61–72.
Foster, Ian, and Florian Krobb (eds.), *Arthur Schnitzler: Zeitgenossenschaften/Contemporaneities* (Bern, 2002).
Grimstad, Kari, 'The Institution of Marriage in Schnitzler's *Komtesse Mizzi oder der Familientag* and *Das weite Land*', *Modern Austrian Literature*, 25/3–4 (1994), 141–56.
Lorenz, Dagmar C. G. (ed.), *A Companion to the Works of Arthur Schnitzler* (Rochester, NY, 2003).
Nehring, Wolfgang, 'Schnitzler, Freud's alter ego?', *Modern Austrian Literature*, 10/3–4 (1977), 179–94.
——'Arthur Schnitzler and the French Revolution', *Modern Austrian Literature*, 25/3–4 (1994), 75–94.
Ossar, Michael, 'Individual and Type in Arthur Schnitzler's *Liebelei*', *Modern Austrian Literature*, 30/2 (1997), 19–34.
Otis, Laura, 'The Language of Infection: Disease and Identity in Schnitzler's *Reigen*', *Germanic Review*, 70 (1995), 65–75.
Robertson, Ritchie, 'Schnitzler's Honesty', in Alan Deighton (ed.), *Order from*

Confusion: Essays presented to Edward McInnes on the Occasion of his Sixtieth Birthday (Hull, 1995), 162–85.

Roe, Ian F., 'The Comedy of Schnitzler's *Reigen*', *Modern Language Review*, 89 (1994), 674–88.

Schwarz, Egon, '1921: The staging of Arthur Schnitzler's play *Reigen* in Vienna creates a public uproar that draws involvement by the press, the police, the Viennese city administration, and the Austrian parliament', in Sander L. Gilman and Jack Zipes (eds.), *The Yale Companion to Jewish Writing and Thought in German Culture, 1096–1996* (New Haven, 1997), 412–19.

Stern, Guy, 'From Austria to America via London: Tom Stoppard's Adaptations of Nestroy and Schnitzler', in Wolfgang Elfe, James Hardin, and Gunther Holst (eds.), *The Fortunes of German Writers in America: Studies in Literary Reception* (Columbia, SC, 1992), 167–83.

Swales, Martin, *Arthur Schnitzler: A Critical Study* (Oxford, 1971).

—— 'Schnitzler's Tragi-Comedy: A Reading of *Das weite Land*', *Modern Austrian Literature*, 10/3–4 (1977), 233–45.

Thompson, Bruce, *Schnitzler's Vienna: Image of a Society* (London, 1990).

Wisely, Andrew C., *Arthur Schnitzler and the Discourse of Honor and Duelling* (New York, 1996).

Yates, W. E., 'Changing Perspectives: The "doppelte Sexualmoral" in 1841 and 1895. *Das Mädl aus der Vorstadt* and *Liebelei*', in Hanne Castein and Alexander Stillmark (eds.), *Erbe und Umbruch in der neueren deutschsprachigen Komödie: Londoner Symposium 1987* (Stuttgart, 1990), 17–31.

—— 'The Tendentious Reception of *Professor Bernhardi*', *Austrian Studies*, 1 (1990), 108–25.

—— *Schnitzler, Hofmannsthal, and the Austrian Theatre* (New Haven, 1992).

Cultural and Historical Background

Barea, Ilsa, *Vienna: Legend and Reality* (London, 1966).

Beller, Steven, *Vienna and the Jews, 1867–1938: A Cultural History* (Cambridge, 1989).

Finney, Gail, *Women in Modern Drama: Freud, Feminism, and European Theater at the Turn of the Century* (Ithaca, NY, 1989).

Frevert, Ute, *Men of Honour: A Social and Cultural History of the Duel*, trans. Anthony Williams (Cambridge, 1995).

Geehr, Richard S., *Karl Lueger, Mayor of Fin de Siècle Vienna* (Detroit, 1990).

Hamann, Brigitte, *Hitler's Vienna: A Dictator's Apprenticeship*, trans. Thomas Thornton (New York, 1999).

Janik, Allan, and Stephen Toulmin, *Wittgenstein's Vienna* (London, 1973).

Le Rider, Jacques, *Modernity and Crises of Identity: Culture and Society in Fin-de-Siècle Vienna*, trans. Rosemary Morris (Cambridge, 1993).

Otis, Laura, *Membranes: Metaphors of Invasion in Nineteenth-Century Literature, Science, and Politics* (Baltimore, 1999).

Pauley, Bruce F., *From Prejudice to Persecution: A History of Austrian Anti-Semitism* (Chapel Hill, NC, 1993).

Robertson, Ritchie, *The 'Jewish Question' in German Literature, 1749–1939: Emancipation and its Discontents* (Oxford, 1999).

Ryan, Judith, *The Vanishing Subject: Early Psychology and Literary Modernism* (Chicago, 1991).

Schorske, Carl E., *Fin-de-siècle Vienna: Politics and Culture* (Cambridge, 1981).

Yates, W. E., *Theatre in Vienna: A Critical History 1776–1995* (Cambridge, 1996).

Further Reading in Oxford World's Classics

Freud, Sigmund, *The Interpretation of Dreams*, trans. Joyce Crick, ed. Ritchie Robertson.

The German-Jewish Dialogue, trans. and ed. Ritchie Robertson.

A CHRONOLOGY OF
ARTHUR SCHNITZLER

1862   15 May: Arthur Schnitzler born in Vienna, son of Dr Johann
        Schnitzler (1835–93), a laryngologist, and Louise Schnitzler née
        Markbreiter (1838–1911).

1865   13 July: birth of AS's brother Julius (d. 1939).

1867   20 December: birth of AS's sister Gisela (d. 1953).

1879   AS begins studying medicine at Vienna University.

1885   Graduates from the Vienna Medical School; begins work in the
        Allgemeines Krankenhaus (General Hospital).

1887   Becomes editor of the medical journal *International Clinical Review*
        (*Internationale Klinische Rundschau*), founded by his father.

1888   Becomes an assistant in the Allgemeine Poliklinik, directed by his
        father. Visits Berlin and London.

1889   Publishes a paper, 'On functional aphonia [loss of speech] and its
        treatment by hypnotism and suggestion', in the *International Clin-
        ical Review*. Meets Marie Glümer (1873–1925): their relationship
        lasts intermittently till 1899.

1892   The series of one-act plays, *Anatol*, published in book form.

1893   2 May: death of Johann Schnitzler. AS leaves the Poliklinik and
        henceforth confines his medical work to private practice. 14 July:
        première of the one-act play 'Farewell Supper' ('Abschiedssouper'),
        from the *Anatol* cycle. 1 December: première of the play *The Fairy-
        Tale* (*Das Märchen*), with the famous actress Adele Sandrock
        ('Dilly') as the leading lady; beginning of a relationship between her
        and AS that lasts till spring 1895.

1894   12 July: AS meets Marie Reinhard (1871–99), initially one of his
        patients; their relationship begins in March 1895. Onset of deafness
        and tinnitus, an increasing problem for the rest of AS's life. The
        story *Dying* (*Sterben*), AS's first substantial prose work, appears in
        the prominent literary monthly *New German Review* (*Neue deutsche
        Rundschau*); published in book form in 1895. October: completes
        Flirtations (*Liebelei*).

1895   9 October: première of *Flirtations* in the Vienna Burgtheater, with
        Adele Sandrock as Christine.

1896   July and August: journey to Scandinavia; visits Ibsen.

1897   February: completion of *Round Dance* (*Reigen*). 24 September:
        Marie Reinhard bears AS a stillborn child.

1899   1 March: première of *The Green Cockatoo* (*Der grüne Kakadu*) in the Burgtheater (with two other one-acters, *Paracelsus* and *The Woman Friend* (*Die Gefährtin*). 18 March: death of Marie Reinhard. 11 July: AS meets the actress Olga Gussmann (1882–1970), initially a patient.

1900   *Reigen* privately printed. 25 December: publication of the story *Lieutenant Gustl* (*Leutnant Gustl*) in the prominent Vienna newspaper *The New Free Press* (*Neue Freie Presse*); as a satire on an army officer, it unleashes a scandal, resulting in AS's being cashiered as a reserve officer (14 June 1901).

1902   4 January: première of *Living Hours* (*Lebendige Stunden*), a cycle of one-act plays including *The Last Masks* (*Die letzten Masken*). 9 August: birth of Olga's and AS's son Heinrich.

1903   26 August: marries Olga. First publication of *Round Dance* by the Wiener Verlag.

1904   *Round Dance* banned in Germany.

1908   Publication of the novel *The Road to the Open* (*Der Weg ins Freie*), dealing with the 'Jewish question'.

1909   5 January: première of *Countess Mizzi* (*Komtesse Mizzi*) in the Deutsches Volkstheater. 13 September: birth of Olga's and AS's daughter Lili.

1910   AS buys the house (Sternwartestrasse 71, Eighteenth District of Vienna) where he will reside for the rest of his life.

1911   9 September: death of Louise Schnitzler. 14 October: première of *The Vast Domain* (*Das weite Land*) at the Vienna Burgtheater and simultaneously at theatres in Prague and throughout Germany.

1912   28 November: première of *Professor Bernhardi* in the Kleines Theater in Berlin; the play is banned in Austria.

1914   Première of the first film based on a work by AS: *Elskovsleg*, a Danish version of *Flirtations*. August: the outbreak of the First World War finds AS and his family on holiday in Switzerland; AS notes: 'World War. World ruin. Prodigious and appalling news' (diary, 5 August).

1918   21 December: first Austrian production of *Professor Bernhardi* in the Deutsches Volkstheater.

1920   23 December: first performance of *Round Dance* in the Kleines Schauspielhaus in Berlin.

1921   1 February: first performance of *Round Dance* in Vienna in the chamber theatre of the Deutsches Volkstheater. Banned by the Vienna police on 17 February as a threat to public order. 26 June: AS and Olga have their marriage dissolved.

1922   16 June: first extended meeting between AS and Sigmund Freud.

1924   Publication of *Fräulein Else*, an innovative story in interior monologue (a technique already used in *Lieutenant Gustl*).

1925–6 *Dream Story* (*Traumnovelle*) published in instalments in a magazine, *The Lady* (*Die Dame*).

1927   15 March: première of the silent film *Flirtations* in Berlin.

1928   26 July: death by suicide of AS's daughter Lili, a year after her marriage to an Italian Fascist, Arnoldo Cappellini. Publication of AS's second novel, *Therese: Chronicle of a Woman's Life* (*Therese: Chronik eines Frauenlebens*).

1931   21 October: Schnitzler dies in Vienna.

FLIRTATIONS
(*Liebelei*)

A Play in Three Acts

CAST

HANS WEIRING, *violinist at the Theatre in the Josefstadt*
CHRISTINE, *his daughter*
MIZI* SCHLAGER, *milliner*
KATHARINA BINDER, *wife of a stocking-maker*
LINA, *her nine-year-old daughter*
FRITZ LOBHEIMER, *young man*
THEODORE KAISER, *young man*
A GENTLEMAN

Vienna—the Present

Act One

Fritz's room. Elegant and comfortable.
Fritz, Theodore. Theodore enters first, his coat on his arm, takes his hat off as he comes in but retains his walking-stick.

FRITZ (*talking off stage*) No one called then?

VOICE OF SERVANT No, Sir.

FRITZ (*entering*) We can dismiss the cab, can't we?

THEODORE Of course, I thought you'd already done so.

FRITZ (*going out again, in the doorway*) Dismiss the cab, would you. And... you can leave too now, I won't be needing you again today. (*He comes in. To Theodore*) Won't you take off your things?

THEODORE (*is by the desk*) A few letters for you. *He throws his coat and hat onto a chair, but retains his walking-stick.*

FRITZ (*hastens over to the desk*) Ah!...

THEODORE Well now!... You seem positively alarmed.

FRITZ From Papa... (*opens the other*) from Lensky.

THEODORE Don't let me interrupt.

Fritz scans the letters.

THEODORE What does your Papa have to say?

FRITZ Nothing much... I'm supposed to go out to the estate at Whitsun for a week.

THEODORE It would do you a world of good. I'd send you for six months.

Fritz standing in front of the desk, turns towards him.

THEODORE Certainly!—riding, coach outings, fresh air, dairy maids—

FRITZ There aren't any dairies among the maize fields!

THEODORE Well, you know what I mean...

FRITZ Will you come with me?

THEODORE Afraid I can't.

FRITZ Why not?

THEODORE My dear fellow, my exams are just round the corner! If I came, it would only be to help you settle in.

FRITZ Don't worry about me!

THEODORE All you need, you know—I'm quite convinced—is a bit of fresh air. I noticed it again today. Out there in the real spring countryside, you were your dear, likeable self again.

FRITZ Thanks.

THEODORE And now—now you're going all to pieces. We're too close to the torrid zone again.

> *Fritz makes a gesture of annoyance.*

THEODORE You don't know how cheerful you were out there—you were your normal sensible self—it was like the good old days...— And lately, with those two delightful young girls, you were such good company again, but now of course—all that's over, and you seem to find it impossible not to (*with ironic pathos*)—brood over that woman.

> *Fritz gets up irritably.*

THEODORE You misjudge me, my friend. I don't intend to put up with it much longer.

FRITZ My God, how you go on!...

THEODORE I'm not asking you to (*again with pathos*) forget that woman... all I want, (*sincerely*) my dear Fritz, is that you see this maudlin affair, which makes one tremble for you, as just a conventional adventure... Look Fritz, one day, when you stop worshipping 'that woman', you'll be surprised how much you like her. You'll suddenly realize there's nothing demonic about her, and that she's an attractive little woman one can have a good time with, just like any other pretty young thing with a bit of temperament.

FRITZ Why do you say 'makes one tremble for me'?

THEODORE Well... to be frank, I am always worrying that one fine day you might simply decide to run off with her.

FRITZ Is that really what you meant?...

THEODORE (*after a short pause*) That's not the only danger.

FRITZ You are right, Theodore,—there are others.

THEODORE Of course, one has to avoid doing anything stupid.

FRITZ (*to himself*) There are others sure enough...

THEODORE What's the matter... You've something specific on your mind.

FRITZ Ah no, nothing special... (*with a glance toward the window*) She deluded herself once before.

THEODORE How do you mean?... what?... I don't understand.

FRITZ Ah nothing.

THEODORE What's all this? Come on, talk sensibly.

FRITZ She's been having misgivings recently... now and then.

THEODORE Why?—There must be a reason.

FRITZ Not at all. The jitters—(*ironically*) a guilty conscience, if you will.

THEODORE You say she deluded herself once before—

FRITZ That's right—and again today.

THEODORE Today—But what's all this supposed to mean—?

FRITZ (*after a short pause*) She thinks... we are being watched.

THEODORE What?

FRITZ She gets these frights, you know, real hallucinations. (*Near the window*) Through the gap in the curtains here, she thinks she sees someone standing on the corner, and imagines—(*interrupts himself*) Is it possible to recognize a face at this distance?

THEODORE Hardly.

FRITZ That's what I said too. But then it all gets so awful. She's afraid to leave, she gets in a panic, weeps hysterically, wants us to die together—

THEODORE Naturally.

FRITZ (*short pause*) Today I was obliged to go downstairs and look around. All very casually, as if I were going out myself,—of course there wasn't a familiar face in sight...

> *Theodore remains silent.*

FRITZ That's fairly reassuring, don't you think? People can't just sink into the ground, can they?... Well, answer me!

THEODORE What do you want me to say? Of course they can't sink into the ground. But they can hide in an entrance hall if need be.

FRITZ I checked inside all of them.

THEODORE That must have looked very innocent.

FRITZ There was no one there. Hallucinations, I tell you.

THEODORE No doubt. But it should teach you to be more careful.

FRITZ But I'd have been sure to notice if he suspected anything. Yesterday I had supper with them after the theatre—the two of them together—and I tell you, it was all perfectly sociable and friendly!—Ridiculous!

THEODORE Please, Fritz—do me a favour, be sensible. Give the whole damned thing up—for my sake. I get edgy, too, you know... I understand you're not the man to make a clean break when it comes to ending an affair, that's why I've made things easy for you by giving you the chance to escape into another one...

FRITZ You?...

THEODORE Well, didn't I take you along on my rendezvous with Fräulein Mizi just the other week? And didn't I ask Mizi to bring her prettiest friend along? And can you deny you found the little woman very attractive?...

FRITZ Certainly, she was very sweet!... So sweet! And you've no idea how I've longed for such tenderness free of pathos, longed to be enveloped by such sweetness and tranquillity to help me recuperate from all the endless torments and histrionics.

THEODORE That's it precisely! Recuperate! That's the essence of it. They are there for our recuperation. That's why I've always been against your so-called interesting women. Women should not be interesting but pleasing. You must seek happiness where I have always found it, where there are no grand scenes, no dangers, no tragic complications, where the beginning has no special difficulties and the end no special torments, where one receives the first kiss with a smile and parts with gentle tenderness.

FRITZ Yes, that's right.

THEODORE Women are perfectly happy as ordinary healthy human beings—so what possesses us to make them into angels or demons at all cost?

FRITZ She's a real treasure. So sweet, so clinging. I sometimes almost think she is too nice for me.

THEODORE You are quite incorrigible. If you intend to start taking her seriously too—

FRITZ Not in the least. We've agreed already: recuperation.

THEODORE Just as well, because I'd wash my hands of you. I've had enough of your tragic love affairs. You bore me with them. And in case you decide to come to me with your famous guilty conscience, let me explain the simple principle I use: rather me than someone else. Because it's as sure as fate that there'll be someone else.

The door bell rings.

FRITZ Who can that be?...

THEODORE Have a look—You've turned pale again! Well, calm down. It's our two sweet young girls.

FRITZ (*pleasantly surprised*) What?...

THEODORE I took the liberty of inviting them over to your place this evening.

FRITZ (*going out*) But—why didn't you tell me! Now I've dismissed the servant.

THEODORE All the more intimate.

FRITZ'S VOICE (*outside*) Hello, Mizi!—

Theodore, Fritz, Mizi enters, carrying a package.

FRITZ And where's Christine?—

MIZI She'll be here shortly. Hello, Dori.

Theodore kisses her hand.

MIZI You must excuse me, Herr Fritz, but Theodore invited us—

FRITZ Of course, it was a splendid idea. There's just one thing Theodore's forgotten—

THEODORE Theodore has not forgotten anything! (*Takes the package from Mizi*) Have you managed to get everything I jotted down?—

MIZI Of course I have! (*To Fritz*) Where shall I put it?

FRITZ Give it to me, Mizi, we'll leave it on the sideboard for the time being.

MIZI I bought something extra, which you didn't put down, Dori.

FRITZ Give me your hat, Mizi, there—(*puts it on the piano along with her fur boa*).

THEODORE (*suspiciously*) What is it?

MIZI A coffee cream cake.

THEODORE You little glutton!

FRITZ But tell me, why didn't you and Christine come together?—

MIZI Christine is walking her father to the theatre. Then she'll catch the tram here.

THEODORE Such a loving daughter...

MIZI Well yes, especially lately, since they've been in mourning.

THEODORE Who was it that died, actually?

MIZI The old gentleman's sister.

THEODORE Ah, the aunt!

MIZI She was an elderly spinster who had always lived with them— Well, and so now he feels quite lonely.

THEODORE Christine's father is a small man, isn't he, with short grey hair—

MIZI (*shakes her head*) No, he has long hair.

FRITZ How come you know him?

THEODORE I went to the Theatre in the Josefstadt with Lensky recently, and I watched the double basses playing.

MIZI He doesn't play the double bass, he plays the violin.

THEODORE I see, I thought it was the double bass. (*To Mizi, who is laughing*) It isn't funny, how could I possibly have known that?

MIZI You've a very nice place here, Herr Fritz, very nice indeed! What's the view like?

FRITZ That window looks out onto the Strohgassse, and from the next room—

THEODORE (*quickly*) Tell me, why are you so formal with each other? Surely you could call each other 'du'.

MIZI We'll drink a pledge to that at supper.

THEODORE A sound principle! Relaxing anyway.——And how is your dear mother?

MIZI (*turns to him with a sudden expression of concern*) Do you know, she has—

THEODORE Toothache—I know, I know. Your mother is always having toothache. She should really go and see a dentist some time.

MIZI But the doctor says it's just rheumatic.

THEODORE (*laughing*) Well then, if it's just rheumatic—

MIZI (*with a photo album in her hand*) You've got such nice things here!... (*Leafing through it*) Who's that then?... But that's you, Herr Fritz... In uniform!? Were you in the army?

FRITZ Yes.

MIZI A dragoon!—Were you in the yellow or the black brigade?

FRITZ (*smiling*) In the yellow.

MIZI (*dreamily*) In the yellow brigade.

THEODORE Look, she's gone all dreamy! Mizi, wake up!

MIZI But now you're a lieutenant in the reserves?

FRITZ That's correct.

MIZI You must look splendid in your fur-trimmed uniform.

THEODORE A positively encyclopaedic knowledge!—I say, Mizi, I was in the army too, you know.

MIZI Were you also a dragoon?

THEODORE Yes.—

MIZI But why didn't you tell me all this...

THEODORE I wanted to be loved for my own sake.

MIZI Go on, Dori, next time we go out together somewhere, you must wear your uniform.

THEODORE In August I'll be having weapons training anyway.

MIZI God, by August—

THEODORE Of course—eternal love can't be expected to last as long as that.

MIZI In May who wants to be thinking about August. Don't you agree, Herr Fritz—By the way, Herr Fritz, why did you stand us up yesterday?

FRITZ How do you mean...

MIZI Well, after the theatre.

FRITZ Didn't Theodore pass on my apologies?

THEODORE Of course I made your apologies.

MIZI What good are your apologies to me—or more to the point, to Christine! If one makes an arrangement, one should stick to it.

FRITZ I would honestly rather have been with you...

MIZI Is that true?...

FRITZ But I simply couldn't. You saw for yourself, I was in a box with acquaintances of mine, and afterwards I couldn't get away.

MIZI Yes, you couldn't get away from all those lovely ladies. Do you think we couldn't see you from the gallery?

FRITZ I could see you too...

MIZI You were sitting at the back of your box.—

FRITZ Not the whole time.

MIZI But most of it. You were sitting behind a lady in a black velvet dress, and you kept on (*with a parodic gesture*) peeping forward.

FRITZ You were certainly watching me pretty carefully.

MIZI Nothing to do with me! But if I were Christine... How is it Theodore has time after the theatre? How is it he doesn't need to have supper with acquaintances? How is it I don't need to have supper with acquaintances?...

The door bell rings.

MIZI That's Christine.

Fritz hurries out.

THEODORE Mizi, do me a favour, will you.

Mizi a questioning expression.

THEODORE Forget about your military reminiscences—at least for a little while.

MIZI But I don't have any.

THEODORE Come now, one can tell you didn't learn all that from a military manual.

Theodore, Mizi, Fritz, Christine holding a bunch of flowers.

CHRISTINE (*greets the others with a touch of embarrassment*) Good evening. (*They reciprocate. To Fritz*) Are you pleased we've come?—You're not angry?

FRITZ But my dear girl!—Sometimes Theodore's quicker off the mark than me, that's all.

THEODORE Your Papa is playing his fiddle by now, I imagine?

CHRISTINE He is indeed; I walked with him to the theatre.

FRITZ Mizi was just telling us.—

CHRISTINE (*to Mizi*) And then Katharina held me up.

MIZI Oh no, that devious woman.

CHRISTINE Oh, I'm sure she isn't devious, she is very good to me.

MIZI But then you trust everyone.

CHRISTINE Why would she be devious with me?

FRITZ Who is this Katharina?

MIZI The wife of a stocking-maker, and she's always getting worked up if anyone is younger than she is.

CHRISTINE She's still a young woman herself.

FRITZ Let's forget about Katharina, shall we?—What have you got there?

CHRISTINE I bought you a few flowers.

FRITZ (*takes them from her and kisses her hand*) You're a little angel. Wait, we'll put them over there in the vase...

THEODORE Oh no! You obviously have no idea how things are done at banquets. Flowers must be strewn artlessly about the table... later of course, after we've laid it. What one should really do is let them flutter from the ceiling. But perhaps that wouldn't work.

FRITZ (*laughing*) Hardly.

THEODORE Well, for the time being we'll put them in here after all. (*Places them in the vase*)

MIZI It's getting dark already!

FRITZ (*has been helping Christine off with her jacket, she has also taken off her hat, he puts the things on a chair at the back*) Let's light the lamp at once then.

THEODORE Lamp! Nonsense! We'll light the candles. That'll be much nicer. Come, Mizi, you can help me. (*He and Mizi light the candles; all the candles in the two candelabra on the chest, one candle on the desk, then two candles on the sideboard*)

   While this is being seen to, Fritz and Christine talk together.

FRITZ Well, how are you, my love?

CHRISTINE I'm fine now.—

FRITZ And apart from that?

CHRISTINE I've been longing for you so.

FRITZ But we saw each other only yesterday.

CHRISTINE Saw each other... from a distance... (*shyly*) You know, it wasn't very nice of you to...

FRITZ Yes, I know; Mizi already told me. But you're such a child as usual. I couldn't get away. Surely you can understand.

CHRISTINE Tell me... Fritz... who were those people in your box?

FRITZ Acquaintances—It really doesn't matter what they're called.

CHRISTINE Who was the lady in the black velvet dress?

FRITZ Well, I can never remember what people wear.

CHRISTINE (*flatteringly*) Go on!

FRITZ That is... I can remember sometimes—in very special cases. For example, I remember the dark grey blouse you had on the first time we went out together. And the black and white bodice you wore yesterday... to the theatre—

CHRISTINE But I'm also wearing that today!

FRITZ So you are... it looks quite different from a distance—seriously! Oh, and your locket, I recognize that too!

CHRISTINE (*smiling*) When was I wearing it?

FRITZ Let me see—well, that time we walked in the park on the edge of town, where all those children were playing... wasn't it...?

CHRISTINE Tell me... Do you ever think about me?

FRITZ Very often, my sweet...

CHRISTINE Not as often as I think about you. I think about you constantly... all day... and yet I'm only really happy when I'm seeing you!

FRITZ Don't we see each other often enough—

CHRISTINE Often...

FRITZ Certainly. We'll see less of one another in the summer though... Supposing, for instance, I were to go away for a few weeks, what would you say then?

CHRISTINE (*anxiously*) What? You're going away?

FRITZ No... But even so, it's possible the mood might one day take me to spend a week or so alone...

CHRISTINE Whatever for?

FRITZ I'm merely talking about possibilities. I know the way I am, you see, I have these moods. And you too might not want to see me for a few days... I should always understand that.

CHRISTINE I'll never be in a mood like that, Fritz.

FRITZ One can never tell.

CHRISTINE I'm sure of it... I love you.

FRITZ I love you too, a lot.

CHRISTINE But you are my all, Fritz, for you I could... (*she breaks off*) No, I can't imagine a time when I wouldn't want to see you. As long as I live, Fritz——

FRITZ (*interrupts her*) My love, please... don't say things like that... I can't stand all those grand sentimental phrases. Don't let's talk about eternity...

CHRISTINE (*smiling sadly*) Don't worry, Fritz... I know very well it's not forever...

FRITZ You misunderstand me, my sweet. It's possible of course, (*laughing*) that one day we may find we can't live without each other, but we can hardly know that in advance now, can we? We are only human.

THEODORE (*indicating the candles*) Would you be good enough to take a look... Don't they look better than that stupid lamp?

FRITZ You are truly a past master at arranging banquets.

THEODORE Incidentally, everyone, should we not be thinking about a little supper?...

MIZI Yes... Come along Christine!...

FRITZ Wait, I must show you where to find things.

MIZI First we need a tablecloth.

THEODORE (*putting on a foreign accent the way clowns do sometimes*) 'A tablescloth.'

FRITZ What?...

THEODORE Don't you remember the clown at the Orpheum?* 'She is a tablescloth'... 'He is a trumpet.' 'She is a little piccolo.'

MIZI I say, Dori, when are you going to take me to the Orpheum? You did promise the other day. But then Christine must come, and Herr Fritz too. (*She takes the tablecloth from Fritz, which he has just produced from the sideboard*) Then we will be the acquaintances in your box...

FRITZ Yes, yes...

MIZI And the lady in the black velvet dress can find her own way home.

FRITZ You both have this thing about the woman in black, it's really so stupid.

MIZI Oh, but it's not we who have a thing about her... There... and the cutlery?... (*Fritz shows her everything in the open drawer of the sideboard*) Yes... and the plates?... yes, thank you... Well, now we can manage by ourselves... off you go, off you go, you'll just be in our way now.

THEODORE (*has meanwhile stretched out lengthways on the divan; Fritz comes forward and joins him*) You don't mind my...

   Mizi and Christine lay the table.

MIZI Have you seen the photograph of Fritz in uniform?

CHRISTINE No.

MIZI You must have a look. Really smart!... (*they go on talking*)

THEODORE You see, Fritz, evenings like this are my idea of heaven.

FRITZ They're very nice.

THEODORE I really feel at ease... Don't you?

FRITZ I only wish I always felt like this.

MIZI Herr Fritz, do you know if there's any coffee in the machine?

FRITZ Yes... You might as well light the spirit lamp now too—that machine takes hours before the coffee's ready...

THEODORE (*to Fritz*) I'd give ten demonic women for one sweet young girl like that.

FRITZ You can't compare the two.

THEODORE We hate the women we love—and only love the women we're indifferent about.

    Fritz laughs.

MIZI What was all that? We want to hear too!

THEODORE Nothing for you, ladies. We're philosophizing. (*To Fritz*) If this were to be our last evening with these two, it wouldn't make us any less cheerful, would it?

FRITZ Our last evening... Well that certainly has a melancholy ring to it. Parting is always painful, even if one has long been looking forward to it!

CHRISTINE I say, Fritz, where are the dessert spoons?

FRITZ (*goes back to the sideboard*) Here they are, my love.

    Mizi has meanwhile come forward to where Theodore is lying on the divan, and runs her fingers through his hair.

THEODORE You kitten, you!

FRITZ (*opens the package Mizi has brought*) Magnificent...

CHRISTINE (*to Fritz*) How nicely you've arranged everything!

FRITZ Yes... (*lays out the things Mizi has brought,—tins of sardines, cold meats, butter, cheese*)

CHRISTINE Fritz... won't you tell me?

FRITZ What?

CHRISTINE (*very shyly*) Who the lady was?

FRITZ No; don't irritate me. (*More gently*) Look, we did explicitly agree: there would be no interrogations. After all, that is what's so beautiful. When I'm with you, the whole world vanishes—full stop. I don't ask you any questions either.

CHRISTINE You may ask me anything you like.

FRITZ But I don't. I just don't want to know.

MIZI (*comes over again*) Lord, what a mess you're making—(*takes over the various dishes, puts them out on plates*) There...

THEODORE I say, Fritz, have you anything to drink in the house?

FRITZ Oh yes, I think I can find something. (*Goes into the adjoining room*)

THEODORE (*gets up and surveys the table*) Splendid.—

MIZI There, I don't think there's anything missing now!...

FRITZ (*returns with several bottles*) Well, here's something to drink.

THEODORE Where are the roses fluttering from the ceiling?

MIZI Of course, we forgot the roses! (*She takes the roses from the vase, climbs on a chair and scatters them over the table*)

CHRISTINE Goodness, she's in a giddy mood.

THEODORE But not onto the plates...

FRITZ Where would you like to sit, Christine?

THEODORE Where's the corkscrew?

FRITZ (*fetches one from the sideboard*) Here's one.

    Mizi tries to open the wine.

FRITZ You'd better give that to me.

THEODORE Let me do it... (*takes the bottle and corkscrew from him*) Meanwhile, you could provide a bit of (*imitates playing the piano*)

MIZI Yes, yes, that would be nice!... (*She runs to the piano and opens it, having put the things lying there onto a chair*)

FRITZ (*to Christine*) Should I?

CHRISTINE Yes do, I've been longing to hear you for ages.

FRITZ (*at the piano*) You play a little too, don't you?

CHRISTINE (*defensively*) Oh God.

MIZI Christine plays beautifully... and she can sing as well.

FRITZ Really? You never told me that!...

CHRISTINE Did you ever ask me?

FRITZ Where did you study singing?

CHRISTINE I didn't really study. My father taught me a little—but I don't have much of a voice. And you know, since my aunt died, the one who always lived with us, it's been even quieter at home.

FRITZ So what do you do all day?

CHRISTINE Oh God, I've more than enough to do!—

FRITZ About the house—is that right?—

CHRISTINE Yes, And then I copy scores a good deal,—

THEODORE Musical scores?—

CHRISTINE Of course.

THEODORE That must be stupendously well paid. (*When the others laugh*) Well, I would pay stupendously high rates for it. I imagine transcribing scores must be a laborious task!—

MIZI It's ridiculous, her slaving away like that. (*To Christine*) If I had a voice as good as yours, I'd be working in the theatre.

THEODORE You wouldn't even need a voice... You of course don't do anything all day, right?

MIZI Do you mind! I have two little brothers who both go to school, and I get them dressed in the morning; then later I do their homework with them—

THEODORE Not a word of it is true.

MIZI Well, you don't have to believe me!—And until last autumn I even worked in a shop, from eight in the morning till eight at night—

THEODORE (*mocking slightly*) Where was that?

MIZI In a milliner's shop. Mother wants me to go back there.

THEODORE (*in the same tone*) So why did you leave?

FRITZ (*to Christine*) Well, you must sing something for us!

THEODORE Shouldn't we perhaps eat first, and then you can play later?...

FRITZ (*standing up, to Christine*) Come, my love! (*Leads her to the table*)

MIZI The coffee! The coffee's boiling over already, and we haven't even started eating!

THEODORE It doesn't really matter either way!

MIZI But it's boiling over! (*Blows out the spirit lamp. They sit down at the table*)

THEODORE What will you have, Mizi? But let me tell you something: the cake comes last!... You have to start with all the savoury things.

> Fritz pours out the wine.

THEODORE Not like that: nowadays it's done quite differently. Don't you know the latest fashion? (*Stands up, and affecting a grand manner, to Christine*) Vintage Vöslau eighteen hundred and... (*mumbles the next lines incoherently. Pours, then turns to Mizi*) Vintage Vöslau eighteen hundred and... (*as before. Pours, then turns to Fritz*) Vintage Vöslau eighteen hundred and... (*as before. Returning to his seat*) Vintage Vöslau... (*as before. Sits down*)

MIZI (*laughing*) He's always clowning like that.

THEODORE (*raises his glass, they all clink*) Cheers!

MIZI To your health, Theodore!...

THEODORE (*getting to his feet*) Ladies and gentlemen...

FRITZ Come on, not right away!

THEODORE (*sits down again*) I can wait. (*They eat*)

MIZI I really love it when there are speeches at table. I have a cousin who always speaks in rhyme.

THEODORE Which regiment is he in?...

MIZI Go on, stop teasing... He always speaks off the cuff in rhyme; I tell you, Christine, he's absolutely marvellous. And he's an older gentleman.

THEODORE Oh, that happens you know, older gentlemen do still speak in rhyme.

FRITZ But nobody's drinking. Christine! (*He clinks glasses with her*)

THEODORE (*clinks glasses with Mizi*) To the old gentlemen who speak in rhyme.

MIZI (*merrily*) To the young gentlemen, even if they never say a word... to Herr Fritz, for instance... I say, Herr Fritz, if you like we could pledge our friendship now—and Christine must also drink a pledge with Theodore.

THEODORE But not with this wine, this is no wine for drinking pledges. (*Gets up, takes another bottle—goes through the same routine as before*) Jerez de la frontera eighteen fifty—Jerez de la frontera— Jerez de la frontera

MIZI (*sips*) Ah—

THEODORE Can't you wait till we're all ready to drink?... Well, every-one... before we formally pledge our friendship, let's first drink to our good fortune, to hers, hers... and so on...

MIZI Yes, a good idea! (*They drink*)
> *Holding their glasses, Fritz links arms with Mizi, Theodore with Christine, as is customary when drinking pledges.*
> *Fritz kisses Mizi.*
> *Theodore tries to kiss Christine.*

CHRISTINE (*smiling*) Is this necessary?

THEODORE Absolutely, otherwise it doesn't count... (*kisses her*) There, and now pray be seated!

MIZI But the room's getting frightfully hot.

FRITZ That's from all the candles Theodore lit.

MIZI And the wine. (*She leans back in her chair*)

THEODORE Come over here, now you can try the pièce de résistance. (*He cuts a little of the cake and pops it in her mouth*) There, my kit-ten—good?—

MIZI Delicious!... (*He gives her more*)

THEODORE Well, Fritz, the moment has arrived. Why don't you play us something!

FRITZ Would you like me to, Christine?

CHRISTINE Please!—

MIZI But something jolly!
> *Theodore fills the glasses.*

MIZI No more for me. (*Drinks*)

CHRISTINE (*sipping*) This wine's really strong.

THEODORE (*pointing to the wine*) Fritz!
> *Fritz empties his glass, goes to the piano.*
> *Christine seats herself beside him.*

MIZI Herr Fritz, play the 'Double Eagle'.

FRITZ The 'Double Eagle'*—how does that go?

MIZI Dori, can you play the 'Double Eagle'?

THEODORE I can't play the piano at all.

FRITZ I know it, but it just won't come to me.

MIZI I'll sing it for you... La... la... lalala... la...

FRITZ Aha, I know the one. (*But he doesn't play it quite correctly*)

MIZI (*goes to the piano*) No, like this... (*plays the tune with one finger*)

FRITZ Yes, yes... (*he plays, Mizi sings along*)

THEODORE Brings back sweet memories, what?...

FRITZ (*plays it wrong again and stops*) It won't work. I just don't have a good ear. (*He improvises*)

MIZI (*after the first few bars*) That's all rubbish!

FRITZ (*laughs*) Don't swear, that's my composition!—

MIZI But one can't dance to it.

FRITZ Well, try it and see...

THEODORE (*to Mizi*) Come on, let's have a go. (*He takes her by the waist, they dance*)

> *Christine stands by the piano watching the keys. The door bell rings. Fritz suddenly stops playing: Theodore and Mizi continue dancing.*

FRITZ That was the door bell... (*to Theodore*) Did you invite anyone else?

THEODORE Certainly not—you don't have to open.

CHRISTINE (*to Fritz*) What's the matter?

FRITZ Nothing...

> *The bell rings again.*
> *Fritz gets up, but doesn't move.*

THEODORE You are simply not at home.

FRITZ But the piano can be heard all down the passage... One can also see the lights on from the street.

THEODORE Why are you being so ridiculous? You are simply not at home.

FRITZ It just makes me nervous.

THEODORE Well, what do you expect it's going to be? A letter!—Or a telegram—You won't be getting visitors at (*looking at his watch*) nine o'clock at night.

> *The bell rings again.*

FRITZ Oh confound it, I'll have to go and see— (*goes out*)

MIZI Nobody is being very jolly—(*bangs out a few notes on the piano*)

THEODORE Come now, stop that!—(*To Christine*) What's the matter? Does the bell make you nervous too?—

> *Fritz comes back with an assumed air of calm.*

THEODORE *and* CHRISTINE (*together*) Well, who was it?—Who was it?

FRITZ (*with a forced smile*) You must be good enough to excuse me for a minute. If you wouldn't mind going in here.

THEODORE What's up?

CHRISTINE Who is it?!

FRITZ Nothing, my love, I must just have a word with a certain gentleman in private... (*Opening the door into the adjoining room, he ushers
the girls in; Theodore as he follows them gives Fritz a questioning look*)

FRITZ (*in an undertone, with a horrified expression*) It's him!...

THEODORE Ah!...

FRITZ Go inside, go inside.—

THEODORE Now please, don't do anything stupid, it may be a trap...

FRITZ Get in... get in...

> *Theodore goes into the next room. Fritz walks swiftly across the
> room out into the passage, leaving the stage empty for a few
> moments. Then he re-enters, making way for an elegant
> gentleman of about thirty-five.—The gentleman appears in a
> yellow overcoat, wearing gloves, and holding his hat in his hand.
> Fritz, Gentleman.*

FRITZ (*as they enter*) Sorry to keep you waiting... after you...

GENTLEMAN (*in a casual tone*) Oh, that's all right. I'm sorry to have
disturbed you.

FRITZ Not at all. Won't you have a—(*points to a chair*)

GENTLEMAN But I see I have indeed disturbed you. A little get-
together, what?

FRITZ A few friends.

GENTLEMAN (*sitting down, still affably*) A fancy dress party perhaps?

FRITZ (*embarrassed*) How do you mean?

GENTLEMAN Well, your friends seem to have ladies' hats and shawls.

FRITZ Ah yes... (*smiling*) There might be a lady friend or two as well...
(*Silence*)

GENTLEMAN Life can be great fun sometimes... certainly... (*He looks
hard at the other man*)

FRITZ (*holds his gaze for a while, then looks away*) ... Might I ask to
what I owe the honour of your visit?

GENTLEMAN Certainly... (*calmly*) My wife forgot her veil while she
was here with you.

FRITZ Your wife with me?... her... (*smiling*) This is rather an odd
joke...

GENTLEMAN (*suddenly getting up, very loudly, almost wildly, supporting
himself on the back of the chair with one hand*) —She forgot it, Sir.
> *Fritz rises, and the two of them stand face to face.*

GENTLEMAN (*raises his fist as if to strike Fritz;—in fury and revulsion*)
Oh...!

Fritz preparing to defend himself, takes a short step back.

GENTLEMAN (*after a long pause*) Here are your letters. (*He takes a packet from his coat pocket and throws it onto the desk*) In return I request the ones that you received...

Fritz gesture of denial.

GENTLEMAN (*violently, with meaning*) I don't want them found in your possession—later.

FRITZ (*very loudly*) They won't be found.

Gentleman looks at him. Pause.

FRITZ Is there anything more I can do for you?...

GENTLEMAN (*contemptuously*) Anything more—?

FRITZ I'm at your disposal...

GENTLEMAN (*bows coolly*) Good.— (*He casts his eye round the room; when he again sees the set table, ladies' hats etc., his face becomes convulsed, as though he were on the point of another outbreak of fury.*)

FRITZ (*who notices this, repeats*) I am completely at your disposal.—I shall be at home tomorrow until noon.

Gentleman bows and turns to go.

FRITZ (*accompanies him to the door, though the gentleman protests. Once he has left, Fritz goes to the desk and stands there a while. Then he rushes to the window and peeps out through a chink in the blind, following the gentleman down the pavement with his gaze. Then he leaves the window, halts for a moment staring at the ground, then goes to the door of the adjoining room, opens it halfway and calls out*) Theodore... could I see you for a moment.

Fritz, Theodore.

This scene should be very rapid.

THEODORE (*excitedly*) Well...

FRITZ He knows.

THEODORE He knows nothing. You must have fallen for his trick. Don't tell me you admitted it. You're a fool, I tell you... You're a—

FRITZ (*pointing to the letters*) He brought my letters back.

THEODORE (*stunned*) Oh... (*after a pause*) I've always said, one should never write letters.

FRITZ It must have been him in the street outside this afternoon.

THEODORE So what happened?—Get on with it.

FRITZ You must do me a great favour, Theodore.

THEODORE I will smooth matters over.

FRITZ There's no question of that now.

THEODORE Well then...

FRITZ It's for the best, one way or another... (*breaking off*) —but we mustn't keep the girls waiting any longer.

THEODORE Let them wait. What were you going to say?

FRITZ It would be good if you could contact Lensky before tomorrow.

THEODORE Right away, if you wish.

FRITZ You won't catch him now... but he's sure to drop by the coffee house between eleven and twelve... perhaps both of you could then come over here...

THEODORE Come now, don't make a face like that... in ninety-nine cases out of a hundred these things turn out all right.

FRITZ They'll make sure this case does not turn out all right.

THEODORE For goodness sake, remember last year the affair between Doctor Billinger and young Herz—that was exactly the same.

FRITZ Spare me, you know yourself,—he might as well have shot me here in this room,—it would have come to the same thing.

THEODORE (*pretending*) Ah, now that's really splendid! That's what I call a terrific attitude... And I suppose Lensky and I don't count for anything? You think we'd agree to——

FRITZ Spare me the rhetoric, please!... You'll simply accept whatever terms are offered.

THEODORE Ah,—

FRITZ Why pretend, Theodore. As if you didn't know...

THEODORE Nonsense. Anyway, it's all in the hands of fate... You could just as well end up killing him...

FRITZ (*without listening to him*) She had a premonition. We both had a premonition. We somehow knew...

THEODORE Come now, Fritz...

FRITZ (*goes to the desk and locks away the letters*) What can she be doing at this moment? Could he have... Theodore... tomorrow you must find out what has happened to her.

THEODORE I will do my best...

FRITZ And make sure there are no unnecessary postponements...

THEODORE It can hardly take place before the day after tomorrow.

FRITZ (*almost tremulously*) Theodore!

THEODORE Come now... chin up.—There's something to be said for inner conviction too, don't you agree—and I'm convinced everything will turn out all right. (*Talks himself into a better mood*) I don't know why myself, but I just have this firm conviction!

FRITZ (*smiling*) What a good-natured fellow you are!—But what are we going to say to the girls?

THEODORE That is not important surely. We can simply send them packing.

FRITZ Oh no. In fact, we should try to be as merry as possible. Christine mustn't suspect anything. I'll sit down at the piano again, while you go and call them in. (*Theodore, looking dissatisfied, turns to do so*) So what are you going to tell them?

THEODORE That it's none of their business.

FRITZ (*having resumed his seat at the piano, turns toward him*) No, no—

THEODORE That it concerns a friend—that should do the trick.

    Fritz plays a few chords.

THEODORE (*opening the door*) This way, ladies.

    Fritz, Theodore, Christine, Mizi.

MIZI At last! Has he gone?

CHRISTINE (*hurrying to Fritz*) Who was it, Fritz?

FRITZ (*at the piano, continuing to play*) She's getting curious again.

CHRISTINE Please, Fritz, do tell me.

FRITZ My love, I honestly can't tell you, it concerns people you don't know at all.

CHRISTINE (*wheedling*) Come on, Fritz, tell me the truth!

THEODORE She's not going to leave you in peace, of course... Just make sure you don't tell her anything! You promised him!

MIZI Don't be such a bore, Christine, let them do as they please! They're just trying to impress us!

THEODORE I must finish that waltz with Fräulein Mizi. (*With the emphasis of a clown*) Conductor—a little music if you please.

    Fritz plays while Theodore and Mizi dance; after a few beats:

MIZI I can't go on! (*She falls back in an armchair*)

    Theodore kisses her, sits on the arm of her chair.

    Fritz still at the piano, takes Christine's hands and gazes at her.

CHRISTINE (*as if awakening*) Why aren't you playing?

FRITZ (*smiling*) Enough for today...

CHRISTINE You see, that's how I'd like to be able to play...

FRITZ Do you play a lot?...

CHRISTINE I don't get round to it much; there's always something to be done in the house. And then, you see, we have such a miserable upright piano.

FRITZ I'd like to try it some time. I'd love to see your room anyway some time.

CHRISTINE (*smiling*) It's not as nice as your place!...

FRITZ And there's one other thing I'd like: for you to tell me more about yourself... much more... I know so very little about you.

CHRISTINE There's not much to tell really.—I don't have any secrets—unlike some people...

FRITZ Haven't you loved anyone before?

> *Christine just looks at him.*
> *Fritz kisses her hands.*

CHRISTINE And I'll never love anybody else...

FRITZ (*with an almost pained expression*) Don't say that... don't say that... how can you tell?... Is your father very fond of you, Christine?—

CHRISTINE O God!... And to think that I once used to tell him everything.—

FRITZ Well, my love, don't reproach yourself... Now and then one just has secrets—that's the way of the world.

CHRISTINE If only I were sure you're fond of me—then everything would be all right.

FRITZ Well, aren't you sure?

CHRISTINE If you always talked to me in this tone of voice, perhaps...

FRITZ Christine! But you're sitting so uncomfortably.

CHRISTINE Oh don't worry—I'm all right. (*She leans her head against the piano*)

> *Fritz stands up and strokes her hair.*

CHRISTINE Oh, that feels so nice.

> *Quiet in the room.*

THEODORE Where are those cigars, Fritz?—

> *Fritz goes over to where he's standing at the sideboard looking for them.*
> *Mizi has fallen asleep.*

FRITZ (*holds out a small box of cigars to him*) And some black coffee! (*He pours out two cups*)

THEODORE Anyone else for black coffee?

FRITZ Mizi, shall I pour you a cup...

THEODORE Let her sleep...—By the way, you'd better not have coffee yourself tonight. You should go to bed early and get a good night's rest.

> *Fritz looks at him and laughs bitterly.*

THEODORE Ah well, like it or not, that's how matters stand... now it's a question of being not as grand or melancholy, but as sensible as possible... that's crucial... in these matters.

FRITZ You'll come over tonight with Lensky, won't you?

THEODORE Nonsense! Tomorrow morning is quite soon enough.

FRITZ Please.

THEODORE Very well...

FRITZ And will you see the girls home?

THEODORE Yes, right away in fact... Mizi!... up you get!—

MIZI You're drinking black coffee—! I'd like some too!—

THEODORE Here you are, my dear...

FRITZ (*going to Christine*) Are you tired, my love?...

CHRISTINE You're so sweet, when you talk like that.

FRITZ Really tired?—

CHRISTINE (*smiling*) —It's the wine.—I've got a bit of a headache too...

FRITZ Well, in the fresh air that will soon clear!

CHRISTINE Are we off now? Will you see us home?

FRITZ No, my love. I'm staying here... I have a few things still to see to.

CHRISTINE (*whose memory is coming back*) Now... what have you to see to at this late hour?

FRITZ (*almost severely*) Look, Christine, you must really get out of this habit!—(*Gently*) I'm completely whacked you see... Earlier today, Theodore and I spent two whole hours in the country—

THEODORE Ah, and delightful it was too. Next time we'll all have a country jaunt together.

MIZI Yes, that will be fun! And both of you can wear your uniforms.

THEODORE That's what I call a feeling for nature!

CHRISTINE So when shall we see each other again?

FRITZ (*a little nervously*) I'll write to you.

CHRISTINE (*sadly*) Goodbye then. (*Turns to go*)

FRITZ (*notices her sadness*) We'll see each other tomorrow, Christine.

CHRISTINE (*happily*) Really?

FRITZ In the park... beside the tram-lines like last time... at—let's say at six... perhaps? Is that all right with you?
    Christine nods.

MIZI (*to Fritz*) Are you coming with us, Fritz?

THEODORE She has a flair for using 'du'—!

FRITZ No, I'm staying at home now.

MIZI Lucky you! To think of the long trek home we have...

FRITZ But Mizi, you're not going to leave all this nice cake behind. Wait, I'll wrap it up for you—all right?

MIZI (*to Theodore*) Would that be polite?
    Fritz wraps up the cake.

CHRISTINE She's like a little girl...

MIZI (*to Fritz*) Wait, for that I'll help you put the candles out. (*Puts out one candle after another, the candle on the desk remaining lighted*)

CHRISTINE Shouldn't I open the window for you?—it's so stuffy.
  (*She opens the window and looks out at the house opposite*)

FRITZ Well, there we are. I'll light the way for you.

MIZI Are the lights out on the stairs already?

THEODORE Of course.

CHRISTINE Ah, isn't the fresh air from the window marvellous!...

MIZI A May breeze... (*by the door, Fritz with the candle in his hand*)
  Well, thank you, kind Sir, for the reception!—

THEODORE (*urging them*) Out you go. Out you go...

> Fritz shows the others out. The door remains open, their voices
> are heard talking in the hall. The apartment door is heard
> opening.

MIZI Tut! Tut!—

THEODORE Mind the stairs.

MIZI Thank you for the cake...

THEODORE Shush, you'll wake the neighbours up!—

CHRISTINE Good night!

THEODORE Good night!

> Fritz is heard in the hall, closing and locking the apartment
> door.—As he returns and puts the candle on the desk, the front
> door downstairs is heard opening and closing.
> Fritz goes to the window and waves goodbye.

CHRISTINE (*from the street*) Good night!

MIZI (*likewise, cheekily*) Good night, joy of my life...

THEODORE (*scolding*) Look here, Mizi...

> His words and her laughter are heard as their footsteps recede.
> Theodore whistles the tune of the 'Double Eagle,' which fades
> away last. Fritz continues to look out for a few seconds, then
> sinks into the armchair near the window.
> Curtain.

Act Two

Christine's room. Modest and pleasant.
Christine is just getting dressed to go out. Katharina enters, after knocking on the outside door.

KATHARINA Good evening, Fräulein Christine.

CHRISTINE (*who is standing in front of the mirror, turns round*) Good evening.

KATHARINA Are you just going out?

CHRISTINE I'm not in any hurry.

KATHARINA Well, my husband sent me to ask if you'd like to go out for supper with us in the Lehner Garden,* as there will be music there today.

CHRISTINE Thank you, Frau Binder... I can't today... another time, perhaps?—You're not offended, are you?

KATHARINA Not a bit... why should I be? You'll be able to enjoy yourselves much better on your own.

Christine gives her a look.

KATHARINA Your father's already at the theatre, is he?...

CHRISTINE Oh no; he'll be coming home first. The show doesn't start till half past seven now!

KATHARINA Of course, I keep forgetting. In that case I might as well wait, I've been wanting to ask him about free tickets to the new play... Surely they'll be available by now?...

CHRISTINE Certainly... no one wants to be indoors, now the evenings are so lovely.

KATHARINA The likes of us never get to go... unless we happen to know someone in the theatre... But don't let me hold you up, Fräulein Christine, if you really must be going. My husband will be very sorry of course... as will someone else...

CHRISTINE Who?

KATHARINA Herr Binder's cousin will be coming naturally... and did you know, Fräulein Christine, he's now got a permanent position?

CHRISTINE (*indifferently*) Ah.—

KATHARINA With a very good wage as well. And such an upright young man. And he does admire you so—

CHRISTINE Well—goodbye, Frau Binder.

KATHARINA People could say what they liked to him about you—he wouldn't believe a word of it...

Christine gives her a look.

KATHARINA Some men are like that...

CHRISTINE Good day, Frau Binder.

KATHARINA Good day... (*in a slightly less malicious tone*) Don't be late for your rendezvous, Fräulein Christine.

CHRISTINE What do you really want from me?—

KATHARINA Nothing, nothing, you're quite right of course! One's only young once!

CHRISTINE Goodbye.

KATHARINA But let me give you a piece of advice, Fräulein Christine: you might be a little more cautious!

CHRISTINE What's that supposed to mean?

KATHARINA Look—Vienna is a big enough town... so why d'you have to have your rendezvous a hundred yards from home?

CHRISTINE That's none of your business.

KATHARINA When Herr Binder told me, I refused to believe him. He was the one who spotted you, you see... Go on, I said to him, you must have been mistaken. Fräulein Christine is not the kind of girl to go walking with smart gentlemen at night, and if she did she'd have more sense than to do so just up our street! Well he said, you can ask her yourself! And it's hardly surprising, he said, she never comes to see us any more, and yet she goes the rounds with that slut Mizi, what sort of company is that for a respectable young girl?— Men are so vulgar, Fräulein Christine!—And of course he would have to go and tell Franz all about it straight away; but Franz got very angry—would vouch for Fräulein Christine any day, and anyone saying anything against her would have him to reckon with. And how much of a home bird you were, and how kind you'd always been to your old maiden aunt—God rest her soul—, and how modestly and retiringly you lived, and so on... (*Pause*) Perhaps you'll come and listen to the music with us after all?

CHRISTINE No...

Katharina, Christine: Enter Weiring with a sprig of lilac in his hand.

WEIRING Good evening... Ah, it's Frau Binder. Well now, how are you?

KATHARINA Very well, thank you.

WEIRING And little Lina?—And your husband?...

KATHARINA All in good health, thank goodness.

WEIRING Well, that's fine then.—(*To Christine*) Still at home in beautiful weather like this—?

CHRISTINE I was just going out.

WEIRING You couldn't do better! The air outside is something wonderful today, isn't it, Frau Binder? I just came through the park on
the edge of town—the lilac's in full bloom—really glorious! I even
stepped outside the law a bit! (*Presents the sprig of lilac to Christine*)

CHRISTINE Thank you, Father.

KATHARINA Be thankful the watchman didn't catch you.

WEIRING Go past yourself some time, Frau Binder—it smells just as
nice as if I never plucked that sprig.

KATHARINA But if everybody took that attitude—

WEIRING Well, that would certainly be wrong!

CHRISTINE Goodbye, Father!

WEIRING If you'd like to wait a few minutes, you could walk me to the
theatre.

CHRISTINE I... I promised Mizi I would call for her...

WEIRING I see.—Well, perhaps that's best. Youth belongs to youth,
you know. Goodbye, Christine...

CHRISTINE *kisses him. Then* Goodbye, Frau Binder! (*Exit; Weiring
gazes fondly after her*)
     Katharina, Weiring.

KATHARINA She seems to have struck up quite a close friendship with
this Fräulein Mizi.

WEIRING Yes.—I'm really glad Tina's made a few contacts and
doesn't sit at home all day now. What's the poor girl getting out of
life!...

KATHARINA That's true.

WEIRING I can't tell you, Frau Binder, how much it pains me sometimes when I get home from my rehearsal—and she's just sitting
here and sewing—then in the afternoon, we've hardly finished our
meal when she sits down again to copying those scores...

KATHARINA Ah well, millionaires are better off than the likes of us of
course. But how is her singing coming on?—

WEIRING Not much doing there. In a private room her voice is
adequate, and she sings well enough to please her father—but one
can't make a living out of that.

KATHARINA What a pity.

WEIRING I'm glad she's realized it herself. At least she will be spared
the disappointments. I could get her an audition for the chorus in
our theatre of course—

KATHARINA Certainly, with a figure like hers!

WEIRING But that has no long-term prospects.

KATHARINA Girls are always a worry! To think that in five or six years time, my little Lina too will be a fully grown woman—

WEIRING But won't you sit down, Frau Binder!

KATHARINA Oh, thank you, but my husband will be calling for me shortly—I just came by to invite Christine...

WEIRING Invite her—?

KATHARINA Yes, to come and listen to the music in the Lehner Garden. I thought it would cheer her up a little—she certainly could do with it.

WEIRING It wouldn't do her any harm at all—especially after such a sad winter. So why won't she go out with you—?

KATHARINA I don't know... Perhaps because Herr Binder's cousin will be coming with us.

WEIRING Ah, very likely. She can't stand him, you know. She told me so herself.

KATHARINA Why ever not? Franz is a decent enough fellow—and now he's even got a permanent position, and these days that's a real blessing for a...

WEIRING For a... penniless girl—

KATHARINA It's a blessing for any girl.

WEIRING Now, tell me, Frau Binder, does a blooming girl like her exist just to wed a fellow who happens to have a permanent position?

KATHARINA Still, it would be wise! One can't wait around for a count, and even if one did come along, he'd probably bow out before he ever proposed marriage... (*Weiring is standing by the window. Pause*) Oh well... That's why I always say, you can't be too careful with a young girl—especially when it comes to the company she keeps—

WEIRING Is there nothing for it, but to throw away one's youth?—and what does a poor girl have to show for all her virtue, if—after years of waiting—a stocking-maker is all that comes along!

KATHARINA Herr Weiring, even if my husband is a stocking-maker, he is a good and honest man whom I've never had reason to complain about...

WEIRING (*soothingly*) But Frau Binder—you don't think I meant you! You didn't throw your youth away now, did you?

KATHARINA I don't remember anything about those days.

WEIRING Don't say that—You can tell me anything you like now—memories are the best part of life.

KATHARINA I don't have any memories at all.

WEIRING Come, now...

KATHARINA And even if a woman does have the kind of memories you're thinking of, what is she left with?... Regrets.

WEIRING Well, and what is she left with—if she—doesn't have any fond memories at all—? If her whole life has just slipped by (*very simply, without any pathos*) one day much like another, without happiness or love—is that supposed to be better?

KATHARINA Indeed, Herr Weiring, one only has to think of your own sister!... It still distresses you, Herr Weiring, to even hear her mentioned...

WEIRING Yes, it does indeed distress me...

KATHARINA Of course it does... When two people have been so devoted to each other... I've always said, it's not that easy to find a brother like you.

Weiring makes a deprecating gesture.

KATHARINA Indeed it's true. After all, at such a young age, you had to act as both father and mother to her.

WEIRING True enough, true enough—

KATHARINA At least that must be some sort of consolation. Knowing one has always been the guardian and benefactor of a poor thing like that—

WEIRING Yes, I once fondly imagined so myself—while she was still young and pretty,—and God only knows I thought myself very wise and noble. But later, as grey hair and wrinkles gradually appeared, and day followed day, until youth itself had slipped away and—one scarcely notices these things—the young maiden turned into an old maid,—then I began to realize what I had done!

KATHARINA But Herr Weiring—

WEIRING I can still see her sitting opposite me of an evening by the lamp, looking at me with her quiet smile of resignation,—as if she still had something she wished to thank me for;—and I—well, I just wanted to throw myself on my knees, and beg her forgiveness for having protected her so well from every danger—and from every happiness!

Pause.

KATHARINA And yet many a woman would be happy if she'd always had a brother like you beside her... and nothing to regret...

Katharina, Weiring, Mizi enters.

MIZI Good evening!... It's quite dark already... one can hardly see.— Ah, Frau Binder. Your husband's downstairs waiting for you, Frau Binder... Isn't Christine at home...

WEIRING She went out quarter of an hour ago.

KATHARINA Didn't you see her? I thought she had arranged to meet you?

MIZI No... anyway we missed each other... You and your husband are off to the music in the park, he tells me—?

KATHARINA Yes, he's always raving about it. But I say, Fräulein Mizi, that's a charming little hat you're wearing. New, is it?

MIZI Not a bit.—Don't you recognize the shape? It was all the rage last spring; just the trimming's new.

KATHARINA Did you trim it yourself?

MIZI Certainly.

WEIRING So clever with her hands!

KATHARINA But of course—I keep forgetting you were in that milliner's shop for a whole year.

MIZI I shall probably have to go back again too. That's what mother wants—so there's not much I can do about it.

KATHARINA How's your mother, by the way?

MIZI Not too bad—she gets a bit of toothache—but the doctor says it's just rheumatic...

WEIRING Well, it's high time I was off...

KATHARINA I'll come down with you, Herr Weiring...

MIZI I'll come too... You'd better take your coat, Herr Weiring, it'll get quite chilly later.

WEIRING Do you think so?

KATHARINA Certainly... How can anybody be so careless.

          The above—Christine.

MIZI Here she is.

KATHARINA Back from your walk already?

CHRISTINE Yes. Hello, Mizi... I've such a splitting headache... (*sits down*)

WEIRING What?...

KATHARINA It's probably the weather...

WEIRING Goodness, Christine, what's the matter!... Light the lamp for us, would you, Fräulein Mizi.

          Mizi proceeds to do so.

CHRISTINE But I can do that myself.

WEIRING Let me have a look at your face, Christine!

CHRISTINE But Father, it's nothing, I'm sure it's just the weather.

KATHARINA Some people just can't take spring weather.

WEIRING You'll stay here with Christine now, won't you, Fräulein Mizi?

MIZI Of course I'll stay...

CHRISTINE But it's really nothing, Father.

MIZI My mother makes such a fuss over me when I have headaches...

WEIRING (*to Christine, who is still sitting*) Can you really be that tired?...

CHRISTINE (*getting up from the armchair*) There I am, back on my feet. (*Smiling*)

WEIRING Well now—you're looking better already. (*To Katharina*) She looks quite different when she smiles, doesn't she...? Well, goodbye, Christine, my dear... (*kisses her*) And make sure that little head of yours is better by the time I get home!... (*He is at the door*)

KATHARINA (*in an undertone to Christine*) Did you two have a quarrel?
        Christine's reluctance is apparent.

WEIRING (*from the door*) Frau Binder...!

MIZI Goodbye!...
        Weiring and Katharina exeunt.
        Mizi, Christine.

MIZI D'you know what's caused your headache? All that sweet wine last night. I'm surprised I haven't felt anything myself... But it was good fun, don't you think...?
        Christine nods.

MIZI They are such smart gentlemen, the two of them—there's no denying that now, is there?—And Fritz's place is really nicely furnished, quite resplendent! Now Dori's place... (*breaks off*) Oh nothing... I say, is your headache very bad still? Can't you say something?... What's the matter?...

CHRISTINE Do you know what—he never came.

MIZI He stood you up? Well serves you right!

CHRISTINE What's that supposed to mean? What have I done?

MIZI You spoil him, you're too good to him. That way a man's certain to get arrogant.

CHRISTINE You don't know what you're talking about.

MIZI I know very well what I'm talking about. All this time I've been getting more and more impatient with you. He's late for every rendezvous, he doesn't see you home, he hob-nobs with strange women at the opera, and now he stands you up—and you put up with all of this without a murmur, and then to top it all (*mimicking her*) you gaze at him with big sheep's eyes.—

CHRISTINE Come, don't talk like this, don't pretend to be worse than you are. You know you're pretty fond of Theodore too.

MIZI Fond of—certainly I'm fond of him. But neither Dori nor any other man is going to see me make myself miserable over him—the whole pack of them are not worth that, your men.

CHRISTINE I've never heard you talk like this before, never!—

MIZI Well, Chrissie—we've never talked about these things before.— What, you think I didn't respect how you were feeling!... But I've always known that once you were smitten you'd be swept off your feet. The first time always leaves one pretty shaken!—But then be thankful that with your first love, you've got such a good friend to see you through.

CHRISTINE Mizi!

MIZI Don't you think I'm a good friend? If I weren't here to say: my dear, he's a man just like the rest and the whole pack of them are not worth one hour's misery, you'd go getting all sorts of notions in your head. But mark my word! One should never believe anything men say.

CHRISTINE Why do you go on like this—men, men—what do I care about men! I'm not interested in other men.—And I won't be interested in anybody else for as long as I live.

MIZI What's got into you... has he already...? Of course—it's already happened; you see, you should have gone about things differently...

CHRISTINE Oh do be quiet!

MIZI Well, what d'you expect me to say? I can't do much about it,— one needs to think about these things a little sooner. One just has to wait till someone comes along, whose serious intentions are written on his face...

CHRISTINE Mizi, I can't bear this sort of talk today. It's really hurt-ful.—

MIZI (*kindly*) There, now—

CHRISTINE I'd rather you left... don't be offended... but I need to be alone!

MIZI Why should I be offended? Well, I'm off then. I didn't mean to upset you, Christine, really... (*as she is turning to go*) Ah, it's Herr Fritz.

    The above—Fritz enters.

FRITZ Good evening!

CHRISTINE (*joyfully*) Fritz, Fritz! (*Runs into his arms*)

    Mizi slips out, with an expression that says, I'm not needed here.

FRITZ (*disengaging himself*) Well now—

CHRISTINE They're all saying you're going to leave me! It's not true is it, you won't—just yet—not just yet...

FRITZ Who says that?... What's wrong with you... (*stroking her*) My darling!... I thought you might get a fright, if I suddenly came barging in here.—

CHRISTINE Oh—thank goodness you've come!

FRITZ Well then, calm yourself—were you waiting long for me?

CHRISTINE Why didn't you meet me?

FRITZ I was held up and got there late. I was in the park just now but didn't find you—and was on the point of going home. But then I was suddenly seized by such a yearning for you, such a longing to see this dear, sweet face...

CHRISTINE (*happily*) Is that true?

FRITZ And then I suddenly had an incredible urge to see where you live—yes seriously—I just had to see it—and then I couldn't bear it any longer and so came up... you don't mind, do you?

CHRISTINE Oh God!

FRITZ No one saw me—and I knew of course that your father would be at the theatre.

CHRISTINE What do I care what people think!

FRITZ So here is—? (*Looks round the room*) So this is your room? Very pretty...

CHRISTINE But you can't see anything. (*Is on the point of removing the shade from the lamp*)

FRITZ No, don't bother, it would only dazzle me, it's better like this... So this is it? This is the window you told me about, where you always work, is it?—And what a splendid view! (*Smiling*) Amazing, the number of roofs one can see across... And over there—tell me, what is that dark mass over in the distance?

CHRISTINE That's the Kahlenberg!*

FRITZ I see! You're more nicely situated here than I am.

CHRISTINE Oh!

FRITZ I'd like to live as high up as this, and look out across the roofs, I find it all quite beautiful. And it must be quiet in the street?

CHRISTINE Ah, there's noise enough during the day.

FRITZ Do coaches ever drive past here?

CHRISTINE Not often, but there's a locksmith's workshop in the house opposite.

FRITZ O, that must be unpleasant. (*He takes a seat*)

CHRISTINE One gets used to it! We no longer hear it.

FRITZ (*gets up again quickly*) Can this really be the first time I've been here—? Everything seems so familiar!... It's all exactly as I imagined it. (*As he begins to look round the room more closely:*)

CHRISTINE No, you're not allowed to look at things.—

FRITZ What are these pictures?...

CHRISTINE Stop it!...

FRITZ Ah, I'd like to have a look at these. (*He takes the lamp and illuminates the pictures*)

CHRISTINE ... 'Parting'—and 'Homecoming'!

FRITZ I see—'Parting'—and 'Homecoming'!

CHRISTINE I know these pictures are not particularly good.— There's one in my father's room which is much better.

FRITZ What's that a picture of?

CHRISTINE It's of a girl looking out of a window, and outside, you see, it's winter—and it's called 'Forsaken.'—

FRITZ There... (*puts the lamp down*) Ah, and there's your library. (*Sits down next to the little bookcase*)

CHRISTINE I'd rather you didn't look at those——

FRITZ Why not? Ah!—Schiller...* Hauff...* an encyclopaedia... Well I'll be blowed!—

CHRISTINE It only goes as far as G...

FRITZ (*smiling*) I see... 'A Book for Everyone'...* You like looking at the pictures in this one, I suppose?

CHRISTINE Of course I like looking at the pictures.

FRITZ (*still seated*) Who's the gentleman on top of the stove?

CHRISTINE (*instructively*) Now that's Schubert.

FRITZ (*getting up*) I see—

CHRISTINE Because father's so fond of him. Father used to compose songs too once, very lovely ones.

FRITZ Not any more?

CHRISTINE Not any more. (*Pause*)

FRITZ (*sits down*) It's so cosy in here!—

CHRISTINE Do you really like it?

FRITZ Very much... What's this then? (*Picks up a vase with artificial flowers standing on the table*)

CHRISTINE Well, if he hasn't found something else!...

FRITZ These don't belong here, child,... they look so dusty.

CHRISTINE They're certainly not dusty.

FRITZ Artificial flowers always look dusty... In this room you must have real flowers, all fresh and fragrant. From now on I shall... (*breaks off, turns away to hide his emotion*)

CHRISTINE Well what?... What were you going to say?

FRITZ Nothing... nothing...

CHRISTINE (*gets up, tenderly*) What?—

FRITZ I was going to say I would send you some fresh flowers tomorrow...

CHRISTINE And you're regretting it already?—Of course! Tomorrow you won't give me a thought.

Fritz makes a defensive gesture.

CHRISTINE It's true, it's out of sight, out of mind with you.

FRITZ What are you talking about?

CHRISTINE O yes, I know it's true. I can feel it.

FRITZ How can you imagine such a thing.

CHRISTINE You yourself are to blame. Because you're always keeping secrets from me!... Because you never tell me anything about yourself.—What do you do the whole day anyway?

FRITZ Look, my love, that's all quite simple. I go to lectures—occasionally—then I drop in at a coffee house... then I read a little... sometimes I also play the piano—then I chat to whoever it might be—then I call on friends... it's all utterly inconsequential. It's positively boring to even talk about.—But now I really must be going, dearest...

CHRISTINE Already—

FRITZ Your father will be here soon.

CHRISTINE Not for ages yet, Fritz.—Stay a little longer—a few more minutes—please—

FRITZ And then I have to... Theodore is expecting me... I have things to talk over with him.

CHRISTINE Today?

FRITZ Today, of course.

CHRISTINE You'll be seeing him tomorrow anyway!

FRITZ Tomorrow I may not be in Vienna at all.

CHRISTINE Not in Vienna?—

FRITZ (*noticing her anxiety, calmly reassuring*) Well, these things happen, don't they? I shall just be gone for the day—or perhaps for a couple of days, my love.—

CHRISTINE Where to?

FRITZ Where to!... Somewhere—Oh, God, don't make a face like that... I'm going out to the estate to see my parents... there... is that so very odd?

CHRISTINE You see, you never tell me about them either!

FRITZ I can't believe you're such a child... You don't seem to appreciate how marvellous it is, our being so totally alone together. Tell me, don't you feel that at all?

CHRISTINE No, it's not marvellous your never telling me anything about yourself... Look, I'm interested in everything about you, yes really... everything,—I want more of you than just the odd hour we sometimes spend together in the evening. Afterwards you're gone again, and I know nothing... Then the whole night goes by and then another day with all those hours—and I don't know a thing. Sometimes it all makes me so sad.

FRITZ Why should you be sad about it?

CHRISTINE Why, because then I get to longing for you so, as if you weren't even in the same town, but somewhere else entirely! I feel as if you'd vanished and were somewhere far away...

FRITZ (*a little impatiently*) Come now...

CHRISTINE But look, it's true!...

FRITZ Come over here a minute. (*She goes to him*) The one thing you and I do know, is that at this moment we're in love... (*When she tries to speak*) Don't talk to me about eternity. (*More to himself*) Perhaps some moments really do give off an aroma of eternity.—... This is the only eternity we can comprehend, the only one that truly belongs to us... (*He kisses her.—Pause.—He gets up.—Expostulating*) Oh, how marvellous it is here, how simply marvellous!... (*He stands by the window*) One is so remote from the world, in the very midst of all these houses... I feel so lonely, so alone with you... (*softly*) so sheltered...

CHRISTINE When you talk like this... I almost believe...

FRITZ What, my love?

CHRISTINE That you love me as much as I dreamed you did—the day you gave me that first kiss... do you remember?

FRITZ (*passionately*) Oh, I love you so much!—(*He embraces her, then tears himself away*) But now let me go—

CHRISTINE Are you regretting having told me so already? You are free, you know, quite free—you can leave me when you like... You haven't promised me anything—and I haven't asked you for anything... What becomes of me later—is all the same to me—I have been happy once, I don't ask more of life. I just want you to know that I never loved anyone before, and won't love anyone again—if one day you no longer want me.

FRITZ (*more to himself*) Don't say that, don't say that—it sounds... too beautiful...

     There is a knock on the door.

FRITZ (*starts*) That'll be Theodore...

CHRISTINE (*surprised*) Does he know you are here at my place—?

     Christine, Fritz, Theodore enters.

THEODORE Good evening.—A bit of a nerve, what?

CHRISTINE Do you really have such important things to discuss with him?

THEODORE Certainly—and I've been looking for him everywhere.

FRITZ (*in an undertone*) Why didn't you wait downstairs?

CHRISTINE What's that you're whispering?

THEODORE (*deliberately loud*) Why didn't I wait downstairs?... Well, if I'd known for sure that you were here... But as I· didn't want to risk spending two hours walking up and down for nothing...

FRITZ (*hinting*) Well... So you'll be leaving with me tomorrow then?

THEODORE (*cottoning on*) Yes, that's right...

FRITZ A sound decision...

THEODORE But I've been running around so much, I wonder if I might sit down a minute.

CHRISTINE Please do— (*busies herself near the window*)

FRITZ (*in an undertone*) Any news?—Have you discovered how she is?

THEODORE (*in an undertone to Fritz*) No. I only came to fetch you because you're being so thoughtless. Why needlessly excite yourself like this! You should be getting some sleep... You need to rest!... (*Christine rejoins them*)

FRITZ By the way, don't you find this room enchanting?

THEODORE Yes, it's very nice... (*To Christine*) Are you stuck at home all day?—It's very cosy, I might add. A little too high up for my taste.

FRITZ That's just what I find so attractive.

THEODORE But now I must carry off your Fritz, we have an early start tomorrow.

CHRISTINE So you're really going away?

THEODORE He'll be back, Fräulein Christine!

CHRISTINE Will you write to me?

THEODORE But if he's coming back tomorrow—

CHRISTINE Ah, I know he's going to be away much longer...
        Fritz winces.

THEODORE (*who has noticed this*) Does that mean you have to write at once? I'd never have thought you quite so sentimental... I may address you as 'du', by now, I take it... Well then... give each other a goodbye kiss, since it's going to be such a long... (*breaks off*) Pretend I'm not here. (*Fritz and Christine kiss*)

THEODORE (*takes out a cigarette case and puts a cigarette in his mouth, then gropes in his overcoat pocket for a match. Not finding one*) I say, Christine my dear, you don't have a match, do you?

CHRISTINE O yes, there are some over there. (*Pointing to a box on the dresser*)

THEODORE None left.—

CHRISTINE I'll fetch some. (*Runs quickly into the adjoining room*)

FRITZ (*gazing after her, to Theodore*) O God, how such moments lie!

THEODORE Moments such as what!

FRITZ I almost believe I might have found happiness here, that this sweet young girl (*he breaks off*)—but this moment is all a monstrous lie...

THEODORE Sentimental rubbish... How you will laugh about it later.—

FRITZ I haven't much time left for that.

CHRISTINE (*returns with the matches*) Here you are!

THEODORE Thank you... Well, goodbye,—(*To Fritz*) What is it now?—

FRITZ (*looks about the room, as though he wanted to take in everything again*) It's hard to tear oneself away.

CHRISTINE Don't mock.

THEODORE (*emphatically*) Come on.—Goodbye, Christine.

FRITZ Farewell...

CHRISTINE Goodbye!—(*Theodore and Fritz exeunt*)

CHRISTINE (*stands there looking depressed, then goes to the door which is standing open; half aloud*) Fritz...

FRITZ (*comes back one last time and clasps her to his heart*) Farewell!...
          Curtain.

Act Three

The same room as before. It is about midday.
Christine alone. She is sitting at the window:—she sews a little,
then lays her work aside.
Lina, the nine-year-old daughter of Katharina, enters.

LINA Good day, Fräulein Christine!

CHRISTINE (*very distracted*) Hello, child, what do you want?

LINA Mother sent me to ask if I may pick up the tickets for the theatre now.—

CHRISTINE Father is not home yet, my child; do you want to wait?

LINA No, Fräulein Christine, I'll come by again after we've eaten.

CHRISTINE Fine.—

LINA (*about to go, turns round again*) And mother sends her greetings to Fräulein Christine, and asks if she's still got a headache?

CHRISTINE No, my child.

LINA Adieu, Fräulein Christine!

CHRISTINE Adieu!—

As Lina goes out, Mizi appears at the door.

LINA Good day, Fräulein Mizi.

MIZI Hello, little monkey!

Lina exit.
Christine, Mizi.

CHRISTINE (*gets up as Mizi enters and goes towards her*) So are they back?

MIZI How should I know?

CHRISTINE And you don't have a letter or anything for me—?

MIZI No.

CHRISTINE And you haven't had one either?

MIZI What would we have to say to each other?

CHRISTINE They've been gone since the day before yesterday!

MIZI Well, that's not really all that long! There's no need to make such a fuss over it. I don't understand you... What a sight you are. You've been crying your eyes out. Your father is bound to notice something's wrong when he gets home.

CHRISTINE (*simply*) My father knows everything.—

MIZI (*almost frightened*) What?—

CHRISTINE I told him.

MIZI That was another clever move. But of course, with you one can see it all in your face anyway.—Does he also know who it is, by the way?

CHRISTINE Yes.

MIZI And did he curse?

Christine shakes her head.

MIZI So what did he say?—

CHRISTINE No... He went away quietly, as usual.—

MIZI Even so, it was stupid of you to say anything. You'll see... Do you know why he didn't say anything—? Because he thinks Fritz is going to marry you.

CHRISTINE Why do you even mention that!

MIZI Do you know what I think?

CHRISTINE Well, what?

MIZI That they made up that whole story about going on a trip.

CHRISTINE What?

MIZI Perhaps they haven't gone away at all.

CHRISTINE They've gone—I know.—I went past his place last night and the blinds are let down; he isn't there.—

MIZI Well, maybe you're right. They must have gone away after all.— But they won't be coming back—not to us, at least.—

CHRISTINE (*anxiously*) Don't say that—

MIZI Well, it's possible, isn't it!—

CHRISTINE You say that so calmly—

MIZI Ah well—what if it happens today or tomorrow—or in six months' time, it all comes to the same thing in the end.

CHRISTINE You don't know what you're saying... You don't know Fritz,—he's not the way you think—I could tell when he was here in my room. Sometimes he pretends he doesn't care—but he really does love me... (*as though anticipating Mizi's answer*)—Yes, yes— not forever, I know—but such feelings don't just end all of a sudden—!

MIZI I don't know Fritz that well.

CHRISTINE He'll come back, Theodore will come back too, I'm sure!

Mizi: gesture which says: I don't care much either way.

CHRISTINE Mizi, do something for me.

MIZI Don't get so het up—well what is it then?

CHRISTINE Go over to Theodore's and take a look, it's so close by... You can ask if he's back yet, and if he's not, perhaps someone in the building will know when he's expected.

MIZI I'm not running after any man.

CHRISTINE But he needn't ever know about it. Perhaps you'll meet him accidentally. It's almost one o'clock;—now is when he goes to lunch—

MIZI Why don't you go and inquire at Fritz's house?

CHRISTINE I wouldn't dare—he can't stand that sort of thing... And he's certainly not there yet. Theodore may be there already and know when Fritz is due back. Please, Mizi!

MIZI You're so childish sometimes—

CHRISTINE Do it for me! Go and see! There's nothing to it.—

MIZI Well, if it means so much to you, all right I'll go. But it won't be any use. They are sure not to be there yet.

CHRISTINE And you'll come straight back... all right?...

MIZI Oh well, mother will just have to wait a little with the meal.

CHRISTINE Thank you, Mizi you're so good...

MIZI Of course I'm good;—now you be sensible... promise?... well I won't be long!

CHRISTINE Thank you!—

Mizi exit.

Christine, later Weiring.

Christine alone. She tidies up the room. She puts away the sewing things etc. then she goes to the window and looks out. A minute later Weiring comes in, though she does not notice him at first. He is deeply agitated and anxiously observes his daughter standing at the window.

WEIRING She doesn't know yet, she doesn't know yet... (*He remains standing in the doorway, not daring to take another step*)

Christine turns round, notices him and gives a start.

WEIRING (*tries to smile. He comes further into the room*) Christine... (*as if calling her to him*)

Christine goes to him and tries to prostrate herself before him.

WEIRING (*won't allow this*) Come now,... Christine, what's all this? Let's (*with resolve*) let's forget all about it, shall we?

Christine raises her head.

WEIRING Come now... me—and you!

CHRISTINE Father, didn't you understand this morning?...

WEIRING But what do you expect, Christine?... I have to tell you what I think about it! Don't you agree? Well then...

CHRISTINE Father, what do you mean?

WEIRING Come here, my child... and listen patiently. Now look, I listened patiently to what you had to say too.—We shall have to—

CHRISTINE Please don't talk this way, Father... if you've thought it over and decided you cannot forgive me, then throw me out—but don't talk this way...

WEIRING Just listen to me quietly, Christine! Afterwards you can still do as you please... Look, after all you're very young, Christine.— Have you never thought... (*very hesitantly*) that perhaps the whole thing might be a mistake—

CHRISTINE Why are you saying this, Father?—I know what I've done—and I don't expect anything—from you or anybody else, if it has been a mistake... I've already said to you, throw me out, but...

WEIRING (*interrupting her*) How can you talk such nonsense... even if it was a mistake, is that any reason for someone as young as you are to despair?—Just think for a moment how wonderful life is. Just think how much there is to enjoy, how much youth and happiness still lie ahead of you... Look at me, I don't have the world at my doorstep any longer, yet even for me life is still worth while—and there's so much to look forward to. Just think how you and I will be together—how we'll arrange our lives—just you and me... how you'll again take up your singing—now the good weather's here, and how, come the holidays, we'll drive out into the country for the day—yes—oh, there are so many wonderful things... so many.— It's just nonsense to give up everything, because one has to surrender one's first happiness, or what one mistook for it—

CHRISTINE (*anxiously*) Why... must I surrender it...?

WEIRING And was it ever truly happiness? Do you think, Christine, you needed to tell your old father this today? I knew it all along.— And I also knew you'd tell me. No, he never meant happiness to you!... Do you think I don't know your eyes? They would not have been so tearful or your cheeks so pale if you had loved someone who deserved it.

CHRISTINE How can you... What do you know... What have you heard?

WEIRING Nothing, nothing at all... but you've already told me what he's like... A young fellow like that—What does he know?—Does he have the least appreciation of what just falls into his lap like that—does he know the difference between impurity and purity— and as to all your simple-minded love—how much understanding did he show of that?

CHRISTINE (*more and more anxious*) You've been to see...—You were at his place?

WEIRING What are you talking about! He's left town, hasn't he? Come now, Christine, I haven't taken leave of my senses, I still have eyes in my head! Look, child, forget the whole thing! Forget it! Your future lies somewhere else entirely! You can, you shall still be happy, as you deserve to be. And one day you will also find someone who knows how to appreciate you properly—

> *Christine has hurried to the dresser to get her hat. The ensuing exchange is very rapid.*

WEIRING What are you doing?—

CHRISTINE Leave me alone, I must go...

WEIRING Where are you going?

CHRISTINE To him... to him...

WEIRING What's come over you...

CHRISTINE You are keeping something from me—let me go.—

WEIRING (*firmly restraining her*) Now come to your senses, child. He isn't here at all... he may have gone on a long trip... stay with me, why do you want to go there now... Tomorrow or perhaps this evening I'll go over with you. You can't go out on the street like that... you look a sight.

CHRISTINE Will you come with me then—?

WEIRING I promise.—But stay here for the moment, just sit down and pull yourself together. It almost makes one laugh, to see you in this state... and all for nothing, nothing at all. Can't you stand living with your father any longer?

CHRISTINE What do you know?

WEIRING (*increasingly at a loss*) What am I supposed to know... I know I love you, that you're my only child, that you ought to stay with me—that you always should have stayed with me—

CHRISTINE Enough————leave me alone—(*she tears herself away from him and opens the door, behind which Mizi appears*)

> *Weiring, Christine, Mizi, then Theodore.*

MIZI (*gives a little cry as Christine nearly collides with her*) You gave me such a fright...

> *Christine shrinks back when she sees Theodore.*
> *Theodore remains standing in the door; he is dressed in black.*

CHRISTINE What... what's happened... (*She receives no answer; she looks Theodore in the face, but he avoids her eye*) Where is he, where is he? (*With mounting anxiety—she looks at their sad, embarrassed faces, but still receives no answer*) Where is he? (*To Theodore*) Answer me!

> *Theodore tries to speak.*

CHRISTINE (*looks at him intently, looks round at the others, understands the expression on their faces, and after her face has announced that the truth has gradually dawned on her, she gives a terrible scream*) Theodore!... He is...

> *Theodore nods.*

CHRISTINE (*clutches her temples, seems unable to take it all in, goes up to Theodore, seizes him by the arm—like a mad woman*) ... He is... dead...? ... (*as if asking herself*)

WEIRING My child—

CHRISTINE (*repulses him*) Well, say something, Theodore.

THEODORE You know everything.

CHRISTINE I know nothing... I don't know what's happened... don't you think... I should now hear everything... how did it happen... Father... Theodore... (*to Mizi*) You know too...

THEODORE A chance misfortune—

CHRISTINE What, what?

THEODORE He fell.

CHRISTINE What does that mean: He...

THEODORE He fell fighting a duel.

CHRISTINE (*cries out*) Ah!... (*She is on the verge of collapsing, but Weiring holds her up, signalling to Theodore that he should leave now*)

CHRISTINE (*notices and grabs Theodore*) Wait... I must know everything. Do you think you should conceal things from me now...

THEODORE What else do you want to know?

CHRISTINE Why—why did he fight a duel?

THEODORE I don't know the reason.

CHRISTINE With whom, with whom—? Surely you must know who killed him?... well, well—

THEODORE No one you know...

CHRISTINE Who, who?

MIZI Christine!

CHRISTINE Who? You tell me then... (*to Mizi*)... You, Father (*no answer. She tries to leave. Weiring holds her back*) I must be allowed to find out who killed him, and what for—!

THEODORE It was... a trifling matter...

CHRISTINE You are not telling me the truth... why, why...

THEODORE My dear Christine...

CHRISTINE (*as if intending to interrupt, goes up to him—says nothing at first, looks at him and then suddenly screams*) Over a woman?

THEODORE No—

CHRISTINE Yes—over a woman... (*turning to Mizi*) for that woman— for the woman he had been in love with—And her husband—yes, yes, her husband killed him... and I... What am I then? What was I to him...? Theodore... don't you have anything for me... didn't he jot down anything...? Didn't he entrust you with a few words for me...? Didn't you find anything... a letter... or a note...

Theodore shakes his head.

CHRISTINE And the night... he was here, when you called for him... he already knew, he already knew that he perhaps might never see... And he went away to get himself killed for another woman—No, no,—I just can't believe it... didn't he know how much he meant to me... did he...

THEODORE He did know.—On the last morning as we drove out... he talked about you too.

CHRISTINE He talked about me too! About me too! And what else did he talk about? About how many other people, how many other things, that meant just as much to him as I did?—About me too! Oh God!... And about his father and his mother and his friends and his room and springtime in the city, and everything else which was part and parcel of his life and had to be left behind along with me... he talked to you about all that... and about me too...

THEODORE (*moved*) He was certainly very fond of you.

CHRISTINE Fond!—Him?—I was nothing to him but a pastime—yet for another woman he was prepared to die—! And I—adored him!—Didn't he know that?... Did he never notice that I gave him everything it was in my power to give him, that I would have died for him—that he was my Lord and God, my happiness and bliss? And yet he could leave me with a smile, leave this room, and get himself shot for another woman... Father, Father—can you understand that?

WEIRING Christine! (*Beside her*)

THEODORE (*to Mizi*) I say, you really could have spared me this...

Mizi gives him an angry look.

THEODORE I've had enough commotions... in the last few days...

CHRISTINE (*with sudden resolve*) Theodore, take me there... I want to see him—I want to see him one last time—his face—Theodore, take me there.

THEODORE (*hesitates, resisting*) Well...

CHRISTINE Why not?—Surely you can't refuse me that—Surely I may see him one last time—?

THEODORE It's too late.

CHRISTINE Too late?—It's too late... to see his corpse? Goodness— (*she fails to comprehend*)

THEODORE He was buried this morning.

CHRISTINE (*with the utmost expression of horror*) Buried... Without my knowing anything about it? They shot him... and laid him in his coffin and buried him in the ground—and I wasn't even allowed to see him one last time?—He's been dead for two whole days—and yet you didn't come to tell me—?

THEODORE (*much moved*) In the last two days I've had to... You've no idea, the things I've had to see to... Remember, it was also my duty to inform his parents—I had a lot to cope with—and my own feelings on top of everything...

CHRISTINE Your...

THEODORE Besides, the funeral... was a very quiet affair... Only the closest relatives and friends...

CHRISTINE Only the closest—! And what about me—?... What am I then?...

MIZI That's what the others would have wondered too.

CHRISTINE What am I then—? Less than all the others—? Less than his relatives, less than... you?

WEIRING My child, my child. Come to me, to me... (*He embraces her. To Theodore*) Go now... leave her alone with me!

THEODORE I am very... (*in a tearful voice*) I had no idea...

CHRISTINE No idea of what?—That I loved him?—(*Weiring draws her to him. Theodore looks straight ahead. Mizi stands beside Christine*)

CHRISTINE (*freeing herself from Weiring*) Take me to his grave!

WEIRING No, no—

MIZI Don't go, Christine—

THEODORE Christine... later... tomorrow... wait until you're calmer—

CHRISTINE Tomorrow?—When I'm calmer?!—and within a month I'll have consoled myself, right?—And in six months I'll be able to laugh again as usual, right—? (*Laughing out loud*) And when will my next lover be arriving?...

WEIRING Christine...

CHRISTINE Well stay here then... I can find the way myself...

THEODORE Don't go.

MIZI Don't go.

CHRISTINE Indeed it's better... if I... leave me alone, leave me alone.

WEIRING Christine stay...

MIZI Don't go!—You might just find the other woman there— praying.

CHRISTINE (*stares fixedly ahead*) I have no wish to pray there... no... (*she rushes out... leaving the others at first speechless*)

WEIRING Follow her, quick.

Theodore and Mizi go after her.

WEIRING I can't cope, I can't cope... (*He walks painfully from the door to the window*) What does she want... what does she want... (*He looks out of the window into the void*) She'll never come back—she'll never come back! (*He sinks to the floor sobbing loudly*)

Curtain.

ROUND DANCE
(*Reigen*)

CAST

PROSTITUTE
SOLDIER
CHAMBERMAID
YOUNG MASTER
YOUNG WIFE
HUSBAND
SWEET MAID
POET
ACTRESS
COUNT

I THE PROSTITUTE AND THE SOLDIER

Late evening. By the Augarten Bridge.*
Soldier enters whistling, on his way home.

PROSTITUTE Come here, my handsome angel.

Soldier turns round then continues on his way.

PROSTITUTE Don't you want to come with me?

SOLDIER Ah, so I'm the handsome angel?

PROSTITUTE Of course, who else? Go on, come with me. I live just down the road.

SOLDIER I don't have time. I must get back to barracks!

PROSTITUTE You'll still get back to barracks in good time. It's nicer at my place though.

SOLDIER (*close to her*) That may be.

PROSTITUTE Shh. A policeman may come by at any moment.

SOLDIER Ridiculous! Policeman! Besides, I've got my bayonet!

PROSTITUTE Go on, come with me.

SOLDIER Leave me alone, I've got no money.

PROSTITUTE I don't want money.

SOLDIER (*stops short. They are by a street lamp*) You don't want money? Who are you anyway?

PROSTITUTE Civilians have to pay up. But a fellow like you can always come with me for nothing.

SOLDIER Perhaps you're the one Huber told me about.

PROSTITUTE I don't know any Huber.

SOLDIER You must be the one. You know—the coffee house in the Schiffgasse—he went home with you from there.

PROSTITUTE I've gone home with many from that coffee house, you know... oh! oh!—

SOLDIER Come on then, let's go, let's go.

PROSTITUTE So now you're in a hurry?

SOLDIER Well, what's the point in dawdling? And I've got to be back at the barracks by ten.

PROSTITUTE How long have you been in the army?

SOLDIER What's that got to do with you? Is your place far?

PROSTITUTE Ten minutes' walk.

SOLDIER That's too far. Give us a kiss.

PROSTITUTE (*kisses him*) For me that's the best part anyway, if I really like someone!

SOLDIER Not for me. I can't come with you, it's too far.

PROSTITUTE I'll tell you what, come tomorrow afternoon.

SOLDIER Good. Give me your address.

PROSTITUTE But then maybe you won't come.

SOLDIER If I say I will!

PROSTITUTE D'you know what, if my place is too far tonight—how about down there... look... (*points towards the Danube*)

SOLDIER What's that?

PROSTITUTE It's nice and quiet down there too... no one comes past as late as this.

SOLDIER Ah. That wouldn't be right.

PROSTITUTE It's right enough with me at any time. Go on, stay a while. Who knows if we'll be alive tomorrow.

SOLDIER Come on then—but hurry!

PROSTITUTE Watch out, it's dark down there. If you slip, you'll end up in the Danube.

SOLDIER Best place for me anyway.

PROSTITUTE Hey, slow down a bit. There's a bench here somewhere.

SOLDIER You know your way around here.

PROSTITUTE I'd like to have a fellow like you for a sweetheart.

SOLDIER You'd find me a bit too jealous.

PROSTITUTE I'd soon get you out of that.

SOLDIER Ha—

PROSTITUTE Not so loud. Sometimes, policemen do wander down here. D'you think we're in the middle of Vienna?

SOLDIER Over here, come over here.

PROSTITUTE What's the idea, if we slip we'll end up in the water.

SOLDIER (*has taken hold of her*) Ah, that's good—

PROSTITUTE Watch you don't slip.

SOLDIER Don't worry...

— — — — — — — — — — — — — — — — — — — —

PROSTITUTE It would have been better on the bench.

SOLDIER One place is as good as another... Come on, climb up here.

PROSTITUTE What's the big hurry—

SOLDIER I've got to get back to barracks, I'm late anyway.

PROSTITUTE I say, what's your name?

SOLDIER What's that got to do with you?

PROSTITUTE Mine's Leocadia.

SOLDIER Ha!—That's a name I've never heard before.

PROSTITUTE I say!

SOLDIER Well, what is it?

PROSTITUTE I say, at least give me something for the house porter!

SOLDIER Ha!... Thought you could con me, did you. Bye! Leocadia...

PROSTITUTE You rotten bastard!—

He disappears.

II THE SOLDIER AND THE CHAMBERMAID

The Prater.* Sunday evening.
A road leading away from the Wurstelprater off into dark
narrow paths. One can still hear the confused music from the
Wurstelprater, as well as a vulgar polka played by a brass band
coming from the dance floor.
The Soldier. The Chambermaid.

CHAMBERMAID Come on, tell me why you have to leave so early.

Soldier embarrassed, laughs stupidly.

CHAMBERMAID It was wonderful. I do love dancing.

Soldier clasps her round the waist.

CHAMBERMAID (*yields*) We are not dancing now. Why are you holding
me so tight?

SOLDIER What's your name? Kathy?

CHAMBERMAID You always have some Kathy on the brain.

SOLDIER Wait, I remember now... Marie.

CHAMBERMAID I say, how dark it is. I'm getting really frightened.

SOLDIER No need to be afraid when you're with me. I'm no pushover,
by God!

CHAMBERMAID But where is this leading? There's nobody about.
Come, let's go back!—Goodness, it's so dark!

SOLDIER (*draws on his Virginia cigar, making the end glow*) There, it's
lighter now! Ha! Ha! Oh, you little darling!

CHAMBERMAID Ah. What are you doing? If I'd known you'd be like
this!

SOLDIER I'll be damned if any of the girls at Swoboda's* today were
better padded, Fräulein Marie.

CHAMBERMAID Do you sample all the girls like this?

SOLDIER Only what one notices while dancing. And one notices a fair
bit! Ha!

CHAMBERMAID You danced much longer with that blonde girl than
with me—the one with the lopsided face.

SOLDIER She's an old acquaintance of a friend of mine.

CHAMBERMAID You mean the corporal with the turned-up moustache?

SOLDIER Ah no, my friend was the civilian, you know, the one who sat next to me at table and spoke in a hoarse voice.

CHAMBERMAID Ah, I know who you mean. He was a cheeky fellow, right enough.

SOLDIER Did he do anything to you? I'll show him! What did he do to you?

CHAMBERMAID Oh, nothing—I just noticed the way he was carrying on with the other girls.

SOLDIER I say, Fräulein Marie...

CHAMBERMAID You're going to burn me with that cigar.

SOLDIER Apologies!!—Fräulein Marie. Let's call each other 'du'.

CHAMBERMAID But we're not that well acquainted.

SOLDIER Plenty of people who can't stand each other do so.

CHAMBERMAID Well perhaps next time, if we... But Herr Franz—

SOLDIER So you noticed my name?

CHAMBERMAID But, Herr Franz...

SOLDIER Just call me Franz, Marie.

CHAMBERMAID Now don't you get too cocky—but shh, what if someone were to come!

SOLDIER Well even if they did, one can hardly see two steps ahead.

CHAMBERMAID But for heaven's sake, where's this leading?

SOLDIER Look, two others just like us.

CHAMBERMAID Where? I can't see anyone.

SOLDIER There... up ahead of us.

CHAMBERMAID Why do you say: two others just like us?—

SOLDIER Well, I mean they like each other too.

CHAMBERMAID But do be careful, what's this here, I nearly tripped just now.

SOLDIER Ah yes, it's the boundary fence into the meadow.

CHAMBERMAID Don't push like that, I'm going to topple over.

SOLDIER Shh, not so loud.

CHAMBERMAID Look, I'm really going to scream in a minute.—But what are you doing... but—

SOLDIER There's nobody for miles around.

CHAMBERMAID Let's go back to where the other people are.

SOLDIER We don't need other people, what, Marie, all we need... is this... ha ha.

CHAMBERMAID But, Herr Franz, please, for heaven's sake, look, if I had... known... oh... oh... come!...

— —

SOLDIER (*blissfully*) My God, that was really something... ah....

CHAMBERMAID ... I can't see your face at all...

SOLDIER Ah, so what—my face...

— —

SOLDIER I say, Fräulein Marie, you can't just lie there in the grass.

CHAMBERMAID Well, help me up then, Franz.

SOLDIER Come on then.

CHAMBERMAID O God, Franz.

SOLDIER Well, what's wrong with Franz then?

CHAMBERMAID You're a wicked man, Franz

SOLDIER All right, all right. I say, wait a minute, will you.

CHAMBERMAID Why are you letting go my hand?

SOLDIER I suppose I'm allowed to light my cigar?

CHAMBERMAID It's so dark.

SOLDIER Don't worry, it'll be light again tomorrow morning.

CHAMBERMAID Tell me then at least, do you love me?

SOLDIER Well, you must have felt that, Fräulein Marie, ha!

CHAMBERMAID Where are we going now?

SOLDIER Back of course.

CHAMBERMAID Not so fast, I beg you.

SOLDIER What's the matter now? I don't like walking in the dark.

CHAMBERMAID Tell me, Franz, do you love me?

SOLDIER I just told you I love you!

CHAMBERMAID Well then, will you give me a kiss?

SOLDIER (*magnanimously*) There... Listen—one can hear the music again.

CHAMBERMAID I suppose you want to go and dance some more?

SOLDIER Of course, what else?

CHAMBERMAID You see, Franz, it's just that I have to get back. They'll be cursing me already, my mistress is such a... she'd much prefer me not to go out at all.

SOLDIER Well, go home then.

CHAMBERMAID I just thought, Herr Franz, you might see me home.

SOLDIER See you home? Ah!

CHAMBERMAID Go on, it's so sad, walking home alone.

SOLDIER Where do you live then?

CHAMBERMAID It's not far at all—in the Porzellangasse.

SOLDIER Is that so? Well, that's a fair way... but it's too early for me yet... with overtime I've got a bit of time still... I don't have to be back at the barracks before twelve. I'm going to dance some more.

CHAMBERMAID I know, of course, now it's her turn—that blonde with the lopsided face!

SOLDIER Ha!—Her face isn't that lopsided.

CHAMBERMAID My God, men are really wicked! So you do it with just anyone then, do you?

SOLDIER That would be overdoing things a bit!—

CHAMBERMAID Please, Franz, not tonight—stay with me, just for tonight—

SOLDIER Yes, yes, all right. But I'm still going to dance a little longer.

CHAMBERMAID I'm not going to dance with anybody else tonight!

SOLDIER Look, there it is...

CHAMBERMAID What?

SOLDIER Swoboda's of course! How quickly we've got back. The band's still playing that same piece... tadarada tadarada... (*sings along*) Well, if you want to wait, I'll walk you home... if not... then I'll be seeing you—

CHAMBERMAID Yes, I'll wait.

They enter the dance hall.

SOLDIER Tell you what, Fräulein Marie, order yourself a glass of beer. (*Turning to a blonde just dancing past with a young fellow, in very formal German*) May I have the honour, Fräulein?

III THE CHAMBERMAID AND THE YOUNG MASTER

Hot summer afternoon.—The parents are already in the country. The cook is out on her day off.—The Chambermaid is in the kitchen writing to her soldier lover. The bell rings from the Young Master's room. She gets up and goes to the Young Master's room. The Young Master is lying on the divan, smoking and reading a French novel.

CHAMBERMAID You rang, Sir?

YOUNG MASTER Ah yes, Marie, quite right, I rang, now... what was it... yes, of course, could you let the blinds down, Marie... It's cooler when the blinds are down... yes...

The Chambermaid goes to the window and lets down the blinds.

YOUNG MASTER (*continues reading*) What are you doing, Marie? Oh yes, of course. But now one can't see at all to read.

CHAMBERMAID You're always so hard-working, Sir.

YOUNG MASTER (*formally ignores this*) That will be all then. (*Marie exit*)

> *The Young Master tries to continue reading; soon he drops the book and rings again.*
>
> *Chambermaid appears.*

YOUNG MASTER Oh, Marie... yes, now what was I going to ask... oh yes... is there any cognac in the house?

CHAMBERMAID I think it might be locked away.

YOUNG MASTER Well then, who has the key?

CHAMBERMAID Lini has the key.

YOUNG MASTER Who is Lini?

CHAMBERMAID She's the cook, Herr Alfred.

YOUNG MASTER Well, go and tell Lini then.

CHAMBERMAID But it's Lini's day off today.

YOUNG MASTER I see...

CHAMBERMAID Should I get you some from the coffee house, Sir?

YOUNG MASTER Ah no... it's hot enough as it is. I don't need any cognac. I'll tell you what, Marie, bring me a glass of water. Pst, Marie—make sure you let the tap run until it's nice and cold.—

> *The Chambermaid withdraws.*
>
> *The Young Master watches her go; at the door the Chambermaid turns round towards him; the Young Master looks in the air.—*
>
> *The Chambermaid turns on the tap and lets it run. While waiting, she goes into her little closet, washes her hands and adjusts her curls before the mirror. Then she brings the Young Master his glass of water. She goes over to the divan.*
>
> *The Young Master half sits up, the Chambermaid hands him the glass, their fingers touch.*

YOUNG MASTER Ah, thank you.—Well, what's the matter?—Careful now; put the glass back on the tray... (*He lies back and stretches himself*) What time is it?—

CHAMBERMAID Five o'clock, Sir.

YOUNG MASTER I see, five o'clock.—That will be all.—

> *The Chambermaid withdraws; at the door she turns round; the Young Master has been watching her; she notices and smiles.*
>
> *The Young Master lies there for a while, then suddenly gets up. He goes as far as the door, then back again and stretches out on the divan. He again tries to read. After a few minutes he rings again. Chambermaid reappears and doesn't try to hide her smile.*

YOUNG MASTER I say, Marie, I meant to ask you something. Was Doctor Schüller here this morning, by any chance?

CHAMBERMAID No, no one came this morning.

YOUNG MASTER I see, that's very strange. So Doctor Schüller wasn't here then? Do you know Doctor Schüller?

CHAMBERMAID Certainly. He's the tall dark gentleman with the full beard.

YOUNG MASTER Yes, that's right. You're sure he wasn't here?

CHAMBERMAID No, nobody was here, Sir.

YOUNG MASTER (*resolutely*) Come here, Marie.

CHAMBERMAID (*comes a bit closer*) Yes, Sir.

YOUNG MASTER Closer... that's right... ah... I was just thinking...

CHAMBERMAID What's the matter, Sir?

YOUNG MASTER Thinking... I was just thinking—about your blouse... what sort is it?... Well, come a bit closer. I'm not going to bite you.

CHAMBERMAID (*comes up to him*) What's wrong with my blouse? Don't you like it, Sir?

YOUNG MASTER (*stretches out to feel the blouse and at the same time pulls the Chambermaid down close to him*) Blue? That's a really pretty blue. (*Simply*) You dress very nicely, Marie.

CHAMBERMAID But Sir...

YOUNG MASTER Well, what is it?... (*He has opened her blouse. Matter-of-factly*) You have beautiful white skin, Marie.

CHAMBERMAID You're trying to flatter me, Sir.

YOUNG MASTER (*kissing her breasts*) Surely that didn't hurt.

CHAMBERMAID Oh no.

YOUNG MASTER Because you're sighing so! What are you sighing for?—

CHAMBERMAID Oh, Herr Alfred...

YOUNG MASTER And what nice slippers you have...

CHAMBERMAID But Sir... look... it's so light...

YOUNG MASTER You don't need to feel embarrassed in front of me. You've no need to be embarrassed in front of anyone... when you're as lovely as this. My word, yes; Marie, you are... Do you know, even your hair smells fragrant.

CHAMBERMAID Herr Alfred...

YOUNG MASTER Don't make such a fuss, Marie... I've seen you responding very differently. The other night when I came home late and got myself a glass of water; the door to your room was open and... well...

CHAMBERMAID (*covers her face*) O God, I didn't know you could be so naughty, Herr Alfred.

YOUNG MASTER I saw a great deal too... this... and this... and this... and—

CHAMBERMAID But, Herr Alfred!

YOUNG MASTER Come, come... like this... yes, that's right.

CHAMBERMAID But what if someone were to ring now—

YOUNG MASTER Stop this shilly-shallying, will you... if it comes to that we just won't open...

— —

The doorbell rings.

YOUNG MASTER Goodness gracious... And what a noise the fellow's making.—Perhaps he rang earlier and we didn't notice.

CHAMBERMAID Oh, I was listening the whole time.

YOUNG MASTER Well, hurry up and have a look—through the peep-hole, mind.

CHAMBERMAID Herr Alfred... but you're really... well... so naughty.

YOUNG MASTER Please, go and see who it is...

The Chambermaid goes out.

The Young Master hastily raises the blinds.

CHAMBERMAID (*reappears*) Whoever it was has gone away. There's no one there now. Perhaps it was Doctor Schüller.

YOUNG MASTER (*is disagreeably affected*) Just as well.

The Chambermaid approaches him.

YOUNG MASTER (*withdraws from her*) Oh, Marie,—I'm off to the coffee house now.

CHAMBERMAID (*tenderly*) Already... Herr Alfred.

YOUNG MASTER (*severely*) Look, I'm off to the coffee house now, all right. If Doctor Schüller should come—

CHAMBERMAID He won't come today now.

YOUNG MASTER (*more severely*) If Doctor Schüller does come, I, well, I... I'm—in the coffee-house.—(*Goes into the other room*)

The Chambermaid takes a cigar from the table, pockets it and leaves.

IV THE YOUNG MASTER AND THE YOUNG WIFE

Evening.—A sitting room furnished with vulgar elegance in a house in the Schwindgasse. The Young Master has just come in, and with his hat and overcoat still on, he proceeds to light the candles. Then he opens the door into the adjoining room and looks in. The light from the candles in the sitting room stretches across the parquet floor to a four-poster bed against the back wall. A reddish light falls on the bed curtains from the fireplace in the corner of the bedroom. The Young Master also inspects the bedroom. He takes a siphon from the dresser and sprays the pillows with a fine mist of violet-scented perfume. Then he goes through both rooms with the siphon repeatedly squeezing the little bladder, so that everything soon smells of violets. Then he takes his hat and overcoat off. He sits down in the blue velvet armchair, lights a cigarette and smokes. After a short while he gets up again and checks that the blinds are closed. Suddenly he goes into the bedroom again and opens the drawer of the commode. He feels inside and finds a tortoise-shell hair comb. He casts around for somewhere to hide it, and finally puts it in the pocket of his overcoat. Then he opens a cupboard in the sitting room, takes out a silver tray with a bottle of cognac and two liqueur glasses and puts them on the table. He goes back to his coat and this time takes out a little white box of confectionery. He opens it and puts it beside the cognac, then goes back to the cupboard and takes out two plates and some cutlery. He takes a candied chestnut from the box and eats it. Then he pours himself a glass of cognac and swigs it down hastily. Then he looks at his watch. He paces up and down the room.—He pauses for a while in front of the large wall mirror and combs his hair and little moustache with his pocket comb.—He now goes to the hall door and listens. Nothing is stirring. The doorbell rings. The Young Master starts a little. Then he sits down in the armchair and only gets up when the door opens and the Young Wife enters.

The Young Wife, heavily veiled, closes the door behind her, and stands there a moment with her hand to her heart, as if trying to overcome her tumultuous emotions.

YOUNG MASTER *(approaches her, takes her left hand and imprints a kiss on her white glove with its black stitching. He says softly)* Thank you.

YOUNG WIFE Alfred—Alfred!

YOUNG MASTER Come, Frau Emma, come...

YOUNG WIFE Leave me alone a moment—please... oh please, Alfred!
(She continues to stand at the door)

The Young Master stands in front of her, holding her hand.

YOUNG WIFE Where am I really?

YOUNG MASTER At my place.

YOUNG WIFE This house is so awful, Alfred.

YOUNG MASTER But why? It's a very respectable house.

YOUNG WIFE I met two gentlemen on the stairs.

YOUNG MASTER Acquaintances?

YOUNG WIFE I don't know. Possibly.

YOUNG MASTER Pardon me, dear Emma—but surely you recognized your own acquaintances.

YOUNG WIFE But I couldn't see a thing.

YOUNG MASTER Well, even if they'd been your best friends,—they could hardly have recognized you. Even I... if I weren't expecting you... with that veil—

YOUNG WIFE There are two.

YOUNG MASTER Won't you come a bit closer?... And at least take off your hat!

YOUNG WIFE What are you thinking of, Alfred? I told you: five minutes... No, not a moment longer... I swear—

YOUNG MASTER What about your veil—

YOUNG WIFE There are two.

YOUNG MASTER Very well then, both veils—

YOUNG WIFE Do you love me, Alfred?

YOUNG MASTER (*deeply hurt*) Emma—how can you ask...

YOUNG WIFE It's so hot in here.

YOUNG MASTER But you've still got your fur stole on—you're sure to catch a cold like this.

YOUNG WIFE (*at last steps into the room and throws herself into the armchair*) I'm exhausted.

YOUNG MASTER Allow me. (*He takes off her veil; takes the hat-pin out of her hat, and puts hat, pin and veil aside*)

> *Young Wife allows him to.*
> *The Young Master stands in front of her, shaking his head.*

YOUNG WIFE What's the matter?

YOUNG MASTER You've never been more beautiful.

YOUNG WIFE How so?

YOUNG MASTER Alone... alone with you—Emma—(*He gets down on his knees beside her chair, takes both her hands and covers them with kisses*)

YOUNG WIFE And now... you must let me go. I've done what you asked me.

> *The Young Master lays his head in her lap.*

YOUNG WIFE You promised you'd be good.

YOUNG MASTER Yes.

YOUNG WIFE It's really stifling in here.

YOUNG MASTER (*gets up*) You've still got your stole on.

YOUNG WIFE Put it with my hat.

> *The Young Master takes her stole from her and puts it on the divan too.*

YOUNG WIFE And now—adieu—

YOUNG MASTER Emma—! Emma!—

YOUNG WIFE Your five minutes were up long ago.

YOUNG MASTER Not even one yet!—

YOUNG WIFE Alfred, tell me exactly now, what time is it?

YOUNG MASTER It's precisely a quarter past six.

YOUNG WIFE I should have been at my sister's long ago.

YOUNG MASTER You can see your sister any time...

YOUNG WIFE O God, Alfred, why did you talk me into this.

YOUNG MASTER Because I... adore you, Emma.

YOUNG WIFE How many others have you said that to before?

YOUNG MASTER Since setting eyes on you, none.

YOUNG WIFE What a frivolous person I am! Who would have foretold this of me... even a week ago... even yesterday...

YOUNG MASTER Though you'd already promised me the day before, if you recall...

YOUNG WIFE You kept on pestering me so. And I didn't want to come. God is my witness—I really didn't want to come... Yesterday I was quite determined not to... Do you know, last night I even wrote you a long letter?

YOUNG MASTER I didn't receive anything.

YOUNG WIFE I tore it up again. Oh, I wish I'd sent that letter off to you.

YOUNG MASTER It's better this way.

YOUNG WIFE O no, it's shameful... of me. I can't understand myself. Adieu, Alfred, let me go.

> *The Young Master embraces her and covers her face with passionate kisses.*

YOUNG WIFE Is this... how you keep your word...

YOUNG MASTER One more kiss—just one more.

YOUNG WIFE The last one. (*He kisses her; she returns his kiss; their lips remain pressed together for some time*)

YOUNG MASTER Shall I tell you something, Emma? For the first time I know what true happiness is.

> *The Young Wife sinks back in an armchair.*

YOUNG MASTER (*seats himself on the arm of the chair and puts his arm lightly round her neck*) ... or rather, I now know what true happiness could be.

The Young Wife sighs deeply.
The Young Master kisses her again.

YOUNG WIFE Alfred, Alfred, what are you doing to me!

YOUNG MASTER Don't you think—it's really quite cosy here... and we're so safe! It's ten times nicer than all our meetings out of doors...

YOUNG WIFE Oh, don't remind me of them.

YOUNG MASTER I too shall always remember them with infinite pleasure. Every minute I've been allowed to spend beside you is for me a cherished memory.

YOUNG WIFE Do you remember the Industrialists' Ball?

YOUNG MASTER Do I remember...? I sat next to you at supper, so close beside you. And your husband ordered the champagne...
    The Young Wife looks at him reproachfully.

YOUNG MASTER I was only going to talk about the champagne. By the way, what about a glass of cognac, Emma?

YOUNG WIFE Just a drop, but first give me a glass of water.

YOUNG MASTER Let me see... Now where's the—ah yes... (*He draws back the curtain and goes into the bedroom*)
    The Young Wife watches him.
    The Young Master returns with a carafe of water and two tumblers.

YOUNG WIFE Where were you?

YOUNG MASTER In the... next room. (*Pours out a glass of water*)

YOUNG WIFE Now I'm going to ask you something, Alfred—and you must swear to tell the truth.

YOUNG MASTER I swear.

YOUNG WIFE Did any other woman ever come here?

YOUNG MASTER But Emma—this house was built at least twenty years ago!

YOUNG WIFE You know what I mean, Alfred... with you! For you!

YOUNG MASTER With me—here—Emma! How could you think such a thing?

YOUNG WIFE So you did... how shall I... But no, I'd rather not ask. It's better I don't ask you. It's my fault anyway. Everything has to be atoned for.

YOUNG MASTER But what's the matter? What's wrong with you? What must be atoned for?

YOUNG WIFE No, no, no, I mustn't come to my senses... otherwise I'd be so ashamed I'd just sink into the ground.

YOUNG MASTER (*holding the carafe, shakes his head sadly*) Emma, if only you knew how sorry I feel for you.

The Young Wife pours herself a glass of cognac.

YOUNG MASTER Let me tell you something, Emma. If you are ashamed of being here—if you don't care about me—if you can't feel that you mean all the world to me—then you'd better go.

YOUNG WIFE Yes, that's what I'll do.

YOUNG MASTER (*taking her by the hand*) But if you could only understand that I can't live without you, that kissing your hand means more to me than all the caresses all the women in the world could... Emma, I'm not like other men, who know how a lady should be courted—perhaps I'm too naive... I...

YOUNG WIFE What if you really are like other men?

YOUNG MASTER Then you wouldn't be here—because you're not like other women.

YOUNG WIFE How do you know that?

YOUNG MASTER (*has meanwhile drawn her to the divan and seated himself beside her*) I have thought about you. I know you are unhappy.

The Young Wife looks pleased.

YOUNG MASTER Life is so empty, so worthless—and then—so short—so horribly short! The only possibility of happiness is... to find somebody who'll love one—

The Young Wife takes a candied pear from the table and pops it in her mouth

YOUNG MASTER Give me half! (*She offers it him between her lips*)

YOUNG WIFE (*takes hold of the Young Master's hands, which have begun to wander*) What are you doing, Alfred... Is this how you keep your promise?

YOUNG MASTER (*swallowing the pear, more boldly*) Life is so short.

YOUNG WIFE (*weakly*) But that's no reason—

YOUNG MASTER (*mechanically*) Of course.

YOUNG WIFE (*more weakly*) Look, Alfred, you did promise to be good... And it's so light...

YOUNG MASTER Come, come, my one and only... (*He gets up from the divan*)

YOUNG WIFE What are you doing?

YOUNG MASTER It's not light at all in there.

YOUNG WIFE Is that another room through there?

YOUNG MASTER (*draws her with him*) A really nice one... and it's dark.

YOUNG WIFE Perhaps we'd better stay in here.

The Young Master is by now beyond the dividing curtain and inside the bedroom with her, unlacing her bodice.

YOUNG WIFE You are so... O God, what are you doing to me!— Alfred!

YOUNG MASTER I am worshipping you, Emma!

YOUNG WIFE Well, wait a moment, at least give me a minute... (*weakly*) Go away... and then I'll call you.

YOUNG MASTER Can I help you—can you help me—(*He gets tangled up*)... can you—I—help?

YOUNG WIFE You'll tear my things.

YOUNG MASTER Aren't you wearing a corset?

YOUNG WIFE I never wear a corset. Frau Odilon* doesn't wear one either. But you could undo my shoe.

The Young Master undoes her shoes and kisses her feet.

YOUNG WIFE (*slips into bed*) Oh, I'm so cold.

YOUNG MASTER Everything will warm up in a minute.

YOUNG WIFE (*laughing softly*) Do you think so?

YOUNG MASTER (*disagreeably affected, to himself*) She shouldn't have said that. (*Undresses in the dark*)

YOUNG WIFE (*tenderly*) Come, come, come.

YOUNG MASTER (*his mood restored by this*) Coming——

YOUNG WIFE There's such a smell of violets here.

YOUNG MASTER You are my sweet violet... Yes—(*joining her*)—you.

YOUNG WIFE Alfred... Alfred!!!!!!

YOUNG MASTER Emma...

– –

YOUNG MASTER I'm obviously too much in love with you... indeed... I'm quite beside myself.

YOUNG WIFE ...

YOUNG MASTER These last few days I've been almost driven mad. I had an inkling this might happen.

YOUNG WIFE Don't worry about it.

YOUNG MASTER Of course not. It's to be expected, if one...

YOUNG WIFE Don't... don't... You are all excited. Just calm down...

YOUNG MASTER Do you know Stendhal?*

YOUNG WIFE Stendhal?

YOUNG MASTER His 'De l'Amour'?

YOUNG WIFE No, why do you ask?

YOUNG MASTER There's a story in there that's really quite revealing.

YOUNG WIFE What sort of story?

YOUNG MASTER Well, there's this group of cavalry officers who have got together—

YOUNG WIFE I see.

YOUNG MASTER And they tell each other stories about their amorous adventures. And each of them relates how, with the woman he loved best, most passionately that is... he, his—in short how each of them experienced the same problem with this favourite woman as I had just now.

YOUNG WIFE I see.

YOUNG MASTER It's very common.

YOUNG WIFE I see.

YOUNG MASTER That's not the end of the story. Only one of the officers claims... that this had never happened to him in his life: but then Stendhal adds that he was a notorious braggart.

YOUNG WIFE I see.

YOUNG MASTER And yet it's so frustrating, that's the stupid thing, even though it's not important.

YOUNG WIFE Certainly. But after all, you know... you did promise you'd be good.

YOUNG MASTER Don't laugh at me, that doesn't make things any easier.

YOUNG WIFE No, no, I'm not laughing. What Stendhal has to say is really interesting. I always thought this only happened with older... or with very... you know, men who have lived it up a lot...

YOUNG MASTER What curious ideas you have. That has nothing to do with it. By the way, I completely forgot the nicest story in Stendhal. One cavalry officer even tells how he spent three whole nights, or was it six... I can't remember, with a woman he'd been yearning for some weeks—désirée—as one might say—and all they did each night was simply cry for joy... both of them...

YOUNG WIFE Both of them?

YOUNG MASTER Yes. Does that surprise you? To me it's so very understandable—especially when two people are in love.

YOUNG WIFE But there must be many who don't cry.

YOUNG MASTER (*irritably*) Certainly... that case was exceptional, of course.

YOUNG WIFE Ah—I thought Stendhal was saying, all cavalry officers in that situation cry.

YOUNG MASTER You see, now you're making fun of me again.

YOUNG WIFE You're imagining things! Don't be so childish, Alfred!

YOUNG MASTER Well, it just gets on my nerves. And I also have the feeling you're thinking about it the whole time. And that really is embarrassing.

YOUNG WIFE I'm not thinking about it at all.

YOUNG MASTER Of course. If only I were sure you loved me.

YOUNG WIFE Do you want more proof than this?

YOUNG MASTER You see... you're always making fun of me.

YOUNG WIFE But how? Come, give me your sweet little head.

YOUNG MASTER Ah, that feels so good.

YOUNG WIFE Do you love me?

YOUNG MASTER O, I'm so happy.

YOUNG WIFE But you don't have to cry about it too.

YOUNG MASTER (*withdrawing from her, extremely irritated*) There you go again. And I asked you specially...

YOUNG WIFE When I say there's no need to cry for happiness...

YOUNG MASTER You said: cry about it too.

YOUNG WIFE You're overwrought, my love.

YOUNG MASTER I know that.

YOUNG WIFE But you shouldn't be. I'm even glad that it... that we'll be as it were parting as good friends.

YOUNG MASTER There you go again already.

YOUNG WIFE Don't you remember! That was one of our very first discussions. We were just going to be good friends and nothing more. Oh, that was so nice... it was at my sister's, in January during the grand ball, while we were dancing the quadrille... Heavens above, I should have left ages ago... my sister is expecting me— what am I going to say to her... Adieu, Alfred—

YOUNG MASTER Emma—! Are you going to abandon me like this!

YOUNG WIFE Well now!—

YOUNG MASTER Just five more minutes...

YOUNG WIFE All right. Five more minutes. But will you promise... not to move?... Yes?... I'll give you one more farewell kiss... Shh... quiet... don't move, I said, or I'll get up at once, my sweet... sweet...

YOUNG MASTER Emma... my adora...

YOUNG WIFE My Alfred—

YOUNG MASTER Ah, it's heaven, just lying in your arms.

YOUNG WIFE But now I really must be off.

YOUNG MASTER Oh, let your sister wait.

YOUNG WIFE I must get home. It's far too late to go and see my sister. What time is it?

YOUNG MASTER How should I know?

YOUNG WIFE Look at your watch of course.

YOUNG MASTER It's in my waistcoat pocket.

YOUNG WIFE Well go and get it then.

YOUNG MASTER (*heaves himself to his feet*) Eight.

YOUNG WIFE (*gets up hastily*) Goodness gracious... Quick Alfred, give me my stockings. What am I going to say? They're bound to be expecting me at home by now... eight o'clock...

YOUNG MASTER When shall I see you again?

YOUNG WIFE Never.

YOUNG MASTER Emma! Don't you love me any more?

YOUNG WIFE That's precisely why. Give me my shoes.

YOUNG MASTER Never again? Here are your shoes.

YOUNG WIFE There's a button-hook in my bag. Please, hurry...

YOUNG MASTER Here's the button-hook.

YOUNG WIFE Alfred, this could cost both of us our necks.

YOUNG MASTER (*very disagreeably affected*) How do you mean?

YOUNG WIFE Well, what am I to say if he asks me where I've been?

YOUNG MASTER To your sister's.

YOUNG WIFE If only I could lie.

YOUNG MASTER Well, you'll just have to.

YOUNG WIFE Anything for a man like you. Ah, come here... let me kiss you one more time. (*She embraces him*)—And now——leave me alone, go into the other room. I can't get dressed with you here.

> *The Young Master goes into the sitting room and gets dressed. He eats some of the confectionery and drinks a glass of cognac.*

YOUNG WIFE (*calls out after a while*) Alfred!

YOUNG MASTER My darling.

YOUNG WIFE Just as well we didn't cry over it.

YOUNG MASTER (*smiling with a touch of pride*) How can you be so flippant—

YOUNG WIFE But what are we going to do if we chance to meet in company one day?

YOUNG MASTER Chance to meet—one day... Surely you'll be at the Lobheimers' tomorrow?

YOUNG WIFE Yes. You too?

YOUNG MASTER Of course. May I ask you to put me down for the cotillion?

YOUNG WIFE Oh, I shan't be going. How can you expect me to?—I would just... (*she comes fully dressed into the sitting room, and helps herself to a chocolate cake...*) sink into the ground.

YOUNG MASTER Well then, tomorrow at the Lobheimers', that's settled.

YOUNG WIFE No, no... I shall cry off, I'm sure to—

YOUNG MASTER All right, the day after tomorrow... here.

YOUNG WIFE Can't you be serious?

YOUNG MASTER About six.

YOUNG WIFE There are cabs here on the corner, aren't there?—

YOUNG MASTER As many as you want. Well then, here at six the day after tomorrow. Do say yes, my darling.

YOUNG WIFE ...We'll talk about it during the cotillion tomorrow.

YOUNG MASTER (*embraces her*) My angel.

YOUNG WIFE Don't ruin my hair now.

YOUNG MASTER Tomorrow at the Lobheimers' and then, the day after in my arms!

YOUNG WIFE Farewell...

YOUNG MASTER (*suddenly concerned again*) And what are you going to tell—him tonight?—

YOUNG WIFE Don't ask... don't ask... it's just too awful.—Why do I love you so!—Adieu.—I'll have a fit if I meet someone on the stairs again—Pah!—

> The Young Master kisses her hand again.
> The Young Wife departs.

YOUNG MASTER (*is left behind alone. He sits down on the divan. He smiles and says to himself*) So here I am, having an affair with a respectable married woman.

V THE YOUNG WIFE AND THE HUSBAND

> *A comfortable bedroom.*
> *It is half past ten at night. The Young Wife is lying in bed reading.*
> *The Husband enters the room in his dressing gown.*

YOUNG WIFE *without looking up* Aren't you working any more?

HUSBAND No, I'm too tired. And besides...

YOUNG WIFE Well?—

HUSBAND I suddenly felt so lonely sitting at my desk. I found myself longing for you.

YOUNG WIFE (*looks up*) Really?

HUSBAND (*sits beside her on the bed*) Don't read any more tonight. You'll ruin your eyes.

YOUNG WIFE (*closes the book*) So what's the matter?

HUSBAND Nothing, my dear. I'm in love with you! You know that!

YOUNG WIFE Sometimes one might almost forget it.

HUSBAND Sometimes one needs to forget it.

YOUNG WIFE Why?

HUSBAND Because otherwise marriage would be something less than perfect. It would... how shall I say... it would lose its sanctity.

YOUNG WIFE Oh...

HUSBAND Believe me—it is so... If in the five years we've been married we hadn't occasionally forgotten we're in love—we would no longer be so.

YOUNG WIFE That's too lofty for me.

HUSBAND As it is, we've had perhaps ten or twelve love affairs, all with each other... Doesn't it seem like that to you as well?

YOUNG WIFE I can't say I've been counting!—

HUSBAND If we'd savoured our first one to the very dregs, if I'd surrendered to my passion for you from the very start, we'd have fared no better than a million other couples. Our relationship would by now be over.

YOUNG WIFE Ah... so that's what you think?

HUSBAND Believe me—Emma—for the first few days of our marriage, I was afraid that's what would happen.

YOUNG WIFE Me too.

HUSBAND You see? Wasn't I right? That's why now and then it's good to live as just good friends together.

YOUNG WIFE I see.

HUSBAND That way we can keep on having new honeymoons, because I never let the honeymoons...

YOUNG WIFE Go on for months.

HUSBAND Precisely.

YOUNG WIFE And so now... another period of being just good friends would seem to have expired—?

HUSBAND (*drawing her to him tenderly*) That may well be.

YOUNG WIFE But supposing... it were different for me.

HUSBAND It isn't any different for you. You're the cleverest and most charming little woman in the world. I am very happy to have found you.

YOUNG WIFE It's sweet, the way you pay court to me—now and then.

HUSBAND (*gets into bed too*) For a man who's seen a little of the world—here, put your head on my shoulder—the significance of marriage is more of a mystery than for you young ladies from good families. You come to us pure and... at least to a certain degree ignorant, and consequently you have a much clearer vision of the true nature of love than we do.

YOUNG WIFE (*laughing*) Oh!

HUSBAND Certainly. For we become uncertain and confused by the manifold experiences we've had to go through before marriage. Of course you hear a lot, and know more than you should, and probably read too much about these things as well, but still you don't have a true grasp of what we men actually experience. We become utterly disgusted by what is commonly called love; but then what sort of creatures are we obliged to turn to!

YOUNG WIFE What sort of creatures are they then?

HUSBAND (*kisses her on the forehead*) Be thankful, my dear, that you're ignorant of such matters. Besides, they are unfortunate wretches for the most part—so let's not be the first to cast a stone.

YOUNG WIFE Come now—all this pity.—It doesn't seem to me called for in the least.

HUSBAND (*with fine indulgence*) Ah but they deserve it. You young ladies from good families waiting calmly in the shelter of your parents' home for someone respectable to ask your hand in marriage;—you have no idea of the poverty that drives these wretches into the arms of sin.

YOUNG WIFE So do they all do it just for money?

HUSBAND I wouldn't say that. I don't only mean material poverty of course. There is also—if I may say so—such a thing as moral poverty; a deficient sense of what's permissible, and more especially of what is noble.

YOUNG WIFE But why should they be pitied?—They have quite a good life, after all.

HUSBAND You have some curious notions, my dear. Don't forget such wretches are doomed by nature to fall lower and lower. There is no stopping them.

YOUNG WIFE (*nestling close to him*) Evidently they quite enjoy falling.

HUSBAND (*painfully affected*) How can you talk like that, Emma. I'd have thought that for you respectable women in particular, nothing could be more repellent than women who are not so.

YOUNG WIFE Of course, Karl, of course. I was just being flippant. Go on, tell me more. It's so nice when you talk like this. Talk to me.

HUSBAND What about?

YOUNG WIFE Well—about these wretched creatures.

HUSBAND What's got into you?

YOUNG WIFE Well, you know I've asked you often enough, ever since the very beginning in fact, to tell me all about your youth.

HUSBAND Why are you so interested in that?

YOUNG WIFE Well, you are a man, aren't you? And isn't it rather unfair that I don't know anything about your past?—

HUSBAND You don't think me so tasteless as to—Enough of this, Emma... it's a sort of desecration.

YOUNG WIFE And yet who knows... how many more young ladies you have held in your arms like this.

HUSBAND Don't use the word 'ladies'. It's you who are the lady.

YOUNG WIFE But you must answer me one question... otherwise... no more honeymoon.

HUSBAND The way you talk... kindly remember you're a mother... and it's our little girl asleep through there...

YOUNG WIFE (*cuddling up to him*) But I'd like a boy as well.

HUSBAND Emma!

YOUNG WIFE Go on, don't be such a... of course I'm your wife... but I also want to be... your lover occasionally too.

HUSBAND Do you?...

YOUNG WIFE But—first my question.

HUSBAND (*indulgently*) Well?

YOUNG WIFE Was... a married woman—one of them?

HUSBAND Why?—What d'you mean?

YOUNG WIFE You know.

HUSBAND (*a little uneasily*) What makes you ask?

YOUNG WIFE I would like to know whether... that is—such women do exist... I know. But whether you...

HUSBAND Do you know any such woman?

YOUNG WIFE Why, I wouldn't know myself.

HUSBAND Are there any such women among your friends, by any chance?

YOUNG WIFE Well, how can I confirm that for certain—or deny it?

HUSBAND Have any of your friends ever... People discuss all sorts of things in certain situations—I mean, when women are alone together—has anyone admitted to you that they—?

YOUNG WIFE (*uncertainly*) No.

HUSBAND Do you have any suspicions about any of your friends...

YOUNG WIFE Suspicions... oh... suspicions.

HUSBAND Evidently so.

YOUNG WIFE Of course not, Karl, I'm quite sure not. When I think about it—I can't believe any of them capable of such a thing.

HUSBAND None of them at all?

YOUNG WIFE None of my friends.

HUSBAND Promise me one thing, Emma.

YOUNG WIFE Well?

HUSBAND That you won't associate with any woman you in the least suspect of... not leading a completely blameless life.

YOUNG WIFE Do I really need to promise that?

HUSBAND Of course I realize you'd never associate with such women knowingly yourself. But fate might contrive things so that you... In fact it's often precisely women of far from unsullied reputation who seek out the company of decent women, partly to enhance their social standing, but also from a... how shall I put it... a certain homesickness for virtue.

YOUNG WIFE I see.

HUSBAND Yes, I think what I just said is absolutely true. Homesickness for virtue. Because take my word for it, all these women are thoroughly unhappy.

YOUNG WIFE Why?

HUSBAND What a question, Emma!—How can you ask?—Just imagine the kind of existence these women are obliged to lead. Full of lies, deceit and baseness, not to speak of danger.

YOUNG WIFE Yes indeed. You're right about that.

HUSBAND Truly—they pay dearly for their bit of happiness... their bit of...

YOUNG WIFE Pleasure.

HUSBAND Why pleasure? What makes you call it pleasure?

YOUNG WIFE Well—it must be something—! Otherwise they wouldn't do it, surely.

HUSBAND It's nothing but... a drug.

YOUNG WIFE (thoughtfully) A drug.

HUSBAND No, it's not even a drug. Whatever it is—it's paid for dearly, that much is certain!

YOUNG WIFE So... you yourself took part in all this once—didn't you?

HUSBAND Yes, Emma.—It's my most painful memory.

YOUNG WIFE Who was it? Tell me? Do I know her?

HUSBAND What are you talking about?

YOUNG WIFE Was it quite some time ago? Was it long before you married me?

HUSBAND Don't ask. Please, don't ask.

YOUNG WIFE But Karl!

HUSBAND She is dead.

YOUNG WIFE Seriously?

HUSBAND Yes... it sounds almost ridiculous, but I have a feeling all these women die young anyway.

YOUNG WIFE Did you love her very much?

HUSBAND One doesn't love women who lie.

YOUNG WIFE So why...

HUSBAND A drug...

YOUNG WIFE Is that so?

HUSBAND Don't let's discuss it any more, please. All that's over long ago. I've only loved one woman—and that's you. One can only love where purity and truth reside.

YOUNG WIFE Karl!

HUSBAND Oh, how safe, how good one feels in such arms. Why didn't I know you as a child? I'm sure I would never have looked at another woman then.

YOUNG WIFE Karl!

HUSBAND And you're so beautiful!... beautiful!... Oh come... (*He turns the light out*)

— — — — — — — — — — — — — — — — — — — —

YOUNG WIFE Do you know what tonight reminds me of?

HUSBAND What, my love?

YOUNG WIFE Of... of... of Venice.

HUSBAND Our first night...

YOUNG WIFE Yes... you were so...

HUSBAND What—? Go on, say it!

YOUNG WIFE You were so loving tonight.

HUSBAND Loving, of course.

YOUNG WIFE Ah... If only you'd always...

HUSBAND (*in her arms*) What?

YOUNG WIFE My sweet Karl!

HUSBAND What did you mean? If only I'd always...

YOUNG WIFE Well, you know.

HUSBAND Well, what would happen, if I always...

YOUNG WIFE Then I'd always know you loved me of course.

HUSBAND Yes. But you'll have to know it without that sometimes. One can't always be the loving husband, one also has to venture forth into the hostile world* sometimes, one has to fight the good fight! Don't ever forget that, my child! There's a time for everything in marriage—that is what's so beautiful. There are not that many people who, after five years, still—remember their Venice.

YOUNG WIFE Certainly.

HUSBAND And now... good night... my child.

YOUNG WIFE Good night!

VI THE HUSBAND AND THE SWEET MAID

A private room in the Riedhof.* Subdued comfortable elegance.
The gas stove is burning.
The Husband, the Sweet Maid.
On the table the remains of a meal can be seen—cream puffs,
fruit, cheese. In the glasses, a white Hungarian wine.
The Husband is smoking a Havana cigar, leaning back in one
corner of the divan.
The Sweet Maid is sitting in an armchair beside him, as she
spoons whipped cream out of the cream puff and slurps it up with
evident satisfaction.

HUSBAND Taste good?

SWEET MAID (*without pausing*). Mmh!

HUSBAND Would you like another?

SWEET MAID No. I've had too many already.

HUSBAND You've finished your wine. (*He replenishes her glass*)

SWEET MAID No more, Sir... please, I'll just leave it anyway.

HUSBAND You're being so formal again.

SWEET MAID Well—you see, Sir—it's hard to get out of the habit.

HUSBAND You see.

SWEET MAID What?

HUSBAND Just say, you see, and forget the Sir,—Come and sit over
here with me.

SWEET MAID In a moment... I've not quite finished.
    The Husband gets up, goes behind the chair and embraces the
    Sweet Maid, turning her head towards him.

SWEET MAID Well, what is it?

HUSBAND I want you to kiss me.

SWEET MAID (*gives him a kiss*) You're very forward, Sir... oh sorry, I
forgot.

HUSBAND Have you only just noticed that?

SWEET MAID Oh no, I suspected as much earlier... even on the street,
Sir.

HUSBAND There you go again.

SWEET MAID You must have a fine opinion of me.

HUSBAND But why?

SWEET MAID My coming to a private room with you at once like this.

HUSBAND Well, one can hardly say at once.

SWEET MAID But you do have a way of asking nicely.

HUSBAND You think so?

SWEET MAID And besides, what does it matter?

HUSBAND Certainly.

SWEET MAID Whether one goes walking or—

HUSBAND It's much too cold for walking anyway.

SWEET MAID Of course it was too cold.

HUSBAND But in here it's nice and warm, don't you find? (*He resumes his seat, putting his arm round the Sweet Maid and drawing her down beside him*)

SWEET MAID (*weakly*) Ah well.

HUSBAND Now tell me something... You'd noticed me earlier, hadn't you?

SWEET MAID Of course. In the Singerstrasse already.

HUSBAND I don't mean today. But when I followed you the day before yesterday, and the day before that.

SWEET MAID I get followed quite a bit.

HUSBAND I can imagine. But I wondered if you'd noticed me.

SWEET MAID Well, Sir... oh, sorry... do you know what happened to me recently? My cousin's husband followed me in the dark, but didn't recognize me.

HUSBAND And did he approach you?

SWEET MAID How can you say that? Do you think everyone's as forward as you?

HUSBAND But it does happen.

SWEET MAID Of course it happens.

HUSBAND Well, what do you do when it does?

SWEET MAID Well, nothing.—I just don't respond.

HUSBAND Hmm... But you responded to me.

SWEET MAID Are you angry then?

HUSBAND (*kisses her hard*) Your lips taste of whipped cream.

SWEET MAID Oh, they're sweet by nature.

HUSBAND Have many others told you that?

SWEET MAID Many others! I don't know what you imagine!

HUSBAND Come on, be honest. How many others have kissed that mouth of yours?

SWEET MAID Why bother asking then? You won't believe me anyway, if I tell you!

HUSBAND Why not?

SWEET MAID Well then, guess!

HUSBAND I would say—but you mustn't be angry?!

SWEET MAID Why should I be angry?

HUSBAND All right then, I would guess... twenty.

SWEET MAID (*disengaging herself from him*) Well—why not a hundred while you're about it?

HUSBAND But it was only a guess.

SWEET MAID Well, it was a poor one.

HUSBAND All right, ten.

SWEET MAID (*offended*) Why not! A girl who lets herself be accosted in the street and taken to a private room at once!

HUSBAND Don't be so childish. What does it matter whether one wanders about the streets or sits inside a room... Anyway, we're in a restaurant here. The waiter could come in at any minute—nothing really to get so upset about...

SWEET MAID That's what I've just been thinking too.

HUSBAND Have you been in one of these private rooms before?

SWEET MAID Well, to tell the truth: yes.

HUSBAND I like that, you know, at least you're honest.

SWEET MAID But not—the way you're imagining again. I was invited by a friend and her fiancé once during Carnival this year.

HUSBAND It wouldn't be a tragedy if you'd been to one with—your sweetheart—

SWEET MAID Of course it wouldn't be a tragedy. But I don't have a sweetheart.

HUSBAND Come on.

SWEET MAID I swear, I haven't.

HUSBAND But you're not going to persuade me that I'm the...

SWEET MAID What?... I haven't had one—for more than six months now.

HUSBAND I see... But before that? Who was he?

SWEET MAID Why are you so curious?

HUSBAND I'm curious because I'm fond of you.

SWEET MAID Is that true?

HUSBAND Certainly. You must be aware of that. So tell me. (*Draws her close to him*)

SWEET MAID What am I supposed to tell you?

HUSBAND How many times do I have to ask. I'd like to know who he was.

SWEET MAID (*laughing*) Well, a man of course.

HUSBAND Well then—so—tell me about him?

SWEET MAID He looked a bit like you.

HUSBAND I see.

SWEET MAID If you hadn't looked a bit like him—

HUSBAND What then?

SWEET MAID Well, don't ask me then, if you can see already that...

HUSBAND (*understands*) So that's why you didn't mind when I approached you.

SWEET MAID I suppose so.

HUSBAND Now I really don't know whether I should be pleased or annoyed.

SWEET MAID Well, if I were you, I would be pleased.

HUSBAND Perhaps so.

SWEET MAID And the way you speak reminds me so much of him... and the way you look at me...

HUSBAND What was his occupation?

SWEET MAID Your eyes, I can't believe it—

HUSBAND What was his name?

SWEET MAID No, please don't look at me like that.

> *The Husband embraces her and gives her a long fervent kiss.*
> *The Sweet Maid shakes herself and starts to get up.*

HUSBAND Why are you getting up?

SWEET MAID It's time I was going home.

HUSBAND Later.

SWEET MAID No, I really must be going home now. What do you suppose my mother's going to say.

HUSBAND You live with your mother?

SWEET MAID Of course I live with my mother. What did you imagine?

HUSBAND I see—with your mother. Do you live alone with her?

SWEET MAID Oh yes of course, alone! There are five of us! Two boys and two more girls.

HUSBAND Don't sit so far away from me. Are you the eldest?

SWEET MAID No, I'm the second. First comes Kathy; she goes out to work in a flower shop, then I'm next.

HUSBAND And where are you?

SWEET MAID Well, I'm at home.

HUSBAND All the time?

SWEET MAID One of us has to stay at home.

HUSBAND Well—and what do you tell your mother when you—come home as late as this?

SWEET MAID It doesn't happen very often.

HUSBAND What about tonight for instance? Your mother will ask you, won't she?

SWEET MAID Of course she'll ask me. However careful I am—she always wakes when I come in.

HUSBAND So what will you say to her?

SWEET MAID Well, that I've been to the theatre perhaps.

HUSBAND And will she believe that?

SWEET MAID Well, why shouldn't she believe it? I often go to the theatre. Only last Sunday I was at the opera with my friend and her fiancé and my older brother.

HUSBAND Where did you get the tickets?

SWEET MAID But my brother's a hairdresser!

HUSBAND But what do hairdressers... oh, a hairdresser at the theatre, you mean.

SWEET MAID Why are you cross-examining me like this?

HUSBAND It all intrigues me. And what does your other brother do?

SWEET MAID He's still at school. He wants to become a teacher. Goodness... I don't believe this!

HUSBAND And then you've got another, younger sister?

SWEET MAID Yes, she's just a little brat still, but even with her one has to be so careful these days. You've no idea how they neglect young girls at school. Can you imagine! The other day I caught her on a rendezvous already.

HUSBAND What?

SWEET MAID Yes! She was out walking in the Strozzigasse with a boy from the school opposite, at seven-thirty in the evening. The little brat!

HUSBAND And what did you do?

SWEET MAID Well, she got a spanking.

HUSBAND Are you always as severe as that?

SWEET MAID Well, what else is one to do? My older sister is at work, my mother does nothing but complain;—so everything falls on my shoulders.

HUSBAND God, how sweet you are! (*Kisses her and becomes more intimate*) You remind me of someone too.

SWEET MAID Really—of whom?

HUSBAND Oh no one in particular... of the time when... well, of my youth. Anyway, drink up, my dear!

SWEET MAID So how old are you then? You know... I don't even know your name.

HUSBAND Karl.

SWEET MAID I don't believe it! You're called Karl?

HUSBAND He was called Karl too?

SWEET MAID Well that's quite miraculous... it's hard to—incredible, the eyes... the look... (*shakes her head*)

HUSBAND And you still haven't told me anything about him.

SWEET MAID He was a wicked man—no doubt about that, otherwise he wouldn't have abandoned me.

HUSBAND Were you very fond of him?

SWEET MAID Of course I was.

HUSBAND I know what he was—a lieutenant.

SWEET MAID No, he wasn't in the army. They wouldn't take him. His father has a house in the... but why do you need to know that?

HUSBAND (*kisses her*) Your eyes are grey in fact; at first I thought that they were black.

SWEET MAID Does that mean they're not pretty enough for you?
          The Husband kisses her eyes.

SWEET MAID Don't, don't—I really can't bear that... oh please—Oh God... no, let me get up... just for a minute—please.

HUSBAND (*tenderly*) Oh no.

SWEET MAID Please, Karl.

HUSBAND How old are you?—eighteen?

SWEET MAID Over nineteen.

HUSBAND Nineteen... and I am—

SWEET MAID You are thirty...

HUSBAND Plus a few.—Don't let's talk about it.

SWEET MAID He was thirty-two already when I met him.

HUSBAND How long ago was that?

SWEET MAID I don't remember any more... You know, I think there must be something in the wine.

HUSBAND What makes you say that?

SWEET MAID I'm really quite... you know—my head's spinning.

HUSBAND Well then hold me tight. There... (*he draws her closer to him and caresses her more and more intimately, she scarcely resisting*) I'll tell you what, my love, we could go now if you like.

SWEET MAID Yes... home.

HUSBAND Well not straight home...

SWEET MAID What do you mean?... Oh no, oh no... I'm not going anywhere, what are you thinking of—

HUSBAND Now listen, my love, next time we meet we'll arrange things so that... (*he has sunk to the floor and put his head in her lap*) That feels good, oh, that feels so good.

SWEET MAID What are you doing? (*She kisses his hair*)... You know, there must have been something in the wine—so sleepy... I say,

what's going to happen if I can't stand up? But, but, listen Karl...
what if someone comes in... please... the waiter.

HUSBAND No waiter... is ever going to come in here... don't worry...

— —

> *The Sweet Maid is leaning back with eyes closed in the corner of
> the divan.*
> *The Husband is pacing up and down the little room, having
> lighted a cigar. Protracted silence.*

HUSBAND (*to himself, after considering the Sweet Maid for some time*)
Who knows what sort of girl she really is—Good heavens... All so
quick... Was rather careless of me... Hm...

SWEET MAID (*without opening her eyes*) There must have been something in the wine.

HUSBAND But why?

SWEET MAID Otherwise...

HUSBAND Why do you blame everything on the wine?

SWEET MAID Where are you? Why are you so far away? Come over
here to me.

> *The Husband goes over to her and sits down.*

SWEET MAID Now tell me if you really love me.

HUSBAND But you know very well I... (*breaks off quickly*) of course I
do.

SWEET MAID You know... it's really... Come on, tell me the truth,
what was in the wine?

HUSBAND Now what do you take me for... a poisoner?

SWEET MAID You see, I don't understand. I'm not like this... we've
only known each other since... I'm not like this... I swear to God—
if you thought that of me—

HUSBAND Come—what are you getting all upset for. I don't think any
the worse of you. I just think you're fond of me.

SWEET MAID Yes...

HUSBAND After all, when two young people wine and dine alone in a
room together... there doesn't have to be anything in the wine...

SWEET MAID It was just something I said anyway.

HUSBAND But why?

SWEET MAID (*a shade defiantly*) Because I was ashamed.

HUSBAND That's ridiculous. There's no reason for that at all. The
more so, since I remind you of your first lover.

SWEET MAID Yes.

HUSBAND Your very first.

SWEET MAID Well...

HUSBAND Now I'd really be interested to know about the others.

SWEET MAID There weren't any.

HUSBAND That's not true, that can't be true.

SWEET MAID Come now, please don't nag me.—

HUSBAND Do you want a cigarette?

SWEET MAID No thank you.

HUSBAND Do you know how late it is?

SWEET MAID Well?

HUSBAND Half past eleven.

SWEET MAID Is it!

HUSBAND Well... and how about your mother? She's used to it, what?

SWEET MAID Do you really want to send me home already?

HUSBAND But earlier you said yourself—

SWEET MAID Goodness, how you've changed. What have I done to you?

HUSBAND But what's the matter with you, child, you're imagining things.

SWEET MAID And it was only the way you look, otherwise I swear you wouldn't have... plenty of others have asked me to come to private rooms with them before.

HUSBAND Well, would you like to... come here with me again soon... or perhaps go somewhere else—

SWEET MAID I don't know.

HUSBAND What's that supposed to mean: you don't know.

SWEET MAID Well you haven't asked yet, have you?

HUSBAND All right, when? Only I must first explain to you that I don't live in Vienna. I just come here for a few days from time to time.

SWEET MAID Go on, don't tell me you're not Viennese?

HUSBAND I'm Viennese all right. But I now live near...

SWEET MAID Near where?

HUSBAND Ah God, does it matter!

SWEET MAID Well, don't worry, I shan't be coming.

HUSBAND Oh God, come by all means if you like. I live in Graz.

SWEET MAID Seriously?

HUSBAND Well, why should that surprise you?

SWEET MAID You're married, aren't you?

HUSBAND (*completely taken aback*) What makes you think that?

SWEET MAID I just get that impression.

HUSBAND And wouldn't that embarrass you at all?

SWEET MAID Well, I'd prefer you to be single.—But you are married, aren't you?

HUSBAND Come on now, tell me, what makes you think so?

SWEET MAID When a man says he doesn't live in Vienna and doesn't have time—

HUSBAND But that's surely not all that improbable?

SWEET MAID I don't believe it.

HUSBAND And don't you have any qualms about seducing a married man?

SWEET MAID Get away, your wife is sure to be up to the same tricks as you.

HUSBAND (*outraged*) I forbid you to talk like that. Such remarks—

SWEET MAID But I thought you didn't have a wife.

HUSBAND Whether I have or not—such remarks are quite uncalled for. (*He has stood up*)

SWEET MAID Karl, come now Karl, what's the matter? Are you angry? Look, I really don't know whether you are married. I was just saying things. Go on, come and be nice to me again.

HUSBAND (*comes to her after a few seconds*) You really are strange creatures, you... women. (*Beside her, he resumes his intimate caresses*)

SWEET MAID Come... don't... it's really too late—

HUSBAND All right, now listen to me. We need to talk seriously. I want to see you again, see you often.

SWEET MAID Is that true?

HUSBAND But that entails... well, I must be able to rely on you. I can't look after you.

SWEET MAID Oh, I can look after myself already, thank you.

HUSBAND You are... well, one can hardly say inexperienced—but you are young—and—men are generally an unscrupulous lot.

SWEET MAID Oh dear!

HUSBAND And I don't mean that just from a moral point of view— I'm sure you understand me.

SWEET MAID Tell me, what do you think I am?

HUSBAND Well then—if you want me to be your lover—me and no one else—we can get ourselves a little place—even though I shall normally be living in Graz. Here, where someone might come in at any time, is not quite the thing for us.

    The Sweet Maid cuddles close to him.

HUSBAND Next time... we'll go somewhere else, agreed?

SWEET MAID Yes.

HUSBAND Where we'll be completely undisturbed.

SWEET MAID Yes.

HUSBAND (*embraces her ardently*) We'll talk about the other matter on the way home. (*Gets up, opens the door*) Waiter... the bill!

VII THE SWEET MAID AND THE POET

> *A small room, tastefully and comfortably furnished. Curtains, which leave the room in semi-darkness. Red muslin outer curtains. Large writing desk strewn with books and papers. An upright piano against the wall. The Sweet Maid. The Poet. They are just coming in together. The Poet locks the door.*

POET There we are, my darling. (*Kisses her*)

SWEET MAID (*wearing a hat and shawl*) Ah! But this is really lovely! Except that one can't see a thing!

POET Your eyes have to adjust to the half-light.—These sweet eyes—(*kisses her on the eyes*)

SWEET MAID These sweet eyes are not going to have time for that.

POET But why?

SWEET MAID Because I can only stay a minute.

POET Take your hat off, all right?

SWEET MAID Just for one minute?

POET (*Takes the pin out of her hat and puts the hat aside*) And the shawl—

SWEET MAID What's the point of that?—I've got to be off again at once.

POET But you must rest a little! We've been walking for three hours.

SWEET MAID We were driving.

POET We drove home, yes—but in Weidling* we walked a good three hours along the river. So sit down a moment, my love... anywhere you like;—here at the desk;—no, perhaps not, it's a bit uncomfortable. Come and sit on the divan.—There. (*He helps her sit*) If you're very tired you can stretch out too. There. (*He helps her lie down on the divan*) Now your sweet head on this cushion.

SWEET MAID (*laughing*) But I'm not tired at all!

POET You only think that. There—and if you feel sleepy, you can go to sleep. I shall be very quiet. I can even play you a lullaby... I wrote... (*goes to the piano*)

SWEET MAID You wrote?

POET Yes.

SWEET MAID But Robert, I thought you were a doctor.

POET How so? I told you I'm a writer.

SWEET MAID But all writers are called Doctor something, aren't they?

POET No, not all of them. I'm not, for instance. But what made you think of that suddenly?

SWEET MAID Why, because you said you wrote that piece you're playing.

POET Well... perhaps I didn't write it. It doesn't matter, does it? Anyway, it never matters who wrote a thing. As long as it's beautiful— don't you agree?

SWEET MAID Certainly... as long as it's beautiful—that's the main thing!—

POET Do you understand what I meant by that?

SWEET MAID By what?

POET Well, what I just said.

SWEET MAID (*sleepily*) But of course.

POET (*gets up; goes over to her, strokes her hair*) You didn't understand a word.

SWEET MAID Go on, I'm not that stupid.

POET Of course you are that stupid. But that's exactly what's so adorable about you. Ah, it's so marvellous when you women are stupid. I mean, the way you are.

SWEET MAID Come now, why all these insults?

POET My little angel. The Persian rug makes the couch really comfortable, don't you find?

SWEET MAID Oh, it does. I say, aren't you going to go on playing?

POET No, I'd rather sit right here beside you. (*Caresses her*)

SWEET MAID I say, wouldn't it be better if you put a light on?

POET Oh no... This twilight is so soothing. Today we spent the whole day bathed in sunlight. Now we have as it were got out of the bath and swathed ourselves... in twilight, like a bath-robe— (*laughs*)—ah no—there must be a better way of saying it... Wouldn't you agree?

SWEET MAID I don't know.

POET (*withdrawing from her lightly*) What divine stupidity! (*Takes a notebook and scribbles a few words in it*)

SWEET MAID What are you doing? (*Turning towards him*) What are you jotting down?

POET (*in an undertone*) Sun, bath, twilight, robe... there. (*Puts the notebook away. Aloud*) Nothing... tell me now, my darling, wouldn't you like something to eat or drink?

SWEET MAID I'm not really thirsty, but I've an appetite all right.

POET Hm... I would rather you were thirsty. I've got some cognac, but there's no food in the house.

SWEET MAID Can't you order some?

POET That's a bit difficult, the maid has left already—wait—I'll go myself... what would you like?

SWEET MAID It really isn't worth the trouble, as I must be getting home.

POET No trouble at all, my love. But I tell you what: when we leave, why don't we go and eat somewhere together.

SWEET MAID Oh, no. I don't have time for that. And besides, where would we go? We might be seen by some acquaintance.

POET Do you have that many acquaintances?

SWEET MAID All it takes is for one of them to see us, and the damage is done.

POET What sort of damage might that be?

SWEET MAID You know, what if my mother were to hear things...

POET But we could go somewhere nobody would see us, after all, there are restaurants with private rooms.

SWEET MAID (*singing*) Yes, supper with you, in a room for two!

POET Have you been in one of those private rooms before?

SWEET MAID To tell the truth—yes.

POET Who was the lucky man?

SWEET MAID Oh, it wasn't what you think... I was with my friend and her fiancé. They took me along with them.

POET I see. And am I supposed to believe you?

SWEET MAID You don't have to believe me!

POET (*close to her*) Tell me, are you blushing now? It's too dark to see! I can't make out your features. (*Feels her cheeks with his hand*) But I can also tell like this.

SWEET MAID Well, just make sure you're not confusing me with someone else.

POET It's strange. I can't remember how you look any more.

SWEET MAID Well, thank you!

POET (*seriously*) D'you know, this is quite uncanny. I just can't picture you.—In a sense, I've forgotten you already.—Supposing I couldn't remember the sound of your voice either... what would you be then?—Near and far at once... uncanny.

SWEET MAID What are you talking about—?

POET Nothing, my angel, nothing. Where are your lips... (*he kisses her*)

SWEET MAID Shouldn't you put a light on?

POET No... (*becomes very affectionate*) Tell me, do you love me?

SWEET MAID Very much... oh so very much!

POET Have you ever loved anyone as much before?

SWEET MAID I've already told you—no.

POET Come now... (*he sighs*)

SWEET MAID Well, he was my fiancé.

POET I'd rather you didn't think about him now.

SWEET MAID I say... what are you doing... look...

POET Let's imagine we're in a palace somewhere in India.

SWEET MAID They certainly wouldn't be as naughty there as you.

POET How stupid! Divine—ah, if only you knew how much you mean to me...

SWEET MAID Well?

POET Don't keep pushing me away; I'm not doing anything to you— for the moment.

SWEET MAID I say, my corset's hurting.

POET (*simply*) Take it off then.

SWEET MAID All right. But you mustn't get naughty then.

POET No.

> *The Sweet Maid gets up and takes off her corset in the dark.*

POET (*who meanwhile sits down on the divan*) By the way, aren't you interested at all in knowing my surname?

SWEET MAID Well, what is your name then?

POET I'd prefer to tell you what I call myself, rather than my name.

SWEET MAID So, what's the difference?

POET Well, what I call myself as a writer.

SWEET MAID Ah, so you don't write under your real name.

> *The Poet moves very close to her.*

SWEET MAID Ah!... come on... don't.

POET What fragrance ascends to greet one. How sweet.

> *He kisses her breasts.*

SWEET MAID You're tearing my blouse.

POET Off... off... all this is superfluous.

SWEET MAID But Robert!

POET And now come inside our Indian palace.

SWEET MAID First, tell me if you really love me.

POET But I worship you. (*Kisses her fervently*) I worship you, my darling, my springtime... my...

SWEET MAID Robert... Robert...

– –

POET That was transcendent bliss... I call myself...

SWEET MAID Robert, my own Robert!

POET I call myself Biebitz.

SWEET MAID Why do you call yourself Biebitz?

POET Biebitz is not my name—that's just what I call myself... well, perhaps you've never heard the name before?

SWEET MAID No.

POET You've never heard the name Biebitz? Ah—divine! Really? You're not just saying that, are you?

SWEET MAID I swear, I've never heard it!

POET Don't you ever go to the theatre then?

SWEET MAID Oh yes—just the other day I was with a—with my friend and her uncle, you know, and we all went to the opera to see 'Cavalleria Rusticana'.*

POET Hm, so you never go to the Burgtheater then.

SWEET MAID I never get free tickets there.

POET I'll have tickets sent you shortly.

SWEET MAID Oh yes! Don't forget! But make sure it's something funny.

POET Let's see... something funny... so you don't want something sad?

SWEET MAID I'm not too keen.

POET Even if it's a play by me?

SWEET MAID Really—a play by you? So you write for the theatre?

POET Excuse me, I'll just get a light. I've not yet seen you since we've become lovers.—My darling angel! (*He lights a candle*)

SWEET MAID Do you mind, it makes me feel ashamed. At least give me a rug.

POET Later! (*He approaches her with the light and contemplates her for a long while*)

SWEET MAID (*covers her face with her hands*) Come on, Robert!

POET You're so beautiful, you're beauty incarnate, perhaps you're Nature herself even, you're divine simplicity.

SWEET MAID Ouch, you're dripping wax on me! Why don't you look what you're doing!

POET (*puts the candle to one side*) You are what I've long been looking for. You love me for myself, you would love me even if I were a draper's clerk. That's very comforting. But I confess there's one suspicion I still can't quite shake off. Tell me honestly, did it really never cross your mind that I was Biebitz?

SWEET MAID Look, I've no idea what you want me to say. I don't know anyone at all called Biebitz.

POET Such is fame! Never mind, forget everything I said, forget the name I gave you even. I'm Robert and to you I will remain so. I was only joking. (*Lightly*) I'm not a writer anyway, I'm a clerk and in the evenings I accompany folk singers on the piano.

SWEET MAID Well I must say, now I'm completely lost... and goodness, the way you look at one. What's wrong, what's the matter with you?

POET It's very strange—this has almost never happened to me before, my love, but I find myself close to tears. I am profoundly moved by you. Yes, we must stay together, you and I: we must cherish one another deeply.

SWEET MAID Tell me, is that true about the folk singers?

POET Yes, but don't ask me any more. If you love me, don't ask me anything at all. Incidentally, couldn't you get away entirely for a few weeks?

SWEET MAID How do you mean, get away entirely?

POET Well, from home?

SWEET MAID Now I ask you!! How can I possibly do that! What would Mother say? And then, everything would go wrong at home without me.

POET I imagined it all being so very beautiful, alone with you together for a week or two, somewhere out there in the seclusion of the woods in communion with nature. Nature... alone with nature... And then one day, adieu—we would part from one another, bound we know not whither.

SWEET MAID So now you're talking about saying goodbye already! And I thought you were so fond of me.

POET That's precisely why—(*bends over her and kisses her forehead*) You sweet creature!

SWEET MAID Come, hold me tight, I feel so cold.

POET It's time you got dressed. Wait, I'll light you some more candles.

SWEET MAID (*gets up*) Don't look.

POET No. (*At the window*) Tell me, my love, are you happy?

SWEET MAID How do you mean?

POET I was asking whether in general you're happy?

SWEET MAID Things could be better.

POET You misunderstand me. You've told me about your domestic situation often enough already. I know you're no princess. I mean, when you stand back from all of that, when you simply feel yourself alive. Do you even feel yourself alive?

SWEET MAID I say, have you got a comb?

POET (*goes to the dressing table, gives her the comb, contemplates the Sweet Maid*) My God, you look ravishing!

SWEET MAID Now... don't!

POET Come, stay a bit longer, stay. I'll go and fetch something for supper and...

SWEET MAID But it's already far too late.

POET It's not yet nine.

SWEET MAID Look, if you don't mind, I really have to hurry.

POET When shall we see one another again?

SWEET MAID Well, when would you like to see me?

POET Tomorrow.

SWEET MAID What day is it tomorrow?

POET Saturday.

SWEET MAID Oh, I can't in that case, I have to take my little sister to her guardian.

POET Well then, Sunday... hmm... Sunday... on Sunday... now I must explain something to you.—I'm not Biebitz, but Biebitz is my friend. One day I'll introduce you to him. But on Sunday Biebitz's play is being performed; I'll send you a ticket and then pick you up outside the theatre afterwards. And you must tell me how you liked the play, all right?

SWEET MAID Well I must say, what with all this Biebitz business— I'm completely stupefied.

POET I will only truly know you, once I know what you think about this play.

SWEET MAID There... now I'm ready.

POET Come along, my darling! (*Exeunt*)

VIII THE POET AND THE ACTRESS

A room at an inn in the country. It is an evening in spring, the hills and meadows are bathed in moonlight, the windows are open. Deep quiet. The Poet and the Actress enter; as they do so, the candle the Poet is holding goes out.

POET Oh...

ACTRESS What's wrong?

POET The light.—But we don't need one. Look how bright it is. Marvellous!

The Actress suddenly sinks to her knees at the window, her hands clasped.

POET What's the matter?

The Actress remains silent.

POET (*goes over to her*) What are you doing?

ACTRESS (*exasperated*) Can't you see I'm praying?—

POET Do you believe in God?

ACTRESS Certainly, I'm not totally beyond redemption.

POET I see!

ACTRESS Come here, kneel down beside me. You can pray too. You've nothing to lose.

The Poet kneels beside her and embraces her.

ACTRESS Libertine!—(*she gets to her feet*) And do you know who I was praying to?

POET To God, I take it.

ACTRESS (*with great scorn*) Oh naturally! I was praying to you!

POET Then why were you gazing out of the window?

ACTRESS Why don't you tell me where you've dragged me to, seducer!

POET But this was your idea, my love. It was you who insisted on coming to the country—and to this place in particular.

ACTRESS Well, wasn't I right?

POET Certainly, it's quite enchanting here. To think, just two hours from Vienna—and total solitude. And such splendid countryside.

ACTRESS Don't you think? You could certainly compose a few things here, if only you had any talent.

POET Have you been here before?

ACTRESS Have I been here before? Ha! I lived here for years.

POET With whom?

ACTRESS Well, with Fritz of course.

POET I see!

ACTRESS I worshipped that man!—

POET As you've already told me.

ACTRESS Pardon me—I can leave at once, if I'm boring you!

POET You boring me?... You have no idea how much you mean to me... You are the world to me... You are a goddess, you are genius incarnate... You are... You are in fact divine simplicity... True, my love... But no more talk about Fritz now.

ACTRESS That was a mistake, admittedly! Ah well!—

POET I'm glad you see that.

ACTRESS Come here, give me a kiss!

The Poet kisses her.

ACTRESS But now we must say good night! Farewell, my treasure!

POET How do you mean?

ACTRESS Well, I'm going to bed!

POET Yes—of course, but all that about saying good night... Where am I supposed to spend the night?

ACTRESS No doubt the hotel still has plenty of rooms.

POET But other rooms don't appeal to me at all. By the way, we could do with some light now, don't you think?

ACTRESS Yes.

POET (*lights the candle standing on the commode*) What a beautiful room... pious people in these parts too. All these images of saints... It would be interesting to spend time among these people... another world entirely. We know so little about other people really.

ACTRESS Don't talk nonsense and pass me my bag from the table.

POET Here you are, my one and only love!

The Actress takes a small framed picture out of her little bag and places it on top of the commode.

POET What's that?

ACTRESS That's the Madonna.

POET Do you always take that with you?

ACTRESS Well, she's my talisman. And now please go, Robert!

POET What sort of a joke is that? Shouldn't I help you?

ACTRESS No, you should go.

POET And when should I come back?

ACTRESS In ten minutes.

POET (*kisses her*) See you soon!

ACTRESS Where are you off to?

POET I shall be walking up and down outside your window. I love wandering about under the stars at night. My best ideas come to me then. Especially when you're near at hand, when I'm swathed in the sighs of your longing, so to speak... wafted on the current of your art.

ACTRESS You talk like a fool...

POET (*peevishly*) Some women would perhaps say... like a poet.

ACTRESS Well, get along with you. But don't start any hanky-panky with the waitress.—

The Poet exits.

ACTRESS (*undresses. She hears the Poet going down the wooden stairs, then his footsteps underneath the window. As soon as she has undressed, she goes to the window and looks down at him outside; she calls out to him in a whisper*) Come!

The Poet comes rapidly back upstairs and bursts into the room; she meanwhile has got into bed and blown out the light; he proceeds to lock the door.

ACTRESS There, now you can sit here beside me and tell me something.

POET (*sits down beside her on the bed*) Shouldn't I close the window? Aren't you cold?

ACTRESS Oh, no!

POET What am I to tell you?

ACTRESS Well then, who are you being unfaithful to this very moment?

POET Not to anyone as yet, unfortunately.

ACTRESS Console yourself, I'm being unfaithful to somebody too.

POET I can well imagine.

ACTRESS And who do you suppose it is?

POET Well, my love, I really wouldn't have any idea.

ACTRESS Come on, guess.

POET Let me see, now... Well, your director.

ACTRESS My dear man, I'm not a chorus girl.

POET Well, it was just an idea.

ACTRESS Have another guess.

POET Let me think, you're being unfaithful to your colleague... Benno—

ACTRESS Ha! That man isn't interested in women at all... didn't you know? He's having an affair with his postman!

POET I don't believe it!—

ACTRESS Well anyway, give me a kiss.

The Poet embraces her.

ACTRESS What are you doing?

POET Don't torture me like this.

ACTRESS Listen, Robert, I'll make you a suggestion. Get into bed with me.

POET Accepted!

ACTRESS Come on then, hurry, hurry!

POET Well... if it had been up to me, I would have long ago been... Can you hear that...

ACTRESS What?

POET It's the crickets chirping outside.

ACTRESS You must be mad, my dear, there are no crickets around here.

POET But one can hear them.

ACTRESS Well, are you coming or not!

POET Here I am. (*Joins her*)

ACTRESS There, now just lie quietly... Shh... don't move.

POET But what's the idea?

ACTRESS Do you want to have an affair with me, or don't you?

POET That should be obvious by now.

ACTRESS Well, you're not the only one, you know...

POET Yes, but clearly at the moment I have the inside chance.

ACTRESS Come then, my chattering little cricket! From now on I shall call you my cricket.

POET Fine...

ACTRESS Now then, who am I being unfaithful to?

POET Who... Me perhaps...

ACTRESS My dear, you need your head examining.

POET Or someone... you have never seen... someone you don't know, someone—destined for you and who you never seem to find...

ACTRESS Please don't talk such romantic rubbish.

POET Isn't it strange... even you—despite what one wants to believe.—But no, it would mean denying the best in you if one were to... come, come——come—

— —

ACTRESS That was more fun than acting in some stupid play... don't you agree?

POET Well, I'd say you're lucky you still get parts in decent plays occasionally.

ACTRESS I suppose you mean yours again, you arrogant dog?

POET I do indeed!

ACTRESS (*seriously*) Well, it certainly is a splendid play!

POET There you are then!

ACTRESS Yes, you're a true genius, Robert!

POET Incidentally, now's your chance to tell me why you cried off two nights ago. There was absolutely nothing wrong with you.

ACTRESS Well, I wanted to annoy you.

POET But why? What did I do to you?

ACTRESS You were arrogant.

POET In what way?

ACTRESS Everyone in the theatre agrees.

POET I see.

ACTRESS But I told them: the man has a right to be arrogant.

POET And what did they reply?

ACTRESS Why should they reply to me? I never talk to anyone.

POET I see.

ACTRESS They would all like to poison me. But they won't succeed.

POET Don't think about other people now. Instead enjoy our being here tonight, and tell me you love me.

ACTRESS Do you need further proof?

POET One can never prove a thing like that.

ACTRESS That's a bit rich... What more do you want?

POET How many others have you tried to prove it to this way... did you make love to all of them?

ACTRESS Oh no. I only loved one.

POET (*embracing her*) My...

ACTRESS Fritz.

POET My name is Robert. So what am I to you, if you're now thinking about Fritz?

ACTRESS You are a passing mood.

POET Good of you to say so.

ACTRESS Well now tell me, aren't you proud?

POET Why should I be proud?

ACTRESS I think you have good reason.

POET Ah that.

ACTRESS Yes that, my pale little cricket!—Well, how's the chirping going? Are they still chirping out there?

POET Incessantly. Can't you hear it?

ACTRESS Of course I can, but those are frogs, my love.

POET You're mistaken, frogs croak.

ACTRESS Of course they croak.

POET But not out there, my love, out there they're chirping.

ACTRESS You're the most obstinate creature I've ever had to put up with. Give me a kiss, my little frog.

POET Please don't call me that, it's really quite irritating.

ACTRESS Well, what am I to call you?

POET I do have a name: Robert.

ACTRESS Ah, this is so stupid.

POET Still, I would ask you to call me by my real name.

ACTRESS All right then, Robert, give me a kiss... Ah! (*She kisses him*) Are you satisfied now, my frog? Hahahaha.

POET Do you mind if I light a cigarette?

ACTRESS Give me one too.

> He takes his cigarette case from the top of the commode, takes out two cigarettes, lights both of them, and gives her one.

ACTRESS Incidentally, you haven't said a word to me yet about my triumph yesterday.

POET About what triumph?

ACTRESS Come on.

POET I see. I wasn't at the theatre.

ACTRESS You're pulling my leg.

POET Not at all. After you cried off the day before, I assumed you wouldn't be in top form yesterday either, and decided not to go.

ACTRESS You really missed something.

POET Did I?

ACTRESS It was a sensation. The audience went pale.

POET You could see that clearly, could you?

ACTRESS Benno said: my dear, you gave the performance of a goddess.

POET Hm!... And yet you were so sick the day before.

ACTRESS Certainly; and I was too. And do you know why? Because I was yearning for you.

POET Just now you told me you wanted to annoy me, and that's why you cried off.

ACTRESS What do you know about my love for you? All this leaves you cold. Yet I spent nights on end in the grip of fever. Forty degrees!

POET That's a pretty high temperature for a passing mood.

ACTRESS You call that a mood? I'm dying of love for you, and you call it a mood—?!

POET And Fritz...?

ACTRESS Fritz... Don't mention that galley-slave to me!—

IX THE ACTRESS AND THE COUNT

The Actress's bedroom. Very opulently furnished. It is noon, the blinds are still down, a candle is burning on the commode, the Actress is still lying in her four-poster bed. The counterpane is strewn with a quantity of newspapers. The Count enters in the uniform of a captain of dragoons. He stands waiting at the door.

ACTRESS Ah, Count.

COUNT Your dear mother granted me permission, otherwise I would not have—

ACTRESS Please, do come in.

COUNT How do you do. Pardon me a moment—coming in from the street like this... I still can't see anything at all. Ah... that's better— (*at her bedside*)—How do you do.

ACTRESS Please be seated, Count.

COUNT Your dear mother tells me you're a little out of sorts. Nothing serious, I hope.

ACTRESS Nothing serious? I've been at death's door.

COUNT Goodness gracious, how can that be?

ACTRESS Anyway, it's very good of you to be concerned.

COUNT At death's door! And just last night you gave the performance of a goddess.

ACTRESS It was a triumph, certainly.

COUNT Stupendous!... The audience was carried away. To say nothing of myself.

ACTRESS Thank you for the lovely flowers.

COUNT Don't mention it, Fräulein.

ACTRESS (*indicating with her eyes a large basket of flowers on a little table in the window*) They're over there.

COUNT You were publicly showered with flowers and garlands yesterday.

ACTRESS They're all still in my dressing room. Your basket was the only one that I brought home with me.

COUNT (*kisses her hand*) That is very good of you.

> *The Actress suddenly seizes his in turn and kisses it.*

COUNT But Fräulein.

ACTRESS Don't be alarmed, Count, that doesn't commit you to anything.

COUNT You are a strange creature... enigmatic, one might almost say.—(*Pause*)

ACTRESS Fräulein Birken is no doubt easier to fathom.

COUNT Yes, that little Birken woman's not a problem, although... I only know her slightly.

ACTRESS Ha!

COUNT Take my word for it. But you're a problem. That is something I have always had a yearning for. I have been deprived of a great pleasure, in as much as yesterday... was the very first time I've seen you acting.

ACTRESS Is that possible?

COUNT Indeed. You see, Fräulein, it's so difficult with the theatre. I'm used to dining late... and if one gets there after dinner, the best of it is over. Don't you agree?

ACTRESS Well, from now on you'll have to dine a little earlier.

COUNT Yes. I have already thought of that. Or not at all. Dining is really not much of a pleasure.

ACTRESS What do you know about pleasure, you who are old before your time?

COUNT I sometimes ask myself the same question! But it's not that I'm old. There must be some other reason.

ACTRESS Do you think so?

COUNT Yes. Lulu for example would say I'm a philosopher. You know, Fräulein, he thinks I brood too much.

ACTRESS Yes... thought, that brings unhappiness all right.

COUNT I have too much time on my hands, that's why I brood a lot. You know, Fräulein, I thought if they transferred me to Vienna, things might improve. Here there are plenty of distractions and excitement. But when it comes down to it, it's no different from up there.

ACTRESS Where is up there, might one ask?

COUNT Down there, I should say, Fräulein, in Hungary, in those backwater towns where I was garrisoned most of the time.

ACTRESS What on earth were you doing in Hungary?

COUNT Well, as I say, Fräulein, service with the army.

ACTRESS And why did you stay in Hungary so long?

COUNT Well, these things happen.

ACTRESS It must drive one mad.

COUNT But why? There's more to do down there than here, in fact. You know the sort of thing, Fräulein, training recruits, riding remounts... and then the countryside down there is not as bad as people say. The low-lying plains are really splendid—and such glorious sunsets, it's a pity I am not a painter; I've sometimes thought if I were a painter, that's what I'd paint. We had an artist in our regiment, a young fellow by the name of Splany, he was good at that.—But why am I boring you with all my reminiscing, Fräulein.

ACTRESS Not at all, I'm being entertained right royally.

COUNT You know, Fräulein, a fellow can talk to you, Lulu said so too, and that's something one doesn't often come across.

ACTRESS Well, in Hungary certainly.

COUNT But in Vienna it is just the same! People are the same everywhere; where there are more of them, the crowds are bigger, that's the only difference. Tell me, Fräulein, do you like people?

ACTRESS Like them—?? I hate them! I can't face seeing them. Nor do I see anyone. I am always alone, no one sets foot inside this house.

COUNT You know, I thought you might be a misanthropist. It must be fairly common in the world of art. When one is exploring higher things... anyway, you're fortunate. At least you know why you are living!

ACTRESS Who told you that? I've no idea what I'm living for!

COUNT But surely, Fräulein—famous—celebrated—

ACTRESS Do you suppose that that brings happiness?

COUNT Happiness? Pardon me, Fräulein, but there's no such thing. In general, it's precisely the things that are talked most about which don't exist... for example, love. That's another one.

ACTRESS You're right about that.

COUNT Enjoyment... intoxication... fair enough, one can't fault that... it's something certain. Supposing I'm enjoying... very well, I know that I'm enjoying. Or supposing I'm intoxicated, fine. That too is something certain. And when it's over, well, it's over and there's an end of it.

ACTRESS (*grandly*) It's over!

COUNT But as soon as one, how should I put it, as soon as one refuses to surrender to the moment, begins that is to think about before and after... well then it's quickly over. Before... is sad... and after is uncertain... in short, one only gets confused. Don't you agree?

ACTRESS (*with brimming eyes*) You've understood the way things are all right.

COUNT And you see, Fräulein, once one is clear about that, it doesn't really matter whether one lives in Vienna or on the puszta* or in Steinamanger.* Take, for example... where may I put my cap? Ah, thank you... what were we talking about?

ACTRESS About Steinamanger.

COUNT That's right. Well as I say, the difference is not that great. Whether I spend the evening in the casino or the club, it's all the same.

ACTRESS And how does this relate to love?

COUNT If one believes in it, there will always be somebody to love one.

ACTRESS Fräulein Birken for example.

COUNT I really don't know, Fräulein, why you keep bringing up that little Birken woman.

ACTRESS But she's your mistress.

COUNT Who says so?

ACTRESS Everyone knows that.

COUNT Except me, strangely enough.

ACTRESS But you fought a duel over her!

COUNT Perhaps I was even shot dead, and failed to notice.

ACTRESS Well, Count, you're a man of honour. So sit a little closer.

COUNT With your permission.

ACTRESS Right over here. (*She draws him to her and ruffles his hair with her hand*) I knew you'd come today.

COUNT How was that?

ACTRESS I already knew in the theatre yesterday.

COUNT Could you see me from the stage?

ACTRESS Good God, man! Didn't you notice it was you alone that I was playing for?

COUNT How could that be so?

ACTRESS When I saw you in the front row, I started trembling all over!

COUNT Trembling all over? Because of me? I had no idea you'd noticed me!

ACTRESS You could drive one to distraction, you and your formality.

COUNT But Fräulein...

ACTRESS 'But Fräulein'!... Well, unbuckle your sword at least!

COUNT With your permission. (*Unbuckles it and leans it against the bed*)

ACTRESS And now give me a kiss at last.
    The Count kisses her, she doesn't let him go.

ACTRESS I wish I'd never set eyes on you.

COUNT But it's better this way!—

ACTRESS Count, you're a poseur!

COUNT Me—but why?

ACTRESS To think how happy many a man would be if he could be in your position!

COUNT But I'm very happy.

ACTRESS I thought there was no such thing as happiness. Why are you looking at me like that? Count, I think you are afraid of me!

COUNT As I say, Fräulein, you're a problem.

ACTRESS Ah, don't bother me again with your philosophy... come to me. And now ask me for something... you may have anything you wish. You're so handsome.

COUNT Then I would beg permission (*kissing her hand*)—to come again this evening.

ACTRESS This evening... but I'm performing.

COUNT After the theatre.

ACTRESS Couldn't you ask for something else?

COUNT I shall ask for everything else after the theatre.

ACTRESS (*offended*) You can ask until you're blue in the face then, you miserable poseur.

COUNT Look here now, we've been completely frank with one another so far... I would find all this much more pleasant in the evening after the theatre... cosier than now when... I keep having the feeling the door might open...

ACTRESS It's not going to open from outside.

COUNT You see, I don't think one should thoughtlessly spoil something in advance, which might possibly be very beautiful.

ACTRESS Possibly!...

COUNT To tell the truth, I find love gruesome in the morning.

ACTRESS I must say—you're the queerest fish I've ever come across!

COUNT I'm not talking about women of convenience... ultimately they're all the same. But women like you... well, call me a fool if you like. Women like you... should not be enjoyed before breakfast. And so... you see... and so...

ACTRESS God, you're so sweet!

COUNT You understand what I've been saying, don't you. I imagine it like this—

ACTRESS Go on then, how do you imagine it?

COUNT I thought... after the theatre, I'd wait for you in my coach, then we could drive somewhere for supper—

ACTRESS I am not your Fräulein Birken.

COUNT I didn't say that. I just think there's a right mood for everything. I'm never in the mood before supper. It's nicest when one drives home together after supper, and then...

ACTRESS And then what?

COUNT Well, then... things develop naturally.

ACTRESS Sit a bit closer. Closer.

COUNT (*sitting on the bed*) I must say, the fragrance coming from the pillows... Reseda—is it not?

ACTRESS It's very hot in here, don't you find?
          The Count leans over and kisses her neck.

ACTRESS Oh, Count, but that's upsetting your programme.

COUNT Who says so? I don't have any programme.
          The Actress draws him to her.

COUNT It really is quite hot.

ACTRESS You think so? And so dark, as if it were evening already... (*draws him closer*) It's evening... it's night time... close your eyes if it's too light for you. Come!... Come!...
          The Count ceases to resist.

— —

ACTRESS What happened about waiting for the right mood there, you old poseur?

COUNT You're a little devil.

ACTRESS What's that supposed to mean?

COUNT Well, an angel then.

ACTRESS And you should have been an actor! Truly! You know women! And do you know what I'm going to do now?

COUNT Well?

ACTRESS I'm going to declare I never want to see you again.

COUNT But why?

ACTRESS No, no. You're too dangerous for me. You're enough to drive a woman mad. Now you're suddenly standing there as if nothing had happened.

COUNT But...

ACTRESS May I remind you, Count, that we have just made love.

COUNT I shall never forget it!

ACTRESS And what about this evening?

COUNT How do you mean?

ACTRESS Well—weren't you going to wait for me after the theatre?

COUNT Very well, what about the day after tomorrow?

ACTRESS What do you mean, the day after tomorrow? We were talking about this evening.

COUNT There wouldn't be much point in that.

ACTRESS Old man!

COUNT You don't quite understand me. I meant that more, how shall I put it, in relation to the soul.

ACTRESS What do I care about your soul?

COUNT Believe me, that is part of it all. In my view, it is a mistake to think one can separate these things.

ACTRESS Don't bother me with your philosophy. When I want it, I'll read books.

COUNT One never learns anything from books.

ACTRESS That's very true! And that's why you can wait for me tonight. We'll get together for the good of our souls, you scoundrel!

COUNT Well then, with your permission, I shall await you in my carriage...

ACTRESS You'll await me here in my apartment—

COUNT ... After the theatre.

ACTRESS Of course. (*He buckles on his sword*)

ACTRESS What are you doing there?

COUNT I think it's time for me to go. For a formal call, I have rather overstayed my welcome.

ACTRESS Well, tonight won't be a formal call.

COUNT You think so?

ACTRESS Leave me to see to that. And now give me one more kiss, my
    little philosopher. There, you seducer, you... sweet child, you ven-
    dor of souls, you swallow... you... (*after kissing him fervently a few
    times, she pushes him violently away*) Count, it has been an honour!
COUNT My compliments, Fräulein. (*At the door*) Good day to you.
ACTRESS Adieu, Steinamanger!

X THE COUNT AND THE PROSTITUTE

Morning, about six o'clock.
*A dingy room with one window, its dirty yellowing blinds let
down. Worn, greenish curtains. A commode on which are a few
photographs and a cheap, tastelessly garish lady's hat. A few
cheap Japanese fans are stuck behind the mirror. On the table
covered with a reddish cloth is a petroleum lamp, burning fitfully
under its yellow paper shade, and beside it are a jug with a little
beer and a half-empty glass. On the floor by the bed a woman's
clothes are strewn untidily, as if they had just been hastily
discarded. In the bed the Prostitute is lying fast asleep and
breathing calmly.—On the divan the Count is stretched out fully
clothed in his camel overcoat, his hat on the floor at the head of
the divan.*

COUNT (*stirs, rubs his eyes, sits up and looks about*) Now how on earth
    did I get... Oh yes... So I did go home with that hussy after all (*he
    quickly gets to his feet, sees her bed*) And there she is... The things that
    can happen to one at my age. I've no idea now, did they have to
    carry me up here? No... I remember noticing—as I came into the
    room... yes... I was still awake then or had woken up... or... or
    perhaps it's only that the room reminds me of something? My God,
    but... of course, I only saw it yesterday... (*looks at his watch*) What!
    Yesterday, that's only a few hours ago—But I knew something was
    bound to happen... I sensed it... When I started drinking yesterday,
    I sensed that... And so what did happen?... Nothing... Or did it?...
    My God,... it's been... ten years since something like this happened
    to me—not knowing whether... Well, clearly I was drunk. If only I
    knew from what point on. I remember entering that whore-ridden
    coffee house with Lulu... no, no... we left the Hotel Sacher... and
    then on the way... That's right, Lulu and I drove in my carriage...
    Why am I racking my brains over this? What does it matter? Better

be getting along. (*Gets up. The lamp wobbles*) Oh! (*Looks at the sleeping girl*) She's sleeping soundly. I don't remember anything— but I'll leave the money on the commode for her... and so goodbye... (*stands beside her and looks at her for some time*) I've known many who didn't look as virtuous as that, even when asleep. My God... Lulu would probably say I'm philosophizing again, but it's true, as I see it, Sleep is a great leveller;—like his brother, Death... Hm, if I only knew whether... No, surely I'd remember that... No, no, I fell onto the divan over there at once... and nothing happened... It's incredible how all women look alike sometimes... Well, must be off. (*He starts to go*) I almost forgot. (*He takes out his wallet and proceeds to take a banknote from it*)

PROSTITUTE (*wakes up*) Well now... who's this so bright and early—? (*Recognizes him*) Hello, ducky.

COUNT Good morning. Did you sleep well?

PROSTITUTE (*stretches*) Ah, come here. Give us a kiss.

COUNT (*bends towards her, has second thoughts, straightens up again*) I was just leaving...

PROSTITUTE Leaving?

COUNT It really is high time.

PROSTITUTE Just like that?

COUNT (*almost embarrassed*) Well...

PROSTITUTE Well, bye-bye then; another time perhaps.

COUNT Yes, goodbye. Won't you give me your sweet little hand?
          The Prostitute holds out her hand from under the cover.

COUNT (*takes her hand and kisses it automatically, notices, and laughs*) Like a princess. Indeed, when all one can see...

PROSTITUTE Why are you looking at me like that?

COUNT When all one can see is their little head like this... they all look innocent on waking up... my God, one could imagine all sorts of things, if the place didn't stink so of petroleum...

PROSTITUTE Yes, that lamp is always giving trouble.

COUNT How old are you then?

PROSTITUTE Well, how old would you say?

COUNT Twenty-four.

PROSTITUTE Oh, thanks.

COUNT Are you older?

PROSTITUTE I'm nearly twenty.

COUNT And how long have you been...

PROSTITUTE I've been in this business a year now.

COUNT You certainly started early then.

PROSTITUTE Better too early than too late.

COUNT (*sits down on the bed*) Tell me, are you happy?

PROSTITUTE What?

COUNT I meant, are things all right with you?

PROSTITUTE Oh, things are all right just now.

COUNT I see... tell me, have you ever thought of doing anything else with your life?

PROSTITUTE What else could I do?

COUNT Well... You're a really beautiful girl. You could take a lover for instance.

PROSTITUTE D'you think I don't have one already?

COUNT Yes, I know that—but I mean one who, you know, would keep you, so you didn't have to go out with just anyone.

PROSTITUTE I don't go out with just anyone now. I don't need to, thank God, I can pick and choose.

    The Count looks round the room.

PROSTITUTE (*notices this*) Next month we're moving into town, to the Spiegelgasse.

COUNT We? Who's we?

PROSTITUTE Well, the woman in charge of us and a few other girls who lodge here.

COUNT So there are more of you—

PROSTITUTE In the next room... can't you hear... that's Milly, who was also at the coffee house.

COUNT I hear snoring.

PROSTITUTE That's Milly, she'll go on snoring all day till ten at night. That's when she gets up and goes out to the coffee house.

COUNT But that must be a dreadful life.

PROSTITUTE Certainly. The woman curses her enough too. I'm always on the street by noon.

COUNT What do you do on the street at noon?

PROSTITUTE What else would I be doing? Looking for business.

COUNT I see... of course... (*gets up, takes out his wallet, and leaves a banknote on the commode for her*) Goodbye then!

PROSTITUTE Are you off already... bye-bye then... come again soon.

COUNT (*stops short again*) Tell me, it's all the same to you now, right?

PROSTITUTE What?

COUNT I mean, you don't enjoy it any more.

PROSTITUTE (*yawns*) I'm so sleepy.

COUNT It's all the same to you, whether someone's young or old, or whether someone's...

PROSTITUTE What are you asking?

COUNT ...Well (*suddenly struck by something*)—my God, now I know who you remind me of, it's...

PROSTITUTE Do I look like someone?

COUNT Incredible, incredible, but now I beg you, don't say a word for at least a minute... (*gazes at her*) Exactly the same face, exactly the same face. (*He kisses her eyes suddenly*)

PROSTITUTE Well...

COUNT My God, it's a pity you are... nothing more... You could make your fortune!

PROSTITUTE You're just like Franz.

COUNT Who is Franz?

PROSTITUTE Well, the waiter at the coffee house...

COUNT In what way am I like Franz?

PROSTITUTE He too keeps telling me I could make my fortune and ought to marry him.

COUNT Why don't you?

PROSTITUTE No, thank you very much... I don't want to get married, not at any price. Later perhaps.

COUNT The eyes... exactly the same eyes... Lulu would probably say that I'm a fool—let me kiss your eyes again... there... and now goodbye, I must go.

PROSTITUTE 'Bye...

COUNT (*at the door*) I say... tell me... aren't you surprised at all...

PROSTITUTE At what?

COUNT That I don't want you to do anything.

PROSTITUTE There are plenty of men who aren't in the mood in the morning.

COUNT Oh well... (*to himself*) How stupid to expect she'd be surprised... Well, goodbye then... (*he's again at the door*) I'm annoyed in fact. Of course I know it all comes down to money with such women... why do I say—such... it was nice of her... not to pretend at least, one should be pleased about that... Look—I'll come and see you again soon.

PROSTITUTE (*with eyes closed*) Good.

COUNT When are you usually at home?

PROSTITUTE I'm always at home. Just ask for Leocadia.

COUNT Leocadia... Very well—Goodbye then. (*At the door*) I can still feel the effects of that wine in my head. Well this really beats the band... I've spent the night with a whore, and done nothing more than kiss her eyes because she reminded me of someone... (*turns to her*) I say, Leocadia, does this often happen, someone leaving you like this?

PROSTITUTE Like what?

COUNT Like me?

PROSTITUTE In the morning?

COUNT No... have you ever had anyone—who didn't want you to do anything for him?

PROSTITUTE No, that's never happened.

COUNT So what do you think? Don't you think I like you?

PROSTITUTE Why shouldn't you like me? You liked me well enough last night.

COUNT I like you now as well.

PROSTITUTE But last night you liked me even more.

COUNT What makes you say that?

PROSTITUTE Why all these silly questions?

COUNT Last night... tell me, didn't I fall on the bed at once?

PROSTITUTE You did indeed... with me.

COUNT With you?

PROSTITUTE Don't you remember?

COUNT I fell... we were together... and so...

PROSTITUTE But then you went to sleep at once.

COUNT I went to sleep at once... I see... So that's what happened!...

PROSTITUTE Yes, ducky. You must have been blind drunk though, not to remember anything.

COUNT I see...—And yet... there is a faint resemblance... I'm off... (*listens*) What's going on?

PROSTITUTE The chambermaid's arrived. Give her something on your way out. It means the front door's open, so you won't need to tip the porter too.

COUNT Very well. (*In the hall*) Well now... It would have been nice though, if I'd only kissed her eyes. That would almost have made it a romantic adventure... But my fate ruled otherwise. (*The Chambermaid stands there and opens the door*) Ah—for you... Good night.—

CHAMBERMAID Good morning.

COUNT Yes of course... good morning... good morning.

THE GREEN COCKATOO
(*Der grüne Kakadu*)

A Grotesque in One Act

CAST

ÉMILE, DUKE OF CADIGNAN
FRANÇOIS, VISCOUNT NOGEANT
ALBIN, CHEVALIER DE LA TREMOUILLE
THE MARQUIS OF LANSAC
SEVERINE, *his wife*
ROLLIN, *poet*
PROSPÈRE, *landlord, former theatre director*

Prospère's troupe:
HENRI
BALTHASAR
GUILLAUME
SCAEVOLA
JULES
ÉTIENNE
MAURICE
GEORGETTE
MICHETTE
FLIPOTTE
LÉOCADIE, *actress, Henri's wife*
GRASSET, *philosopher*
LEBRÊT, *tailor*
GRAIN, *a vagabond*
THE COMMISSIONER
ARISTOCRATS, ACTORS, ACTRESSES, CITIZENS & THEIR WIVES

The action takes place in Paris on the evening of 14 July 1789, in Prospère's tavern

Public bar at 'The Green Cockatoo'.
A moderately large cellar, accessed on the right—fairly far back—by a flight of seven steps, closed off at the top by a door. There is a second door, barely visible, in the background on the left. Almost the entire floor space is taken up by a number of plain wooden tables with chairs grouped round them. The bar runs from the middle over to the left; behind it are a number of barrels with taps. The room is lit by oil lamps suspended from the ceiling.
Prospère the landlord; citizens Lebrêt and Grasset enter.

GRASSET (*still on the steps*) In here, Lebrêt; I know this place. My old friend and director always manages to hide a barrel of wine somewhere, even if the rest of Paris is dying of thirst.

LANDLORD Good evening, Grasset. So you've decided to show your face again? Done with philosophy? Would you like to sign up again with me?

GRASSET Certainly! But bring out some wine. I am the guest here— you the landlord.

LANDLORD Wine? Where would I get wine from, Grasset? Last night all the wine shops in Paris were raided. And I wouldn't mind betting you were among the looters.

GRASSET Out with the wine. The rabble will be here within the hour... (*listening*) Do you hear anything, Lebrêt?

LEBRÊT It sounds like distant thunder.

GRASSET Bravo—citizen of Paris... (*to Prospère*) You're sure to have plenty stashed away for the rabble. So out with it. My friend and admirer here is paying—citizen Lebrêt, tailor from the Rue St Honoré.

LEBRÊT Of course, of course, I'll pay.
          The landlord hesitates.

GRASSET Show him your money, Lebrêt.
          Lebrêt pulls out his purse.

LANDLORD Well, I'll just see whether... (*he taps a barrel and fills two glasses*) Where have you come from, Grasset? The Palais Royal?*

GRASSET That's right... I gave a speech there. Yes, my friend, it's my turn now. Do you know who my speech came after?

LANDLORD Well?

GRASSET After Camille Desmoulins!* My word, yes. And tell me, Lebrêt, who was applauded more, Desmoulins or me?

LEBRÊT You... no doubt about it.

GRASSET And how did I look?

LEBRÊT Splendid.

GRASSET Are you listening, Prospère? I climbed onto a table... I looked impressive as a monument... my word, yes—and the whole crowd, maybe five or ten thousand of them, gathered round—just as they had round Camille Desmoulins... and cheered for me as well.

LEBRÊT The cheers were definitely louder.

GRASSET My word, yes... not by much, but they certainly were louder. Now they are marching on the Bastille... and I don't mind saying, they have responded to my call. Take my word for it, before nightfall it will be in our hands.

LANDLORD Why certainly, if the walls cave in at your speech!

GRASSET What do you mean... speech!—Are you deaf?... The shooting has begun. Our brave soldiers are primed. They're as fiendishly enraged over the damn prison as we are ourselves. They know their own fathers and brothers are prisoners behind those walls... But they'd never have brought themselves to shoot if we hadn't made our speeches. The power of the spirit is great, my dear Prospère. I say—(*to Lebrêt*) where did you put those booklets?

LEBRÊT Here... (*pulls some pamphlets out of his pocket*) Here are the latest pamphlets being distributed at the Palais Royal this very moment. Here's one by my friend Cerutti,* an address to the people of France; here's another by Desmoulins, who one must admit speaks better than he writes... 'Free France.'

LANDLORD And when is yours finally coming out, the one you're always talking about?

GRASSET We don't need any more pamphlets. The time for action has arrived. Anyone who stays inside his own four walls today is a rogue. If he's a man, he should be taking to the streets!

LEBRÊT Bravo, bravo!

GRASSET In Toulon they've already killed the mayor, in Brignolles they've plundered a dozen or so houses... it's only we in Paris who are still half asleep and willing to put up with anything.

LANDLORD That can't be said any longer.

LEBRÊT (*who has been drinking continually*) Arise, citizens, arise!

GRASSET Arise!... Close up shop and come with us now!

LANDLORD I'll come when the time is ripe.

GRASSET Of course you will, once the danger's over.

LANDLORD My good friend, I love freedom as much as you—but I have my profession and that comes first.

GRASSET Today there's only one profession for the citizens of Paris: liberating their brothers.

LANDLORD Yes, for those who have nothing better to do!

LEBRÊT What did he say!... He's making fun of us!

LANDLORD It never entered my head.—You'd better get out of here now... my show is about to begin, and I can do without you then.

LEBRÊT What sort of show?... Is this a theatre?

LANDLORD Certainly it's a theatre. Your friend was acting here just two weeks ago.

LEBRÊT Were you acting here, Grasset?... Why let this fellow get away with making fun of you!

GRASSET Calm down... it's true; I was acting here all right, and this is no ordinary tavern... it's a refuge for criminals... come, let's go...

LANDLORD Pay up first.

LEBRÊT If it's a refuge for criminals, I won't pay a sou.

LANDLORD Explain to your friend where he is.

GRASSET It's a rum place! Some people come here and pretend to be criminals—while others are so, without even suspecting it.

LEBRÊT Really?

GRASSET May I alert you to the wittiness of my last remark; it could form the basis for an entire political speech.

LEBRÊT I don't know what you're talking about.

GRASSET As I told you, Prospère is my former director. And he and his troupe continue to put on performances, only different from the ones we did before. Now my former actor colleagues sit around here, pretending to be criminals. Do you follow? They recount hair-raising escapades they never in fact experienced—talk about crimes they never in fact committed... and the audience gets a thrill out of sitting next to the most dangerous riff-raff in Paris—sharpsters, burglars, murderers—and—

LEBRÊT What sort of audience?

LANDLORD Paris high society.

LEBRÊT Aristocrats...

LANDLORD Gentlemen from court—

LEBRÊT Down with the lot of them!

GRASSET It's just what they need. It'll shake their jaded sensibilities all right. Here is where I got my start, Lebrêt, here is where I gave my maiden speech, as if it were all just a joke... and this is where I began to hate those perfumed, ravaged dogs, sitting among us in their finery... and I'm pleased, my good Lebrêt, that you too are seeing the place your famous friend set out from. (*In a different tone*) I say, Prospère, what if the whole business were to go wrong...

LANDLORD What business?

GRASSET Why, my political career... would you sign me up again?

LANDLORD Not for the world!

GRASSET (*lightly*) Why not?—You could use another actor as a side-kick to Henri.

LANDLORD Maybe... but I'd be worried you might forget yourself some day—and attack one of my paying guests in earnest.

GRASSET (*flattered*) That would certainly be possible.

LANDLORD Me now... I keep myself well under control—

GRASSET Frankly, Prospère, I'm bound to say I'd admire your self-control more, if I didn't happen to know that you're a coward.

LANDLORD Ah well, my friend, I am content with what I can achieve in my own small way. I get enough pleasure telling these people to their face what I think, and cursing them to my heart's content—while they just take it as a joke. That's a way of venting one's anger too.—(*He pulls out a dagger and lets it gleam*)

LEBRÊT What's the meaning of this, citizen Prospère?

GRASSET Don't worry. I bet his dagger hasn't even been sharpened.

LANDLORD You might be mistaken about that, my friend; sooner or later the day will come when jesting turns to earnest—and then I shall be ready, come hell or high water.

GRASSET That day is fast approaching. We are living in momentous times! Come, citizen Lebrêt, we'll go and join our brothers. Farewell, Prospère, you'll next see me as a great man, or not at all.

LEBRÊT (*Tipsily*) A great man... or... not at all—(*They depart*)

LANDLORD (*remains behind, seats himself on a table, opens a pamphlet and reads aloud*) 'Now that the beast is caught in the noose, it will choke itself to death!'—He doesn't write badly, this young Desmoulins. 'Never before have the victors been offered such rich booty. Forty thousand palaces and castles, two-fifths of all the estates in France, will be the reward for their bravery,—the self-appointed conquerors will be brought to heel, the nation will be purged.'

The commissioner enters.

LANDLORD (*looks him over*) I see the riff-raff are turning up early today?

COMMISSIONER My good Prospère, you don't make jokes with me. I am your district police commissioner.

LANDLORD How may I be of service?

COMMISSIONER I've been instructed to spend the evening in your tavern.

LANDLORD It will be a special honour.

COMMISSIONER It's not a question of that, my good Prospère. The authorities want clarification as to what is actually going on here. For some weeks now—

LANDLORD This is a place of entertainment, Commissioner, nothing more.

COMMISSIONER Let me finish. Your tavern is reputed to have been the scene of wild orgies for several weeks now.

LANDLORD You have been misinformed, Commissioner. We have a bit of good clean fun here, that's all.

COMMISSIONER That's how it all starts, I know. But it ends rather differently, according to my report. You were once an actor?

LANDLORD A director, Commissioner, the director of an outstanding troupe, which last performed in St Denis.

COMMISSIONER That's immaterial. And then you came into a fortune?

LANDLORD Nothing to speak of, Commissioner.

COMMISSIONER Your troupe was dissolved?

LANDLORD So was my fortune.

COMMISSIONER (*smiling*) Not bad. (*Both smile.—Suddenly serious*) And so you set up in business as a publican?

LANDLORD A business which went from bad to worse.

COMMISSIONER At which point you had an idea, that one can't deny has a certain originality.

LANDLORD You make me feel proud, Commissioner.

COMMISSIONER You reassembled your troupe here, and now have them perform a strange and not altogether unobjectionable play.

LANDLORD If it were objectionable, Commissioner, I would not retain my audience—the most respectable audience in Paris, I might add. Viscount Nogeant is a daily guest. The Marquis of Lansac drops in frequently; and the Duke of Cadignan, Commissioner, is a fervent admirer of my leading actor, the famous Henri Baston.

COMMISSIONER And no doubt also of the art, or rather the arts of your young actresses.

LANDLORD If you knew my little actresses, Commissioner, you would not hold that against anybody in the world.

COMMISSIONER Enough of that. It has been reported to the authorities that the entertainment provided by your—how should I say—

LANDLORD The word 'artists' should be adequate.

COMMISSIONER I think I would choose the word 'riff-raff'—that the entertainment provided by your riff-raff exceeds what is permissible in all respects. It is alleged that—how should I say—your artist-criminals are delivering speeches which—what was it I put in my report? (*He consults his notebook as before*)—are not only immoral, which would not cause much embarrassment, but highly seditious in their tendency—and that is not something the authorities can remain indifferent to in so turbulent an age.

LANDLORD The only way I can answer this charge, Commissioner, is by cordially inviting you to come and have a look at things yourself some time. You will see that nothing seditious is going on, for the good reason that my audience could never be stirred into rebellion. What's going on here is simply play-acting—nothing more.

COMMISSIONER I can't of course accept your invitation, but by the authority invested in me by my office I shall stay.

LANDLORD I think I can promise you some outstanding entertainment, Commissioner, but permit me to recommend that you take off your official clothes and come back dressed as a civilian. If a police commissioner in uniform were seen around here, both the spontaneity of my actors and the mood of my audience would suffer.

COMMISSIONER You have a point, Prospère, I'll slip out and return as a young man of fashion.

LANDLORD That should come naturally, Commissioner, but you'd also be welcome as a rogue—that too would not look out of place—anything except as a commissioner.

COMMISSIONER Adieu. *Exit*

LANDLORD (*bows*) Roll on the blessed day, when you and the likes of you...

COMMISSIONER (*meets Grain at the door, an extremely ragged individual who gives a start on seeing the commissioner. The latter looks him over, then smiles, and turns affably to Prospère*) One of your artists, I presume?... *Exit*

GRAIN (*in a pathetic whining voice*) Good evening.

LANDLORD (*after looking at him for some time*) I don't wish to deny you my acknowledgement, if you are one of my troupe, but I can't say I recognize you.

GRAIN How do you mean?

LANDLORD No funny business now, take off your wig, I want to know who you are. (*He tugs at his hair*)

GRAIN Ouch, that hurt!

LANDLORD But that's real—well I'll be damned... who are you?... You seem to be a genuine tramp?

GRAIN Of course.

LANDLORD So what d'you want from me?

GRAIN Do I have the honour of addressing citizen Prospère?... Landlord of the Green Cockatoo?

LANDLORD That's me.

GRAIN I'm called Grain... and sometimes Carniche... and occasionally the Screaming Pumice-stone—but it was under the name of Grain that I was jailed, Citizen Prospère—and that's what counts.

LANDLORD Ah—I see. You want me to sign you up, and so you're putting on a little demonstration of your acting skills. Good idea. Carry on.

GRAIN Citizen Prospère, don't mistake me for a crook. I'm an honest man. When I say I was jailed, then that's the honest truth.

The landlord looks at him suspiciously.

GRAIN (*pulls a paper from his coat*) Here, Citizen Prospère, this shows that I was discharged yesterday afternoon at four o'clock.

LANDLORD After two years in prison—well I'll be damned, but this is genuine—!

GRAIN Are you now convinced, Citizen Prospère?

LANDLORD What did you get up to, to receive two years in—

GRAIN They would have hanged me; but luckily for me, when I murdered my poor aunt I was still half a child.

LANDLORD But for God's sake, how can anyone murder their aunt?

GRAIN I wouldn't have done it, Citizen Prospère, if my aunt hadn't betrayed me with my best friend.

LANDLORD Your aunt?

GRAIN Yes—we were rather closer than aunts and nephews usually are. Relationships in our family were a bit peculiar... I was bitter, extremely bitter. May I tell you all about it?

LANDLORD Go ahead, perhaps we can do business after all.

GRAIN My sister was still half a child when she ran away from home—and can you guess who with?

LANDLORD Hard to imagine.

GRAIN With my uncle. And he abandoned her—with a child.

LANDLORD Not half a child—I hope.

GRAIN It's not very nice of you to joke about such matters, Citizen Prospère.

LANDLORD Let me tell you something, young Screaming Pumice-stone. Your family stories bore me. Do you think I have nothing better to do than listen to just any passing tramp who wants to tell me who he's murdered? What's it all got to do with me? I take it you want something from me—

GRAIN Of course, Citizen Prospère, I've come to ask for work.

LANDLORD (*jeeringly*) I must point out that there are no aunts waiting to be murdered here; this is a place of entertainment.

GRAIN Oh, once was quite enough for me. I want to be respectable— and they recommended me to you...

LANDLORD Who, if I may ask?

GRAIN A nice young man they locked in my cell three days ago. He was called Gaston... and I believe you know him.—

LANDLORD Gaston! Now I know why he's been absent for the last three nights. He's one of my best actors when it comes to imitating pickpockets.—The stories he tells;—they set one trembling in one's boots.

GRAIN They do indeed. And now they've caught him!

LANDLORD How d'you mean, they've caught him? He didn't really steal.

GRAIN Certainly he did. But it must have been his first time, because he seems to have gone about things incredibly ineptly. Imagine, (*confidingly*)—he just put his hand into a lady's handbag on the Boulevard des Capucines and removed her purse—a complete amateur.—I feel I can trust you, Citizen Prospère—so I don't mind admitting—there was a time when I used to put on such side-shows myself, but never without my dear father. When I was still a child, when we all lived together, when my poor aunt was still alive—

LANDLORD What are you snivelling for? That's absurd! You never should have killed her!

GRAIN Too late. But as I was going to say—why don't you sign me up. I'll do things the opposite way round from Gaston. He acted the part of a criminal and then became one—whereas I shall...

LANDLORD I'll give you a try. Your clothes alone will make an impact. And all you'll have to do is tell them the story of your aunt at an appropriate moment. And how it really felt. Somebody is bound to ask you that.

GRAIN Thank you, Citizen Prospère. And as regards my wages—

LANDLORD Today will be a guest appearance, and I can't pay you a wage for that.—You'll get plenty to eat and drink... and I might even throw in a few francs for a night's lodging.

GRAIN Thank you. And I'll introduce myself to the rest of your troupe as a guest artist from the provinces.

LANDLORD Ah no... we'll tell them straight away that you're a real murderer. They'd much prefer that.

GRAIN Excuse me, I don't want to get myself into trouble—I don't understand at all.

LANDLORD When you've been with this theatre a little longer, you'll understand all right.

Scaevola and Jules enter.

SCAEVOLA Good evening, Director!

LANDLORD Landlord... How often must I tell you, you'll give the whole game away if you go on calling me 'Director'.

SCAEVOLA Whatever you are, I don't think we'll be putting on a show today.

LANDLORD Why not?

SCAEVOLA People won't be in the mood——. All hell has broken loose out on the streets, and outside the Bastille especially they are shouting like a lot of madmen.

LANDLORD What's that got to do with us? They've been shouting for months and our audience has never stayed away. People go on enjoying themselves as much as ever.

SCAEVOLA Yes, they display the cheerfulness of people waiting to be hanged.

LANDLORD If only I may live to see the day!

SCAEVOLA In the meantime give me a drink to get me in the mood. I'm not in the mood at all today.

LANDLORD That happens to you too frequently, my friend. Yesterday, I must tell you, I was thoroughly dissatisfied with your perform-ance. Your send-up of that burglar story was utterly inept.

SCAEVOLA Inept?

LANDLORD Certainly. Completely unconvincing. Just bellowing isn't going to do the trick.

SCAEVOLA I wasn't bellowing

LANDLORD You always bellow. I may have to rehearse your act with you. I can't rely on you to improvise. Henri's the only one.

SCAEVOLA Henri, always Henri. Henri's a ranter. My burglary act yesterday was a masterpiece. Henri couldn't put that together to save his life.—If you're not satisfied with me, my friend, then I'll simply transfer to a proper theatre. This is just a troupe of strolling players... Ah... (*notices Grain*) And who is this?... He doesn't belong to us, does he? Or have you recently engaged him? What's that costume the fellow's wearing?

LANDLORD Calm down, he's not an actor by profession. He's a genuine murderer.

SCAEVOLA I see... (*goes up to him*) Very pleased to meet you. Scaevola's the name.

GRAIN I'm called Grain.

> *Jules has been pacing about the tap-room the whole time, stopping now and then like someone inwardly tormented.*

LANDLORD What's the matter, Jules?

JULES I'm memorizing.

LANDLORD What?

JULES Pricks of conscience. Today I'm playing someone plagued by pricks of conscience. Look at me. How d'you like these wrinkles on my brow? Don't I look as if all the furies in hell were... (*paces up and down*)

SCAEVOLA (*bellows*) Wine—Bring some wine!

LANDLORD Calm down... the audience has not arrived yet.

> *Henri and Léocadie enter.*

HENRI Good evening! (*He greets those sitting further back with an airy wave*) Good evening, gentlemen!

LANDLORD Good evening, Henri! What's this I see! With Léocadie!

GRAIN (*has been looking attentively at Léocadie; to Scaevola*) But I know her... (*Talks to the others in an undertone*)

LÉOCADIE Yes, my dear Prospère, it's me!

LANDLORD I haven't seen you for a while. Allow me to welcome you. (*Tries to kiss her*)

HENRI Steady on!—(*His eye lingers proudly and passionately, but also a little apprehensively on Léocadie*)

LANDLORD Come now, Henri... We're old colleagues!... Léocadie... I'm your former director!

LÉOCADIE How the time has flown, Prospère!...

LANDLORD What's the sigh for! If ever anyone made good, it's you! Of course, a beautiful young woman always has an easier time of it than we do.

HENRI (*angrily*) Enough of that.

LANDLORD Why do you keep on raising your voice at me? Just because you and she are back together?

HENRI Silence!—Since yesterday she's been my wife.

LANDLORD Your...? (*To Léocadie*) Is he joking?

LÉOCADIE He has really married me. Yes.—

LANDLORD Well congratulations. I say... Scaevola, Jules—Henri has just got married.

SCAEVOLA (*comes forward*) My congratulations! (*Winks at Léocadie*)
    Jules also shakes hands with both of them.

GRAIN (*to the landlord*) Ah, how very strange—I noticed this
woman... just a few minutes after my release.

LANDLORD How come?

GRAIN She was the first attractive woman I'd set eyes on for two
years. I was very excited. But she was with another man— (*goes on
talking to the landlord*)

HENRI (*in a high-pitched rapturous tone, without becoming declamatory*)
Léocadie, my beloved, my bride!... The past is behind us. Much is
effaced at a moment like this. (*Scaevola and Jules have retreated and
the landlord again comes forward*)

LANDLORD A moment like what?

HENRI Now we are united by a holy sacrament. That is something
stronger than mere human vows. Now God is with us, and everything that has happened in the past should be forgotten. A new age
is dawning, Léocadie. Everything is sanctified, Léocadie, and our
kisses too, however wild, henceforth are sanctified. Léocadie, my
beloved, my bride!... (*He contemplates her with an ardent gaze*)
Doesn't she look quite different from how you remember her,
Prospère? Is her brow not purer now? The past has been effaced. Is
that not so, Léocadie?

LÉOCADIE Of course, Henri.

HENRI And everything is fine. We leave Paris tomorrow, Léocadie
appears at the Porte St Martin for the last time tonight, and this
will be my last performance here with you.

LANDLORD (*astounded*) Have you taken leave of your senses, Henri?—
Surely you can't want to leave me? And do you imagine it won't
occur to the director of the Porte St Martin to lure Léocadie back?
She's made that theatre's fortune. They say the young men simply
flock to see her.

HENRI Silence. Léocadie is coming with me. She will never leave
me. Tell me you'll never leave me, Léocadie. (*Brutally*) Tell
me!

LÉOCADIE I'll never leave you!

HENRI If you ever should, then I'd... (*Pause*) I've had enough of this
life. I need peace and quiet, I tell you.

LANDLORD But what will you do, Henri? This is all preposterous. I'll
make you a suggestion. Take Léocadie away from the Porte St
Martin theatre if you must,—but let her stay on here with me. I'll
sign her up. I'm short of female talent anyway.

HENRI I've made up my mind, Prospère. We're leaving town. We're off to the country.

LANDLORD The country? Where to?

HENRI To my old father living alone in our poor village,—whom I haven't seen for seven years. He has almost given up hope of seeing his long lost son again. He'll receive me with open arms.

LANDLORD But what are you going to do in the country? People starve out there. They are a thousand times worse off than here in town. What are you going to do there? You're not the man to go tilling fields. So don't imagine that.

HENRI I shall prove I'm man enough for that too.

LANDLORD Soon there'll be no more corn left anywhere in France. You are heading for certain misery.

HENRI For happiness, Prospère. Is that not so, Léocadie? We've often dreamed about it. I yearn for the peace of the wide plains. Yes, Prospère, in my dreams I see myself walking with her in the evening through the fields, surrounded by infinite quietude, the wonderful consoling heavens above us. Yes, we'll escape this terrible and dangerous city, and true peace will descend on us. We've often dreamed about it, isn't that so, Léocadie?

LÉOCADIE Yes, we've often dreamed about it.

LANDLORD Listen, Henri, you should think it over. I'll gladly raise your wage, and I'll pay Léocadie the same as you.

LÉOCADIE Did you hear, Henri?

LANDLORD Frankly, I don't know who could replace you here. No one in my troupe has such brilliant ideas as you, no one is as popular with the audience as you... Don't go away!

HENRI I can well believe that I am irreplaceable.

LANDLORD Stay with me, Henri! (*Throws a glance at Léocadie, who indicates that she would certainly agree to this*)

HENRI And I assure you my departure will be hard to bear—for the audience, not for me. I have prepared something for my last appearance, which will put the fear of God into them all... it will give them a glimpse of how their world will end... for the end of their world is indeed approaching. But that is something I shall experience only from a distance... out there, Léocadie, they will report it to us many days after the event... I can tell you though, they are going to be absolutely horrified. And you yourself will say: never before did Henri perform so splendidly.

LANDLORD What are you going to perform for us? What is it? Do you know, Léocadie?

LÉOCADIE I never know anything, of course.

HENRI Does anyone even suspect what a great artist dwells within me?

LANDLORD Of course we do, that's why I keep saying, with talent like that, you shouldn't just go and bury yourself in the country. What an injustice to yourself! And to art!

HENRI I don't give a fig for art. I want peace and quiet. You cannot understand that, Prospère. You have never been in love.

LANDLORD Oh!—

HENRI Not the way that I'm in love.—I want to be alone with her— that's the point... Léocadie, that's the only way we can forget things. But we will be happier than anyone has ever been. We shall have children, and you, Léocadie, will become a good mother and a virtuous wife. The past, everything, will be effaced. (*Long pause*)

LÉOCADIE It's getting late, Henri, I must be leaving for the theatre. Farewell, Prospère, I'm pleased to at last have seen your famous tavern, where Henri has celebrated all his triumphs.

LANDLORD Why did you never come before?

LÉOCADIE Henri wouldn't hear of it—well, you know, because of all those young men I'd have had to sit among.

HENRI (*has moved back a little*) Give me a swig, Scaevola. (*He drinks*)

LANDLORD (*to Léocadie, while Henri is not listening*) A real fool, that Henri—if only you'd come and sat among them.

LÉOCADIE Look, I won't put up with remarks like that.

LANDLORD Take my advice and watch your back, you stupid trollop. One of these days he's going to murder you.

LÉOCADIE Why, what's up?

LANDLORD Only yesterday you were seen with one of your old customers again.

LÉOCADIE That wasn't a customer, you blockhead, that was...

HENRI (*turns round suddenly*) What's going on? No jokes, if you don't mind. And stop that whispering. We have no secrets any more. She's now my wife.

LANDLORD What did you give her as a wedding gift?

LÉOCADIE Ah God, he doesn't think of things like that.

HENRI Very well, you shall have one tonight.

LÉOCADIE What?

SCAEVOLA, JULES What are you going to give her?

HENRI (*quite seriously*) When you've finished your show, you may come back here and watch me acting. (*They laugh*)

HENRI Never before has a woman received such a splendid wedding gift. Come Léocadie; goodbye, Prospère, I'll be back shortly.

> *Henri and Léocadie exeunt.—At the same time there enter: François Viscount Nogeant, Albin Chevalier de la Tremouille.*

SCAEVOLA What a pathetic braggart.

LANDLORD Good evening, you swine.

> *Albin starts back.*

FRANÇOIS (*without taking any notice*) Wasn't that little Léocadie from the Porte St Martin I saw leaving with Henri?

LANDLORD It was indeed.—And if she really put her mind to it, perhaps she might even remember you're what passes for a man.

FRANÇOIS (*laughing*) It's not inconceivable. We've arrived a little early today, it seems?

LANDLORD Well, while you're waiting you can amuse yourself with your lover boy here. (*Albin is on the point of flaring up*)

FRANÇOIS Come now, forget it. I told you the way things are set up here. Bring us some wine.

LANDLORD By all means. The time will come when you'll be more than happy with water from the Seine.

FRANÇOIS No doubt, no doubt... but today I would prefer to order wine, and make it of the best.

> *The landlord goes over to the bar.*

ALBIN He's really an atrocious fellow.

FRANÇOIS Remember now, it's all in jest. After all, there are places where you'll hear such things in earnest.

ALBIN But isn't it against the law?

FRANÇOIS (*laughs*) One can see you're from the provinces.

ALBIN Ah, things have come to a pretty pass with us too lately. The peasants are becoming insolent to the point where... it's hard to know where to turn for help.

FRANÇOIS What do you expect? The poor devils are hungry; that's the secret.

ALBIN But what can I do about it? What can my great-uncle do about it?

FRANÇOIS What makes you think of your great-uncle?

ALBIN Well, I mention him because they held a meeting—quite openly—in our village, and denounced my great uncle, the Count of Tremouille, for hoarding corn.

FRANÇOIS Is that all...?

ALBIN Well, isn't that enough!

FRANÇOIS We should go past the Palais Royal tomorrow, and you'll hear the kind of infamous speeches those scoundrels are making there. But let them rant; it's the wisest thing to do; they are basically good people and one just has to let them vent their anger.

ALBIN (*pointing to Scaevola etc.*) Who are those suspicious-looking tykes? Just look at the way they're eyeing us.

He reaches for his sword.

FRANÇOIS (*pulls his hand back*) Don't make yourself ridiculous! (*To the threesome*) No need to start yet, wait until more people have arrived. (*To Albin*) Actors are the most respectable people in the world, you know. I guarantee you've sat at the same table with worse rogues.

ALBIN But then they were better dressed.

The landlord brings wine.

Michette and Flipotte enter.

FRANÇOIS Hello girls, come and sit with us.

MICHETTE Well, here we are. Come on, Flipotte. She's still a bit shy, you know.

FLIPOTTE Good evening, sir.

ALBIN Good evening, madam.

MICHETTE The little fellow's rather sweet. (*She sits herself in Albin's lap*)

ALBIN Please explain, François, are these decent women?

MICHETTE What's he saying?

FRANÇOIS No, that's not the way it is, the young ladies who drop in here—God, you're dense, Albin!

LANDLORD What would the Duchesses like to drink?

MICHETTE Bring me a nice sweet wine.

FRANÇOIS (*indicating Flipotte*) A friend of yours?

MICHETTE We live together. In fact, we share a bed!

FLIPOTTE (*blushing*) That won't bother you when you come to see her, will it? (*Sits herself on François's lap*)

ALBIN But she isn't the least bit shy.

SCAEVOLA (*gets up, scowling, and goes over to the young people's table*) So I've finally caught you again! (*To Albin*) And as for you, you miserable seducer, I'll show you... She is mine! (*The landlord looks on*)

FRANÇOIS (*to Albin*) It's all in fun, all in fun...

ALBIN You mean, she isn't his?

MICHETTE Come on, let me sit where I please.

Scaevola stands there with fists clenched.

LANDLORD (*behind him*) Well, well!?

SCAEVOLA Ha, ha!

LANDLORD (*seizes him by the collar*) Ha, ha! (*Aside to him*) So that's the best you can come up with! You haven't an ounce of talent. Bellowing. That's all you're good for.

MICHETTE (*to François*) He did everything much better recently—

SCAEVOLA (*to the landlord*) I'm still not in the mood. I'll run through it again later when more people have arrived; you'll see, Prospère; I just need an audience.

    The Duke of Cadignan enters.

DUKE Very busy already!

    Michette and Flipotte approach him.

MICHETTE My darling Duke!

FRANÇOIS Good evening, Émile!... (*Introduces*) My young friend Albin Chevalier de la Tremouille—the Duke of Cadignan.

DUKE I am very pleased to make your acquaintance. (*To the girls hanging on his arm*) Let me go, girls!—(*To Albin*) So you've come to have a look at this curious alehouse too?

ALBIN I find it all thoroughly bewildering!

FRANÇOIS The Chevalier just arrived in Paris a few days ago.

DUKE (*laughing*) You've certainly chosen a fine time to come.

ALBIN How so?

MICHETTE What perfume he's wearing again! There's not a sweeter smelling man in Paris. (*To Albin*)... It's not one you often come across.

DUKE She's just thinking of the seven or eight hundred others she knows, besides me.

FLIPOTTE Do you mind if I play with your sword—(*She draws the sword from its scabbard and tilts it this way and that, making it gleam*)

GRAIN (*to the landlord*) He's the one!... He's the one I saw her with!—

    The landlord listens, evidently astonished.

DUKE Isn't Henri here yet? (*To Albin*) When you see him acting, you won't regret you came.

LANDLORD (*to the Duke*) Well, so you too are back again. That's good. We won't be having the pleasure for much longer.

DUKE Why not? I feel very much at home here.

LANDLORD I'm sure you do. But as you will certainly be among the first...

ALBIN What does that mean?

LANDLORD I think you understand me.—The most favoured by fortune will be the first in line!... (*Withdraws towards the back*)

DUKE (*after some reflection*) If I were the king, I would make him my court jester, or at least, I would maintain several, and he'd be one of them.

ALBIN What did he mean about your being too fortunate?

DUKE What he meant, Chevalier...

ALBIN Please, don't call me Chevalier. Everyone calls me Albin, just plain Albin, because I look so young.

DUKE (*smiling*) Very well... but then you must call me Émile, agreed?

ALBIN Willingly, Émile, if that's all right with you.

DUKE They are getting uncannily witty, these people.

FRANÇOIS Why uncannily? I find it rather reassuring. As long as the rabble are disposed to jest, matters won't take a more serious turn.

DUKE They are such peculiar jokes sometimes. Again today I heard a case that gives one pause for thought.

FRANÇOIS Tell me about it.

FLIPOTTE, MICHETTE Yes, do tell us, darling Duke!

DUKE You know Lelange?

FRANÇOIS Of course—the village... the Marquis of Montferrat has one of his most splendid hunting grounds near there.

DUKE That's right; my brother is staying at the castle with him at the moment, and wrote to me about this incident. Now, in Lelange they have a mayor who apparently is most unpopular—

FRANÇOIS Can you name me a mayor who is popular—

DUKE Yes, but listen.—Well, the women of the village assembled outside the mayor's house—with a coffin...

FLIPOTTE What?... They carried it? A coffin? I wouldn't carry a coffin if it were to save my life.

FRANÇOIS Do be quiet—no one's asking you to carry a coffin. (*To the Duke*) Well then?

DUKE And then a couple of the women entered the mayor's residence and explained to him that he was about to die—but that they would do him the honour of burying him—

FRANÇOIS And so did they murder him?

DUKE No—at least, my brother doesn't say anything about that in his letter.

FRANÇOIS There you are, you see! Ranters, chatterers, buffoons, the lot of them—that's all they are. Today instead, they are braying outside the Bastille in Paris—as they've done half a dozen times before.

DUKE Well—if I were the king, I would have put an end to it... long ago...

ALBIN Is the king really as benevolent as they say?

DUKE Haven't you been introduced yet to his Majesty?

FRANÇOIS It's the first time the Chevalier has been to Paris.

DUKE How amazingly young you are. How old, if one may ask?

ALBIN I'm seventeen already, I just look very young...

DUKE Seventeen—you have so much to look forward to. I'm already twenty-four... I'm beginning to regret how much of my own youth I've wasted.

FRANÇOIS (*laughs*) That's a good one! You, Duke... to you, every day you fail to make a female conquest or stab a man to death is wasted.

DUKE The unfortunate thing is, one almost never conquers the right woman—and invariably kills the wrong man. And so one wastes one's youth. It's just as Rollin says.

FRANÇOIS What does Rollin say?

DUKE I was thinking of his recent play, which is running at the Comédie Française—somewhere in that he makes a beautiful analogy. Don't you remember?

FRANÇOIS I have no memory for verse—

DUKE I'm afraid I don't either... All I can remember is the gist... He says, the youth one fails to enjoy is like a shuttlecock one buries in the sand, instead of hitting it into the air.

ALBIN (*sagely*) I think that's very true.

DUKE Isn't it?—The feathers slowly lose their colour and fall out. It would be even more apt if it were to fall into the bushes and get lost.

ALBIN How should that be understood, Émile?

DUKE It's more a matter of feeling. If I could only remember the lines, you'd understand at once.

ALBIN I'm sure, Émile, you could write poetry yourself, if you really wanted to.

DUKE Why do you say that?

ALBIN Ever since you've been here, I've felt as if life were bursting into flame—

DUKE (*smiling*) Really? Bursting into flame?

FRANÇOIS Are you sure you won't join us?

> *Meanwhile two aristocrats have entered and sat down at a table a little way off; the landlord seems to be addressing them crudely.*

DUKE I can't stay now. But I'll look in again later.

MICHETTE Stay with me!

FLIPOTTE Take me with you!

> *They try to hold him back.*

LANDLORD (*comes forward*) Let him go! You are not wicked enough for him by a long shot. Let him run along to his little whores where he feels most at home.

DUKE I'll be back without fail, I don't want to miss Henri.

FRANÇOIS By the way, Henri was just leaving with Léocadie when we arrived.

DUKE I see.—He has married her, did you know?

FRANÇOIS Really?—What will the others have to say about that?

ALBIN What others?

FRANÇOIS She is widely admired.

DUKE And he intends to leave town with her... or at least... that's what they tell me.

LANDLORD So? Is that what they tell you?—(*Gives the Duke a look*)

DUKE (*gives the landlord a look, then*) It's so stupid. Léocadie was created to be the greatest, most gorgeous whore on earth.

FRANÇOIS Everyone knows that.

DUKE Can anything be more imprudent than to deprive someone of their profession? (*As François laughs*) I don't mean that as a joke. One is born to be a whore—just as one is born to be a conqueror or poet.

FRANÇOIS You are being paradoxical.

DUKE I'm sorry for her—and for Henri. He should stay here—not this pub—I would like to get him into the Comédie Française— though even there—I've always felt no one could appreciate him as deeply as I do. That may be an illusion by the way, as I have the same feeling about most artists. But I must say, if I were not the Duke of Cadignan, I would like to be an actor—like...

ALBIN Like Alexander the Great...

DUKE (*smiling*) Yes—like Alexander the Great. (*To Flipotte*) Give me my sword. (*He puts it in its scabbard. Slowly*) It's the best way to ridicule the world; a man who can enact anything he wants before us is greater than all the rest of us. (*Albin looks at him wide-eyed*)

DUKE Don't ponder what I say: it's true, but only for the moment.— Goodbye!

MICHETTE Give me a kiss before you go!

FLIPOTTE Me too!

> They cling to him, the Duke embraces both at once and kisses them, then goes.—During this:

ALBIN A wonderful fellow!...

FRANÇOIS True enough... but the fact that such people exist is almost reason enough not to marry.

ALBIN By the way, could you explain what sort of women these are.

FRANÇOIS Actresses. They're also members of the troupe started by Prospère, now the landlord of this tavern. But even then they behaved much as they do now.

GUILLAUME (*rushes in, out of breath. He staggers to the table where the actors are seated, clutching his heart and reaching out for support*) Saved, thank God, I'm saved!

SCAEVOLA What's up, what's wrong?

ALBIN What's happened to the man?

FRANÇOIS This is all an act. Pay attention!

ALBIN Ah—?

MICHETTE, FLIPOTTE (*hasten over to Guillaume*) What's up? What's wrong with you?

SCAEVOLA Sit down, have a swig!

GUILLAUME More! More!... Prospère, more wine!——I've been running. My throat's dry. They were on my heels.

JULES (*starts*) Ah, beware, they are after all of us.

LANDLORD Well, out with it, what happened? (*To the actors*) Get a move on! Move!

GUILLAUME Women!... fetch the women!—Ah—(*embraces Flipotte*) that brings one back to life all right! (*To Albin, who is utterly perplexed*) I'll be damned if I ever thought I'd see you alive again, my lad... (*appears to listen*) They're coming, they're coming!—(*Going to the door*) No, it's nothing after all.—They...

ALBIN How strange!... That noise really does sound like people dashing past outside... Is all that directed from in here as well?

SCAEVOLA (*to Jules*) He's always adding nuances... it's so stupid!—

LANDLORD Well, are you finally going to tell us why they're after you.

GUILLAUME Nothing serious. But even so, if they caught me, it would cost me my neck—I set a house on fire.

> *During this scene more young aristocrats arrive and sit down at the tables.*

LANDLORD (*in an undertone*) Go on, go on!

GUILLAUME (*likewise*) What d'you mean go on? Isn't that enough, my setting a house on fire?

FRANÇOIS Tell me, my friend, why did you set this house on fire?

GUILLAUME Because the President of the Supreme Court lives there. We wanted to start with him. We want to deter our good Parisian landlords from letting their houses to people who send the likes of us poor devils to jail.

GRAIN That's good! That's good!

GUILLAUME (*looks at Grain and gives a start; he then continues talking*) All the houses must be set ablaze. Three more incendiaries like me, and there won't be a judge left in Paris!

GRAIN Death to all judges!

JULES Well... there is perhaps one we can't get rid of.

GUILLAUME I'd like to meet him.

JULES The judge within us.

LANDLORD That's preposterous. Forget it. Scaevola! Start bellowing! Now's your cue!

SCAEVOLA Bring some wine, Prospère, we'll drink to the death of every last judge in France!

> *During these last words, enter:*
> *The Marquis of Lansac with his wife Severine and Rollin the poet.*

SCAEVOLA Death to anyone in power today! Death!

MARQUIS You see, Severine, this is how we're greeted.

ROLLIN I did warn you, Marquise.

SEVERINE What for?

FRANÇOIS (*gets up*) What's this I see! The Marquise! Permit me to kiss your hand. Good evening, Marquis! Hello, Rollin! So you've taken the risk of coming to this tavern, Marquise!

SEVERINE I've heard so much about it. Besides, we seem to be having an adventurous time today—don't we, Rollin?

MARQUIS Yes, just imagine, Viscount—where do you think we've come from?—The Bastille.

FRANÇOIS Are those demonstrations still going on outside there?

SEVERINE They are indeed!—It looks as though they want to overrun the place.

ROLLIN (*declaims*) Like to a flood that burgeons o'er its banks
And deep resents the staunch resisting flanks
Of its own child, the Earth—

SEVERINE Don't, Rollin!—We had our coach pull up near by. It's such a glorious sight; huge crowds are always rather splendid.

FRANÇOIS I suppose so, if only they didn't smell so foul.

MARQUIS So now my wife won't give me a moment's peace... and I was obliged to bring her here.

SEVERINE Well, what's so special about the place?

LANDLORD (*to Lansac*) So you're here too, you dry old stick? Have you brought the wife along because she's not safe enough to leave at home?

MARQUIS (*with a forced laugh*) He's quite a card, isn't he!

LANDLORD Just make sure she doesn't get filched from under your nose in here instead. Fine ladies like her sometimes have a damnable urge to try it with a real tramp.

ROLLIN Severine, I'm suffering unspeakably.

MARQUIS My dear, I did forewarn you—there is still time to leave.

SEVERINE Whatever for? I find it quite intriguing. Do let's finally sit down!

FRANÇOIS Permit me, Marquis, to introduce you to the Chevalier de la Tremouille. He too is here for the first time. The Marquis of Lansac; Rollin, the well-known poet.

ALBIN Pleased to meet you. (*Compliments all round; everyone sits down*)

ALBIN (*to François*) Is she one of the actresses, or... I am completely lost.

FRANÇOIS Don't be so obtuse! That's the real Marquise of Lansac... a highly respectable lady.

ROLLIN (*to Severine*) Tell me you love me.

SEVERINE Yes, yes, but don't keep asking me every other minute.

MARQUIS Have we missed any of the show already?

FRANÇOIS Not much. The fellow over there is playing an arsonist, apparently.

SEVERINE Chevalier, you must be the cousin of young Lydia de la Tremouille, who was getting married today?

ALBIN Indeed, Marquise, that was one of the reasons why I came to Paris.

SEVERINE Yes, I do seem to remember seeing you in church.

ALBIN (*embarrassed*) I'm extremely flattered, Marquise.

SEVERINE (*to Rollin*) What a sweet young boy.

ROLLIN Ah, Severine, you've never met a man you didn't like.

SEVERINE Oh, but I have; and I promptly went and married him.

ROLLIN Ah, Severine, I'm so afraid—there are times when even your own husband is a danger to you.

LANDLORD (*brings wine*) There you are! I wish it were poison, but for the moment we're not allowed to serve that to you scoundrels.

FRANÇOIS The day will come, Prospère.

SEVERINE (*to Rollin*) What's the matter with those two pretty girls? Why don't they come closer? Since we're here, I want to join in everything. So far, the proceedings all seem rather staid.

MARQUIS Just be patient, Severine.

SEVERINE To me it's on the streets that life's most entertaining these days. Do you know what happened to us yesterday, while we were driving down the Longchamps promenade?

MARQUIS Now look, Severine my dear, what's the point in...

SEVERINE Well, this ruffian leapt onto our carriage step and shouted: next year you'll be standing behind your coachman and we'll be sitting in your carriage.

FRANÇOIS Well, that's a bit much.

MARQUIS Ah God, to my mind, these things are not even worth discussing. Paris is a little feverish at the moment, but that will soon subside.

GUILLAUME (*suddenly*) I see flames, flames everywhere I look, towering red flames.

LANDLORD (*across to him*) You're supposed to be playing a madman, not a criminal.

SEVERINE Can he really see flames?

FRANÇOIS None of this is the real thing yet, Marquise.

ALBIN (*to Rollin*) I can't tell you how confused I am by all of this.

MICHETTE (*approaches the Marquis*) I've not even said hello to you yet, you darling old swine.

MARQUIS (*embarrassed*) She's joking of course, Severine my dear.

SEVERINE I don't see it that way at all. Tell me, young lady, how many lovers have you had?

MARQUIS (*to François*) It's remarkable how the Marquise, my wife, finds her feet at once, in whatever situation.

ROLLIN Yes, it is indeed remarkable.

MICHETTE Have you counted yours?

SEVERINE When I was as young as you... certainly.—

ALBIN (*to Rollin*) Tell me, is the Marquise play-acting or is she really like this—I'm absolutely lost.

ROLLIN Play-acting... reality... can you tell the difference that precisely, Chevalier?

ALBIN Even so.

ROLLIN I can't. And what I find so curious here is that all apparent differences are so to speak suspended. Reality merges into play-acting—play-acting into reality. Just look at the Marquise. The way she's chatting with those wretched creatures, as if they were her equals. And the whole time she's...

ALBIN Something else entirely.

ROLLIN Thank you, Chevalier.

LANDLORD (*to Grain*) Well then, how did it feel?

GRAIN What?

LANDLORD All that business with your aunt you spent two years in jail for?

GRAIN But I told you, I strangled her.

FRANÇOIS He's pretty feeble. Must be an amateur. I've never seen him here before.

GEORGETTE (*enters hastily, dressed as a whore of the lowest order*) Good evening, everyone! Isn't my Balthasar here yet?

SCAEVOLA Georgette! Come and sit by me! Your Balthasar will get here on time.

GEORGETTE If he isn't here in ten minutes, he'll not be here on time—he'll not be back at all.

FRANÇOIS Keep an eye on her, Marquise. She's actually the wife of this Balthasar she's talking about, who will be here shortly.—She plays the part of a low-class whore, and Balthasar plays her pimp. But in fact she's the most devoted wife one could hope to find in Paris.

> *Balthasar enters.*

GEORGETTE It's my Balthasar! (*She runs to meet him and embraces him*) Why, there you are!

BALTHASAR Everything's been seen to. (*Silence all round*) It wasn't worth the candle. I almost felt sorry for him. You should check out your customers a bit more thoroughly, Georgette—I'm fed up with bumping off young hopefuls for the sake of a few francs.

FRANÇOIS Splendid...

ALBIN What?—

FRANÇOIS He puts it so succinctly.

> *The commissioner enters, disguised, and sits down at a table.*

LANDLORD (*to him*) You've come at a good moment, Commissioner. That is one of my most outstanding actors.

BALTHASAR I ought to find another way to make a living altogether. By God, I'm no coward, but it's a bitter way to earn a crust.

SCAEVOLA I can believe that.

GEORGETTE What's the matter with you today?

BALTHASAR Well I'll tell you straight, Georgette;—I think you're a bit too intimate with the young gentlemen.

GEORGETTE See what a child he is. Be reasonable, Balthasar! I have to be sweet to them to gain their trust.

ROLLIN What she says is quite profound.

BALTHASAR If I ever thought you were enjoying it when they were...

GEORGETTE Well, how d'you like that! His stupid jealousy will be the death of him one day.

BALTHASAR I heard you sighing today, Georgette, after his trust was already firm enough.

GEORGETTE But one can't just suddenly stop playing the adoring mistress.

BALTHASAR Beware, Georgette, the Seine is deep. (*Savagely*) If you betray me.—

GEORGETTE Never, never!

ALBIN I don't understand all this at all.

SEVERINE Now that's the right attitude, Rollin!

ROLLIN Do you think so?

MARQUIS (*to Severine*) We can still go if you'd like, Severine.

SEVERINE What for? I'm really beginning to enjoy myself.

GEORGETTE My own Balthasar, I adore you. (*They embrace*)

FRANÇOIS Bravo! Bravo!—

BALTHASAR Who is that cretin?

COMMISSIONER This is really a bit much—this is—

> *Maurice and Étienne enter; they are dressed as young aristocrats, but one can see they are only wearing cast-off theatre costumes.*

FROM THE ACTORS' TABLE Who are they?

SCAEVOLA I'll be damned if it isn't Maurice and Étienne.

GEORGETTE Of course it's them.

BALTHASAR Georgette!

SEVERINE God, what an absolutely gorgeous young couple!

ROLLIN It's really hurtful, Severine, when you get excited like this over every pretty face.

SEVERINE What else have I come here for?

ROLLIN Well, at least tell me you love me.

SEVERINE (*with a look*) You have a very short memory.

ÉTIENNE Well now, guess where we've just come from?

FRANÇOIS Pay attention, Marquis, they're a really artful couple.

MAURICE From a wedding.

ÉTIENNE One has to dress up a little for such occasions, you know. Otherwise the damned secret police are onto one at once.

SCAEVOLA Have you made a decent haul at least?

LANDLORD Let's have a look.

MAURICE (*takes various watches from his jacket*) What'll you give me for these?

LANDLORD For that? One louis!

MAURICE Get away!

SCAEVOLA It's not worth more!

MAURICE What will you give me for it?

MICHETTE Take a look at me!... Is this enough for you?—

FLIPOTTE No, me;—look at me—

MAURICE Listen girls, I can get plenty of that without risking my neck.

MICHETTE You're a conceited ape.

SEVERINE I'll swear this is no play.

ROLLIN No, glimpses of reality keep flashing through. That's what's so intriguing.

SCAEVOLA Whose wedding was it then?

MAURICE Lady de la Tremouille's—she has married the Count of Banville.

ALBIN Did you hear that, François—Take my word for it, these are real villains.

FRANÇOIS Calm down, Albin. I know these two. I've seen them perform a dozen times. Their speciality is imitating pickpockets. (*Maurice pulls several purses from his jacket*)

SCAEVOLA Well, you can afford to be magnanimous tonight.

ÉTIENNE It was a grand wedding all right. The entire aristocracy of France was there. Even the king sent his representative.

ALBIN (*excited*) That's all quite true!

MAURICE (*lets money roll out onto the table*) This is for you, my friends, so you can see we stick together.

FRANÇOIS Just props, my dear Albin. (*He gets up and takes a few coins*) We might as well pick up something too.

LANDLORD Help yourself... you've never earned a more honest penny in your life!

MAURICE (*holds a garter set with diamonds in the air*) And who shall I give this to?

> *Georgette, Michette, Flipotte grab at it.*

MAURICE Patience, little darlings, we'll talk about it later. I'll give it to whoever can invent a new caress.

SEVERINE (*to Rollin*) Don't you want me to compete?

ROLLIN Severine, you'll drive me mad.

MARQUIS Shouldn't we be going Severine? I think...

SEVERINE Oh no. I'm feeling absolutely fine. (*To Rollin*) Ah, I'm really getting in the mood for—

MICHETTE But how did you manage to get the garter off?

MAURICE There was such a crush in church... and when a woman thinks you're paying court to her...

> *All laugh. Grain has relieved François of his purse.*

FRANÇOIS (*showing Albin the coins*) They're only counters. Does that reassure you?

> *Grain starts to withdraw.*

LANDLORD (*follows him; in an undertone*) Give me that purse you've just taken from the gentleman.

GRAIN I—

LANDLORD At once... or you'll regret it.

GRAIN You don't have to be so rough about it. (*Gives it to him*)

LANDLORD And make sure you stay around. I don't have time to search you now. Who knows what else you've pocketed. Go back to your seat.

FLIPOTTE I'm going to win that garter.

LANDLORD (*to François, tossing him his purse*) Here's your purse. It must have dropped out of your pocket.

FRANÇOIS Thank you, Prospère. (*To Albin*) You see, in reality we are among the most respectable people in the world.

> *Henri has been there for some time, sitting at the back; now he suddenly stands up.*

ROLLIN Henri, there's Henri.—

SEVERINE Is he the one you've been telling me so much about?

MARQUIS Indeed. He's the one we came to see.

> *Henri steps forward with great stage presence; doesn't say a word.*

THE ACTORS Henri, what's the matter?

ROLLIN Observe his eye. A world of passion. He's playing someone guilty of a crime of passion.

SEVERINE Now that's something I can appreciate!

ALBIN So why doesn't he say anything?

ROLLIN He seems to be withdrawn. Just watch. Pay attention... he has committed some appalling act.

FRANÇOIS He is being a little theatrical. It looks as if he might be working up to a soliloquy.

LANDLORD Henri, Henri, where have you been?

HENRI I've just murdered someone.

ROLLIN What did I tell you?

SCAEVOLA Who?

HENRI My wife's lover.

> *The landlord looks at him, and in that instant evidently has the feeling that it might be true.*

HENRI (*looks up*) Well, it's done now, so why stare at me like that. That's how things are. Is it so surprising? You all know the kind of woman my wife is; it was bound to end like this.

LANDLORD And her—where is she?

FRANÇOIS You see, the landlord's actively participating. Notice how that makes the whole thing seem more natural.

Noise outside, moderately loud.

JULES What's that noise out there?

MARQUIS Can you hear anything, Severine?

ROLLIN It sounds like troops marching past.

FRANÇOIS Oh no, it's our old friends the people of Paris, just listen to them bawling. (*Disquiet in the cellar; things quieten down outside*) Go on, Henri, go on.

LANDLORD Well, tell us, Henri!—Where is your wife? What have you done with her?

HENRI Ah, I'm not worried about her. It's not going to kill her. One man's as good as the next, what do women care? There are a thousand more good looking men running around Paris—one as good as the next—

BALTHASAR May the same thing happen to all who take away our wives.

SCAEVOLA To all who take what belongs to us.

COMMISSIONER (*to the landlord*) Those are provocative remarks.

ALBIN It's quite frightening... these people are in earnest.

SCAEVOLA Down with the profiteers of France! You can bet the fellow he caught his wife with was another of those accursed dogs who take the very bread out of our mouths.

ALBIN I suggest we leave.

SEVERINE Henri! Henri!

MARQUIS Really, Marquise!

SEVERINE Please, my dear Marquis, ask the man how he caught his wife out... or I'll ask him myself.

MARQUIS (*hesitating*) Tell me, Henri, how did you manage to apprehend the two of them?

HENRI (*who has been deep in thought*) Do you know my wife?—She is the most beautiful and depraved creature under the sun.—And I loved her.—We've known each other seven years... but she's only been my wife since yesterday. In seven years, not a day, but not a day went by when she didn't lie to me, for everything about her lies. Her eyes as much as her lips, her kisses and her smile.

FRANÇOIS He's getting a little declamatory.

HENRI Any man, young or old, who charmed her and was prepared to pay, indeed I suspect any man who fancied her at all, enjoyed her favours—and I always knew about it.

SEVERINE Not every man can say as much.

HENRI And yet she loved me; my friends, can any of you understand that? Again and again she would come back to me—from far and wide—from the handsome and the ugly—the clever and the dull, the scoundrels and the cavaliers—always she'd come back again to me.—

SEVERINE (*to Rollin*) If you men only realized that love is just this coming back.

HENRI How I suffered... Torture, torture!

ROLLIN It's quite devastating!

HENRI And then yesterday I married her. We had a dream. No—I had a dream. I wanted to get away from here with her. Away to the countryside and solitude, out into the open fields. We wanted to live like other couples—we even dreamed of having a child one day.

ROLLIN (*softly*) Severine.

SEVERINE Well, that's all right I suppose.

ALBIN François, this fellow is telling the truth.

FRANÇOIS Certainly, the love story is true, but it's the murder story that's at issue.

HENRI I was a day late... and she had forgotten about one man, apart from whom—I believe—there was nobody she missed... but then I caught the two of them together... and the man was... hmm.

THE ACTORS Who?... Who? How did it happen?... What have you done with him?—Are you being followed?... How did it happen?... Where is she?

HENRI (*more and more excited*) I escorted her... to the theatre... today was to have been her last performance... I kissed her... at the door— and she went up to her dressing room, while I departed like a man with nothing to fear.—But I'd not gone a hundred yards when I was seized by a tremendous anxiety... as though driven by some inner compulsion to turn back... and so I began to retrace my steps. But then I felt ashamed and started out again... but within a hundred yards of the theatre I was again overcome by anxiety... and again I went back. Her performance for the night was over... she doesn't have a lot to do, just stands about on stage a while, half-naked—and then she's finished... I stood outside her dressing-room, put my ear to the door and heard whispering. I couldn't make out a single word... the whispering stopped... I broke open the door... (*he bellows like a wild animal*)—it was the Duke of Cadignan and so I murdered him.—

LANDLORD (*who now finally believes it's true*) Madman!

SEVERINE Bravo! bravo!

ROLLIN What are you doing, Marquise? The moment you call out

Bravo! you turn it all into theatre again—and the pleasurable creepy feeling's lost.

MARQUIS I don't find being given the creeps all that pleasurable myself. A round of applause, my friends, that's the best way to shake off the spell.

LANDLORD (*to Henri under the cover of the noise*) Save yourself, Henri, fly.

HENRI What? What?

LANDLORD Call it a day here and get away!

FRANÇOIS Quiet!... Let's hear what the landlord has to say!

LANDLORD (*after a moment's reflection*) I'm telling him he should leave before the watch at the city gates hear anything. The handsome duke was one of the king's favourites—they'll break you on the wheel! If only you'd stabbed that slut of a wife of yours instead!

FRANÇOIS Great collaborative acting...! Splendid!

HENRI Prospère, which of us is mad, you or me?—(*He stands there trying to read the landlord's eyes*)

ROLLIN It's amazing, we all know he's acting, and yet if the Duke of Cadignan were to walk in now, we would think he was a ghost. (*Noise outside—louder and louder. People enter, shouts are heard. Grasset in the lead, followed down the steps by others, Lebrêt among them. Shouts are heard: Freedom, Freedom!*)

GRASSET Here we are, citizens, in here!

ALBIN What's all this? Is this part of it?

FRANÇOIS No.

MARQUIS What does all this mean?

SEVERINE Who are these people?

GRASSET In here! I tell you, my friend Prospère still has a cask of wine or two left, (*noise from the street*) and we have earned it! Friends! Brothers! We have them, we have them!

SHOUTS OUTSIDE Freedom! Freedom!

SEVERINE What's happening?

MARQUIS Let's leave, let's leave, the rabble are approaching.

ROLLIN How are you going to get out though?

GRASSET It's fallen, the Bastille has fallen!

LANDLORD What did you say?—Is that true?

GRASSET Can't you hear?

  Albin starts to draw his sword.

FRANÇOIS Forget about that now, or we'll all be lost.

GRASSET (*comes reeling down the steps*) And if you hurry, you can still

see something comical out there... the head of our good Delaunay*
stuck up on a pole.

MARQUIS Is the fellow mad?

CRIES Freedom! Freedom!

GRASSET We've cut off a dozen heads, the Bastille is in our hands, the
prisoners are free! Paris belongs to the people!

LANDLORD Did you hear that! Did you hear that! Paris belongs to us!

GRASSET You see how he now finds courage. Yes, shout away,
Prospère, nothing can happen to you now.

LANDLORD (*to the nobles*) What do you say to that? You riff-raff! The
game is up.

ALBIN Didn't I say so?

LANDLORD The people of Paris are victorious.

COMMISSIONER Quiet! (*People laugh*) Quiet!... The resumption of
the performance is hereby prohibited!

GRASSET Who is this numbskull?

COMMISSIONER Prospère, I hold you responsible for all seditious
remarks—

GRASSET Is the fellow mad?

LANDLORD The show is over, don't you understand? Henri, tell them
will you, you're now allowed to tell them! We will protect you... the
people of Paris will protect you.

GRASSET Yes, the people of Paris.

Henri stands there looking vacant.

LANDLORD Henri has really murdered the Duke of Cadignan.

ALBIN, FRANÇOIS, MARQUIS What's he saying?

ALBIN AND OTHERS What does all this mean, Henri?

FRANÇOIS Henri, say something!

LANDLORD He caught him with his wife—and murdered him.

HENRI It's not true!

LANDLORD You've no need to be afraid now, you can shout it from
the rooftops. I could have told you she was the Duke's mistress
several hours ago. I came pretty near to doing so, by God... True
isn't it, my Screaming Pumice-stone, we knew all about it?

HENRI Who saw her? Where was she seen?

LANDLORD What do you care about that now! He must be mad... you
murdered him, you can't do more than that.

FRANÇOIS For heaven's sake, is it really true or not?

LANDLORD Yes, it's true!

GRASSET Henri—from now on we are friends for life. Long live
freedom! Long live freedom!

FRANÇOIS Henri, say something.

HENRI She was his mistress? She was the Duke's mistress? I didn't know... he's still alive... he's still alive.—

    Huge uproar.

SEVERINE (*to the others*) Well, now where is the truth?

ALBIN For God's sake!

    The Duke pushes his way through the crowd onto the steps.

SEVERINE (*who sees him first*) The Duke!

SEVERAL The Duke!

DUKE Well now, what's the matter?

LANDLORD Is it a ghost?

DUKE Not that I'm aware. Let me through there!

ROLLIN How much do you bet, it's all arranged? The fellows over there belong to Prospère's troupe. Bravo, Prospère, that was a real triumph!

DUKE What's all this? Still play-acting in here, while out there... don't people know what's going on outside? I've just seen Delaunay's head being paraded on a pole. Well, why are you all looking at me like that—(*comes down*) Henri—

FRANÇOIS Beware of Henri.

    Henri rushes at the Duke like a maniac and thrusts a dagger through his neck.

COMMISSIONER (*stands up*) This is really going too far!—

ALBIN He's bleeding!

ROLLIN A murder's been committed!

SEVERINE The Duke is dying!

MARQUIS I am quite distraught, dear Severine, that today of all days I had to bring you to this tavern.

SEVERINE Why? (*wearily*) It all worked out splendidly. It's not every day that one sees a real duke being really murdered.

ROLLIN I still haven't taken it all in.

COMMISSIONER Quiet!—No one is to leave the premises!—

GRASSET What does he want??

COMMISSIONER In the name of the law, I arrest this man.

GRASSET (*laughs*) We make the laws, you dunderhead! Away with the rogue. Anyone who murders a duke is the people's friend. Long live freedom!

ALBIN (*draws his sword*) Make way! Follow me, friends!

    Léocadie rushes in down the steps.

CRIES Léocadie!

OTHERS His wife!

LÉOCADIE Let me through here! I want to see my husband! (*She comes forward, sees, gives a scream*) Who's done this? Henri! (*Henri looks at her*)

LÉOCADIE Why have you done this?

HENRI Why?

LÉOCADIE Yes, yes, I know why. For my sake. No, no, I mustn't say for my sake. Never in my life have I been worthy of that.

GRASSET (*begins a speech*) Citizens of Paris, let us celebrate our victory. On our way through the streets of Paris, fate led us to this friendly landlord. Things couldn't have worked out better. Nowhere can the cry 'Long live freedom!' sound sweeter than over a duke's corpse.

CRIES Long live freedom! Long live freedom!

FRANÇOIS I think we should leave—the people have gone mad. Let's go.

ALBIN Should we leave the corpse here for them?

SEVERINE Long live freedom! Long live freedom!

MARQUIS Are you mad?

THE CITIZENS, THE ACTORS Long live freedom! Long live freedom!

SEVERINE (*at the head of the nobles, approaching the exit*) Rollin, wait outside my window tonight. I'll throw the key down to you again— we'll have a rare old time—I feel really quite excited.

CRIES Long live freedom! Long live Henri! Long live Henri!

LEBRÊT Just look at the rogues—they've taken to their heels.

GRASSET Let them go for today—let them go.—They won't escape us.

Curtain.

THE LAST MASKS
(*Die letzten Masken*)

A Play in One Act

CAST

KARL RADEMACHER, *journalist*
FLORIAN JACKWERTH, *actor*
ALEXANDER WEIHGAST

Doctors in the Vienna General Hospital:
DR HALMSCHLÖGER
DR TANN
JULIANE PASCHANDA, *nurse*

A smaller room—the so-called 'annexe'—in the General Hospital, connected to a larger sick ward; in place of partition doors there is a movable linen curtain. On the left, a bed. In the middle, an oblong table strewn with papers, little bottles, etc. Two chairs. An armchair beside the bed. A candle is burning on the table. Karl Rademacher, over fifty, very emaciated, completely grey, is sitting in the armchair with eyes closed. Florian Jackwerth, about twenty-eight, thin, clean shaven, with very bright almost feverish eyes, is wearing a linen nightgown, the heavy folds of which he adjusts occasionally. The nurse, Juliane Paschanda, plump, good-natured and still young, is busy doing paperwork.

FLORIAN (*draws the curtain back as he enters from the ward, which is dimly illuminated by a hanging lamp, and goes over to the nurse*) Busy as ever, are we, Fräulein Paschanda.

NURSE So you're out of bed again? What will the doctor say! Now be off and try to get some sleep.

FLORIAN Certainly, indeed I mean to take a long sleep soon.* Can I be of assistance to you, pretty woman? And I don't mean in bed.

The nurse ignores him.

FLORIAN (*creeps over to Rademacher*) Look, Fräulein Paschanda—I say, look at this!

NURSE What do you want?

FLORIAN (*returning to her*) My God, I thought for a moment he was dead already.

NURSE It's going to be a while yet.

FLORIAN Do you really think so? Well good night then, Fräulein Juliane Paschanda.

NURSE Don't call me Fräulein, I'm a married woman.

FLORIAN I see! I've not yet had the honour of meeting your good husband.

NURSE Nor would I wish you to. He's an orderly in the morgue.

FLORIAN Thanks for telling me, but I won't be needing him. I say, Frau Paschanda, (*confidingly*) did you happen to see the young lady who did me the honour of a visit this afternoon?

NURSE Yes; the one in the red hat.

FLORIAN (*annoyed*) Red hat—red hat... She was a colleague of mine—I'll have you know! We had an engagement at the same theatre last year—in Olmütz.* She was the leading lady, and yours truly was the youthful hero. Look at me, please—Need I say more?—Yes, I sent her a card... just a card—and she came at once. Loyalty's not dead yet in the theatre. And she promised she'd keep an eye out for me, talk to an agent or two—just to make sure I get a summer contract when I'm released from this place. So you see, Frau von Paschanda, a young lady can have a heart of gold, even if she does wear a red hat. (*More and more irritably, eventually coughing*) Perhaps she'll be coming by again—so I'd better write and tell her to put on a blue hat at once—because Frau von Paschanda can't stand the colour red.

NURSE Shh! Shh! People are trying to sleep. (*Listens*)

FLORIAN What is it?

NURSE I thought I heard the doctor—

The hospital clock strikes.

FLORIAN What time is it then?

NURSE Nine.

FLORIAN Who is on duty tonight?

NURSE Doctor Halmschlöger.

FLORIAN Ah, Doctor Halmschlöger. A fine man, but a bit conceited. (*Notices that Rademacher has woken up*) Good evening, Herr von Rademacher.

Rademacher nods.

FLORIAN (*imitates Doctor Halmschlöger*) Well, my dear Rademacher, how are you feeling today? (*Pretending to take off his coat and give it to the nurse*) Oh, Frau Paschanda, would you be so good as to... Thank you.

NURSE (*laughing despite herself*) How you can mimic people.

FLORIAN (*in another voice, as if going from bed to bed*) No change? No change? No change? Good—good—good...

NURSE Why, that's the head doctor. If he should get to hear about this!

FLORIAN Just wait a bit, you've seen nothing yet.

He suddenly falls into a chair, his face appears contorted with pain, and he rolls up his eyes.

NURSE But for heaven's sake, that's—

FLORIAN (*interrupting his mimicry for a moment*) Go on then, who?

NURSE The one from bed seventeen, old Engstl—the roof man that died two days ago. Oh, do stop! It's a sin against the dead.

FLORIAN Well, my dear Frau Paschanda, d'you think the likes of me are in hospital for nothing? I have a lot to learn here.

NURSE The doctor's coming.

Exit into the ward.—When she draws back the curtain, Doctors Halmschlöger and Tann can be seen near the back of the stage.

FLORIAN Indeed, Herr Rademacher, I'm putting myself through my own course of studies here.

RADEMACHER Really!

FLORIAN Yes, for the likes of me, it pays to be laid up in hospital a while. D'you think I can't make use of it because I am an actor? Wrong! You see, I've made a discovery, Herr Rademacher. (*Importantly*) Given the intuition of an actor of genius, it is possible to take any sad or pain-racked countenance, and work out the individual's comic mask from it. Once I've seen a dying man, I know exactly how he would have looked after being told a first-rate joke. But what's wrong, Herr Rademacher? Courage! Don't lose your sense of humour. Look at me—ha! A week ago I was despaired of—not only by the doctors, which would not have been so dangerous, but even by myself! And now I'm right as rain again. And in another week—your most obedient servant! And so farewell, thou silent house!* And then I shall take the liberty of inviting your worthy self to my debut performance. (*Coughs*)

RADEMACHER That seems hardly likely.

FLORIAN Isn't it strange? If we'd both remained healthy, we'd probably be mortal enemies.

RADEMACHER How so?

FLORIAN Well, I would have been acting and you would have written reviews pulling me to pieces,—and I've never been able to stomach people criticizing me. While as things are, we have become the best of friends.—Tell me, Herr Rademacher, didn't I look just as sick as you a week ago?

RADEMACHER Maybe your case is different.

FLORIAN Nonsense! All one needs is a little determination. Do you know how I got better? (*Rademacher looks at him*) No need to look at me like that—I'm nearly there. I just kept all those gloomy thoughts at bay.

RADEMACHER How did you manage that?

FLORIAN Well, in my own mind I just hurled abuse at all the people whom I bear a grudge against. That relieves one's feelings, I can tell you! I even worked out who I would return to haunt, once I had passed on.—First in line would be a colleague of yours in Olmütz—a really spiteful fellow! And then there's the director who deducted half my pay because I improvised. What happened was, the audience was always laughing at my jokes instead of at the plays. He should have been grateful, that director. Instead of which—well, he'll see, he'll see! I might have turned out to possess a gift for ghostly visitations—oh, I could have earned a decent living in Heaven all right.—I might even have accepted a contract with the Spiritualists.

Doctor Halmschlöger and Doctor Tann enter with the nurse.

TANN (*a young, rather sloppily dressed man, his hat still on, an extinguished cigar in his mouth*) But this time, Halmschlöger, don't take all night in there.

HALMSCHLÖGER (*a meticulously dressed young man with a pince-nez and a little blonde beard; his overcoat thrown over his shoulders*) No, I won't be long.

TANN Or perhaps I should go on ahead and meet you at the coffee house.

HALMSCHLÖGER I won't be long.

FLORIAN Good evening, Doctor.

HALMSCHLÖGER Why aren't you in bed? (*To the nurse*) Paschanda!

FLORIAN I've been sleeping all day, Doctor, I feel fine. Allow me, Doctor, to invite you to my debut...

HALMSCHLÖGER (*looks at him with amusement for a moment, then turns away*) Yes, yes. (*Turning to Rademacher*) Now then, my dear Rademacher, how are you feeling?

Florian makes a sign to the nurse, referring to his earlier mimicry.

RADEMACHER I'm in a bad way, Doctor.

HALMSCHLÖGER (*consulting the chart at the head of the bed, while the nurse holds up the light*) Let's see 39.4 degrees—well now! Yesterday it was 40. (*Nurse nods*) So that's an improvement. Well, good night. (*Prepares to go*)

RADEMACHER Doctor!

HALMSCHLÖGER Did you want something?

RADEMACHER Please, Doctor, how much longer is this going to go on?

HALMSCHLÖGER Well, you'll have to have a little patience.

RADEMACHER I don't mean that, Doctor. I mean, when will it be all over for me?

Tann has taken a seat at the table and is leafing absent-mindedly through the papers.

HALMSCHLÖGER What are you talking about? (*To the nurse*) Has he had his drops?

NURSE At seven-thirty, Doctor.

RADEMACHER Doctor, I would ask you not to treat me like an idiot. Oh, forgive me, Doctor—

HALMSCHLÖGER (*a little impatiently, but kindly*) Not so loud, not so loud.

RADEMACHER Please, one word more, Doctor. (*Resolutely*) You see, I must know the truth—I really must—for a very specific reason!—

HALMSCHLÖGER The truth... I certainly hope——Well, in a certain sense the future is a closed book to all of us—however I can say——

RADEMACHER But Doctor,—what if there were something very important I still had to—something other people's fate depended on—not just my own peace of mind—in my last hour...

HALMSCHLÖGER Come, come now!—Well, do you want to explain? (*Still kindly*) But be as brief as possible, if you don't mind. I still have two wards to get through. Imagine if everyone took this long— Well, go on.

RADEMACHER I need to speak to someone.

HALMSCHLÖGER Well, you may write to them, if that sets your mind at rest. If you wish you may also receive guests tomorrow between four and five. I have no objection.

RADEMACHER Doctor—that's too late—it may be too late—I can feel it... by tomorrow morning it may all be over.

HALMSCHLÖGER That's highly unlikely. What is all this anyway? If you set so much store by it, surely yesterday would have been...

RADEMACHER (*urgently*) Doctor! You have always been good to me—I know I'm being a little forward—but you see, Doctor, once one's sure the men in white coats will be here in a day or so to carry one downstairs, one thinks one can get cocky and demand more than other people.

TANN Well, Halmschlöger, what's the trouble?

HALMSCHLÖGER Won't be a moment. (*Rather impatiently*) Well, in short, what is it you want?

RADEMACHER I absolutely must speak to this friend of mine. Someone called Herr Weihgast—Alexander Weihgast.

HALMSCHLÖGER Weihgast! You don't mean the well-known poet Weihgast?

RADEMACHER Yes!

HALMSCHLÖGER Is he a friend of yours?

RADEMACHER Was, was—some considerable time ago.

HALMSCHLÖGER Well, write him a card.

RADEMACHER What's the use of that? I'd have passed on before he
    got here. I need to speak to him today—at once...

HALMSCHLÖGER (*firmly*) Herr Rademacher, it's out of the question.
    And there's an end of it. (*Gently*) To set your mind at rest, I'll write
    to Herr Weihgast this evening myself, as I happen to know him
    personally, and leave it to him to look you up when it's convenient.

RADEMACHER Do you know Herr Weihgast, Doctor? (*Suddenly*)
    Fetch him here then—fetch him here!

HALMSCHLÖGER Now listen, Herr Rademacher, I really don't know
    what more—

RADEMACHER (*in great agitation*) Doctor, I know this is utterly pre-
    sumptuous of me,—but you are human, Doctor, and you take a
    human view of things. Unlike some others who judge solely by the
    book. And so, Doctor, you can appreciate the situation: here is
    someone doomed to die tomorrow who has one last wish he lays
    great store by, and it's up to you to fulfil that wish for him... I beg
    you, Doctor, go and fetch him!

HALMSCHLÖGER (*hesitating, looks at his watch*) Well—supposing I
    were to agree—I put it to you, Herr Rademacher, how can I ask
    him—at this late hour... frankly, it's a very odd request. Think
    about it yourself.

RADEMACHER Oh, Doctor, I know my friend Weihgast. If you tell
    him, his old friend Rademacher is dying in the General Hospital
    and wants to see him one last time—oh, he won't ignore that.—I
    beseech you, Doctor—for you it's just the drive,—right? But for
    me—for me...

HALMSCHLÖGER Yes, that's just the point! For me of course, it's of
    no importance. But for you—make no mistake, the excitement
    could be fatal.

RADEMACHER Doctor—Doctor! We are men! What is an hour more
    or less.

HALMSCHLÖGER (*soothingly*) There, there now! (*After short consider-
    ation*) Very well, I'll go and see him.
        Rademacher starts to thank him.

HALMSCHLÖGER (*defensively*) I can't guarantee to bring him back.
    But as you seem so set on it,—(*as Rademacher again tries to thank
    him*) All right, all right. (*Turns away*)

TANN Well, at last!

HALMSCHLÖGER My dear colleague, I must ask a favour—would you
    mind seeing to the other wards? There's nothing much—a couple
    of injections—the nurse will tell you——

TANN But what's wrong, what's wrong?

HALMSCHLÖGER A curious business. The poor devil has asked me to fetch an old friend of his, apparently he has something important to confide to him. And guess who it is? Weihgast, the poet.

TANN What, and you've agreed to go? Come now, you're not a messenger boy! Listen, people here are exploiting your good nature.

HALMSCHLÖGER My friend, one's feelings are involved here too, you know. In my view, it is precisely cases like these that are the most interesting part of our profession.

TANN Well, that's one way of looking at it.

HALMSCHLÖGER So, will you do this for me?

TANN Of course. The coffee house is off tonight then?

HALMSCHLÖGER I might still make it later.

Halmschlöger, Tann, Nurse exeunt.

FLORIAN (*comes back on*) What were you talking to the doctor so long about?

RADEMACHER (*excited, almost light-hearted*) I'm to have a visitor—I'm to have a visitor.

FLORIAN (*interested*) What? A visitor? Now? In the middle of the night?

RADEMACHER Yes, my dear Jackwerth—so pay attention, and you may learn a thing or two... from my visitor, that is. Make sure you watch the fellow as he comes in, and again when he departs... ah! (*More and more excited*) If only I may live to see it!—if only I may live to see it!—Hand me a glass of water, Jackwerth—there's a good fellow. (*Takes the glass and gulps it down*) Thank you—thank you,——Yes, I think the old ticker will hold out all right... (*almost fearfully*) So long as he comes... so long as he comes...

FLORIAN Who are you talking about?

RADEMACHER (*to himself*) Write to him?... No, I'd get no satisfaction out of that. No, I must have him *here*—right here—opposite me... face to face, eyeball to eyeball—ah!...

FLORIAN (*with concern*) Herr Rademacher...

RADEMACHER Don't worry about me—it's totally unnecessary. My God, I'm feeling quite elated, I don't even feel afraid of death now... It won't be hard at all, once he has been here... Ah, Florian Jackwerth, what can I do for you?

FLORIAN (*taken aback*) What do you mean?

RADEMACHER I want to show my gratitude to you. It was you who put me onto this idea—Indeed it was. I shall install you as my heir. The key to my desk is under the cushion.—Perhaps you're

thinking, it can't be anything that special?—Who knows? You
might be mistaken... There might be the odd masterpiece locked
away in there! I'm feeling more and more elated—by God...
Perhaps I'm getting better!

FLORIAN Of course you are!

RADEMACHER If I get better—I swear, if ever I set foot outside this
hospital again, I'll make a fresh start. I'll begin again.

FLORIAN Begin what?

RADEMACHER Why, battling—, battling of course. I'll try again. I
won't give up yet—no indeed. I'm not really all that old,—fifty-
five... Is that so old when one's in good health still? I am somebody,
Florian Jackwerth—I am somebody, I'll have you know. It's just
that I've had bad luck. I'm as good as many another who is riding
his high horse, my good Sir—and I'm a match for many another
who thinks himself my better because he's had more luck. (*Feverishly*) So long as he comes... so long as he comes... Lord God, I beg
you, even though you've abandoned me for fifty years, at least in my
final hour grant me the strength to settle the score, as far as that is
possible. Let me see him sitting here in front of me—pale and
crushed—as insignificant before me as he has felt superior to me all
his life... You see, my dear Jackwerth, the man I am expecting is a
boyhood friend of mine. And twenty-five—even twenty years ago
we were on good terms, having started out from the same spot—
only then we went our separate ways—he to ever new heights and I
to ever more abysmal depths. And today he is a rich and famous
poet, while I am a poor devil of a journalist dying like a dog in hospital.—But no matter, no matter—for now comes the moment
when at last I can crush him... and crush him I will! I know, Herr
Jackwerth, that your sweetheart was here this afternoon—but what
are the ardours of awaiting a loved one, compared to the longing for
a person one hates and has hated all one's life but neglected to tell.

FLORIAN But you're getting awfully upset, Herr Rademacher!—You
seem to be losing your voice.

RADEMACHER Don't you worry—once he's here, I shall be able to
speak all right.

FLORIAN Well, who knows, who knows?—Look, Herr Rademacher,
I'll make you a suggestion. Why don't we hold a little rehearsal.—
Yes, Herr Rademacher, I'm serious. I know what I'm talking about.
Here's the point: everything depends on how things are *presented*,
wouldn't you agree? What satisfaction will you get if you just come
straight out and tell him: 'You're a despicable fellow and I hate

you'—that simply wouldn't work. He will say to himself: curse me as much as you please so long as it's you lying in hospital with a 39 degree fever, and me enjoying my walk and smoking a cigar.

RADEMACHER I have something quite different to tell him as well. Anyone can reconcile himself to being despicable. But if he discovers that all his life he has been derided by the very people he loved most—he won't so easily get over that.

FLORIAN Well, go on, go on. Imagine I'm your boyhood friend. I am standing here, with my wallet full of money and my head full of conceit—(*acting*) 'Here I am, old pal. You wanted to speak to me. I'm listening.' Well then.

RADEMACHER (*feverishly, gradually working himself into a fury*) Yes, certainly I had them call you. But not to say goodbye to you in remembrance of old friendship—not at all, but to tell you about something before it is too late.

FLORIAN (*acting*) 'My curiosity is killing me, old chum. What d'you want to tell me?' Well—well!

RADEMACHER You think you're so much better than me, don't you?—Well let me tell you, my friend, neither of us has ever ranked among the great, and among the dregs where we belong, there's not much to choose between us at moments like this. Your greatness is all vanity, deceit and double-dealing. Your fame—a pile of newspapers blowing in the wind the day after your death. Your friends?—Flatterers who prostrate themselves before success, enviers who clench their fists inside their pockets when your back is turned, fat-heads you are insignificant enough to be admired by. But you're also clever enough to suspect as much yourself from time to time. So I didn't have to get you here to tell you that. It may seem mean of me to want to say more than I already have.—But you'd be amazed how little one cares about being mean, when there's no time left to feel ashamed. (*He stands up*) I've wanted to shout this in your face a hundred times in recent years,—whenever we've chanced to meet each other in the street and you deigned to address a civil word to me. My friend, not only do I know you, as do a thousand others—but your wife too knows you better than you might imagine. She saw through you twenty years ago—in the prime of your success and youth.—Yes, she saw through you all right—and no one knows it better than me... She was my mistress for two years, and a hundred times came running to me, disgusted by your emptiness and triviality, wanting to escape with me. But I was poor and she was cowardly, and so she stayed on with you and continued to betray you. It was more convenient for all concerned.

FLORIAN 'Ha, miserable wretch! You're lying!'

RADEMACHER Me?—(*As if waking up*) Ah, of course... Yes, Jackwerth, you now have the key. If he doesn't believe me—there are letters in the desk as well. You are my executor. There are all sorts of treasures in my desk—and who knows, perhaps all that will be needed to give them value is my death. Especially if I am reported as having died in poverty and wretchedness—and indeed I am dying in poverty and wretchedness as I have lived. But at least somebody will give a speech at my graveside. Just pay attention, would you,—industrious—devoted to duty—a martyr to his profession... Yes, Florian Jackwerth, it's true, ever since I have had a profession I have been a martyr to it—from the very first moment, I've been a martyr to my profession. And do you know what I'm dying of? Do you think I'm dying of whatever those Latin terms stand for on my chart—? Not at all! I am dying of spleen at having had to toady up to people I despised to get a job. Of disgust at having had to write things I did not believe in, so as not to starve. Of rage at having had to do hack work for infamous exploiters who had made their money by swindling and trickery, while I used my talent to assist them. But of course I can't complain: I have always come in for my share of contempt and hatred of the rabble—but unfortunately not of more substantial benefits.

NURSE (*enters*) Doctor Halmschlöger's coming.

RADEMACHER (*startled*) Alone?

NURSE No, there's a gentleman with him.

> *Rademacher looks relieved and gratified.*

FLORIAN Now pull yourself together. A pity I'm not allowed to stay. (*Then he sneaks out*)

> *Halmschlöger and Weihgast enter.*

HALMSCHLÖGER Well, here's the patient.

WEIHGAST (*an elegantly dressed, very well-preserved gentleman of about fifty-five, full grey beard, dark overcoat, walking-stick*) So—in here. (*Addressing Rademacher cordially*) Rademacher—can it be you? Rademacher—so we meet again! My dear friend!

RADEMACHER I'm very grateful to you for coming.

HALMSCHLÖGER (*has just signalled to the nurse; she brings in a chair for Weihgast*) And now if you don't mind, Herr Weihgast, I must ask you as a doctor not to go on for more than a quarter of an hour. After that I shall take the liberty of returning myself to escort you downstairs.

WEIHGAST Thank you, Doctor, you are very kind.

HALMSCHLÖGER Oh, I'm the one who should be thanking you. It's really very generous of you...

WEIHGAST (*deprecatingly*) Not at all, not at all...

HALMSCHLÖGER Well, Herr Rademacher, goodbye for now. (*Makes a kindly doctor's gesture of warning against his getting overexcited. Then he exchanges a few words with the nurse and the two leave together*)

WEIHGAST (*after giving the nurse his coat takes a seat; he comes across as warm, almost sincere*) Now then, tell me, my dear Rademacher, what's the idea, landing yourself in hospital of all places!

RADEMACHER Well, I can't complain, one's very well looked after here.

WEIHGAST Yes, I'm sure you are in the best of hands. Doctor Halmschlöger is a conscientious young doctor, and what's more, a really decent human being. Though of course one can never separate the man himself from his professional qualities. But still—forgive my asking—why ever didn't you get in touch with me?

RADEMACHER How could I...

WEIHGAST Even though you've not bothered about your old friend all these years, you may be sure that under the circumstances I'd be happy to assist in whatever way...

RADEMACHER Never mind about that, never mind about that.

WEIHGAST Very well—as you please. I didn't mean to offend you. In any case even now it's not too late.—Doctor Halmschlöger tells me it's only a matter of time and proper care... in a few weeks you'll be out of hospital, and then as regards your convalescing in the country...

RADEMACHER There's no question of all that now.

WEIHGAST I see, well—Doctor Halmschlöger did also warn me about your hypochondria. (*He shifts uneasily under Rademacher's gaze, but does not look away*) So, you've had me summoned and would like to speak to me. Well, I'm ready. Why do you smile?—No, it must be the play of light. The lighting here leaves something to be desired.—Well, I'm waiting. I'll explain to Doctor Halmschlöger that you didn't make use of our first five minutes. Well?— (*Rademacher has already half opened his lips several times, as if trying to say something. Does so again, but again remains silent.—Pause*) How has the world been treating you anyway? (*Slightly embarrassed*) Hm, the question's perhaps a little ill-considered under the circumstances. I admit I do feel slightly awkward; after all, looking at things externally, one might easily conclude that I'm the one fortune has favoured. And yet—rightly considered—who is it that experiences the greatest disappointments? Always the fellow who apparently has achieved the most.—That sounds paradoxical, and yet so it is.—Ah, if I were to go into everything... endless battles— endless worries—I don't know if you've been following recent literary trends much lately. Well, they're at my throat... Who? The younger generation. To think that ten years ago one belonged to the younger generation oneself. Now they are trying to dethrone me... When one reads the latest reviews... Ah, it's enough to make one sick! They treat me with contempt, with condescension. It's all deplorable! One has worked hard and honestly, and given of one's best—and now... Ah well, be thankful you don't know anything about these things. If I had a choice today,—could start my life afresh tomorrow...

RADEMACHER Well?

WEIHGAST I'd rather be a peasant on the land, a shepherd, a polar explorer—or, what you will!—Anything rather than get involved in literature again.—But there's still plenty of time.

RADEMACHER (*smiling strangely*) So are you planning to go to the North Pole?

WEIHGAST Oh no. But a new play of mine is coming out early next season. That'll show them, that'll show them! I won't be trampled on! Just wait!—Well, if it goes all right, you must come and see it too, old friend. I promise I'll send you tickets. Even though your paper generally takes damned little notice of me. In fact it received my last two books in dead silence. But of course you wouldn't have had anything to do with that department. Oh well!—What trivial rubbish, by the way... Well now, out with it at last. What is it you wanted to say to me? If you find it difficult to raise your voice... I can pull up closer—Hm... (*Pause*) I wonder what my wife will say, when I tell her our old friend Rademacher is laid up in the General Hospital... Your pride, dear Rademacher, your confounded pride... Well, don't let's talk about it... Besides, my wife isn't in Vienna at the moment— she's in Abbazia.* She keeps having trouble with her health.

RADEMACHER Nothing serious, I hope.

WEIHGAST (*pats his hand*) No, thank God. If it were, I'd really be in a bad way, my dear fellow. Frankly, it is thanks to her that I have found myself—found faith in myself when I was on the verge of losing it—found the strength to write, the desire to live. And the older one gets, the more one feels that marriage is the only true relationship there is. Because as regards the children... oh God!

RADEMACHER What's wrong with them? What are they doing?

WEIHGAST My daughter is married. Yes, I'm already a grandfather twice over. You wouldn't think it to look at me, I know. And my boy—I still say boy!!—is doing his military service this year— getting into debt—fought a duel recently with a young Baron Wallerskirch—over some woman... Yes, my friend, the same stupidities all over again. And so one grows old and life goes on.

RADEMACHER Ah well. (*Pause*)

WEIHGAST Well now, time is running out. I'm waiting. What have you to say to me? I'm prepared to do anything you wish... Should I apply to Concordia* on your behalf? Or can I approach the editor of 'New Day' about the chances of your speedy reinstatement... Or— forgive me, won't you, for mentioning such things—can I assist in any way to do with filthy lucre...

RADEMACHER Forget it, forget it. There's nothing I need—nothing... I just wanted to see you one last time, old friend—that's all. Yes. (*They shake hands*)

WEIHGAST Is that so? I'm really touched. Yes.—well, when you're better, I hope we'll see more of one another again... well!

> *Awkward pause.—The clock can be heard ticking in the ward next door.*

HALMSCHLÖGER (*enters*) Well, here I am, not too punctual I hope?

WEIHGAST (*gets up, visibly relieved*) Not at all, we've already finished.

HALMSCHLÖGER Well that's splendid then. And I trust our patient is now feeling calmer—is he?

RADEMACHER (*nods*) Thank you, yes.

WEIHGAST Well then, goodbye, dear friend. With the doctor's permission, I'll look in again in a few days.

HALMSCHLÖGER Certainly. I'll arrange for you to be admitted any time...

WEIHGAST Oh, I don't wish you to make exceptions for my sake.

HALMSCHLÖGER Paschanda!

> *The nurse hands Weihgast his coat.*

WEIHGAST Well goodbye again, get well soon and don't become despondent.

> *Makes for the entrance with Halmschlöger.*

FLORIAN (*comes out from behind the curtain*) Good night, Doctor, good night!

HALMSCHLÖGER Now look here, you're still not in bed!

WEIHGAST Who on earth is that? He's staring at me very strangely...

HALMSCHLÖGER A poor devil of an actor.

WEIHGAST I see.

HALMSCHLÖGER Has no idea that in a week at the outside he'll be dead and buried.

WEIHGAST I see.

 Weihgast's and Florian's eyes meet.

HALMSCHLÖGER That's why I consider being strict with him a little pointless. Regulations for the dying—it doesn't make too much sense.

WEIHGAST Quite right.—Well, I really enjoyed this opportunity to get to know you better, and so to speak eavesdrop on you at work. It was altogether very interesting.

HALMSCHLÖGER If I might ask, was whatever your friend had to tell you really that important?

WEIHGAST I have no idea. We used to be on good terms a long time ago, and he wanted to see me again... that was all. I think my coming did calm him a good deal, though. (*Proceeds to leave*)

NURSE Goodbye, Sir.

WEIHGAST Ah, yes, of course. (*Gives her a tip*)

 Halmschlöger, Weihgast exeunt, followed by the nurse.

FLORIAN (*hurries over to Rademacher*) Well, what happened? That fellow must have immense self-control. I'm an old hand at reading physiognomies—but I didn't notice any change in his. How did he take it?

RADEMACHER (*without listening to him*) How wretched people are who must still go on living tomorrow.

FLORIAN Herr Rademacher—what's the matter? What do you want me to do about the key to your desk?

RADEMACHER (*wakening*) Desk—?—Do what you want. Burn everything, as far as I'm concerned!

FLORIAN And what about the treasures? The masterpieces?

RADEMACHER Masterpieces!—And even if they were... Futurity only exists for the living anyway. (*Like a visionary*) Now he's reached downstairs. Now he's going along the avenue—through the gate— now he's on the street—the lamps are lighted—the coaches are rolling past—people are passing up and down the street... (*he has gradually stood up*)

FLORIAN Herr Rademacher! (*He watches him intently*)

RADEMACHER What has he to do with me? What do I care about his happiness, what do I care about his worries? What did we really have to say to one another? Ha! What?... (*He seizes Florian's hand*)

What do the likes of you and me have to do with people who will still be on this earth tomorrow?

FLORIAN (*in fear*) What do you want from me?—Frau Paschanda!
> *The nurse enters with the candle.*

RADEMACHER (*lets Florian's hand go*) Put it out, Frau Paschanda—I no longer need one... (*He sinks back into the chair*)

FLORIAN (*stands beside the curtain; he clutches at it with both hands; to the nurse*) He is now though—isn't he?
> *Curtain.*

COUNTESS MIZZI

OR

THE FAMILY REUNION

(*Komtesse Mizzi*)

A Comedy in One Act

CAST

COUNT ARPAD PAZMANDY
MIZZI, *his daughter*
EGON PRINCE RAVENSTEIN
LOLO LANGHUBER
PHILIP
PROFESSOR WINDHOFER
WASNER
THE GARDENER
THE SERVANT

Garden of the Count's villa. High fence at the back. Gate roughly in the middle, a little over to the right. On the left in the foreground the two-storey villa, which was once a hunting lodge, built 180 years ago and renovated 30 years ago. Along the length of the elevated ground floor runs a fairly broad terrace, from which three broad steps lead down into the garden. An open glass door leads from the terrace into the sitting room. The first floor has simple windows; above the first floor there is a small balcony decked with flowers which belongs to a sort of attic. Lawn set with flowerbeds in front of the villa. On the right under a tree in the foreground, a garden bench, chairs and a little table.

The Count, an older gentleman with a grey moustache, still very good looking, with the bearing and manner of a former officer, in riding clothes, a riding crop in his hand, enters from the right. The servant accompanies him.

SERVANT What time does your Grace wish to order luncheon for today?

COUNT (*speaks in the clipped manner customary with German-Hungarian officers. Is just lighting a large cigar*) Two.

SERVANT And what time should the coach be ready for, your Grace?

COUNTESS (*appears on the balcony holding a paintbrush and palette. She calls down*) Good morning, Papa.

COUNT Good morning, Mizzi.

COUNTESS You left me to breakfast on my own again, Papa. Where have you been?

COUNT Quite a distance. I rode out past Mauer and Rodaun.* It's a beautiful day. What are you doing? Hard at work already? Are we going to be allowed to see anything again soon?

COUNTESS Oh yes, Papa; but I'm afraid it's only flowers again.

COUNT Isn't your Professor coming today?

COUNTESS Yes, but not until about one.

COUNT Well, don't let me hold you up.

The Countess throws him a kiss and disappears into the attic.

COUNT (*To the servant*) What do you want? Ah yes, the coach. I won't be going out again today. Joseph may take the day off. Or, wait a minute. (*Calls up*) I say, Mizzi...

The Countess reappears on the balcony.

COUNT Sorry to disturb again. Do you need the coach today at all?

COUNTESS No, Papa, thank you. I wouldn't know... But thank you anyway. (*Disappears again*)

COUNT As you were then: Joseph can do what he likes this afternoon. You... and make sure Franz gives the bay a good rubbing down, we were a bit spirited this morning... both of us.

> *Servant exit.*
>
> *The Count, having taken a seat on the bench, picks up a paper lying on the table and reads.*

GARDENER (*enters*) Good morning, your Grace.

COUNT Good morning, Peter. What's up?

GARDENER If it please your Grace, I have just been cutting some tea roses.

COUNT But why so many?

GARDENER The bush is covered with them. It would be unwise, your Grace, to leave them for much longer. If your Grace should have any use for these...

COUNT I have no use for them. Well, what are you looking at me like that for? I'm not going into town today so I don't need a bouquet. Put single flowers into all those vases about the place inside. That's the fashion nowadays. (*Picks up the flowers and smells them. Appears to consider*) Isn't that a coach pulling up?

GARDENER Those are his Excellency's blacks. I recognize them by their trot.

COUNT Well, thank you anyway. (*Gives him back the roses*)

> *The Prince steps in through the gate.*
>
> *The Count advances to meet him.*

GARDENER Good morning, your Excellency.

PRINCE Good day, Peter.

> *Gardener exit right.*
>
> *The Prince in a light summer suit, slim, fifty-five years old, but looking a bit younger. Has the easy accent of a diplomat who uses French as much as German.*

COUNT Nice to see you, old friend. How are you, how are things?

PRINCE Thank you. Splendid weather.

> *The Count offers him a huge cigar.*

PRINCE Thank you, not before a meal. I'll have one of my own cigarettes, if you don't mind. (*Takes one from his cigarette case and lights it*)

COUNT So you've decided to drop round again at last. Do you know how long it's been since you were here? Three whole weeks.

PRINCE (*glances up at the attic*) Has it really been that long?

COUNT Well, why are you making yourself so scarce?

PRINCE Don't be offended. It's true enough, I'm afraid. And today in fact I've only come to bid you goodbye.

COUNT How do you mean, goodbye?

PRINCE I'm leaving tomorrow, you see.

COUNT You're leaving? Where for?

PRINCE For the seaside. And what about you... no plans yet?

COUNT I haven't even thought about it this year.

PRINCE Oh well, it's so beautiful out here anyway... with this huge park! Though I take it you'll go somewhere over the summer.

COUNT I don't know yet. Anyway it's all the same to me.

PRINCE What's the matter?

COUNT Ah, my friend, going downhill, you know.

PRINCE How do you mean? What's this absurd expression, Arpad? What do you mean, 'downhill'?

COUNT Growing old, Egon.

PRINCE Yes. But one gets used to it.

COUNT All very well for you to talk, you're five years younger.

PRINCE Six. But even at fifty-five one's not exactly in the first flush of youth. Anyway—one adjusts.

COUNT You've always been a bit of a psychologist, old friend.

PRINCE Besides, I really don't know what you expect. You look splendid. (*He takes a seat and again glances up at the attic, as he has been doing off and on. Pause*)

COUNT (*with resolve*) Have you heard the latest? She's getting married.

PRINCE Who's getting married?

COUNT Need you ask... who else do you imagine.

PRINCE I see, I thought for a moment you meant Mizzi. Well then, it must be... So Lolo's getting married?

COUNT Yes, Lolo.

PRINCE But that's hardly 'the latest', surely.

COUNT How do you mean?

PRINCE She's been promising you that, or threatening you with that, or however one likes to put it, for at least three years.

COUNT Three? You could say ten. Or eighteen for that matter. True enough. In fact, since our whole affair began. It's always been an idée fixe with her of course. If an honest man were to request her hand, she'd leave the stage tomorrow. That was her second promise. You've no doubt heard her often enough yourself. And now he's materialized, the long awaited one... and so she's getting married.

PRINCE Well, so long as he is in fact an honest man.

COUNT Joking, are you! So much for your concern at a serious moment like this.

PRINCE Come now. (*Lays his hand on his friend's arm*)

COUNT Yes, I assure you, it's a serious moment all right. No small matter after one has been all but living with a woman for twenty years, spent one's best years with her, shared life's happiness and sorrows with her... somehow one comes to believe it could never end... and then one fine day she ups and says 'May God preserve you, dear, I'm about to get married...' It's a damnable business altogether. (*Gets up, paces to and fro*) And yet I can't hold it against her. Because I can fully understand her. So what is one to do!

PRINCE You were always much too good a fellow, Arpad.

COUNT What's goodness got to do with it? Why wouldn't I understand her? She's turned thirty-eight already. And she's bowing out of her profession. So who could blame her if she didn't see much fun in continuing life as a retired ballet dancer and the current mistress of Count Pazmandy, who in time no doubt will become a bit of an old stick. I was certainly forewarned. No, by God, I can't say I hold it against her in the least.

PRINCE So you've parted quite good friends then?

COUNT Of course. Even had quite a jolly farewell party. My word, yes. At first I didn't realize how hard I'd find it. Only dawned on me gradually, you know. It's quite a remarkable story in its way...

PRINCE What's so remarkable about it?

COUNT Well, I'll tell you: as I was driving back from seeing her for the last time one night last week, suddenly I felt, how should I put it... a tremendous sense of relief. Now you're a free man, I thought. You no longer need to drive into the Meyerhofgasse* every blessed evening, only to sit talking or rather listening to Lolo. Sometimes that used to bore me stiff, you know. And then all that business of driving home in the middle of the night, and having to explain yourself if you happened to have supper with a friend at the club, or take your daughter to the opera or the Burgtheater. What more can I tell you, I was all fired up as I drove home. I had all sorts of plans in mind... oh, not what you are thinking... no, but trips I'd long had in mind to make, to Africa or India, as a free man... though, of course I would have taken my little girl along as well. You'll laugh, no doubt, at my still calling her my little girl.

PRINCE I wouldn't dream of it. Mizzi does indeed still look like a young girl. Remarkably so. Especially in that Florentine straw hat the other day.

COUNT Like a young girl! And yet she is exactly the same age as Lolo. Well, you know all that of course! We're growing old, Egon. All of us. Ah well... And lonely too. Though frankly, at the beginning I didn't even notice. It only gradually came over me. For a while after our farewell party it wasn't too bad. It's only been in the last two days, about the time I usually drive into the Mayerhofgasse... and again just now when Peter brought me Lolo's roses, that I've begun to realize that for the second time in my life I've become a widower. Yes, my dear fellow. And now it's permanent. Now comes loneliness. In fact it's here.

PRINCE But that's ridiculous. Loneliness!

COUNT Don't be offended, but you just don't understand. You have led quite a different life from me. You've not let yourself become involved again since your poor wife died ten years ago. In anything serious, I mean. And besides, you have a profession of sorts.

PRINCE How do you mean?

COUNT Well, as a member of the Upper House.

PRINCE Oh that.

COUNT And twice you almost became a minister.

PRINCE Almost...

COUNT Who knows. It might one day really come your way. Whereas I am now completely finished. Even let myself be pensioned off three years ago, ass that I was.

PRINCE (smiling) But then you are now a free man. Completely free. The world is your oyster.

COUNT But I've no urge to do anything. That's the worst of it. Since Lolo, I haven't even been to the casino. Do you know what I did these last few evenings? I sat under a tree with Mizzi and played dominoes.

PRINCE Well, you see, that's hardly loneliness. When one has a daughter one's always been on such good terms with, and such a clever one at that... What does she say about your spending all your evenings at home, by the way?

COUNT Nothing. That sometimes happened earlier too of course. She doesn't say a thing. What should she say anyway? My impression is she doesn't even notice. Do you think she knew anything about Lolo?

PRINCE (laughs) Well, listen to that!

COUNT Yes of course. I know. Of course she knew. But after all, when her poor mother died I was still almost a young man. She can't have held it against me.

PRINCE I'm sure she didn't. (*Lightly*) But I would think she must have felt it sometimes, being left alone so much.

COUNT Has she complained at all about me? Go on, you can tell me.

PRINCE Well, I'm not in Mizzi's confidence. Naturally she has never complained to me. My God, perhaps she never felt like that about it anyway. After all, she's been used to this retired life so long.

COUNT Yes, and she also has a taste for it. And anyway until a few years ago she often went out into society. And between us, Egon, even two or three years ago, I was still convinced that she would take the plunge.

PRINCE Take the plunge? Oh, I see...

COUNT You'd be surprised the sort of people who've been showing a keen interest in her even lately...

PRINCE That's quite understandable.

COUNT But she isn't interested. She simply doesn't want to. Well, all I mean is, she can't have felt that lonely... otherwise she would have, since she has not been short of opportunities...

PRINCE Certainly. After all she's free to choose. Besides, Mizzi has other resources like her painting. It was exactly the same with Fanny Hohenstein, my sainted aunt, who wrote books on into advanced old age, and simply wouldn't hear of marriage either.

COUNT It's possible such things are part and parcel of their artistic aspirations. I sometimes wonder if all such overwrought conditions don't always have a deeper psychological explanation.

PRINCE Overwrought? One surely can't call Mizzi overwrought.

COUNT Well, now she's settled down. But earlier on...

PRINCE I have always found Mizzi very intelligent and self-possessed. If someone paints roses and violets, that hardly indicates she's overwrought.

COUNT You don't think I'm so stupid as to mean her violets and roses. But as a young girl, if you remember...

PRINCE What?

COUNT That whole business when Fedor Wangenheim was courting her.

PRINCE Good God, are you still thinking about that? But that's all ancient history. It must be almost twenty years ago.

COUNT At the time she was quite determined to join the Ursulines,* rather than marry that nice young fellow she was already as good as engaged to.

PRINCE What put you in mind of that whole forgotten business today?

COUNT Forgotten? To me it's as if it happened yesterday. It was just about the time my affair with Lolo was beginning. Looking back, who could have predicted it! You know, it all began like any other adventure. Utterly thoughtless and quite mad. Yes, mad. Well, I don't want to sin against the departed, but it was a blessing for us all that my poor wife had been dead for several years by then. Lolo was my destiny. Mistress and housewife in one. She was such a magnificent cook, you know. How at home one felt in that cosy little apartment of hers. And she was always in a good mood, and never a cross word... anyway, it's over. Don't let's talk about it any more. (*Pause*)... By the way, won't you stay and have a meal with us? I'll ·just go and call Mizzi.

PRINCE (*holding him back*) Wait, I have something else to tell you. (*Lightly, as though being humorous*) There's something I must prepare you for.

COUNT What? Prepare me for what?

PRINCE Today I'm going to present a young gentleman to you.

COUNT (*surprised*) How do you mean, a young gentleman?

PRINCE If you don't object, of course.

COUNT Why should I object? But who is he?

PRINCE My son, my dear Arpad.

COUNT (*thoroughly astonished*) What?

PRINCE Yes, my son. I didn't want to start out on my travels without...

COUNT Your son? You have a son?

PRINCE Yes.

COUNT Well I never... A young gentleman who's your son? Or rather, a son who's a young gentleman. How old is he?

PRINCE Seventeen.

COUNT Seventeen! Now he tells me! Well I must say, Egon... Egon! But tell me... seventeen... Good God! Your wife was still alive then...

PRINCE Yes, my wife was still living then. One can sometimes get entangled in remarkable affairs, my dear Arpad.

COUNT God yes, that's true enough!

PRINCE And then one fine day one finds oneself with a seventeen-year-old son one is going on a trip with.

COUNT So it's him you are travelling with?

PRINCE I have taken that liberty.

COUNT   Well, I don't know what to say... so now he has a seventeen-year-old son!... (*suddenly he shakes him by the hand and embraces him*) And if I might ask... the mother of your son... how was it that... you started to tell me once before—

PRINCE   His mother died a long time ago. It all happened a few weeks after she gave birth. She was in the first blush of womanhood.

COUNT   A girl from the people?

PRINCE   Yes, naturally. But a delightful creature. Well, I don't mind telling you in a little more detail. So far as I can still remember it all myself, that is. The whole affair was so like a dream. If the lad weren't here to prove it...

COUNT   And you only tell me all this now! Today, just before the boy comes to pay a visit.

PRINCE   One never knows how such news will be received.

COUNT   Nonsense. Received! You didn't perhaps think... I'm a bit of a psychologist myself, you know. And I'm supposed to be your friend!

PRINCE   Not a soul knew about it, no one in the world.

COUNT   But you could have told me. I really don't understand how you could... I must say, that was really a bit much.

PRINCE   I wanted to wait and see how the lad turned out. One can never tell...

COUNT   True enough, with a mixed pedigree like that... But now you seem reassured at least?

PRINCE   Yes. He's a fine lad.

COUNT (*embraces him again*) So, where has he been living all this time?

PRINCE   For the first few years, some distance from Vienna. In the Tyrol.

COUNT   With farming people?

PRINCE   With a small landowner. Then he went to primary school in Innsbruck. For the last few years I've been sending him to the grammar school in Krems.*

COUNT   So you did visit him occasionally.

PRINCE   Naturally.

COUNT   And who does he believe he is?

PRINCE   Until a few days ago he thought he had no parents, no father even, and that I was one of his dead father's friends.

COUNTESS (*on the balcony*) Good day, Prince Egon.

PRINCE   Good day, Mizzi.

COUNT   Well, aren't you coming down for a while?

COUNTESS   If I won't be interrupting anything... (*She disappears*)

COUNT So, what are we to tell Mizzi?

PRINCE Of course I'd like to leave all that to you. But since I'm adopting the lad, and in a few days he will bear my name, through special dispensation from his Majesty...

COUNT (*astonished*) What?

PRINCE It might be as well if we told Mizzi the truth at once.

COUNT Of course, of course, anyway why not? Especially as you've gone so far as to adopt him... It's a funny thing, you know. A daughter, even when she's well on the way to becoming an old maid, still remains a little girl in her father's eyes.

COUNTESS (*appears. She is thirty-seven years old and still very good looking in her Florentine straw hat and white dress. She kisses the Count, then shakes hands with the Prince*) How are you, Prince Egon? We see you so seldom.

PRINCE Well, thank you, Mizzi. You seem very busy?

COUNTESS Painting little flowers.

COUNT You are far too modest, Mizzi. Professor Windhofer recently remarked that she ought to be exhibiting. No reason to hide her head alongside Wiesinger-Florian* at all.

COUNTESS Yes, that may be true. But I just have no ambition.

PRINCE I'm not all that much in favour of exhibiting either. One is then exposed to every newspaper reporter.

COUNTESS You'd think they were members of the Upper House too, some of them. At least when they start pontificating.

COUNT And do you think people like us are spared? They poke their noses into everything.

PRINCE Well, the way things are going today, Mizzi, some people would rail against your paintings simply because you are a countess.

COUNT He's right about that.

SERVANT (*enters*) Your Grace is requested on the telephone.

COUNT Who is it? What's up?

SERVANT If your Grace would be good enough to come to the phone personally.

COUNT Excuse me a minute. (*Aside to him*) Tell her now, while I'm not there. I'd much prefer that. (*Exit*)

COUNTESS A telephone call... could Papa be forming new ties again already? (*Sits down*)

PRINCE New ties?

COUNTESS Lolo usually rang about this time. But it's all over now between him and Lolo. You knew, of course?

PRINCE I've just heard.

COUNTESS And what do you have to say about it, Prince Egon? Myself, I'm very sorry. If he takes up with someone else, he's sure to get into deep water. And I fear he's bound to do so. He's too young for his years still.

PRINCE Ah well.

COUNTESS (*turning round to face him*) By the way, you haven't been to see us for some time.

PRINCE You can't have missed me very much... I fear... what with your art... and God knows what besides...

COUNTESS (*simply*) Even so...

PRINCE You're very kind.
          Pause.

COUNTESS Why are you so silent today? Tell me something. Is there nothing new in the world outside?

PRINCE (*as if after some thought*) Our son has just finished his last year at school.

COUNTESS (*with a slight shrug*) I hope you have something more interesting than that to tell me.

PRINCE More interesting...

COUNTESS Or at least, news more related to me personally than the curriculum vitae of a total stranger.

PRINCE Nevertheless, I feel duty bound to keep you abreast of important stages in this young man's development. When he was confirmed, I also took the liberty of conveying as much to you. But we've no need to talk about it further now. (*Pause*)

COUNTESS Well, did he pass at least?

PRINCE With distinction.

COUNTESS Then it looks as though the stock is improving.

PRINCE Let's both hope so.

COUNTESS And so now the great moment is approaching...

PRINCE What moment?

COUNTESS Don't you remember? Once he'd finished his exams, you were going to reveal that you're his father.

PRINCE I've already done so.

COUNTESS You—have told him already?

PRINCE Yes.

COUNTESS (*after a pause, without looking at him*) And so his mother— is dead...

PRINCE Dead for the time being.

COUNTESS Forever. (*Gets up*)

PRINCE As you wish.

The Count and the servant enter.

SERVANT But you gave Joseph the day off yourself, your Grace.

COUNT Yes, yes, very well then.

     Servant exit.

COUNTESS What's the matter, Papa?

COUNT Nothing, nothing, my child. I just needed to go somewhere in a hurry, and Joseph, confound him... Don't be cross, Mizzi, but I must have another word with Egon... (*Takes him aside*) Guess what, apparently she rang me earlier—Lolo, that is. But she couldn't get through, and now Laura, her chambermaid, has rung to say Lolo's on her way out here.

PRINCE She's coming here to see you?

COUNT Yes.

PRINCE But why?

COUNT I can well imagine why. As you know, she has never of course set foot inside the place, and I promised her that before she married she might come out some time and look round the villa and the park. It was her pet grievance that I would not receive her here. You know, because of Mizzi. Which she acknowledged too. And as for bringing her out here secretly when Mizzi's not at home, well I've never gone in for that sort of thing. And so she's just notified me that the wedding's in two days, and she's on her way right now.

PRINCE Well, what harm is there in that? She's not coming as your mistress, so why do you need to feel embarrassed?

COUNT It would have to be today... and especially just now, with your son due any moment.

PRINCE I can answer for him.

COUNT Yes, but it doesn't suit me. I'll go out and meet her coach and see if I can stop her. It's all very annoying. Meanwhile, please make my excuses to your son. Adieu, Mizzi, I'll be back shortly. (*Exit*)

PRINCE Fräulein Lolo has announced she's coming and it doesn't suit your dear Papa.

COUNTESS What? Lolo is coming out here?

PRINCE Apparently your Papa promised her that before she married she might come out and look round the villa. And now he's gone out to intercept her coach.

COUNTESS How childish. How touching, actually. I would have liked to get to know her. Isn't it all too stupid? One has a father who spends almost half his life with a no doubt thoroughly amiable woman... and one never gets to—doesn't even have the right to—

shake her hand. Why shouldn't it suit him? Surely he must realize that I know all about her.

PRINCE My God, it's just the way he is. Perhaps it wouldn't have annoyed him so much, if he'd not been expecting another visitor this very moment...

COUNTESS Another visitor?

PRINCE Whom I took the liberty of announcing.

COUNTESS What sort of visitor?

PRINCE Our son.

COUNTESS Are you... Your son is coming here?

PRINCE He'll be here in half an hour at the latest.

COUNTESS Tell me, Prince... are you playing a joke on me by any chance?

PRINCE Not at all. On a dead woman! How could you think such a thing...

COUNTESS Is it true? He's coming here?

PRINCE Yes.

COUNTESS Evidently you continue to think that my not wanting to have anything to do with the boy is merely a passing mood?

PRINCE A mood...? No. You are much too consistent about it for that. Considering you managed not to ask about him even once during all these years...

COUNTESS That's hardly so remarkable. I've managed to do much harder things. For instance, having to give him up barely a week after he was born.

PRINCE But at the time you had, we had no alternative. What I proposed then, and you eventually agreed to, was decidedly the most sensible thing we could have done in our situation.

COUNTESS Sensible yes, I never doubted that.

PRINCE And not just sensible, Mizzi. You know ours was not the only fate involved. If the truth had come to light, other lives would perhaps also have been wrecked. My wife with her heart condition would scarcely have survived it.

COUNTESS That heart condition of hers...

PRINCE And your father, Mizzi... Your father!

COUNTESS Depend upon it, he would have adjusted. At the time, his affair with Lolo had just begun. Otherwise things would not have gone so smoothly and he might have taken a bit more notice of me. I would not have been able to stay away for months on end, if it hadn't been very convenient for him too. The only danger in the whole situation, my dear Prince, was that Fedor Wangenheim might have shot and killed you.

PRINCE He me? Things could just as well have gone the other way. Or perhaps you believe in divine judgement? Even then the outcome would be doubtful. For we poor mortals can never know what He might think about such matters.

COUNTESS You wouldn't talk like that in the Upper House, that is if you ever opened your mouth there.

PRINCE Possibly. But the important point remains that any amount of honesty and courage at the time would not have helped us in the least. We could scarcely have obtained a special dispensation—and besides, the Princess would never have agreed to a divorce, you know that as well as I do.

COUNTESS As if marriage mattered to me in the least.

PRINCE Oh...

COUNTESS Absolutely not. Surely that's nothing new to you? I told you so at the time as well. You have no idea how I felt about you then... (*with a look*)... and what I would have done for you. I would have followed you anywhere, even as your mistress. Together with our child. To Switzerland or to America. After all, we could have lived anywhere we liked. And in the Upper House perhaps they might not even have noticed you had left.

PRINCE Yes, we could of course have fled and settled in some foreign country... But today you yourself acknowledge you would not have found such a situation pleasant or even tolerable in the long run.

COUNTESS Today perhaps not. Because today I know you. But then I still loved you. And perhaps I could have—gone on loving you a great deal longer, if you hadn't been too cowardly to accept responsibility for what had happened... Too cowardly, Prince Egon...

PRINCE Whether that's exactly the right word...

COUNTESS It is. I have no other. It was not up to me. I was prepared to accept anything joyfully, with pride. I was prepared to be a mother and to acknowledge being the mother of our child. You knew that, Egon! I told you I was prepared for that seventeen years ago, in the little house in the woods where you had hidden me away. But I was never one for half-measures. From the day I had to give up the boy, I also resolved not to bother with him any further. That's why I find it ridiculous that you suddenly want to bring him here. If I may give you a bit of advice, go out and meet him, as Papa is doing with Lolo, and drive home again at once with him.

PRINCE I have no intention of doing that. From all you've obliged me to listen to again, it evidently must remain the case that his mother is dead. But all the more reason I should espouse his cause. He is my son, in the eyes of the world as well. I have adopted him.

COUNTESS You have—

PRINCE By perhaps tomorrow even, he will bear my name. I shall introduce him where I please. And first of all naturally, to my old friend the Count, your Papa. If you find the prospect of seeing the young man disagreeable, you'll have no choice but to withdraw to your room during his visit.

COUNTESS I need hardly say I find your tone uncalled-for—

PRINCE No more so than I your bitterness.

COUNTESS Bitterness? Do I look embittered? Listen... I just happen to find your initiative preposterous. Apart from that, I am in my usual cheerful mood.

PRINCE I'm sure you normally are in a cheerful mood, but I rather doubt so now... Anyway, I'm not unaware that you've long since managed to reconcile yourself to your fate. But I too have had to adjust to mine, and perhaps in its way it has been just as painful.

COUNTESS How so? What's this fate you have had to... Not everyone can become a minister. I see... perhaps you're alluding to the fact that ten years ago, after the death of your sainted wife, your Excellency did me the honour of requesting my hand in marriage?

PRINCE And again seven years ago, if you remember.

COUNTESS Oh yes, I remember well enough. I have never given you cause to doubt my memory.

PRINCE And I hope, Mizzi, that when I renewed my suit, you never suspected my intentions of having anything to do with expiation. I asked you to be my wife because I was convinced I would only find true happiness beside you.

COUNTESS True happiness!... You would have been mistaken.

PRINCE I too think that at the time it would have been a mistake. Ten years ago it was still too early. Even seven years ago perhaps. But surely not today.

COUNTESS Today as much as ever, my dear Prince. It is your destiny never to have known me, never to have understood the slightest thing about me. Neither when I loved you, nor when I hated you, nor even during the long years when I was utterly indifferent to you.

PRINCE I have always understood you, Mizzi. I know more about you than you probably suspect. I am well aware that you have found better things to do with the last seventeen years, than to cry over a man who at the time was perhaps not completely worthy of you. Indeed I even know that after your disappointment over me, you soon took it into your head to have several more.

COUNTESS Disappointments? Well, I can assure you by way of consolation, my dear Prince, there were some very pleasurable ones among them.

PRINCE I know that too. Otherwise, would I dare to claim that I know the story of your life?

COUNTESS And I suppose you imagine that I don't know yours? Do you want me to reel off the list of all your various mistresses? From the wife of the Bulgarian attaché in 1887 to Fräulein Therese Grédun, if that's her real name... who at least until this spring was still in favour with you? I probably know even more than you, as I know about almost all of those she has betrayed you with.

PRINCE I'd rather you didn't tell me about them. If one doesn't discover such things oneself, there's no fun in it at all.

A coach is heard driving up and coming to a halt.

PRINCE It's him. Perhaps you'd like to disappear before he enters the park. I'll detain him while you do so.

COUNTESS Don't bother. I'd prefer to stay. But don't imagine I feel the slightest maternal stirrings... This is just a young gentleman visiting my father. There he is already... The call of the blood? It must be a fable. I don't feel anything at all, dear Prince.

PHILIP (*has come quickly in through the main gate. He is seventeen years old, slim, handsome, elegant but not at all dandified, with an engaging somewhat boyish impudence, as well as a touch of bashfulness*) Good day. (*Bows to the Countess*)

PRINCE Good morning, Philip. Allow me, Countess, to introduce my son. This is Countess Mizzi. The daughter of my old friend and master of this house.

Philip takes the Countess's extended hand and kisses it. A short pause.

COUNTESS Won't you take a seat?

PHILIP Thank you, Countess. (*They all remain standing*)

PRINCE You came out by coach. You could dismiss it, I have mine here.

PHILIP Wouldn't you prefer to drive back with me, Papa? I find Wasner drives better than your Fritz behind those old parliamentary hacks.

COUNTESS Is Wasner your driver?

PHILIP Yes.

COUNTESS The gentleman himself? That's a great honour, you know. Wasner won't drive just anyone. Two years ago he was still driving for Papa.

PHILIP Ah.

PRINCE Incidentally, Philip, you're a little late.

PHILIP Yes, I must apologize. You see I overslept. (*To the Countess*) Last night I went out with a few school friends. As you may have heard, Countess, I passed my exams two weeks ago, and so yesterday we had a bit of a night out.

COUNTESS You seem to have found your feet very quickly in Vienna life, Herr...

PRINCE Just call him Philip, my dear Mizzi.

COUNTESS Shall we sit down then, Philip—(*gives the Prince a look*) Papa should be here any minute now.
      Countess and Prince sit down.

PHILIP (*while still standing*) Well, if I may say so, the park is superb. It's much more beautiful than ours.

COUNTESS You know the park at Ravenstein then?

PHILIP Of course, Countess. I've been living at the castle for the last three days.

COUNTESS What?

PRINCE In town, gardens can't of course develop quite the way they can out here. A hundred years ago, ours was understandably much nicer than it is today. At that time Ravenstein was still outside the city limits too.

PHILIP A pity people were allowed to build their houses all around us.

COUNTESS We're better off in that respect. By the time the city spreads out here, we won't be around to see it.

PHILIP (*in a kindly manner*) Don't say that, Countess...

COUNTESS A hundred years ago, all this was hunting ground. It borders directly on the game preserve. Can you see its walls over there, Philip? And our villa was once a little hunting lodge which belonged to the Empress Maria Theresa. The sandstone statue in the pond there also dates back to the same period.

PHILIP How old is Ravenstein in fact, Papa?

PRINCE (*smiling*) It was built in the seventeenth century, my son. I showed you the room in which the Emperor Leopold once spent the night, if you remember.

PHILIP Emperor Leopold, 1643 to 1705.
      Countess laughs.

PHILIP That's from my history exam. By the time I'm... (*breaks off*) Sorry!... I was just thinking—by next year I shall have forgotten everything. Of course when I was memorizing his dates, I wasn't aware that Emperor Leopold knew our family.

COUNTESS You seem to find the discovery amusing, Philip.

PHILIP Discovery... Well to tell the truth, it wasn't really a discovery. (*Looks at the Prince*)

PRINCE Go on, go on.

PHILIP You see, Countess, I always had the feeling that I was not born Philip Radeiner.

COUNTESS Radeiner? (*To the Prince*) That was the name...?

PRINCE Indeed.

PHILIP Naturally I was delighted when my intuition turned out to be true;—but at heart I always knew. Of course I was no fool. A few of my friends at school also suspected... that I... You see, Countess, all that about Prince Ravenstein driving out to Krems to enquire how the son of his dead friend was doing—, well it just seemed a little too romantic, like something out of a penny-dreadful... To the brighter students it was fairly clear that blue blood runs in my veins. And since I was among the brightest...

COUNTESS So it would appear... So what are your plans for the future, Philip?

PHILIP In October I'm starting my year's military service with the Sixth Dragoons, where we Ravensteins have always served. Who knows what will happen after that, stay in the army perhaps, or become an archbishop—in due course naturally...

COUNTESS That might be just the thing. The Ravensteins were always ardent in their faith.

PHILIP Yes, that's all part of European history. First they were Catholic, then during the Thirty Years War they became Protestant, then they reverted to Catholicism, but their faith was strong at all times. Just that it kept changing.

PRINCE Philip, Philip!

COUNTESS Well, that's the modern world for you, Prince Egon.

PRINCE And a mother's blood.

COUNTESS You have been very industrious, your father tells me, and passed your examinations with distinction.

PHILIP There was nothing to it, Countess. I mastered everything quite quickly. That's probably the bourgeois blood in me. I found time for all sorts of things which were not required at school. I learned to ride and...

COUNTESS And?

PHILIP Play the clarinet.

COUNTESS (*laughs*) Why did you hesitate to mention that?

PHILIP Why?... well because people always laugh when they hear I'm learning the clarinet. You laughed too, Countess. Isn't that odd? Has anyone ever laughed when you told them about your painting, Countess?

COUNTESS You know about that too already?

PHILIP Oh yes, his Excellency... Papa told me. There's even a painting of some flowers in my bedroom at Ravenstein—a Chinese vase with laburnum and some other purple flowers.

COUNTESS The purple ones would probably be lilacs.

PHILIP Lilacs, of course. I recognized them at once, in fact, but couldn't remember the name.

SERVANT (*enters*) There's a lady wishing to speak to the Count. I have shown her into the sitting room.

COUNTESS A lady?... Excuse me a moment, gentlemen. (*Exit*)

PHILIP Well Papa, if it were now entirely up to me, then I'd agree.

PRINCE With what? What are you getting at?

PHILIP I'd agree with your choice.

PRINCE Are you mad, boy?!

PHILIP Come now, Papa, you don't really believe you can conceal things from me. My bourgeois blood...

PRINCE What on earth are you talking about?

PHILIP Look, Papa, when you told me you particularly wanted to introduce me to your old friend, the Count; and that the Count had a daughter—which by the way I've known for quite some time—I was just a bit afraid she might turn out to be too young.

PRINCE (*irritated, but laughing nonetheless*) Too young...

PHILIP Anyway, it was obvious you had a certain fondness for this daughter. Whenever you spoke of her you would become positively bashful. And then you told me all sorts of things about her, which you certainly would not have done about just any woman. Why for example was I supposed to take an interest in some countess's pictures, even if I might be able to distinguish between the colour of lilac and laburnum. So I immediately thought you were bringing me here to see what sort of impression she would make on me. And as I said, my only worry was that she might be too young—to be my mother, not your wife. After all, you still command the attentions of the youngest and the fairest. But I can now say, Papa, that she suits me fine the way she is.

PRINCE You really are the most impudent puppy I've ever come across. Do you think I would ask your permission, if it ever occurred to me to...

PHILIP Not exactly ask, Papa..., but surely a happy family life depends on all the members getting along with one another... wouldn't you agree—?

The Countess and Lolo Langhuber enter.

COUNTESS Won't you come through here, Fräulein. My Papa would certainly be very sorry if he missed you. (*Starts introducing her*) Allow me...

LOLO Oh, Excellency.

PRINCE Ah, Fräulein Pallestri...

LOLO Langhuber, if you don't mind. I just came to thank the Count; he sent such a magnificent bouquet of flowers for my farewell performance.

PRINCE (*introduces*) My son Philip. And this is Fräulein...

LOLO Charlotte Langhuber.

PRINCE Until recently (*to Philip*) known by the name Pallestri.

PHILIP Fräulein Pallestri! I've long had the pleasure of...

PRINCE What?

PHILIP Fräulein Pallestri is in my collection.

PRINCE What... what sort of collection do you have?

LOLO There must be some mistake, Excellency. I don't remember ever having...

PHILIP Of course you can't remember, Fräulein; when I cut your picture out of the paper in Krems, you could not of course have felt it here.

LOLO No, thank goodness.

PHILIP It was all a sort of game we played at school. We had one person cutting out accident and murder cases.

LOLO Well, he must have been a wicked fellow.

PHILIP And another cutting out historical celebrities, north pole explorers, composers and the like; and I collected actresses and dancers. They're so much better looking. Two hundred and thirteen of them, to be precise. I'll show you some time, Papa. Very interesting. There's even an Australian opera singer among them.

LOLO I had no idea you had a son, your Excellency. And such a grown-up one at that.

PHILIP Yes, Fräulein, hitherto I have been blossoming in secret.

PRINCE Well, you're making up for it now, I must say.

LOLO Leave him alone, your Excellency, I like it when young people show a little spirit.

PHILIP So you are withdrawing into private life now, Fräulein? A great shame. Just when I might finally have had the pleasure of admiring you on stage, which as we know is all the world...

LOLO Very charming, Excellency, but unfortunately one has no time to wait for the up and coming generation. And I am already in too high an age-group for those of slightly riper years.

PRINCE I hear you are getting married shortly, Fräulein?

LOLO Indeed, I am entering the state of holy matrimony.

PHILIP And who is the lucky man, Fräulein, if one may ask?

LOLO Who? He's sitting out there on the coach-box.

COUNTESS What? The coachman?

LOLO But Countess—coachman!—No more so than your Papa— forgive me—when he happens to take his bays out for a drive himself. My fiancé is a coach owner, as well as a landlord and respectable citizen of Vienna, and he only mounts the box himself when he feels like it or holds someone in particular esteem. At the moment he's driving for a certain Baron Radeiner. Just a short while ago, he brought him out to visit your Papa, Countess. Though I've not yet noticed him about.

PHILIP Allow me to introduce myself: Baron Radeiner.

LOLO You, Excellency?

PHILIP Since coming to Vienna, I've been driving exclusively with Wasner.

LOLO Under an assumed name, Excellency. You can get into all sorts of trouble like that.

COUNT (*enters, rather hot*) Good day, everybody. (*Surveys the situation*) Ah!

LOLO Good day, Count. I've taken the liberty... I wanted to thank you for the magnificent bouquet.

COUNT Not at all, very good of you, I'm sure.

PRINCE My dear old friend, well here he is, my son Philip.

PHILIP I'm greatly honoured, Count.

COUNT (*shakes hands with him*) Welcome to my home. Consider it your own at any time. Well, it appears there is no need for further introductions.

COUNTESS No, Papa.

COUNT (*somewhat embarrassed*) Well, this is very charming of you, Fräulein. You know yourself how much I always have admired you... But tell me, how did you get out here? I was taking my walk up the main road that all coaches have to come along, and yet I didn't see you.

LOLO Well, Count, what else do you expect! My horse and carriage days are over. Of course I came out on the train, as befits me now.

COUNT I see, I see... But as I understand, your future husband is himself a...

LOLO Well, he has nobler passengers than me of course.

PHILIP I had the pleasure of being driven out here by the Fräulein's fiancé.

COUNT Wasner drove you out here? Then everything makes sense... yes, yes... psychological connections.—(*Offering him the cigar box*) Would you like a cigar?

PHILIP (*taking one*) Thank you.

PRINCE Come now, Philip! A huge cigar like that before a meal!

COUNT Splendid. It's the healthiest thing. I like you, my boy. Shall we sit?

> The Prince, Count and Philip sit down. The Countess and Lolo remain standing near them.

COUNT So you're leaving with Papa tomorrow?

PHILIP Yes, Count. I'm looking forward to the trip immensely.

COUNT Will you be away long?

PRINCE That depends on various circumstances.

PHILIP On the first of October, I have to join my regiment.

PRINCE And I may then possibly continue further south.

COUNT Well that's a new one on me. Where to?

PRINCE (*with a look at the Countess*) Egypt, then perhaps on to the Sudan for a little hunting.

COUNTESS (*to Lolo*) I must show you the park, Fräulein.

LOLO Yes, it looks magnificent. No place for the likes of me. (*They come forward to the left*)

COUNTESS Does your house have a garden too?

LOLO Of course. We have an ancestral home as well... in Ottakring.* Wasner's great-grandfather was already a coach owner. Goodness, how beautiful! The way those flowers hang. I must arrange something like this myself.

COUNT (*uneasily*) Why are the ladies keeping their distance?

COUNTESS Don't worry, Papa, I'm just explaining the façade of our little villa to our guest.

PHILIP Do ladies from the theatre often come out here to see you, Count?

COUNT No, this is more of a coincidence! (*They continue talking*)

COUNTESS (*to Lolo*) How strange that this should be the first day I've had the opportunity of meeting you, Fräulein. I'm really delighted.

LOLO (*with a grateful look*) Me too, Countess. I've known you by sight for ages of course. I often used to look up at your box.

COUNTESS But never visited us.

LOLO Well, that's all over now.

COUNTESS You know, Fräulein, I am a little aggrieved... for him.

LOLO Aggrieved?

COUNTESS It's a hard blow for him. I know better than anyone how much he depended on you. Even though he never said anything to me about it.

LOLO Well, Countess, do you think it's not hard for me too? But I ask you, Countess, what choice does one have after all? I'm no longer all that young now, am I? And one wants to settle down at last. As long as I had a profession, I could afford—how should I put it—to embrace more free and easy attitudes. To some extent that went with my position. But how would it look, now that I'm retiring into private life?

COUNTESS Yes, I completely understand. But what will he do now?

LOLO Perhaps he'll marry too. I can tell you, Countess, there are many who would give their right arm... do you think, Countess, it wasn't a difficult decision for me too?

COUNTESS Do you know what I've sometimes wondered? Whether he mightn't have thought of making you his wife?

LOLO Yes, he wanted to all right, Countess.

COUNTESS What?

LOLO Do you know, Countess, when the last time he asked me was? Not four weeks ago.

COUNTESS And you said no?

LOLO I said no. It wouldn't have done anybody any good. Me as the Countess! Can you imagine it? Me as your stepmother, Countess... We certainly wouldn't have been able to have such cosy conversations then.

COUNTESS If you knew how very much I like you...

LOLO But I don't want to better myself beyond my station. Who knows, I might still be able to have...

COUNTESS Well, what?

LOLO Here's the situation. I've fallen madly in love with Wasner. I hope you don't think the worse of me for that? In all these eighteen years, I've never had cause to reproach your father for anything. But it's hardly surprising if with time passions cool a little. And rather than put your Papa in a... no, no, Countess... I owe your Papa too great a debt of gratitude. Heavens...

COUNTESS What is it?

LOLO He's standing there and looking in.

Countess looks round.

Wasner at the main gate raises his top hat.

LOLO Isn't it silly, Countess, whenever I see him suddenly like that, I get these palpitations. When an old woman's smitten, it's always worse.

COUNTESS Old? You call yourself old? There can't be much difference between us.

LOLO Ah well. (*Gives her a look*)

COUNTESS I am thirty-seven. Well, don't look at me so pityingly. There's absolutely no reason to, I can assure you.

LOLO (*relieved*) One hears so many rumours, Countess... I never believed it of course. Well, thank God it's true. (*Presses her hand*)

COUNTESS I'd like to congratulate your fiancé at once, if you'll permit me.

LOLO How very gracious... but if the Count... perhaps he wouldn't like it.

COUNTESS My dear Fräulein, I've long been accustomed to doing as I please. (*Both make for the entrance*)

WASNER How d'you do, Countess...

COUNT (*to the Prince*) Well look at that.

WASNER How d'you do, Count; it's an honour, Excellency.

PRINCE (*has risen*) Listen, my dear Wasner, you may drive your bride home in your coach now, and I'll take my son with me in mine.

WASNER Your son...

PHILIP Why didn't you tell me you were engaged, Wasner?

WASNER You didn't let on much yourself, Excellency! Herr von Radeiner, indeed!!

COUNT (*to Lolo*) Well, thank you for your kind visit, and I wish you all the very best.

LOLO The same to you, Count. After all, when one has such a daughter...

COUNTESS It's a pity we didn't get to know each other earlier.

LOLO Countess, you are really too...

COUNTESS Dear Fräulein Lolo, well once again, all the very best! (*She embraces her*)

Count surprised, a little touched.

LOLO Well, Count, thank you again for the kind reception—and now farewell!

COUNT Farewell, Fräulein Langhuber. May you be happy... May you be happy, Lolo.

>*Lolo gets into the carriage, which has driven up.*
>*Wasner on the box, top hat in hand. They drive away.*
>*The Countess waves them, goodbye.*
>*The Count stands deep in thought.*
>*Philip and the Prince stand near the front.*

PHILIP My dear Papa, I now see through it all.

PRINCE Well?

PHILIP This Fräulein Lolo is the Count's natural daughter, and so the Countess's sister—her milk-sister.

PRINCE It's called a step-sister, by the way. But, go on, young diplomat.

PHILIP And both of them are in love with you, of course. Both the Countess and the ballet dancer. And this marriage between Wasner and the ballerina is your contrivance.

PRINCE Well, go on.

PHILIP You know, Papa—something has just this minute occurred to me.

PRINCE And what might that be?

PHILIP I don't know if I should say.

PRINCE Well, you're not usually reticent.

PHILIP What if my mother were not dead at all.—

PRINCE Hm...

PHILIP What if it were my mother who, through this remarkable chain of circumstances, is now riding into town in the self-same carriage that brought me out here earlier? What if it were my own mother I cut out of the newspaper—?

PRINCE My boy, you are bound to become at the very least a minister for agriculture.—But come along, we too must take our leave now.

>*The Count and Countess returning from the entrance.*

PRINCE Well, dear friend, I'm afraid we must be saying goodbye.

COUNT But won't you stay the night... it would be splendid if you could stay for a meal...

PRINCE Impossible, I'm afraid. We have a prior engagement at the Sacher.

COUNT That's a shame. And now we won't be seeing you all summer.

PRINCE Well, we're not departing from this world.

COUNT And you're off tomorrow already?

PRINCE Yes.

COUNT Where to exactly?

PRINCE To the coast, Ostend.

COUNT I see, Ostend. I've long wanted to go there.

PRINCE It would certainly be very nice if—

COUNT Well, what do you say, Mizzi, shall we join the fashionable set? Shall we have a look at Ostend too?

COUNTESS I don't know yet. You could go anyway, Papa.

PHILIP It would be really marvellous, Countess, I would be absolutely delighted.

COUNTESS (*smiling*) It's very kind of you to say so, Philip. (*She holds out her hand to him*)

> *Philip kisses her hand.*

COUNT (*to the Prince*) It would seem the children like each other well enough.

PRINCE That's my impression too. Well then, goodbye. Goodbye, dear Mizzi, goodbye, dear friend. I hope at least to see you again in Ostend.

COUNT She'll come, I think. What do you say, Mizzi? After all, one can rent an atelier on the sea front too. Don't you agree, Mizzi?

> *The Countess remains silent.*

PRINCE Well, goodbye again. (*Shakes hands with both of them*)

> *Philip kisses the Countess's hand once more.*

COUNT (*shakes hands with Philip*) It's been a real pleasure.

> *The Prince, Philip exeunt. The coach having drawn up, they get in and drive away.*
> *The Count and Countess come forward and sit down at the table under the tree.*
> *Pause.*

COUNT Quite a remarkable day.

COUNTESS Yes, life is altogether remarkable, only sometimes one forgets that.

COUNT You may well be right there, Mizzi. (*Pause*)

COUNTESS You know, Papa, you really could have introduced us earlier.

COUNT How do you mean. Ah, you and...

COUNTESS Me and Lolo. She's such a nice person.

COUNT You liked her? Ah well, if one could always tell these things in advance... But it can't be helped. Now it's over anyway.

> *The Countess takes his hand.*

COUNT (*stands up and kisses her brow. Takes a few paces to and*

fro) By the way, Mizzi, what do you say to... how do you like the
boy?

COUNTESS Philip? Bit of a smart aleck.

COUNT A smart aleck, but smartly dressed too. Let's hope he stays in
the army. That's a more sensible career than diplomacy. Slow but
steady. If one puts up with it, one gets to be a general. Look at
Egon... he missed becoming a minister three times... And so what if
he had become one? (*Pacing up and down*) Ah well... it's going to be
a little lonely out here over the summer.

COUNTESS But don't you want to go to Ostend, Papa?

COUNT I say,... are you sure you wouldn't like to come? It would be...
well, you know, without you... You don't have to look at me like
that, I know I didn't pay you much attention all those years that I
was...

COUNTESS (*taking his hand*) But Papa, you're not going to start
apologizing? I understand completely.

COUNT Ah well! It's just that, without you I wouldn't enjoy the trip at
all. And what will you do out here all by yourself? Spend the whole
day painting?

COUNTESS Well, the problem is... the Prince has asked me to marry
him.

COUNT What? Is that possible? Well I never... And... and you've said
no?

COUNTESS More or less.

COUNT I see... Oh well... After all, I've never tried to talk you into
anything. Whatever you think best... But I really don't understand
why. I've long noticed that he... In age you're not at all badly suited.
And as regards other matters... six million is not to be sneezed at
either. But whatever you think best.

The Countess remains silent.

COUNT Or is it perhaps because of the boy? Come now, that would be
going a bit far. Such things happen in the best of families. And
especially since his wife was always having trouble with her heart...
Suddenly a man finds himself caught up in some affair or other,
without quite knowing how himself.

COUNTESS And then he abandons the poor girl from the people to her
fate.

COUNT Come come, it's only like that in books. What was Egon supposed to do? These women usually die young anyway,
unfortunately. And who knows, if she hadn't died, whether he
might not have... I find that quite handsome of him actually, the

whole business with the boy. It requires courage. I could name you others... Anyway, let's not talk about it. Well, if that's the only thing that speaks against him... And besides, spending a little time together in Ostend like this wouldn't commit you in any way.

COUNTESS That's true enough.

COUNT Well then. I'll tell you what. You can simply accompany me as far as there. Then if you like, you can stay on. If not, you could perhaps go across to London and visit your aunt Lori. All I mean is, there's not much sense in your letting me go off by myself.

COUNTESS Very well, then.

COUNT How d'you mean?

COUNTESS I'll come with you, Papa. But without committing myself to anything. Obligation free.

COUNT You'll come with me then?

COUNTESS Yes, Papa.

COUNT I am absolutely delighted. Thank you, Mizzi.

COUNTESS No need to thank me, Papa. I'm happy to do it.

COUNT You cannot imagine... without you, Mizzi... The memories, especially just now... You know, I suppose, that I was in Normandy with Lolo last year?

COUNTESS Of course I know...

COUNT And besides, as regards Egon... without trying to persuade you further... people sometimes get to know each other better during a few days in a strange place like that, than after years at home.

COUNTESS It's all settled, Papa, I'm coming with you. As for the rest, don't let's talk about it... for the moment.

COUNT Well then, I'll tell you what, I'll telephone the booking office at once and see about a sleeping-car compartment for tomorrow or the day after.

COUNTESS Why the rush?

COUNT Well, what's the point of sitting about here, once we have decided. So I'll go and telephone... Is that all right with you?

COUNTESS Yes.

The Count embraces her.
Professor Windhofer appears at the garden gate.

COUNT Ah, here comes your Professor. Do you have a lesson today?

COUNTESS I'd completely forgotten too.

Professor Windhofer, a handsome man of about thirty-five, very elegant in his grey suit and goatee beard. He takes off his hat as he enters the park and comes forward.

PROFESSOR Good day, Countess. Good day to you, Count.

COUNT Good day, my dear Professor, how are you? If you'll excuse me, I must make a phone call: we're going on a trip.

PROFESSOR A trip? Please go ahead, Count, don't let me hold you up.

COUNT I'll see you again before you go, Professor.

    Exit inside the house.

PROFESSOR So you're going on a trip then, Countess?

COUNTESS Yes, to Ostend.

PROFESSOR But that's rather sudden.

COUNTESS It is rather. That's the way it is with me.

PROFESSOR Then that will be the end of our lessons for this year? A pity.

COUNTESS Yes, I don't think I can manage today even... I feel rather drained, I'm afraid.

PROFESSOR I see... You do look a little pale, Maria.

COUNTESS Do you think so?

PROFESSOR How long do you intend to be away?

COUNTESS Perhaps until autumn—perhaps until quite late on in the autumn.

PROFESSOR So we won't be resuming our lessons until November then?

COUNTESS (*smiling*) I don't think so.

PROFESSOR You don't think so?... (*They look at each other*)

COUNTESS I don't think so...

PROFESSOR Then... I'm dismissed, Maria.

COUNTESS How can you use that expression, Rudolph. It really isn't very nice of you.

PROFESSOR I'm sorry. Its just come rather more quickly than expected.

COUNTESS Better than its coming too slowly. Don't you think?

PROFESSOR I am far from wishing to reproach you.

COUNTESS Nor have you any reason to. It was wonderful, wasn't it? (*Holds out her hand*)

PROFESSOR (*kisses her hand*) You will be good enough to pay my respects to the Count.

COUNTESS Are you going at once...?

PROFESSOR (*lightly*) Isn't it best that way?

COUNTESS (*after a pause, looking him in the eye*) I think so. (*They shake hands*)

PROFESSOR Farewell then. (*Exit*)

    The Countess stands there for a while gazing after him.

COUNT (*on the terrace*) All organized. Tomorrow evening, nine-thirty from the Westbahnhof. Where is the Professor?

COUNTESS I sent him away.

COUNT Really?—And guess who has the compartment between yours and mine... Egon and his son. That will surprise them.

COUNTESS Yes... enormously. (*Exeunt into the house*)
    Curtain.

THE VAST DOMAIN
(*Das weite Land*)

A Tragicomedy in Five Acts

CAST

FRIEDRICH HOFREITER, *manufacturer*
GENIA, *his wife*
ANNA MEINHOLD–AIGNER, *actress*
OTTO, *her son, naval midshipman**
DOCTOR VON AIGNER, *divorced husband of Frau Meinhold*
FRAU WAHL
GUSTAV, *her son*
ERNA, *her daughter*
NATTER, *banker*
ADELE, *his wife*
DOCTOR FRANZ MAUER, *doctor*
DEMETER STANZIDES,* *first lieutenant*
PAUL KREINDL
ALBERTUS RHON, *writer*
MARIE, *his wife*
SERKNITZ
DOCTOR MEYER
FIRST TOURIST
SECOND TOURIST
ROSENSTOCK, *head porter at the Lake Völs Hotel*
AN ENGLISH LADY
A FRENCH LADY
A SPANISH LADY
PENN, *guide*
THE TWO CHILDREN OF FRAU NATTER
THE ENGLISH GOVERNESS
CHAMBERMAID *at the Hofreiters*
TOURISTS, HOTEL GUESTS, WAITERS, BELL-BOYS *etc.*

Setting of the action: Baden near Vienna;
in the third Act only, the Lake Völs* Hotel*

Act One

Veranda and garden of the Hofreiters' villa. To the right an ample veranda with a balustrade which runs on down the six steps at both ends leading into the upper garden. Double doors from the veranda into the conservatory are wide open.—In front of the veranda, a patch of lawn with rose bushes in bloom.—The garden is enclosed by a tallish green wooden fence, which at the back on the right turns a corner and continues behind the villa. Footpath outside along the fence. Road parallel to the footpath. Bushes along the fence on the inside. The garden gate to the left, opposite the veranda, is open. Benches are grouped about the patch of lawn: one in the foreground opposite the audience, one opposite the gate, a third at the far end of the lawn facing the audience. On the veranda a longish table and six chairs. In the corner at the end of the garden an oleander. The veranda is shaded by a red and white striped awning. An electric lamp on the table. A bracket to the right of the door. Tea things on the table. It is late afternoon after a thunderstorm. Meadows and leaves all wet. The long shadows of the palings fall across the garden.

Frau Genia, thirty-one years old, simply but elegantly dressed in a dark grey skirt and violet silk blouse, is sitting on the chair at the shorter side of the veranda table which faces the audience. She puts down her teacup, gazes in front of her a moment, stands up, pushes her chair back, looks out over the balustrade into the garden, then goes down the steps into the garden, her hands behind her back as is her habit.

The chambermaid comes onto the veranda from the conservatory with a large tray, is about to remove the tea things, hesitates.

GENIA (*still on the steps, turns back towards her*) You may clear the table. The master will probably have had his tea in town. (*After a short pause, during which she looks at the sky*) You can also put up the awning.

CHAMBERMAID (*placing the tray aside and winding up the awning*) Shouldn't I bring Madam something to put on? It's getting chilly.

GENIA Yes. My white coat. (*She sniffs at a rose on its stem, then continues her stroll beside the veranda towards the back*)

The chambermaid, having finished putting up the awning, clears the table and goes out with the tea things.

*Frau Wahl and Erna come up the road along the fence outside
and approach the gate. Genia continuing beside the meadow also
approaches the gate. Frau Wahl and Erna nod greetings while
still outside.*

*Genia waves slightly, hastens her pace a little and meets them
both at the gate.*

*Frau Wahl, slim, supple, about forty-five years old, with a
certain languid but studied formality. Her voice is a little nasal
and she speaks in not quite authentic aristocratic Viennese. Gaze
and speech by turns too weary or too animated. While speaking
she usually looks past her partner, and only when she has finished
observes him with a friendly, searching look, as if seeking
reassurance.*

*Erna, taller than her mother, slim, sure of herself and
straightforward to the point of inconsiderateness, yet without
appearing pert. Direct, unembarrassed gaze.*

GENIA (*shakes hands with both*) Back from the city safe and sound?

FRAU WAHL As you see, my dear Genia. The weather was terrible.

GENIA Out here too, until an hour ago.

FRAU WAHL You were quite right to decide to stay at home. We were
positively inundated at the cemetery. I really only went to please
Erna. Just attending the ceremony in the church would have been
quite enough,—in my opinion! I can't see that it does anybody any
good...

ERNA Mama is absolutely right... it's not as though we could bring
poor Korsakov back to life again.

GENIA Was there a very large turnout?

FRAU WAHL Enormous. One could hardly move in church. And there
must have been a few hundred people at the cemetery too—despite
the miserable weather.

GENIA Many people we know?

FRAU WAHL Yes, of course... The Natters drove up in their new scarlet motor car.

GENIA (*smiling*) I've already heard about that.

FRAU WAHL It made a bizarre impression parked beside the cemetery
wall... well, not exactly bizarre, but a little out of place...

CHAMBERMAID (*enters with Genia's white coat and helps her put it
on*) 'Evening, Frau Wahl, 'evening Fräulein Erna.

FRAU WAHL (*condescendingly*) Good evening my dear Kathy.

GENIA Did you talk to my husband at the cemetery at all?

FRAU WAHL Yes... briefly.

ERNA He was very shaken.

GENIA I can imagine.

ERNA It made me wonder. Normally he is not someone who is easily affected by such things.

GENIA (*smiling*) How well you know him.

ERNA Well, shouldn't I? (*Very simply*) I was already in love with him at seventeen. Long before you, Frau Genia.

GENIA 'Frau' Genia again.

ERNA (*almost affectionately*) Genia then. (*Kisses her hand*)

GENIA He was very fond of Alexei Korsakov, you know.

ERNA Evidently.—Earlier I used to think that Korsakov was merely— his pianist.

GENIA How do you mean... his pianist?

ERNA Well, just as Doctor Mauer is his friend, Herr Natter his bank manager, I his tennis partner, Lieutenant Stanzides... his second.

GENIA Oh...

ERNA I mean, if it should ever come to that... He uses people for his own convenience, and scarcely gives a thought to what else might be going on inside them.

FRAU WAHL Do you know, Genia, what my late husband used to call Erna's remarks like that? Her pirouettes on the tightrope of psychology.

OTTO VON AIGNER (*comes past, greets them from the gate*) Good evening.

GENIA Good evening, Herr von Aigner. Won't you come in and join us for a while?

OTTO If I may. (*He comes into the garden. He is a young man of twenty-five, reserved and amiable in manner; he is wearing the uniform of a naval midshipman. Greetings all round*)

GENIA How is your dear mother? I was actually hoping she might come round this afternoon.

OTTO Wasn't she here yesterday?

GENIA Yes. And the day before as well. (*Smiling*) She has in fact been spoiling me a little.

OTTO My mother went into town two hours ago. She is engaged to play cards this evening. (*To Frau Wahl and Erna*) Have you ladies also been into town today? I saw you driving to the station during that terrible cloudburst this morning.

FRAU WAHL We attended Korsakov's funeral.

OTTO Yes of course, that was today. Does anyone actually know why he killed himself?

ERNA No.

FRAU WAHL Someone at the cemetery today thought it might have been from thwarted ambition.

GENIA What—?... Korsakov...?

FRAU WAHL Yes. Because people were always saying he could play Chopin and Schumann—but not Beethoven or Bach... I thought so too, by the way.

OTTO But it does seem unlikely that a thing like that would drive anyone to suicide. Didn't he leave any farewell letter?

ERNA Korsakov was not the sort to go leaving farewell letters.

FRAU WAHL How can you be so sure of that?

ERNA He was too clever and too much a man of taste for that. He knew full well what being dead meant. And so he didn't care about the looks on people's faces the next morning.

OTTO Somewhere I read that the evening before he killed himself he dined with friends... apparently in the best of spirits...

FRAU WAHL Yes, they always say that in the papers.

GENIA This time it happens to be true.—You see, I know that because my husband was among the friends he dined with.

FRAU WAHL Ah...

GENIA (*casually*) Sometimes he has things to do in town until quite late, and then he always dines at the Imperial*—with members of a sort of fraternity—going back to his bachelor days. Recently Korsakov, who lived in the hotel, was often there as well. And as Friedrich himself told me,—on that last evening there was nothing unusual about his behaviour at all. Afterwards they went on to the coffee house for a game of billiards.

FRAU WAHL What, your husband and Korsakov?

GENIA Yes. They even bet on who would win—and Friedrich lost. The next morning from the office, he sent the servant round to the hotel with the cigars they'd wagered... and—haven't you heard this? The servant was the one who discovered the whole business.

FRAU WAHL So what happened?

GENIA Well, he knocked a few times, there was no answer, so finally he opened the door to deposit the cigars and...

ERNA There lay Korsakov, dead...

GENIA Yes. Dead on the divan, the revolver still in his hand...
          Pause.

FRAU WAHL Your servant must have been quite frightened.—What did he do with the cigars? Did he leave them there?

ERNA Mama is a great one for historical accuracy.

GENIA I'm sorry, Frau Wahl, but I'm afraid I totally forgot to ask about that.

The sound of a car.

FRAU WAHL It's stopping here.

GENIA That's Friedrich...

ERNA Then we can arrange a game of tennis right away. Has the court been put in order yet?

OTTO Of course. I played singles with Herr Hofreiter for two hours yesterday.

FRAU WAHL Was he in the mood for playing tennis?

ERNA Why shouldn't he have been in the mood, Mama? I can't see any reason why not. Anyone may dance the cake walk or even the cancan on my grave... In fact, I find the idea rather appealing.

DOCTOR MAUER (*enters. He is thirty-five, tall with blond full beard, pince-nez, and scar from a sabre on his forehead, he wears a dark lounge suit, and though not elegant, is not at all negligently dressed*) Good evening, one and all.

GENIA Is that you, Doctor?

MAUER (*rapidly greeting everyone*) How nice to see you. (*To Frau Wahl*) Good evening, Fräulein Erna, good evening, Lieutenant. (*To Genia*) Friedrich sends his greetings, Genia, but he still has things to see to at the factory. I drove there with him, and he was kind enough to let me have the car for a few home visits I had to make out here. He'll catch the train later.

FRAU WAHL I'm afraid we must be getting along. (*To Mauer*) I hope you will come and see us as well before too long, Doctor. Even though, praise the Lord, we seem to be enjoying undisturbed good health.

ERNA But you'll have to come soon, Doctor, because in July we are off to Lake Völs in the Tyrol.

MAUER Ah!

FRAU WAHL We have arranged to meet Gustl there. (*To Otto*) He is my son, you know, he spends the whole year travelling. Well, not quite the whole year—but a good deal of it... one could certainly say that... Last year he was in India.

ERNA And I want to do some climbing again.

MAUER Really? Well, perhaps we'll meet again on some mountain top. I am feeling the lure of the Dolomites myself. (*To Genia*) And I must admit, Frau Genia, that I am very keen to borrow Friedrich for a while this summer.

GENIA For a tour of the Dolomites—?... What does he say about it?

MAUER He doesn't seem wholly averse to the idea.

FRAU WAHL I thought, since... since... the accident that time, Friedrich had given up climbing.

MAUER But not for good.

GENIA (*explaining to Otto*) A friend of my husband's, a Doctor Bernhaupt, fell from the rock face next to him and was killed instantly. Though of course that was seven years ago now.

OTTO (*to Genia*) Really? So your husband was a member of that party too?

ERNA (*thoughtfully*) I must say... he doesn't seem to have much luck with his friends.

GENIA (*to Otto*) Have you heard this story before?

OTTO It somehow lodged in my memory, understandably perhaps because it happened on the same peak—my father was the first to climb more than twenty years ago.

GENIA That's right, it was the Aignerturm... Everyone's now forgotten that it's named after a living person. (*Short pause*)

ERNA It must feel rather odd, Herr Otto, knowing there's a rock out there in the Dolomites which in a sort of way you are related to.

OTTO Not all that odd, Fräulein Erna. You see, both my father and the rock seem equally remote. I was only four or five when my parents separated.

FRAU WAHL And haven't you seen your father since?

OTTO That's how things turned out...
        Pause.

ERNA (*getting ready to go*) Well, Mama... I think it's about time.

FRAU WAHL Yes, indeed!... If only we could finally finish our unpacking! (*To Mauer*) We just moved out here on Sunday. Even our domestic arrangements are not yet up and running... we are having to take our meals at that dreadful restaurant in the park.

ERNA But Mama, you know you find them very appetizing.

FRAU WAHL But it's always so crowded, especially in the evening... Well, goodbye, Genia... will you walk with us a little way, Midshipman?

OTTO If I may... Goodbye Frau Genia, my regards to your husband.

ERNA Goodbye, Genia. Goodbye, Doctor.
        Parting courtesies. Frau Wahl, Erna, Otto exeunt.
        Genia, Mauer.

MAUER (*after a short pause, gazing after Erna*) Well there's a girl who almost makes one willing to pardon the existence of the mother.

GENIA She's not the worst of souls, our good Frau Wahl. In fact I find her quite amusing. If only that were all that mattered. (*As they approach the veranda*) As I suggested to you recently Doctor, you should think the matter over.

MAUER (*half in jest*) I don't think I'm quite elegant enough for her. (*Gradually follows her*)

GENIA (*climbing a few steps*) By the way, I didn't know Friedrich had things to see to in the office after hours.

MAUER Oh yes, I forgot to mention, Genia, he had to wait for an important dispatch.

GENIA From America?

MAUER Yes. About a patent for the new electric lights he has invented.

GENIA They're only a refinement, Doctor! (*Sits down*)

MAUER (*leaning against the balustrade*) Be that as it may, the whole business certainly seems to be assuming huge proportions. I hear he intends to build on to the existing factory; to buy up the adjoining block of houses...

GENIA Yes...

MAUER Meanwhile the consortium pursuing him over the factory purchase is knocking on the door again. He has a meeting with his bank manager tomorrow morning.

GENIA With Natter.

MAUER With Natter, of course.

GENIA The Natters were also at the funeral, I hear.

MAUER Yes.

GENIA Apparently their scarlet motor car caused something of a stir.

MAUER Well, what were they supposed to do? It just happens to be scarlet.

    Short pause.
    Genia looks at Mauer, smiling faintly.

MAUER Anyway—their affair is over.

GENIA (*still smiling quietly*) Are you quite certain of that?

MAUER I can assure you, Genia.

GENIA Has Friedrich by any chance...

MAUER No, he never talks about that sort of thing. But one doesn't have a diagnostic eye for nothing. In fact it was all over quite some time ago. I assure you, Genia, Friedrich is always genuinely either in the office or the factory. You know how he is. He must conquer the world with his new electric lights, otherwise he doesn't get any satisfaction out of the whole thing. Frau Natter no longer exists, as far as he's concerned.

GENIA Well, at least it's reassuring to be told that.

MAUER There was never really any cause for alarm. Adele is basically the most harmless person in the world. If one didn't happen to know—

GENIA Yes, she perhaps! There may not be any threat from her. But I think Herr Natter, for all his natural charm and affability, is a brutal man. Even a little spiteful. And I have sometimes been afraid for Friedrich, as you can imagine. Afraid, as for a son,—a fairly grown-up son who lets himself in for dubious adventures.

MAUER (*sits down opposite her*) It's interesting how you perceive these things. I sometimes think women who are born mothers possess the gift—of being so for their husbands too.

GENIA Or of becoming so, my dear Doctor. I've not always been quite so maternally inclined. Earlier, I was on the point of packing up and leaving on more than one occasion.

MAUER Oh!—

GENIA With the boy of course. I could never have left Percy with him, you may be sure of that!

MAUER So you wanted to leave Friedrich...?

GENIA Yes, I did... And once I even wanted to kill myself. Admittedly that was a long time ago. Perhaps I'm now really just imagining I ever would have——

MAUER Certainly... You never would have done it... If only so as not to cause him embarrassment.

GENIA Do you think I'm that considerate? You are mistaken, Doctor... At one time I even intended to do the most inconsiderate thing a woman can do to a man, especially to a vain one. To... have my revenge.

MAUER Your revenge?

GENIA Well, let's say, to get my own back.

MAUER I see... That would certainly have been simpler. And it might also have had other things to recommend it. Well, perhaps it may still happen. The hour of destiny may yet toll for you, Genia.

GENIA Perhaps it wouldn't even need to be an hour of destiny.

MAUER (*seriously*) It would in your case. That's the thing. A pity really. It has long offended my sense of justice that my old friend Friedrich in particular—shouldn't have to pay.

GENIA Who told you, my dear Doctor, that Friedrich doesn't pay? Does it have to be in precisely the same coin? He pays all right— but in his own way! All is not really as well with him as you might think. Not as well as he himself sometimes believes, for that matter.

Sometimes I even feel sorry for him. Yes truly, Doctor, I sometimes think some demon must be driving him.

MAUER A demon—? Well now!... yet some women in your situation would send your husband and his demon packing, and to hell with him,... (*in response to a questioning look from Genia*) as say our Midshipman's mother did once to her demonic husband.

GENIA Perhaps she loved her husband more than me. Perhaps it's always the higher kind of love that can't forgive.

FRIEDRICH HOFREITER (*enters. Slim, medium height, fine narrow face, dark moustache trimmed in the English manner; fair hair flecked with grey parted on the right. He wears a pince-nez without a cord which he sometimes removes, and stoops a little as he walks. Small eyes a little close together. Engagingly soft, almost feminine voice, which sometimes turns sharply ironic. His movements are supple, but suggestive of energy. He is elegantly dressed, without any hint of dandyism; dark lounge suit under an open black overcoat with broad satin lapels, a black bowler hat, and a slender umbrella with a simple handle.—While still at the door*) Good evening. (*As he enters*) Hello Mauer. (*This with a distinctive laugh, which is one of his mannerisms and often sounds as though he wanted to make fun of the person addressed*)

MAUER Back at last, Friedrich. (*Stands up*)

FRIEDRICH (*coming up the steps onto the veranda, kisses Genia lightly on the forehead*) Good evening, Genia, my dear. How is everything? Any news? Letters?

GENIA Nothing at all. The evening post hasn't been yet, though.

FRIEDRICH (*looks at his watch*) Quarter to seven. The postman should be pensioned off. He becomes more tiresome by the year. One can watch it happening. Three years ago, the evening post was always here by half past six. Now, almost never before half past seven. At this rate, he will soon be turning up at midnight.

GENIA Would you like some tea?

FRIEDRICH No thanks... I had some at the office. It wasn't very good, mind. Well, has Mauer told you the latest...?

GENIA Yes... Did the dispatch from America arrive?

FRIEDRICH Of course... And it now looks certain that I shall have to go over in the autumn.

GENIA But you were going to send someone from the office.

FRIEDRICH Ah!—I always have to do everything myself. Would you like to come along then, Genia? Sailing from Liverpool on 29 August or from Hamburg on 2 September. The North German Lloyd* line. If we sail with the King James, I know the captain.

GENIA We can discuss all that later, can't we?

FRIEDRICH My pleasure. (*He sits down*)

GENIA You must be hot in your overcoat.

FRIEDRICH No, I find it rather chilly actually. What amazing weather. Did it pour out here as well? At the cemetery it went on and on!— And I don't mean the speeches. Be thankful you weren't... Frankly, all that ought to be abolished once and for all! What rubbish they manage to come up with.—(*Pause*) Well, Mauer, how was the ride out here? No accidents? How did the driving go? Six miles an hour, what? You wouldn't risk going any faster.

MAUER Pull my leg if you wish. I don't trust chauffeurs. I'm like you, I need to be in control. I've had three car accident victims to treat again this week.

FRIEDRICH Yes of course, how's Stanzides doing?

MAUER Well enough, for someone with an arm fractured in two places. I'm going to call in and see him shortly. He's very impatient. And really he should be thankful he didn't break his neck.

FRIEDRICH So should I, don't forget. I too was flung ten yards down the road.—It's true though, soon insurance companies won't want to take on any acquaintances of mine.

MAUER You certainly don't seem to have much luck with your friends, as Erna Wahl was saying only half an hour ago.

FRIEDRICH So Erna has been here?

GENIA Yes, with her mother. They just left with Herr Otto.

FRIEDRICH And Otto was here too... (*To Mauer*) Did you see him?

MAUER Yes.

FRIEDRICH How do you like him, by the way?

MAUER (*a little disconcerted by the question*) A nice enough young fellow.

FRIEDRICH Remarkable how much he reminds me of his father! The same complexion, but in grey. Don't you agree?

MAUER Possibly... Doctor von Aigner was never my type, of course. Too much of a poseur for my taste.

FRIEDRICH Ah, it's just that he has style. People often confuse the two. It's been a long time since I last saw him. Seven years ago now. In Bozen. Do you remember, Genia?

GENIA Indeed. (*To Mauer*) I liked him very much.

FRIEDRICH Yes, he was having a good time then. At least, he was in better spirits than me. (*To Mauer*) It was only a few days after that whole business over Bernhaupt happened. Aigner had just returned from an election campaign; dressed to the nines; he'd been fired upon by Italian freedom fighters* in some Tyrolean out-

post, after which of course the Germans gave him an ovation... and
the whole time he was having to give two or three speeches every
day...

MAUER Speeches! Yes! That always was his forte. Even in the days
when he was president of the tourist club, and I was on the committee. And again now he is a member of parliament... Plenty of
opportunity there!

FRIEDRICH Ah, but he's not all talk;—he has done something for the
country. But for him, the new roads through the Dolomites would
never have been built. And these gigantic hotels and access roads,
all his work really! Yet at the same time, he has managed to father at
least one child in every village in Tyrol. Even outside his electoral
district.

MAUER Very well then, let us say that he has style. But now I really
must be going. Stanzides will be waiting for me.—

FRIEDRICH Send him my best. Perhaps I'll call by and see him
tomorrow. You'll be back for supper, though?

MAUER I'm not sure.

FRIEDRICH But that goes without saying.

MAUER (*hesitating*) It's very kind of you. But I'd rather go back on the
ten-twenty train. I have things to do at the hospital tomorrow
morning.

FRIEDRICH You're not superstitious, are you, Mauer?

MAUER Why do you ask?

FRIEDRICH Well, I thought perhaps you didn't want to spend the
night in our guest room, because poor Korsakov slept up there a
week ago. But I don't believe the dead can get exit permits their
first night so as to come back and haunt one.

MAUER To hear you talk like that...!

FRIEDRICH (*suddenly serious*) It's all quite awful, actually. Only a week
ago he was sleeping upstairs, and the previous evening he played to
us in there—Chopin—the Nocturne in C sharp minor—and a
piece by Schumann,—and we all dined on the veranda, and Otto
was there, and the Natter couple,—who would have dreamed that
that would happen!—If only one had some inkling why! Well,
Genia,—didn't he say anything to you?

GENIA To me?...

FRIEDRICH (*without ascribing any significance to Genia's response*) Sudden mental derangement, they say. But first I'd like someone to
explain what the term sudden mental derangement means. Well,
Mauer, perhaps you can enlighten us?

MAUER In the first place, I'm not a psychiatrist—and secondly, I am never surprised when someone kills himself. We all come close to it so often... Once when I was fourteen I wanted to kill myself, because a class teacher put my name down in the punishment book.

FRIEDRICH In that case I would have been more inclined to kill the teacher... Except that I then might have been obliged to become a mass murderer.

MAUER An artist more likely! They are all more or less abnormal. Not least because they take themselves so seriously. After all, ambition is in essence a psychological disorder. All that gambling on immortality! And as to performing artists, now they have a raw deal. They may be as famous as you please, yet only their names remain, no trace of what they actually achieved. I think that really might drive a person mad.

FRIEDRICH That's all nonsense! Anyway, you didn't really know him. None of you really knew him. He ambitious...?—He was far too intelligent for that. One might even say too philosophical. His piano playing was really no more than a sideline. Have you any idea of his range of interests? He had Kant, Schopenhauer and Nietzsche at his fingertips, as well as Marx and Proudhon.* He was really quite remarkable. I know where I would turn for decent conversation... And the whole time he was putting in six hours' piano practice every day! Where on earth did he find the time for it?—And only twenty-seven! And yet he kills himself. My God, to think what a fellow like that had to look forward to. Young and famous, and quite good looking too—and then he goes and shoots himself. When some old ass, whom life has nothing more to offer, does that... But it's always those who... Well.—And to think that only the night before one was dining with a man like that—and playing billiards with him... What's the matter, Genia? What is there to laugh about?

GENIA I told the whole story to Frau Wahl just now. The first thing she asked was, what had happened to the cigars you sent him the next day.

FRIEDRICH Ha!... She is really priceless. (*Takes out a cigar case and offers it to Mauer*) So you're not superstitious then. I'll have one too. Franz brought them back, of course.

MAUER Thank you. It's rather a shame before a meal. (*Takes one*)
     Friedrich gives him a light.
     The chambermaid enters with letters.

GENIA (*takes them from her hand*) A card from Percy.

FRIEDRICH 'Dear mother'. For you. Just a card again. What a lazy rascal.

MAUER What does a thirteen-year-old boy want with writing letters. And in English at that.

FRIEDRICH He now knows it almost as well as German.

MAUER Well, goodbye. I'll be back in half an hour. The cigar doesn't seem to be drawing. And I'm not being superstitious. Shan't be long. (*Exit*)

Friedrich, Genia.

FRIEDRICH Yes, just as well you didn't go, Genia. All those speeches... and then the weather. (*He glances through the correspondence and the newspapers*) Did I tell you, as they were lowering the coffin, the sun suddenly came out.—(*Pause*) Isn't today Thursday? He was supposed to have dined with us today. Must mention that to Mauer too... I say, let me have a look at Percy's card.

GENIA (*hands it to him*) He'll be back in four weeks.

FRIEDRICH (*reading*) Yes. So his was the best Greek exercise. That's not bad. Perhaps he'll become a philologist or archaeologist or something. Incidentally, did you read that article in the 'Daily Telegraph' yesterday, about the new excavations in Crete?

GENIA No.

FRIEDRICH Very interesting. One really ought to go there some day. Yes. (*Pause*)

GENIA What you were suggesting earlier about America,—are you serious?

FRIEDRICH Of course. Well, wouldn't you like to go, Genia? I won't have much to do in New York itself. But we'd spend more time in Chicago and Washington, and also in St Louis... And then I think it would be irresponsible not to push on a little further;—across to San Francisco. Do you remember poor Korsakov telling us about his concert tour through California? It must be really glorious out there.

GENIA A trip like that would take several months.

FRIEDRICH If things were running smoothly over here by then, especially the new building, one could easily stay on until next spring... Anyway, think about it.

Genia slowly shakes her head.

FRIEDRICH Are you afraid of the crossing? Come now, with the new ships they have these days! Besides, they've just invented an effective way of overcoming sea-sickness. Electro-vibration.

GENIA I don't think I'd be able to bring myself to go. Despite the electro–vibration. But I have another idea...

FRIEDRICH Which is?

GENIA While you're over there, I'd like to spend some time in England—with Percy.

FRIEDRICH (gives her a sidelong look) Hmm. You wouldn't see much of him.

GENIA But he could continue as a day boy. Just like my sister Mary's boys. And I could live with him.

FRIEDRICH What's all this... What suddenly gave you this idea...

GENIA Not that suddenly. I mentioned it to you quite recently.— Surely you remember. And since you really seem determined to leave him there for several more years...

FRIEDRICH Of course. You can see how splendidly he is developing over there. It would be nothing short of damnable egotism if now, in the middle of his education, we were to bring him back to this continent, where they initiate one into all sorts of brutal and sentimental nonsense, instead of golf and rowing.

GENIA If only one didn't long to see him so...

FRIEDRICH Well, that's part of the price one has to pay. Do you think I don't miss him too? But in my view, longing is a very healthy element in the soul's economy. Longing has the potential to improve human relations. Altogether, I think it's more important for human relations to be based on longing rather than on habit. Besides, we can all go across to England together, and then you can still decide whether to come with me, or stay on with the boy during the winter.

GENIA I would rather you considered my decision today as final.

FRIEDRICH Your decision?

GENIA I'd have all sorts of things to see to before going to England. One can't organize a move like that just overnight.

FRIEDRICH A move?

GENIA Call it what you will.

FRIEDRICH What on earth's the matter, Genia? Why are you so unaccountable?

GENIA What's so strange about it? It's hardly surprising that a mother... that one should want one's only son to... Once he is a little older, I won't see anything of him at all. Two months in the summer, and a week at Christmas and Easter,—that is just too little. I've struggled long enough—I simply can't go on.

FRIEDRICH You know, Genia, one might almost get the impression you were less concerned to spend time with your son, than to leave... than to get away from me.

GENIA I don't think you will miss me particularly... But what's the point in talking about it. (*She stands up*)

FRIEDRICH What's wrong?

GENIA Nothing. I'm going into the garden. (*Goes down the steps*)
   Friedrich gazes after her.
   Genia slowly walks beside the meadow towards the back.

FRIEDRICH (*descends from the veranda, leaving his hat, though still wearing his coat, and stops beside a rose bush. Sniffs*) This year they don't have any scent at all. I don't know what it is. Each year they look more opulent, but they have entirely lost their fragrance.
   Genia slowly strolling off, hands behind her back.

FRIEDRICH (*after a pause*) I say,—Genia.

GENIA What?

FRIEDRICH Well, if you come over here.

GENIA (*approaching slowly*) Here I am.

FRIEDRICH I say, Genia, tell me something. (*Looks her in the eye, very calmly*) Do you know why Korsakov shot himself, by any chance?

GENIA (*calmly*) What's that supposed to mean? You know I was just as astonished as you were.

FRIEDRICH One certainly got that impression. Well then, tell me why you want to leave me... all of a sudden like this?

GENIA I don't want to leave you. I want to visit Percy. And not all of a sudden, but in the autumn. Travelling with Percy.

FRIEDRICH Yes, otherwise it would be rather too conspicuous.

GENIA What would be conspicuous?

FRIEDRICH It would almost look as though you were fleeing.

GENIA Fleeing? Fleeing from you! I would hardly need to do that. We are far enough apart, even at home!—(*Pause*)

FRIEDRICH Look, Genia!—He is dead and buried now,—this Alexei Korsakov...

GENIA Why do you keep coming back to him?

FRIEDRICH Calm down, my dear, just calm down!... All I mean is, that he's no longer in the slightest... Nothing would happen to him even if he were alive, of course, any more than it would to you... But you must admit that this disagreement between us seems to be taking on a curious character... no, that's not quite the word... all I mean is, it seems odd that it should be just today that we are having this discussion, just today, the very day Herr Korsakov is buried, that your mood is so very unaccountable... Even if I am a husband,

Genia, it doesn't mean that I'm a fool. I'll stake my life on it that something isn't right here. Well then—what was there between you?

GENIA I can only look at you.

FRIEDRICH Yes, I notice. But you'll admit that's hardly an answer. Don't misunderstand me, Genia. There may have been nothing serious between you and Korsakov. Perhaps it was only a flirtation. Yes, because if there had been anything more, he would not have had to shoot himself. Unless (*scowling*) there really was more to it— and you————then withdrew your favours. (*He still speaks very calmly, but now takes her by the arm*)

GENIA (*almost smiling*) A jealous scene?!—Come now!... You really should take something to calm your nerves, Friedrich, I'm not to blame if it's over between you and Adele Natter,—and she doesn't yet seem to have any successor.

FRIEDRICH Ah, you are very well informed, I see. Well, for the moment I won't ask where you obtained your information,—but it's not my fault that you never asked me about it directly;—I would never have denied it. I would certainly never have replied that you should take something to calm your nerves. That is altogether... that isn't even like you. I don't understand you at all. You ought to know me better. I really don't understand why you stand there like a statue, instead of answering me reasonably... I have the feeling you don't trust me, Genia?... You are saying to yourself, one never knows with him? But I assure you, Genia—and don't think I am trying to trap you—I would completely understand. After all, you would have been absolutely justified—whether it were Alexei or... well, there's no arguing about taste. It's a well known fact that a wife seldom complies with her husband's taste in such situations.

GENIA Why are you suddenly against him? After all, you were his friend. At the funeral today you were even thought to have been deeply moved.

FRIEDRICH Did Mauer tell you that too?

GENIA Erna Wahl, as it happens. She said she wouldn't have believed anything could have affected you so deeply.

FRIEDRICH Ah, Erna, the connoisseur of human nature. Of course I was affected. I feel more sorry for him than I have ever felt for anyone before. And I would not feel less so if I knew for certain that you—had been his mistress. You can't imagine how—inessential and irrelevant some things become, when one has just returned from a cemetery. I don't tell you that to reassure you, but because it's true.—So answer me finally. I won't leave you in peace until you do. You can lie, but you must answer. I want to know whether it is true. Well then... yes or no?—

GENIA He was not my lover. Unfortunately, he was not my lover. Is that enough for you?

FRIEDRICH Yes, it's enough. Because now I know he was. You have given yourself away! Don't you see?—You said, unfortunately he wasn't. And since you loved him, naturally you were his mistress. What should have prevented you? And then when you—broke it off, he killed himself. Very simple. And the reason you broke it off is even simpler. I'll tell you why: because such things inevitably come to an end. Especially when it's an affair like this with someone a few years younger—who is mainly away on concert tours. And then Percy would soon be coming back, and so you may then have, how shall I put it, felt the need for cleanliness... all very respectable, really. That would make sense of everything, except for your idea of travelling to England. Though actually, I can understand that too. After all, if the affair was over, for you too—then that way of ending things... Even if you didn't love him very passionately—or might not have...

GENIA Don't bother to go on. Read this. (*She pulls a letter out of her belt*)

FRIEDRICH What am I supposed to...?

GENIA Read.

FRIEDRICH What is it... A letter? From him? A letter to you from him?—Ah, keep it then. I don't want to read it. That would look too much like... Thank you. If you had no intention of showing me this letter,—then kindly keep it!

GENIA Read!

> *Friedrich re-enters the veranda. He turns the light on its bracket so that he can see, puts on his pince-nez and begins to read to himself.*
>
> *Genia follows him slowly, but remains standing on the bottom step.*

FRIEDRICH (*reading*) 'Farewell, Genia.' (*Continues reading to himself. Looks up at her, astonished*) What? You didn't have any idea that he... When did you receive this letter?

GENIA An hour before you brought me the news of his death.

FRIEDRICH So you already knew when I got home? One is so... Well, you may think me a complete idiot, but I didn't notice the slightest change in you... (*continues reading to himself, then looks up surprised, then reads half aloud*) 'You were probably right to refuse my presumptuous request. Neither of us was born to lie... I perhaps; you surely not... in spite of everything...' In spite of everything... You must have complained a lot about me?

    Genia gives him a questioning look.

FRIEDRICH (*reading*) 'I can now fully understand that, in spite of everything, you should not want to leave Him'—with a capital H, very flattering.—'You love him, Genia, you still love your husband, that is the solution to the mystery. And perhaps what I mean by the foolish word'... this is getting unreadable...

GENIA 'What I mean by the foolish word fidelity'?...

FRIEDRICH Ah, so you know it by heart. 'What I mean by the foolish word fidelity, is no more than the hope that he will one day return to you.'

GENIA His interpretation. You know I don't hope for anything—or wish for anything.

FRIEDRICH (*looks at her; then*) 'When I spoke to you yesterday, I was already resolved' Yesterday?... Was he here on Sunday? Yes, of course, you strolled up and down the avenue together... yes... (*Reads*) 'When I spoke to you yesterday, I was already firmly resolved to let everything depend on whether you said yes or no. I didn't say anything to you, because I feared that if you suspected how utterly impossible it is for me to live without you...' Our Herr Alexei Ivanovitch certainly has an inflated style (*Faint music coming from the resort*) 'I didn't want to owe my happiness to any compulsion, to any form of blackmail. Therefore'... If you had known it was a matter of life and death, would you have said yes?

GENIA If I had known... how can one know something like that... I wouldn't have believed it. I simply wouldn't have believed it.

FRIEDRICH I'll put the question another way.

PAUL KREINDL (*young, elegant, ostentatiously stylish, appears at the gate*) Good evening! Greetings, Frau Genia.

FRIEDRICH Who is it?... Ah, Paul, it's you! (*Comes down*)

PAUL If I may. (*Approaches*) Don't let me disturb you. I've just come from the park as an emissary from Frau Wahl, Fraülein Erna, Midshipman von Aigner and Lieutenant Stanzides...

FRIEDRICH Is he out and about already?

PAUL We were wondering whether you might like to come across and enjoy the music with us?

GENIA Very kind, but we have a guest to supper, Doctor Mauer.

PAUL Well bring him along too, Frau Genia!

FRIEDRICH You'll all be in the park for some time yet of course.

PAUL Until they put the lights out.

FRIEDRICH That's fine then,—perhaps we'll come a little later... though don't hold us to it.

GENIA But please thank everybody all the same.

PAUL Not at all. We shall all be delighted to see you. Good evening then, Frau Genia, adieu, Herr Hofreiter, a thousand apologies for disturbing you. (*Exit*)

>*Friedrich and Genia in the garden.*
>*Pause.*

FRIEDRICH I'll put the question to you another way. Supposing you could awaken him from the dead,—by declaring that you were willing... to become his mistress.

GENIA I don't know.

FRIEDRICH You forget what you just said. 'Unfortunately, he was not my lover.' If you yourself regret you weren't, surely it would not have taken very much. And now you say you doubt you would become his mistress, even if you could return him from the dead... Why don't you admit it? He would only have had to be patient for a few more days, and you would have... after all, you loved him.

GENIA Not enough, as you see.

FRIEDRICH You say that as if you were reproaching me... I am not to blame.

GENIA Just me, I know.

FRIEDRICH And do you now regret... that you... drove him to his death?

GENIA I am very upset that he is dead. But as to regret, I have nothing to regret! If he had told me what he intended—if he had... Oh, I would have brought him to his senses...

FRIEDRICH But how—?

GENIA I would have made him give his word...

FRIEDRICH You'd have what? Don't talk nonsense! You wouldn't have made him give his word;—you'd simply have become his mistress... of course you would.

GENIA I don't think so.

FRIEDRICH Come now!

GENIA Oh, not because of you. Not even because of Percy.

FRIEDRICH Well then, why?

GENIA For my own sake!

FRIEDRICH I don't understand.

GENIA I couldn't have brought myself to do it. God knows why. I simply couldn't have. (*Pause*)

FRIEDRICH Here's your letter, Genia.

> *Genia takes it.*
> *Mauer enters.*

MAUER Here I am again, my friends. I hope I haven't kept you waiting too long.

FRIEDRICH (*advancing towards him*) Hello, Mauer. Well, Stanzides seems to be feeling better already. He's out enjoying the music in the park.

MAUER Yes, I accompanied him there myself.

FRIEDRICH Paul Kreindl was just here, urging us to join them after dinner.

GENIA I'll just go and see whether it's...

FRIEDRICH I say, Genia, I have an idea... Why don't we go across to the park at once. God knows, I feel in the mood for music and the crowds. You don't mind either way, do you, Mauer?

MAUER Me? It's entirely up to your wife.

GENIA Well I don't want to stop you both, but personally, I would rather stay at home.

FRIEDRICH No, that would really be a bore. Come with us, Genia, it will do you good too.

GENIA I'd have to change...

FRIEDRICH Well, go and change then, we'll wait out here in the garden.

GENIA Does it mean that much to you?

FRIEDRICH (*to Mauer*) What do you think? (*Irritably*) All right then, we'll all stay at home... and there's an end of it.

GENIA I'll be with you in a minute... I must just put on my hat.

> *Exit Mauer, Friedrich.*

FRIEDRICH (*after a pause*) Well, my dear Mauer, there we are...

MAUER I don't understand you... any hostess would find this disagreeable.

FRIEDRICH Well, you'll get quite a good meal in the park too. (*Pause*) Besides—it's perhaps just as well you're going back to town tonight.—The chances of ghostly visitations in this house have increased considerably.

MAUER What?

FRIEDRICH You don't really deserve my confidence, as you let out all sorts of things, even things I haven't told you...

MAUER What's that supposed to mean?

FRIEDRICH Well, what about my affair with Adele Natter being over, how is it Genia knows about that?

MAUER You should be pleased I had something sensible to say about you for a change.

FRIEDRICH Well, whether that was particularly sensible... Ah God, Mauer, life is certainly a complicated business!... But interesting... very interesting!

MAUER What did you mean before about the increased chances of ghostly visitations?

FRIEDRICH Ah yes.—Well, why do you think Korsakov killed himself?—go on, guess!! From unrequited love—for my wife. Why do you look at me like that?! From unrequited love!... It's true... He left her a letter. She just gave it me to read... A remarkable letter, not badly written... for a Russian!

GENIA (*enters wearing a hat. The music is now heard more distinctly*) Here I am. Well, my dear Doctor, now I shall tell you: I'm abandoning our perfectly good dinner entirely for your sake. You see, Erna too is in the park...

FRIEDRICH Oh! Erna! (*To Mauer*) That's splendid then. Well, Mauer, pull yourself together. I wouldn't bestow her on just anyone, you know. Even though she evidently regards me as a heartless rogue, and can't believe that even the death of a friend could...

> *They all go out of the garden and onto the road.*
> *Curtain.*

Act Two

The Hofreiters' villa and the corresponding portion of the garden. On the left, the rear façade of the house. Door leading directly into the garden. Two windows on each side of the door, some of them open. On the first floor, a small balcony. In the centre, an expanse of lawn. Over to the right, a large walnut tree, with benches, a table and chairs under it. Further back in the centre, a clump of trees which partly screen the tennis court in the background from view. Around the tennis court a high wire fence. Outside the fence, benches to left and right. Two small benches either side of the main door under the ground floor windows.— Hot, sunny summer's day.

Frau Genia is sitting under the walnut tree in a white summer dress, a book which she is not reading in her hand.

On the tennis court a game is in progress. On the left Friedrich Hofreiter and Adele Natter, on the right Erna Wahl and Paul Kreindl. Their white tennis clothes gleam in the sun, but their faces are hard to make out. Intermittently there are cries of 'fifteen love, thirty all, out, deuce, second serve' and so on.

Shortly after the curtain rises, Otto von Aigner, this time not in uniform, dressed for tennis, panama hat, racket in hand, enters from behind the house and heads for the tennis court. He notices Genia, who has heard his footsteps, and approaches her. She greets him with a friendly nod.

OTTO Good day, Frau Genia—Aren't you playing?

GENIA As you see, Herr Otto. I'm not quite good enough for them.

A ball flies past Otto, he throws it back.

VOICES FROM THE COURT Thank you!

OTTO They're not exactly brilliant... apart from your husband of course. But pardon me, Frau Genia, I interrupted your reading... I was on my way to the court.

GENIA You're not interrupting me at all. I did try to read, but actually I was on the point of nodding off. It's this weather...

OTTO Yes, it certainly is warm. But the days are really lovely at the moment! Ideal for enjoying our native woods!

GENIA No doubt you've already been for a long walk today?

OTTO Yes; I went as far as the little 'Woodland Shrine' with my mother earlier this morning.

GENIA She must be so happy to have you near her again at last.

OTTO And I'm even happier... The more so since it will be my last leave for some time. I've been assigned to a ship which is going to the South Seas for three years.

GENIA (*conventionally*) Oh!

OTTO The War Ministry has arranged for our ship to link up with a scientific expedition.

GENIA No doubt you are engaged in various fields of study in your spare time, Herr Otto?

OTTO What makes you think that, Frau Genia?

GENIA I can't imagine your finding military life itself completely satisfying.

OTTO (*smiling*) Permit me to observe that in the navy we have numerous tasks which, without exaggeration, may be described as scientific.

GENIA Naturally—I wasn't doubting that. I only meant that you probably have interests outside your profession.

OTTO Well, one doesn't have all that much time left. But on this forthcoming voyage I am hoping to gain a little more insight into one field I've toyed with as an amateur... the expedition we'll be joining is equipped for deep sea exploration; and since I am also on friendly terms with one of the researchers... Oh, here comes Frau von Wahl.

GENIA (*getting up*) You must tell me more about it some time, Herr Otto... this whole deep sea business.

FRAU WAHL (*coming out of the house into the garden*) Greetings, my dear Genia, good day Herr Otto. (*Raising her lorgnette*) The young people are hard at it, I see—?

GENIA If you can still count Friedrich as a young person—

FRAU WAHL Him especially. But also men in general! Herr Otto, would you believe that Herr Hofreiter and I are about the same age? Truly, nature has behaved deplorably towards us women. (*When Genia smiles*) Well, not so kindly anyway. Who else is playing? Adele Natter of course. I saw her scarlet motor parked outside. It doesn't look at all bad out here in the country among all the leaves. Better at least than against a cemetery wall...

GENIA (*smiling faintly*) You don't seem able to forget that impression, Frau von Wahl?

FRAU WAHL Well, it's not all that long ago; barely two weeks.

> *Friedrich and Erna come over from the tennis court with their rackets. Genia, Frau Wahl.*

FRIEDRICH (*in his maliciously humorous way*) How nice to see you, Mama Wahl. Hello, Otto! What's been barely two weeks?

FRAU WAHL Since poor Korsakov was buried.

FRIEDRICH I see... Has it really been as long as that—? Anyway, how did you get onto that morbid topic?

GENIA Frau von Wahl noticed the Natters' motor car—the scarlet one—parked outside just as it was then...

FRIEDRICH I see...

ERNA Otherwise, why would anyone think of talking about a dead pianist on a lovely day like this.

FRAU WAHL Has anybody ever met such a profound young lady? That is another one of her pirouettes on the tightrope of philosophy, as her late lamented father used to say.

FRIEDRICH She'd better make sure she doesn't fall off it one of these fine days...

> *Frau Adele, Paul Kreindl come over from the tennis court with their rackets.*
>
> *Genia, Otto, Frau Wahl, Friedrich, Erna. Greetings all round.*

ADELE (*pretty, plump, dressed in white, with a red belt and red scarf*) What's wrong, aren't we going to continue?

> *Paul Kreindl kisses Frau Wahl's hand.*

FRIEDRICH You could meanwhile have had a game of singles.

ADELE But I don't play well enough to please this gentleman.

PAUL How so, Frau Adele? (*Whining*) Soon everybody will play better than me. I'm playing damned badly at the moment. Oh, pardon me. But it's absolutely true. I simply don't know what's the matter with me. Almost as though I were bewitched. Or perhaps it's just because I'm using a new racket... If you'll excuse me—I'll dash home and fetch my old one. (*Departs. The others laugh*)

FRIEDRICH Why are you all laughing? At least Paul takes things seriously. And that's what counts. Whether it's tennis or skating or painting or curing the sick—To me, a good tennis player is a nobler human specimen than a mediocre poet or a mediocre general. Wouldn't you agree?—(*To Otto*)

ADELE (*to Genia*) So when will Percy be coming back, Frau Genia?

GENIA He should be here in two weeks. And then you must bring your children over too, all right?

ADELE I'd love to, if I may. Though whether such a grown-up boy will still deign to play with the little mites—

> *Doctor Mauer enters, together with Stanzides in uniform.*
> *Greetings all round.*

GENIA (*to Stanzides*) How nice to see you again.

FRIEDRICH How's the arm?

STANZIDES Good of you to ask. Our esteemed Doctor here has just massaged it for the final time... (*Puts his arm on Mauer's shoulder in a friendly way*) But it's not up to playing tennis yet.

MAUER All in good time.

STANZIDES (*to Adele*) You ready for the fray as well, Frau Adele? I just had the pleasure of meeting your husband in the park.

FRIEDRICH What's the matter with you, Mauer, you almost never show your face these days. I thought you must be completely out of reach.

MAUER I've just dropped in today to say goodbye. I'm leaving tomorrow.

GENIA Where to?

MAUER To Toblach.* From there I'm going to do a walking tour across the passes. Falzarego—Pordoi—

FRIEDRICH May I come with you, Mauer?

MAUER But can you get away, and would you want to?

FRIEDRICH Well—why shouldn't I... Are you off tomorrow?

MAUER In the morning, on the express.

ERNA (*to Mauer*) And when shall we have the pleasure of seeing you at Lake Völs?

MAUER In about a week, if that's convenient.

FRIEDRICH (*genuinely indignant*) What's this, you two arranging a little rendezvous...

ERNA Without asking your permission, Friedrich!

FRAU WAHL We shall be leaving the day after tomorrow—travelling direct. (*During what follows Otto stands to one side with Genia and Adele*) Gustl is already there. The things he tells me in his letters, by the way! Do you know who is the manager of the new hotel? Doctor von Aigner.

FRIEDRICH Ah, old Aigner!

FRAU WAHL And he is said to have turned all the ladies' heads there, despite his grey hairs.

FRIEDRICH Yes, women have always fallen for him. So, you be careful, Mama Wahl.

PAUL (*enters*) Well, here I am again! (*Holding up his racket*) I've brought my old one this time. At least I'll now be playing with something decent.

FRIEDRICH Well then, shall we get back to it—(*To Paul*) But no more excuses now! Otherwise you might as well go in for something else... the law perhaps... or hairdressing... (*As they move off*)

Friedrich, Erna, Adele, Otto, Paul go over to the tennis court.
Frau Wahl and Stanzides follow.
Genia, Mauer.

GENIA Shall we go and watch? Erna looks particularly well when playing tennis, you know!

MAUER (*coming to a halt*) Don't you get the impression she doesn't care two hoots about me, Frau Genia?

GENIA That might well be the most promising beginning for a happy marriage.

MAUER Yes, if the indifference were mutual, but as things are—(*breaking off*) By the way, Frau Genia, do you think Friedrich is serious about his travel plans?

GENIA I—I don't really know, I was a little surprised myself. He has certainly been working at such a frenetic pace lately that he deserves a few days to recover. But for that he wouldn't need to—He probably wasn't all that serious. Actually, I don't believe he'll come with you.

MAUER How do things stand then as regards America?

GENIA Friedrich will be going over, that is certain.

MAUER And what about you, Genia?

GENIA Perhaps I will too. (*Smiling*) Yes, dear friend. Perhaps!

MAUER You'll be travelling together?—Splendid. I'm really pleased for you.

GENIA Why the tone of celebration...?! I did say perhaps!...

MAUER Ah, I'm sure it will come off. Besides, it would be just too stupid if poor Korsakov had died in vain.

GENIA (*astonished*) If Korsakov—? How do you mean?—If Korsakov had died in vain?

MAUER I'm convinced Korsakov was destined by Providence to become a sort of sacrifice.

GENIA (*more and more astonished*) A sacrifice?

MAUER For you—and your happiness.

GENIA A sacrifice for my happiness—? Do you believe in such things?

MAUER One doesn't have to believe in them in general. But in this case I sense something like a mystical connection. Have you never had such thoughts yourself?

GENIA Me? To tell the truth, I think about the whole sad business very little.

MAUER That—only appears to be the case.

GENIA And when I—do sometimes think about it, it all seems so curiously remote and indistinct... Believe me—utterly remote! A vague sorrow—no more than that. I can't make myself better or more feeling than I am. Perhaps things will be different later. When autumn comes perhaps. The days are probably too summery for sadness now—or for taking anything too seriously. That's true not only of this business. Most things seem easier to bear. I can't even be angry with the good Adele, for instance. Just now I even asked her to bring her children over next time; I couldn't help it. It seemed so ridiculous to bear her or anyone else a grudge. Indeed I find her rather touching. To me she is like someone who has died long ago and doesn't know it.—

MAUER (*looking at her for some time*) Ah well. (*Pause*) Let's hope Friedrich has now finally come to his senses. Which should not be difficult when good sense and happiness coincide so closely. But if he fails to seize it this time, then—

GENIA (*quickly*) There's nothing to seize at present. You evidently misunderstood me earlier, Doctor. Absolutely nothing has changed between us—so far.

MAUER But it will change. It's impossible to be angry with Friedrich for long! He affects me in exactly the same way. No matter how exasperated I become with him,—as soon as he begins to exert his charm again, I find I'm at his mercy.

GENIA That's certainly not the case with me, Doctor! I have to be courted, courted at length.

> *Otto, Friedrich, Adele, Stanzides, Frau Wahl, Erna and Paul
> returning from the tennis court; Genia and Mauer.*

PAUL (*to Erna, as they approach*) Honestly, Fräulein Erna, it's perfectly true! Your service—it's first class.

FRIEDRICH And—her return?—But then she also practised that with me!—

ERNA Which was—if you'll forgive me, Herr Instructor—a rather doubtful pleasure!

FRIEDRICH ... Oh...?!—

ERNA (*to the others, especially Paul*) He bullies one, you know—bullies one to death!—If one slacks off just a little—one's immediately treated as a lost cause—as a despicable wretch in every respect—

FRIEDRICH (*in passing*) —Well—these things depend on character a good deal too—in my opinion...

GENIA (*who has meanwhile received a message from the chambermaid*) Ladies and gentlemen, tea is served, if you'd like to come this way. There's also ice cream, but no one need feel obligated... This way.

They go into the house, Frau Wahl with Stanzides, Genia with Otto, then Paul, Erna and Mauer. Friedrich and Adele, the last of the company, remain.
Friedrich, Adele.

FRIEDRICH (*to Adele as she is about to go into the house*) Unfortunately I haven't had the opportunity today to enquire about madam's precious state of health. Well, how are you?

ADELE I'm very well, and you, Herr Hofreiter?

FRIEDRICH Not bad. Very busy. We're building again. Next year we'll have six hundred workers. And in the autumn I'm going over to America.

ADELE I see.

FRIEDRICH You don't seem to find that particularly interesting.

ADELE My husband has already told me all about it. And might I suggest that we stop calling each other 'du', once and for all. Over means over. I'm all for relationships being clear.

FRIEDRICH I didn't know our sort of relationship also needed to be clear.

ADELE Kindly don't start joking... Let's be thankful things have ended as well as they have. The time for youthful indiscretions is now over. For both of us, I think. My children are growing up. And your boy too.

FRIEDRICH Yes, that's all very true.

ADELE And if I may give you a piece of advice...

FRIEDRICH I'm listening.

ADELE (*in a different tone*) Seriously though—I think the way you're flirting with that little Wahl girl is quite disgraceful. Don't for heaven's sake think I'm being jealous. I'm honestly not thinking about you at all... but about your wife—

FRIEDRICH (*amused*) Ah!!

ADELE —Who is really the most delightful, touching creature I have come across. Just now, when she asked me to bring the children next time—did you hear her?... I just about sank into the ground!

FRIEDRICH I didn't notice you doing so.

ADELE If I'd known her this well earlier—then—! Honestly, you don't deserve her.

FRIEDRICH I can't pretend you're wrong about that. But if everything on earth went by just deserts...

ADELE And as far as Erna is concerned—you should be careful. A brother is rather different from a husband. A brother can sometimes notice things.

FRIEDRICH What, Gustl! Come now—he couldn't care less!... He's a philosopher... Besides, I've no idea what you're insinuating. You're putting ideas into my head. A girl I've dandled on my knees!

ADELE That doesn't prove a thing. You've probably dandled girls that way in every age group.

FRIEDRICH Well, Adele... without thinking specifically of Erna, whom you've been so good as to suggest... it would certainly be nice!

ADELE What would be nice?—

FRIEDRICH To be young again!

ADELE You've been so long enough already.

FRIEDRICH Yes, but I was young too early... Now I would at last know how one should be young!... Everything in this world is so stupidly arranged. One should become young at forty, then one would at least get something out of it. Shall I tell you something, Adele? I feel as if all my life so far has merely been a preparatory stage, as if life and love were only now beginning.

ADELE I really don't understand you. There are surely other things on earth besides—oneself.

FRIEDRICH Yes,—the intervals between one woman and the next. They too are not uninteresting. If one has time and is in the mood, one builds factories, conquers territories, writes symphonies, becomes a millionaire... but believe me, all that is merely secondary. The main thing is—you women!—every one of you!...

ADELE (*shaking her head*) To think some people actually take you seriously!

FRIEDRICH Ah, do you find my remarks particularly funny?

HERR NATTER (*enters. A tall, quite powerfully built gentleman in a very elegant summer suit, mutton chop whiskers, monocle*) Hello Adele! Good day, my dear Hofreiter.

FRIEDRICH (*shaking hands*) Why so late?

ADELE (*in a friendly tone*) Where have you been roaming?

NATTER I'm sorry, my dear. I've been sitting in the park reading, as normally I never seem to get around to it. Wouldn't you agree, Hofreiter, there's nothing more delightful than sitting out of doors under a tree and reading?

FRIEDRICH It depends... What was the book?

NATTER Don't laugh. The latest Sherlock Holmes! Really terrific! Quite exciting in its way!—

    Mauer and Erna come out of the house.—Greetings.

ERNA (*to Friedrich*) Are we continuing the match?

FRIEDRICH But of course. (*To Natter*) Will you have some tea? We
were just about to...

NATTER If I may... Is Lieutenant Stanzides still here, by the way?

FRIEDRICH Yes, naturally.

NATTER I wanted to invite him to the theatre with us. (*To Adele*) If
you have no objection. I've taken a box in the stadium for today.
(*Mauer and Erna move off towards the right*)

FRIEDRICH Do you really enjoy itinerant shows like that?

NATTER Why not?

ADELE There's nothing on earth he doesn't enjoy. There's no more
appreciative audience than my husband!—

NATTER Yes, that's true. I find life thoroughly amusing. I enjoy myself
immensely. Invariably, and at every opportunity! (*Friedrich, Adele,
Natter go into the house*)

    Mauer, Erna, who have been talking.

ERNA And how did the accident happen?

MAUER It seems a stone worked itself loose under his foot. It was
during their descent from the Aignerturm. Apparently Friedrich
was in the lead, when he heard an ominous rumbling above him.
Almost at once large chunks of rock bounced past him, followed
not two yards away by the unfortunate Bernhaupt himself. Friedrich doesn't like to talk about it. Even though he pretends to be
above it all, at the time it made a deep impression on him.

ERNA You think so?

MAUER The best evidence surely, is that he's not been mountaineering since.

ERNA Well—the Aignerturm is going to be climbed again this year.

MAUER I hope you'll reconsider, Fräulein Erna.

ERNA I've already reconsidered. I always do before I say anything.

MAUER I shall have to write to your brother.

ERNA But my dear Doctor! Surely you don't think that's going to do
any good, once I've got an idea into my head! At most, I might
promise to wait until you join us at Lake Völs.

MAUER So should I come then?

ERNA Certainly you should. I'll hire you as a guide, for the usual fee of
course.

MAUER I never imagined I might be permitted to claim more.

ERNA Was that supposed to be wistful, Doctor Mauer, or just witty?

MAUER Should I come to Lake Völs, Fräulein Erna, yes or no?

ERNA In any case, I see no reason for you to alter your original travel
plans.

MAUER Do you really find it quite impossible to give me a straight answer, Fräulein Erna?

ERNA It's not easy, Doctor. (*She sits down under the walnut tree*) You know I like you very much. So you should come anyway. It would be a good opportunity for us to get to know each other better. But you should not of course feel obligated, any more than I do.

MAUER Very clever, Fräulein Erna.

ERNA I can be even more so. Now look. You've no doubt already got a mistress or some sort of little sweetheart—like all you unmarried men. So don't be in too much of a hurry. What I mean is: don't imagine that after our little conversation here today, you owe it to me to be faithful.

MAUER I'm afraid your courteous admonition comes too late.—I can't of course deny that I, like other men, and so on... But I have... made an end of everything. I am no friend of frivolity in matters of the heart. I would find myself obnoxious.

ERNA You are a decent man, Doctor Mauer! One has the feeling that if one were to entrust one's fate to you... one would have reached safe haven. Nothing could harm one any more.

MAUER One would hope so...

ERNA Only I'm not sure such feelings of security are really that desirable. At least for me. To be perfectly honest, Doctor Mauer, I sometimes feel I have a right to expect something more from existence than security—and peace. Something better or something worse—I don't know which.

MAUER Don't take me for a simpleton, Fräulein Erna, because I happen to believe I could offer you a life which, even if not the most exciting in the world, would have its share of blessings. Life consists of a great deal more than a certain kind of adventure.

ERNA Did I ever—?

MAUER You did not say so, Fräulein Erna, but that is how you feel. No wonder,—in this atmosphere! everywhere about us here! But I assure you, a purer, more bracing one exists—and I am confident that there I can teach you to breathe fresh air more freely.

ERNA You have courage, Doctor. I like you altogether very much. Come to Lake Völs and we shall see.

> Coming from the house: Adele, Natter, Stanzides, gradually followed by Genia, Otto, Paul, Friedrich, Frau Wahl, Mauer and Erna.

STANZIDES Earlier, I sometimes used to watch the show from high up, instead of from the auditorium—a bird's eye view from the little hill behind the stadium.

ADELE   That must have been fun.

STANZIDES   Fun—I don't know about that. It's certainly strange. One can only see a little of the set. A corner of a rock or cut-out of a stove and so on. And one sees next to nothing of the actors, and only occasionally catches the odd word out of context... But what is particularly curious is the effect when one hears a voice one recognizes from among the rest,—some lady one's acquainted with for instance, who might have joined the fun. Suddenly one finds one can understand the words as well. One can't make out anything the others are saying—yet one's acquaintance's voice makes perfect sense.

ADELE (*laughing*)   Acquaintance indeed!

FRIEDRICH   Mistress, you mean. One might say distant acquaintance even, Stanzides—surely more to the point in this case!—

ADELE   Or friend, if one wants to be discreet.

FRIEDRICH   Or enemy.

ERNA   If one is indiscreet.

FRAU WAHL   Erna!———

NATTER   It's getting late, I think we ought to be going if we want to see anything of the show at all. Please don't let us disturb you.

> *Natter, Adele and Stanzides exeunt.*

PAUL (*to Otto*)   Once with Doctor Herz last year I played for nine hours at a stretch. First four hours, then we had some scrambled eggs, and then... (*Goes on talking to Otto*)

MAUER (*taking leave*)   My hour too has come. (*To Genia*) Frau Genia...

FRIEDRICH   But why are you in such a hurry? If you can wait just quarter of an hour, I'll come in with you.

MAUER   What—so you're serious?

FRIEDRICH   Of course... well, can you wait?

GENIA   You mean, you're leaving with the doctor—you want to go into town right now—??—

FRIEDRICH   Yes, it's the most sensible arrangement. All the things I need for the mountains are in town and Joseph can pack them for me in an hour; then I can set off with Mauer early tomorrow morning.

MAUER   That would be splendid.

FRIEDRICH   Will you wait for me then? A quarter of an hour!

MAUER   Yes, I'll wait.

> *Friedrich hurries into the house. Erna, Paul, Otto and Frau*

Wahl stand together.
Erna has been listening off and on.
Genia gazes after Friedrich.

MAUER He is a man of decision.
Genia does not answer.

PAUL Come on, let's take advantage of the last of the evening light.
Erna, Otto, Paul, Frau Wahl move off toward the tennis court.
Mauer after short reflection follows.
Genia continues to stand motionless, and has just decided to go indoors when Frau Meinhold comes towards her.
Frau Meinhold, Genia.

FRAU MEINHOLD (*about forty-four, doesn't look any younger, features somewhat drawn, figure still youthful*) Good evening.

GENIA Oh, Frau Meinhold, so late? I was afraid you wouldn't come at all today. Now I'm doubly delighted you are here. Come and sit down, dear Frau Meinhold. Over there perhaps (*indicating the walnut tree*), that's your favourite spot, isn't it?

FRAU MEINHOLD (*noticing Genia's distracted manner*) Thank you, very kind.

GENIA Or shall we go over to the tennis court? They are still hard at it, and you quite enjoy watching, don't you?

FRAU MEINHOLD (*smiling*) But I've come to see you, Frau Genia. (*Goes over to the walnut tree with her*) But are you sure I'm not disturbing—you seem a little—were you about to go inside?

GENIA No, not at all. It's just that—my husband is going into town with Doctor Mauer shortly. They'll be leaving together tomorrow, you see. They are going on a walking tour. Imagine, only an hour ago he didn't know himself. The Doctor came to say goodbye, and naturally talked about his travel plans—and Friedrich at once got carried away with the idea of walking in the mountains the way he used to do. And so now he's off. (*Looks up at the balcony*)

FRAU MEINHOLD Then I have come at an inconvenient time. You are sure to have things to say to your husband, as he is leaving so suddenly.

GENIA Oh no, it's only for a short while. And we are not sentimental, no, truly.—

FRAU MEINHOLD And you'll also soon have Percy here with you again.

GENIA Oh, my husband will be back before that. Percy is not coming for another two weeks.

FRAU MEINHOLD You are really looking forward to him, aren't you?

GENIA As you can imagine, Frau Meinhold. Well, I haven't seen him since last Christmas. No easy lot, having one's only child overseas like this. But you know something about that yourself, Frau Meinhold.

FRAU MEINHOLD Something, yes.

GENIA Will your son now be leaving you for several years?

FRAU MEINHOLD Yes, it's supposed to be for three years. And so very far away.

GENIA To the South Seas, he was telling me earlier. Yes, that certainly is a long way—And yet I can't help feeling you are more fortunate than I am, Frau Meinhold. You have a profession, and such a fine one too. It seems so completely fulfilling. That must help one over many things.

FRAU MEINHOLD Over some things.

GENIA Don't you agree? When women are just mothers, that isn't really enough, I sometimes feel. I'm sure you wouldn't have agreed to Otto's joining the navy, if you had been just a mother.

FRAU MEINHOLD (*simply*) And what if I hadn't agreed...?

GENIA Then he would have remained with you. Oh, I'm sure he would. If you had wished, if you had asked him! He's so very fond of you. He could have gone in for something else. I can well imagine him as a landowner, say... or—oh yes... as a scholar too.

FRAU MEINHOLD The question is, my dear Frau Genia, would he have belonged to me any more then than he will do now he's off to sea.

GENIA Oh...!

FRAU MEINHOLD I don't think so. (*Unsententiously*) Frau Genia, we can't rid ourselves soon enough of the delusion that we can ever own our children. Especially sons! We belong to them, but they don't belong to us. I sometimes suspect one would become even more painfully aware of this, if one were always living under the same roof with them. When they are little, they will sell us for a toy, and later... for even less.

GENIA (*shaking her head*) That is really... no that... May I say something, Frau Meinhold?

FRAU MEINHOLD (*smiling*) Why shouldn't you? After all we're only chatting. Each of us says what comes into her head.

GENIA You see, I asked myself recently, after one of your—forgive me—gloomy remarks about human nature,—whether the fact that life seems so tragic to you might not have something to do with the roles you play?

FRAU MEINHOLD (*smiling*) Tragic... Do you really think so?

GENIA Because I seem to have a more optimistic view of life than you, Frau Meinhold. In my own mind for instance, I'm convinced that I will always mean a great deal,—a very great deal to Percy. And you too, Frau Meinhold, have in my view every right to expect as much yourself... indeed your son seems unusually affectionate— I'm convinced in fact that he positively adores you.

FRAU MEINHOLD (*smiling*) Let us call it that!

GENIA And if he were ever to 'sell' you, as you put it, it would certainly not be in exchange for anything unworthy. And that is I think the only case in which anything could change in the relationship between a mother and her child. (*After brief reflection*) And probably not even then.

FRAU MEINHOLD (*after a short pause*) He is also a man, have you forgotten that? So how can one predict anything at all... Even sons become men. (*Bitterly*) You too, I think, should have some idea of what that means.

> *Genia lowers her eyes in embarrassment.*

FRIEDRICH (*appears on the balcony above, just tying his cravat, and peers down, screwing up his eyes short-sightedly*) I hear a familiar aristocratic voice down there... I thought so... Greetings, Frau Meinhold.

FRAU MEINHOLD Good evening, Herr Hofreiter.

GENIA Do you need anything, Friedrich?

FRIEDRICH O no, thank you, I've just about finished. I'll come down directly. You see, I'm leaving shortly.

FRAU MEINHOLD Yes, Frau Genia was just telling me.

FRIEDRICH Well, see you anon. (*Leaves the balcony. Pause*)

GENIA May I say something in reply, Frau Meinhold?

FRAU MEINHOLD (*smiling*) Why do you always ask for my permission, Frau Genia—

GENIA It's because you impress me so much, Frau Meinhold. What you say always sounds so assured, so incontrovertible. And one has the feeling that nothing escapes you, nothing at all... and that you understand human nature... But aren't you... aren't you also perhaps a little unjust?

FRAU MEINHOLD That may be so, Frau Genia... But injustice is ultimately our only revenge. (*To a questioning look from Genia*) The only revenge for injustice... done to us at one time or another.

GENIA But eternal injustice in return for some half-forgotten grievance—is that not too much?

FRAU MEINHOLD (*bitterly*) There are things that are never forgotten, and hearts that never forget. (*Pause*) Does that again strike you as tragic, my dear Frau Genia? You are probably thinking to yourself, what's all this nonsense this ageing actress is trying to tell me. What does she want anyway? An eternity ago she parted from her husband, then by all accounts arranged her life to suit herself... and certainly seems to have had absolutely no regrets... so what does she want...? That's what you're thinking, isn't it, Frau Genia?

GENIA (*a little embarrassed*) No one would dispute that you had the right to live your life the way you pleased...

FRAU MEINHOLD Of course I had the right to do so. That is a separate issue. And I'm not trying to suggest that today I feel anything resembling pain over that whole business so long ago.—Or rancour!—Just that I have not forgotten it... that's all. Though you can imagine how much I have forgotten since. Joyous things and sad things... all forgotten—as if they had never been! And yet not what my husband did to me more than twenty years ago!... so it must have meant something after all! I think of it without rancour and without pain—I just remember it—that's all! But I remember it as if it had happened yesterday—just as clearly, just as tenaciously— just as undeniably—that's how it is, my dear Frau Genia...

FRIEDRICH (*enters in his grey travelling suit, ready to go. Kisses Frau Meinhold's hand*) I'm delighted to have this opportunity to say goodbye, Frau Meinhold.

FRAU MEINHOLD Are you going to be away long?

FRIEDRICH That is a little uncertain. It also depends on whether I am needed urgently. At the factory, I mean.

> *Coming from the tennis court Otto, Paul, Erna, Frau Wahl and Mauer. Greetings.*

OTTO Good evening, Mother. (*Kisses her hand*)

FRAU MEINHOLD Good evening, Otto!—

FRIEDRICH Well, how did it go, Paul?

PAUL Please, don't ask. Tomorrow I shall have to return to practising with my trainer.

MAUER Well, then, are you ready?

FRIEDRICH Of course.—Ladies, gentlemen... (*shaking hands all round*)—my dear Genia...

GENIA Forgive me, Doctor, but could you let me have just a few minutes with my husband?

MAUER Oh...

> *Mauer, Erna, Frau Meinhold, Otto, Frau Wahl, Paul withdraw.*

FRIEDRICH Is there anything else you want to say to me, Genia?

GENIA Not really, except that I'm a bit surprised at your decision. I had no idea you intended to leave today.

FRIEDRICH Neither did I, my dear.

GENIA Really, no idea at all?

FRIEDRICH That it would be specifically this evening—absolutely none. If Mauer hadn't happened to come by... But you were aware of my desire to spend a few days in the mountains. So whether I leave today,—or tomorrow or the next day... There's no real reason to be surprised.

GENIA (*her hand to her forehead*) You are right, of course. It's just that there was no discussion.

    Awkward pause.

FRIEDRICH Anyway, I'll be telegraphing every day, both here and to the office. And I'll also write. But I'd ask you to send me regular reports as well. And if anything should come from Percy, please forward it... Even if it's only addressed to 'dear mother'... Well, my dear, it's time I was... Mauer will be getting really impatient.

GENIA Why—why—are you leaving?

FRIEDRICH (*a little impatiently, but not aggressively*) Look, Genia, I think I have already answered that.

GENIA You know very well you haven't answered yet.

FRIEDRICH This mode of enquiry is certainly a novel one—at least in our household.

GENIA You are not obliged to give me an explanation, of course. But I don't see why you should flatly refuse to answer me at all.

FRIEDRICH Look, dear child, if you really think it's necessary to spell things out... very well. For some time now I've not been feeling very well. It will all blow over—probably... certainly. But for the next few days I need a change of air, a new environment. At least, I'm quite sure that I must get away from here.

GENIA From here!?... From me!!

FRIEDRICH From you—Genia—? That's not what I said—But if you insist—very well, from you! Yes, Genia.

GENIA But why? What have I done?

FRIEDRICH Nothing... who said you had done anything?

GENIA Well then explain, Friedrich... I'm so completely... I was prepared for anything except your... so suddenly... By the day, by the hour, I've been expecting we would... talk things over... that we...

FRIEDRICH Yes, Genia, I am aware of that. But... I think it's too early to—talk things over... I still have to get certain things clear in my own mind...

GENIA Clear—? But... where is anything unclear? Didn't you have... the letter in your hand? Didn't you read it? If you'd had any doubts before... which I simply don't believe... surely since then—for heaven's sake, Friedrich—surely since that evening you must have realized—what you meant to... God... is it really necessary to put things into words!...

FRIEDRICH No, of course not... But you've put your finger on it. Ever since that evening I've felt,—forgive me, of course I know you don't intend to—but I've just had the impression you were using this affair... (*hesitates*)

GENIA Well—well—?

FRIEDRICH That you were somehow using Korsakov's suicide as a trump card against me... inwardly of course... And—well, I just find that... a bit irritating...

GENIA Friedrich! Are you mad... Me using his suicide as a... This from you!... I can't believe you mean it!...

FRIEDRICH As I say, you can't help it. You don't mean it that way. I'm sure you're not proud that it was for your sake he... that you so to speak drove him to... you're not proud of your own steadfastness, I know all that...

GENIA Well then, if you know that...

FRIEDRICH Yes, but the fact that it happened...

GENIA What, what?

FRIEDRICH That he felt he had to kill himself... that's what's so terrible... I can't seem to get over it.

GENIA What... that... (*clutches her head*)

FRIEDRICH When you think about it, whichever way one looks at things... poor Korsakov is now lying rotting underground... and you are the direct cause of that!... even though of course you're... innocent—in a double sense.—Another man might go down on his knees to you, worship you—like a saint—for that very reason! I'm simply not like that... To me that's just what makes you... somehow more remote.

GENIA Friedrich!... Remote!... Friedrich!—

FRIEDRICH If you had found him repugnant—then, it would have been the most natural thing in the world. But no, in fact you found him very attractive, as I now know. One might even say, you were a little in love with him. Or—if I had... deserved your... if you had been duty bound to remain true to me, as they say... But I scarcely had the right to expect... well... we don't have to go into that now.— And so I keep asking myself over and over: why did he have to die?

GENIA Friedrich!

FRIEDRICH And you see, I find it really quite uncanny... that a thing which has no real existence—a shadow, a phantom, a delusion, at least when set against so terrible, so irreparable a thing as death— that your virtue—should have driven a man to his death... I don't quite know how else to put it... Well... No doubt I will get over it... with time... in the mountains... and with a few weeks' separation... But at present, that's the way things are—and it can't be helped... So you see, dear Genia... that's how I am... Others might react quite differently...

> *Genia remains silent.*

FRIEDRICH I hope you won't hold it against me if—at your request— I've spelt this out so clearly. So clearly in fact, that it has almost become untrue already...

GENIA It's still true all right, Friedrich...

> *The others slowly approach.*

MAUER (*first*) I'm sorry, Friedrich, but it really is high time I went. I still have things to do in town... Perhaps you could catch a later train...

FRIEDRICH I'm ready now... (*Calling out*) Kathy—hurry up! You'll find my coat and little yellow bag on the couch in my room.

FRAU WAHL Well, have a good journey and we hope to see you again soon.

ERNA On Lake Völs.

FRAU WAHL It would be so nice, Frau Genia, if you could come too.

ERNA Indeed, Frau Genia!—

GENIA I can't, unfortunately! Percy is coming home—

FRIEDRICH But not that soon. (*To Mauer*) When do we arrive?

MAUER In a week or ten days, I would say.

FRIEDRICH Well now, Genia, that would certainly be an idea. You ought to think it over.

GENIA I... will think it over.

> *Chambermaid enters with coat and bag.*

MAUER Well then, adieu, Frau Genia. (*Takes leave of the others as well*)

FRIEDRICH Goodbye, everybody. What are you all going to do this evening?

PAUL I have an idea. We could make a little moonlight excursion to Heiligenkreuz.*

FRAU WAHL On foot—?

FRIEDRICH That wouldn't be necessary. I'll send the car back from the station for you.

PAUL Three cheers for our noble benefactor!

FRIEDRICH No ovations please. Well then, goodbye everyone. Enjoy yourselves. Goodbye, Genia. (*Again takes Genia's hand, which she then lets fall limply by her side*)

> Friedrich and Mauer exeunt through the house.
> Genia stands motionless.
> Paul, Erna, Frau Wahl stand together.
> Otto and Frau Meinhold have exchanged a quick look of understanding.

OTTO (*to Genia, taking leave*) Frau Genia, we too must be——

GENIA (*quickly, with more energy*) Are you going? And you too, Frau Meinhold? But why? We can all fit into the car quite comfortably.

ERNA Of course. Herr Kreindl will sit in front with the chauffeur.

PAUL Delighted to.

OTTO Permit me to observe, however, that a moonlight excursion might be difficult, since the new moon doesn't appear until tomorrow.

ERNA We can make do with just the stars if necessary, Herr Otto.

FRAU MEINHOLD (*gazing at the sky*) I'm afraid you may have to do without them too today.

ERNA Then we shall just hurtle boldly on into the dark.

GENIA Yes, Erna, that will be terrific fun. (*She laughs out loud*)

> Curtain.

Act Three

Lobby of the Lake Völs Hotel.
On the left in the foreground is the entrance (glass revolving doors). On the right opposite the entrance, a lift, with stairs either side of it leading to the upper floors. In the background a wide bay with high glass windows. View out onto a wooded, rocky mountain landscape. To the right at the back a curtained arch, beyond which a passage leads to the dining room. Near the entrance is a large long table, with prospectuses, timetables etc., and behind it a practical wooden panel with shelving for letters and room keys. In both the lobby and bay window areas there are tables and seating arrangements.—Newspapers on some of the tables.—Rocking-chairs.—
Moderate activity in the lobby which continues without disturbing the main action and with suitable intermissions, throughout the act.
Tourists and summer residents come in from outside, guests use the lift, others walk up and down the stairs, occasionally a waiter enters, gentlemen and ladies sit at the tables reading or chatting to each other. The lift is attended by a bell-boy. Behind the table by the entrance is the head porter Rosenstock, a red-cheeked youngish man with dark hair, small dark moustache, sly, good-natured eyes, at once obliging and superior. He is just handing some newspapers to a bell-boy, who takes them and runs up the stairs. Two gentlemen in mountaineering clothes come in from outside and go straight across to the dining room. Rosenstock makes notes in a ledger.—Coming down the stairs, Doctor Meyer, a small, rather shy man in a summer casual suit, approaches the porter. He has a folded map in his hand.

MEYER (*after waiting a short while*) Excuse me...

ROSENSTOCK (*affably, but with a touch of haughtiness*) Yes, Doctor?

MEYER Might I enquire... you see, I wanted to go on a walk tomorrow, so I wondered if I might ask whether a guide would be needed for the Hofbrand hut.

ROSENSTOCK Oh, not at all, Doctor. You can't miss the path, it's all clearly marked.

MEYER And supposing I wanted to go on from the hut and climb a peak? The Aignerturm, for instance.

ROSENSTOCK (*smiling*) The Aignerturm?!... The Aignerturm is the hardest climb in the whole district, it's very seldom attempted. Only by hardy climbers not prone to dizziness. It has not been climbed so far this year.

MEYER I'm sorry, I didn't mean the Aignerturm, (*with the map*) I meant the Rotwand,—Would that be too difficult, do you think?

ROSENSTOCK Not at all. Any child can get up that.

MEYER Never any accidents?

ROSENSTOCK Yes, people have fallen off the Rotwand too.

MEYER What!—

ROSENSTOCK That's how things happen in the mountains. There are always amateurs around...

MEYER Hmm. Well, thank you anyway, for now.

ROSENSTOCK Not at all.

> *Doctor Meyer withdraws, finds a seat at a table in the bay window and studies his map, then later gets up and leaves.*
> *Two young tourists, with rucksacks and walking-sticks, come in from outside.*

FIRST TOURIST (*boisterously*) Good morning. Good evening, rather.

ROSENSTOCK How may I help?

FIRST TOURIST Tell me, do you have either one room with two beds, or two rooms with one bed each?

ROSENSTOCK What was the name, Sir?

FIRST TOURIST What—does one have to introduce oneself in this place? Bogenheimer, law student at Halle.* Birthplace Merseburg, religion Protestant...

ROSENSTOCK (*very courteously and smiling faintly*) I only wanted to enquire whether the gentlemen had booked.

FIRST TOURIST No, we haven't booked.

ROSENSTOCK (*very courteously*) Then I very much regret, we have no vacancies at present.

FIRST TOURIST Nothing at all? That's bad. Not even a straw mattress... one could bed down on for the night?

ROSENSTOCK Unfortunately not.

> *The second tourist has tried two chairs in succession, neither of them comfortable enough for him apparently. Finally he slumps into a rocking-chair.*

FIRST TOURIST (*to the second*) What shall we do now? (*To Rosenstock*) We've been on our legs for fourteen hours, you know.

ROSENSTOCK (*sympathetically*) That's a long time.

SECOND TOURIST I'm not budging from here.

FIRST TOURIST Did you hear that, Cerberus? My colleague isn't budging from here.

ROSENSTOCK As you please. There's room for all, in the hall.

FIRST TOURIST Ah, so you're a poet?

ROSENSTOCK Only in emergencies.

FIRST TOURIST Well, what are we to do?...

ROSENSTOCK Perhaps if the gentlemen were to look in at the Alpenrose...

FIRST TOURIST Is that a hotel too?

ROSENSTOCK So to speak.

FIRST TOURIST D'you think they might still have something there?

ROSENSTOCK They always have something.

FIRST TOURIST Well, let's go and see if we can pluck the Alpenrose. (*To the other*) Up you get, my son.

SECOND TOURIST I'm not budging. Send me a stretcher when you've found something, Bogenheimer... Or a mule. (*He adjusts his position and soon falls asleep*)

FIRST TOURIST (*to Rosenstock*) Make sure my colleague's not disturbed while he's asleep. (*As he leaves*) 'Wandering is the miller's joy!' (*Exit humming*)

> *A married couple enter. A bell-boy follows them with hand luggage.*
>
> *Rosenstock greets them.*

GENTLEMAN Is our room ready?

ROSENSTOCK Of course, Councillor. Room 57. (*Rings. Married couple cross over to the lift with the bell-boy and ascend*)

> *Paul Kreindl enters in an elegant travelling suit, wide cloak, green hat with tuft of chamois hair, red gloves, tennis racket inside its cover in his hand. Bell-boy with hand luggage follows him.*

PAUL Good day.

ROSENSTOCK How may I be of service, Herr von Kreindl?

PAUL Ah, what's this I see...!? You, my dear Rosenstock...?! So you're here now, are you? What is the Semmering Hotel* going to do without you?

ROSENSTOCK One keeps on climbing up and up, Herr von Kreindl. From a thousand... to fourteen hundred metres...

PAUL So do you have anything for me?

ROSENSTOCK Certainly. But only on the fourth floor unfortunately. If only you had telegraphed a day earlier, Herr von Kreindl...

PAUL On the sixth, for all I care. You do have a lift.

ROSENSTOCK When it isn't out of action... Well, Herr von Kreindl, you will find many of your acquaintances up here. Herr von Hofreiter has arrived, then there's Frau von Wahl with her son and daughter, then Doctor Mauer, and of course Herr Rhon the writer, who is here resting on his laurels.

PAUL (*after each name*) I know... I know... I know. (*After Rhon*) Ah, him too... (*To the bell-boy*) Take my things up, will you. (*As the boy tries to take his racket*) Ah no, I'll look after that. Oh by the way, my dear Rosenstock, not a word to Herr Hofreiter about my being here. Or in fact to anyone. I want to surprise them all, you see.

ROSENSTOCK Herr Hofreiter has been on a walk since yesterday.

PAUL A stiff one?

ROSENSTOCK Oh no. Herr Hofreiter gave up the more demanding walks—as everyone knows—after the accident on the Aignerturm seven years ago. The gentlemen have gone up to the Hofbrand hut. There are ladies in the party too. Frau Rhon and Fräulein von Wahl! Ah, here comes her mama.

> *Frau Wahl comes down the stairs in a rather too youthful summer dress.*

PAUL (*advancing to meet her*) How do you do, Frau Wahl.

FRAU WAHL Ah, nice to see you, my dear Paul. (*To Rosenstock*) Aren't they back yet?

ROSENSTOCK Not so far, Frau Wahl.

FRAU WAHL (*to Paul*) I'm in despair... well, not quite despair... but I'm seriously concerned... Erna has been on a walk since yesterday. She was supposed to be back for lunch, but it's five already, and I went all the way up to her room just now, right under the eaves... she's always doing things like that to me! And she still isn't back. I'm quite distraught.

PAUL She's with a larger party, I believe.

FRAU WAHL That's true. Gustl is with her of course and Friedrich Hofreiter, and then there's Doctor Mauer and Frau Rhon.

PAUL Well, nothing can have happened then. But please don't tell anyone I'm here, Frau Wahl. I mean, if everyone gets back while I'm upstairs changing. You see, I would really like to surprise them all. (*Plaintively*) I'm afraid I didn't quite succeed in your case.

FRAU WAHL You must pardon me today, my dear Paul, with all this excitement. What's the news from Baden, by the way? Will Genia be coming?

PAUL Frau Hofreiter? She didn't mention it to me. And I spoke to her just two days ago. We had a little gathering at the stadium, you know. I'll tell you all about it later, if I may. But first I must just go and spruce up the outer man. After a night on the train, and then six more hours by car... (*to Rosenstock*) What a dismal connection!

ROSENSTOCK In three years at the latest we will have a line up here, Herr von Kreindl. Our director will be going to Vienna to see the minister about it in the next few days.

PAUL A wise move. My things should be upstairs by now, shouldn't they, Rosenstock?

ROSENSTOCK Indeed, Herr von Kreindl.

PAUL Splendid. Well, see you soon, Frau Wahl, and remember, mum's the word. (*Goes up in the lift*)

ROSENSTOCK There is no need to get upset, Frau Wahl. The party even took a guide.

FRAU WAHL A guide to the Hofbrand hut? I didn't know about that. I must say, that does seem rather strange.

ROSENSTOCK It's only for the rucksacks. Someone has to do the carrying. And besides, your daughter is such an outstanding walker...

FRAU WAHL So was Bernhaupt...

ROSENSTOCK Yes... swift is Death's approach to man.* He grants him no reprieve...

FRAU WAHL I say—do you mind!

ROSENSTOCK Oh forgive me... that was not of course with reference to your daughter.

FRAU WAHL By the way, I left a book with you, Rosenstock, could you hand it me... it's bound in yellow... by Rhon... yes, that's the one... I'll sit over there and read for a while... If only I can concentrate.

ROSENSTOCK Oh, you will certainly find this book entertaining, Frau Wahl. Herr Rhon writes so adroitly.

Frau Wahl takes a seat at one of the tables.

DOCTOR MEYER (*who has been hovering near by with his folded map, now comes forward*) If I might ask, I notice Baedeker observes that this walk is fairly strenuous, so I wondered whether you would recommend two guides...

ROSENSTOCK Certainly Herr Doctor, you can have two guides if you wish.

SERKNITZ (*comes down the stairs. Tall, strong, casually dressed in a loden suit and outlandish shirt with tassels. To Rosenstock without taking any notice of Meyer*) Letters here yet?

ROSENSTOCK Not yet, Herr von Serknitz. In about half an hour.

SERKNITZ Confound it! The mail came long ago.

ROSENSTOCK But it's the sorting that takes time, Herr von Serknitz.

SERKNITZ The sorting! Set me to it, and I'll sort the whole delivery in fifteen minutes. If I took this long sorting back home in my office!—It's typical Austrian inefficiency. And then you complain about the lack of foreign tourists.

ROSENSTOCK We're not complaining, Herr von Serknitz. We're well over capacity.

SERKNITZ You don't deserve this region, I tell you.

ROSENSTOCK Ah, but we have it, Herr von Serknitz.

SERKNITZ And you can keep your aristocracy, as far as I'm concerned. I'm not going to be taken in by that charade. Anyway, I didn't come about the mail. I came about my laundry.

ROSENSTOCK I'm sorry, Herr Serknitz, I don't have anything to do with...

SERKNITZ I don't care whether you're responsible or someone else. The maid upstairs has referred me to the office, and I've been waiting three days now for my laundry.

ROSENSTOCK I'm really very sorry. By the way, here comes the hotel director.

SERKNITZ Not alone—as usual.

> *Doctor von Aigner comes in from outside with a very beautiful Spanish lady, from whom he now takes leave.*
> *The Spanish lady goes up in the lift.*
> *Doctor von Aigner, a man of over fifty, still very good looking. Elegant traditional Alpine costume with knee-length stockings, dark hair streaked with grey, goatee beard, monocle. Affable, with a touch of affectation. No hat.*

SERKNITZ Herr Director...

AIGNER (*overwhelmingly polite*) I won't be a minute... (*To Rosenstock*) My dear Rosenstock. His Excellency Baron Wondra will be arriving tomorrow instead of Thursday, and as you know, he will be needing four rooms.

ROSENSTOCK Four rooms, for tomorrow, Herr Director... How am I to do that? I would have to... Forgive me, Herr Director, but I would have to murder people.

AIGNER Very well, my dear Rosenstock, but as discreetly as possible. (*To Serknitz, introducing himself*) Doctor von Aigner... How can I be of service?

SERKNITZ (*with some embarrassment, which he tries to conceal beneath an assumed self-confidence*) Serknitz... I have just... I wish to express my exasperation, or at the very least dissatisfaction,—(*breaking off*) In short, the service in your hotel is quite appalling.

AIGNER I should indeed be sorry. What is it you wish to complain about, Herr Serknitz?

SERKNITZ I can't get my laundry back. I've been urging them for the last three days. It's already causing me acute embarrassment.

AIGNER I can see that. But could you not consult the chambermaid...

SERKNITZ You are the director! I am asking you! It has always been my way to go straight to the top. I really don't enjoy appearing in this outfit in the company of your countesses and dollar princesses.

AIGNER Excuse me, Herr Serknitz, there is no compulsory dress code here.

SERKNITZ Not compulsory!... Do you think I don't notice how differently your various guests are treated?

AIGNER Oh...

SERKNITZ I don't mind telling you to your face, Herr Director, if a Lord Chamberlain* or an Excellency Baron Bülow* were standing here complaining, instead of plain Herr Serknitz from Breslau, you would adopt a very different tone. Yes indeed, Herr Director. In fact it would not be inappropriate if you were to put a placard up outside announcing: In this hotel you must be a baron, a banker or an American at least to qualify as human.

AIGNER That would scarcely correspond to the truth, Herr Serknitz.

SERKNITZ Do you think because I didn't drive up here in a motor car, I don't have a right to the same respect as some trust magnate or minister of state? No man alive can presume to treat me with disdain. Whether he wears a monocle or not.

AIGNER (*still calmly*) If, Herr Serknitz, you were to insult anything regarding my personal deportment, I would of course be at your disposal in whatever way you chose.

SERKNITZ Haha! So now I'm supposed to fight you in a duel? That's the very latest. You should get that patented. One complains that one's shirts and—other items haven't been delivered, and has the privilege of being shot dead for one's pains. Look, Herr Director, if you think this is going to do anything to enhance the reputation of your hotel, you are very much mistaken. I would leave this ridiculous dump, this Eldorado of snobs, crooks and stock exchange Jews, by the outgoing mail coach if I intended to make you a present of my laundry. Meanwhile, I'll go and see if it's turned up! Good day to you, Director.

AIGNER Good day, Herr Serknitz. (*Goes over to Frau Wahl, whom he has already acknowledged with a nod during this conversation*) How are you, dear lady.

FRAU WAHL I admire your patience, Herr Director.

AIGNER It's something one learns.

FRAU WAHL I wish I had your self-control.

AIGNER Why, what's the matter?

FRAU WAHL I'm extremely agitated. Our party still hasn't returned.

AIGNER Absolutely no cause for alarm... Everyone returns from the Hofbrand hut. That's just an afternoon stroll... May I? (*He sits down*)

FRAU WAHL Need you ask? It's always gratifying when you're not otherwise engaged,... exotically... erotically...

AIGNER Exotically... erotically...? Surely those are not your words, dear lady. You couldn't be so naughty, lovely lady.

FRAU WAHL True... they are from Rhon.

AIGNER Yes... I thought as much... What a poet, this Herr Rhon... ah well... Yet another charming brooch, I see! Peasant baroque! Really splendid.

FRAU WAHL Yes, quite pretty, isn't it? And not at all expensive. Though it wasn't exactly cheap either. Swatek in Salzburg always puts things aside for me. He knows my taste by now.

ALBERT RHON (*a moderately tall, stout gentleman, with dark, greying, somewhat untidy hair, in a comfortable summer suit, comes down the stairs*) Nice to see you, Frau Wahl. Good evening, Herr Director. Well, have our mountaineers got back yet?

FRAU WAHL What was that? Oh, no!

RHON They'll be here soon enough... they may have had rather an austere breakfast... My wife at any rate.

A BEAUTIFUL ENGLISH LADY (*approaches, and addresses Aigner in an English accent*) Could I have a word with you, Herr Director?

AIGNER Certainly... (*Goes over to her, then together they withdraw*)

RHON (*to Frau Wahl*) Do you know who that is? His latest conquest.

FRAU WAHL Her? But yesterday you pointed out a different woman.

RHON Yesterday it was a different woman. What a man! Have you any idea what havoc he has caused in these parts? Don't tell me you haven't noticed the head waiter's resemblance to Aigner?

FRAU WAHL Really? Do you think the head waiter might be his son?

RHON Or at the very least his nephew. He's such a libertine that— even his nephews look like him.

FRAU WAHL How can you be in the mood for making jokes! They

were supposed to be back for lunch and it's now half past five. I
reproach myself for not having gone with them.

RHON That would have been a mistake. How could you have assisted
with the rescue? We would have just had one more victim to
lament.

FRAU WAHL I find your jokes quite gruesome. You seem to forget
your wife is with them too. How can anyone let his wife go
wandering off so long?

RHON As you know, Frau von Wahl, I don't enjoy mountain climbing.
I lack the talent for—things manual, so to speak. Furthermore, I
am writing a new tragedy.

Aigner has again come forward.

RHON They ought to be back by now though. At least, my wife
should. I've grown accustomed to being welcomed by her when I
step back into mundane existence. We spend the time between the
acts together.

AIGNER Usually at the buffet.

RHON (*slapping him on the back, good-humouredly*) Very true, Director.
Tell me, by the way, is the walk up to the Hofbrand hut really that
safe?

AIGNER As I said earlier: an afternoon stroll. I could still even manage
the Hofbrand hut myself.

FRAU WAHL Why didn't you go with them, Herr Director? It would
have been a real comfort.

AIGNER Unfortunately I have things to do here too, as you saw earlier,
Frau Wahl. And then, as I couldn't get much further than the
Hofbrand hut, I prefer—not even to go as far as that.

RHON That's all very well. But listen, Herr Director, it just occurs to
me, isn't the hut the starting point for climbing your mountain?
The Aignerturm, I mean?

AIGNER Yes, it was mine once! Now it no longer belongs to me... Nor
to anyone else of course.

RHON It must feel quite strange to sit at the foot of a peak one was the
first to scale, and is now no longer up to... Here one might venture
an analogy... which however I had better not pursue. Incidentally,
I'm convinced you are only imagining you can't get up there any
longer, Herr Director. I have been thinking about you and suspect
that you may in fact be hypochondriac.

AIGNER Would you mind if we dropped the subject, Herr Rhon?

Frau Wahl gives a faint scream.

RHON Whatever's the matter, Frau Wahl?

FRAU WAHL Perhaps they went up the Aignerturm.

RHON (*also a little startled*) What makes you think that?

FRAU WAHL It stands to reason. Otherwise they would have been back by now. They took a guide with them as well. There can be no doubt. You are in on the plot, Herr Director, you might as well admit it.

AIGNER I swear that neither by word nor...

RHON There's one of the guides.

FRAU WAHL Where? Ah, that's Penn. Perhaps he was the one...

> *The guide Penn is standing with the Head Porter.*
> *Rhon and Frau Wahl rush over to him.*

FRAU WAHL Were you with the Hofreiter party, Penn?...

PENN Certainly. (*A short volley of rapid questions follows*)

FRAU WAHL Where is my daughter?

RHON Where is my wife?

FRAU WAHL Well, say something.

RHON When did you get back?

FRAU WAHL Where are the others? How come you're alone? What's happened...?

PENN (*smiling*) They're all back safe and sound, Frau Wahl. The young Fräulein handled herself very well.

FRAU WAHL What do you mean?

RHON Where were you?

PENN We were up on the Aignerturm.

FRAU WAHL (*with a faint cry*) I was right! I was right! How frightful.

AIGNER But Frau Wahl, since they are all back safely...

RHON Did my wife go up the Aignerturm as well? Surely that's impossible?

PENN No, the stout one didn't come with us, just Fräulein Erna, Hofreiter and Doctor Mauer.

RHON And what about my wife?

FRAU WAHL And what about my son?

PENN They waited for us in the hut till we got back.

FRAU WAHL But where are they now?

PENN They all went in through the public bar, so they wouldn't attract notice.

FRAU WAHL I must go upstairs at once, I must see Erna. (*To Aigner*) O you... (*goes across to the lift; as it is on another floor she rings for it frantically. To Aigner*) Why does your lift always have to wait on the fourth floor? That's another of the mysteries of your hotel. (*To Rhon*) Well, are you coming?

RHON I can wait.

> *The lift descends with the bell-boy.*

RHON (*aside to Frau Wahl*) Take a look at the bell-boy. A striking resemblance—!

FRAU WAHL To whom?

RHON You know... (*indicates Aigner*)

FRAU WAHL One of his sons too...?

RHON Probably a grandson.

FRAU WAHL Ah God, you and your... (*goes up in the lift*)

AIGNER (*to Penn*) So you really went up the Aignerturm?

PENN Yes, Herr Director. It wasn't easy.

AIGNER I can believe it.

PENN You know, Herr Director, I expected that bad weather last week might mean trouble. We had to duck a few times, I can tell you. And then the last hundred metres, the devil only knows... what's been happening up there since last year. Then one could still find a footing and places to secure the rope, but this time there was nothing for it but to fly...

AIGNER But it must have been beautiful up there.

PENN As you know yourself, Herr Director. It's always beautiful up there. Especially on the Aignerturm.

> *Doctor Meyer with map fully unfolded, hesitantly approaches the Head Porter.*

ROSENSTOCK Here's a guide for you, Doctor.

MEYER Many thanks. (*Approaches Penn*) If I might ask...

GUSTL WAHL (*enters wearing an elegant summer suit, speaks with a certain affected sleepiness, but occasionally becomes deliberately insinuating. Always with a touch of humour*) Greetings, Herr Director. Good evening, Laureate Rhon. I must congratulate you on your wife. She plays an excellent game of dominoes.

RHON You've been playing dominoes with her? But why weren't you up on the Aignerturm? A seasoned climber like yourself. You were in the Himalayas last year, weren't you...

GUSTL I gave up serious climbing long ago, now I merely walk from one hut to the next. Also very pleasant.

RHON And so you sat playing dominoes the whole time? While the others were in mortal danger? It doesn't surprise me of my wife. Women have no imagination. But you...

GUSTL We didn't play the whole time. I tried at first to have a discussion with your wife.

RHON About Buddhist philosophy, no doubt.

GUSTL For the most part.

RHON My wife isn't interested in Buddha.

GUSTL Yes, I got that impression too. So that's why we played dominoes instead. And in the open air, if you please! On a glorious meadow strewn with rarest Alpine plants!

RHON Since when have they had a set of dominoes up there?

GUSTL There are always some around. This time they happened to be in my rucksack. I never leave home for very long without taking a set of dominoes with me.

AIGNER Curious taste.

GUSTL It's the hardest game there is. Harder than chess. Do you know the number of possible combinations in the game?

RHON How should I know?

GUSTL But I do... I've spent years studying the philosophy of games.

RHON And weren't you terribly anxious?

GUSTL But whatever for? Losing is nothing to me.

RHON With your sister suspended between heaven and earth...

GUSTL I can assure you, nothing is going to happen to my sister, she will live to be eighty-four years old.

RHON How can you be so sure of that?

GUSTL I consulted her horoscope. She was born under the sign of Scorpio... she can risk walking up a glacier at eighty-three, if it takes her fancy.

RHON You're not going to persuade me you believe such things?

GUSTL Why not?—I can even recognize at a glance what sign most people were born under...

FRAU RHON (*enters. A short, plump, rather pretty woman, she throws herself on her husband's neck*) I'm back again.

GUSTL (*to Aigner*) Take a look at Frau Rhon, for example...

AIGNER Well—?

GUSTL Unmistakably a Capricorn!...

RHON Well, don't go into it, we are not alone.

AIGNER Don't mind me.

RHON (*coolly*) So, did you enjoy yourself, my dear?

FRAU RHON It was marvellous.

RHON I hear you've been playing dominoes.

FRAU RHON Are you angry? I did win after all.

RHON Well I prefer that to your climbing all over the place.

FRAU RHON You know, I did consider going for a moment. But the others were not keen to take me.

RHON Look, the last thing I need is for you to be getting such ideas into your head. I have no desire to spoil the bliss of being alone by worrying about you. When you are not with me, I don't even want to think about you.

GUSTL She wasn't thinking about you either, Laureate Rhon, I can assure you. One of these days you won't be so lucky. I just happened not to be your wife's type.

RHON Tell me, Gustl, why are you so tactless?

GUSTL Didn't you know, I trade on it? And anyway,—what is tact! A third-rate virtue. Even the word itself is fairly recent. It's not found in Latin, or in Greek, or—very significantly—Sanskrit.

FRAU RHON (*to Rhon*) And what have you been up to all this time? Have you made any progress?

RHON End of Act Three, where, deeply moved, the public storm into the restaurant...

FRAU RHON So I've just got back in time.

RHON Yes, except that this time the intermission won't last very long. From tomorrow morning, I shall be shutting myself away again and keeping out of sight. If you don't have any objections, I shall even be dining at the bar instead of in the restaurant, so that the unwelcome sight of stupid faces doesn't interrupt my mood. Then you can play dominoes again.

GUSTL File for a divorce, dear lady. How can anyone marry a poet? They're all monsters. It was much better in earlier times, when one retained a poet like a slave or barber. Incidentally, similar arrangements still exist in the Azores today. But giving poets a free rein to do just as they please, that's all nonsense.

FRIEDRICH (*enters in an elegant walking outfit*) Good evening, everybody, hail to the poet's lovely wife. What, you've changed already? That was quick.

AIGNER (*standing next to the Head Porter*) Good evening, Hofreiter.

FRIEDRICH Good evening, Herr Director. (*To Rosenstock*) Nothing there for me? No telegrams? No letters? Strange. (*To Aigner*) Well, I can report that there's not the slightest change up there, at least not at the summit. Conditions on the track have admittedly got a little worse. Or is it only that one's getting older? As things are, one is risking life and limb going up there,—but if the face continues to erode, it will be suicidal.

AIGNER Yes, Penn told me the same thing.

FRIEDRICH You know, Aigner, how when one comes into that gully, about three hundred metres from the summit...

AIGNER (*interrupts him*) Please don't go into it. The past is over and done with. How did the young lady cope with everything?

FRIEDRICH Erna? Just splendidly.

AIGNER I must say, though... taking her up there with you...

FRIEDRICH She took us up with her. I never intended to climb the Aignerturm again. Where is Mauer, by the way?

AIGNER I haven't seen him yet.

RHON Tell me, Herr Hofreiter, what were your feelings when you went past the fateful spot?

FRIEDRICH The fateful spot? My God, seven years is a long time. I have almost forgotten things that happened much more recently. I can forget very quickly... when I want to.

RHON Ah well... people probably often go past a place where someone next to them has fallen, just that they are not always aware of it. Don't you agree—?

FRIEDRICH If you only knew how little I am in the mood for philosophizing, Laureate Rhon...

PAUL KREINDL (*comes rapidly down the stairs*) You must be surprised to see me, Herr Hofreiter.

FRIEDRICH (*rather indifferently*) Ah—Paul? How are you?

PAUL Good day, Herr Rhon. I did once have the pleasure... Well, before I go any further, I have a host of greetings to pass on. First from your dear wife, next from Lieutenant Stanzides, then from the Natters, also from Frau Meinhold-Aigner and the young Herr von Aigner...

FRIEDRICH Allow me to introduce you... Herr Paul Kreindl— Director von Aigner.

PAUL Ah... very pleased to... (*He stops, embarrassed, then recovering, to Aigner*) I have the pleasure of being acquainted with your son.

AIGNER (*calmly*) I unfortunately do not.

FRIEDRICH Well, what's the news from Baden? (*Calmly*) You don't happen to know—whether my wife is coming, by any chance?

PAUL I regret to say she didn't mention anything to me.

FRIEDRICH Is everyone having a good time?

PAUL A fabulous time! We all went to the stadium together the other day. Your wife will no doubt have written to you about it.

FRIEDRICH Yes, of course.

PAUL And beforehand we gathered on the meadow near the house, where a sort of folk festival was taking place. We mingled with the people too. We even joined in the dancing.

FRIEDRICH My wife too?

PAUL Yes, naturally, with Herr Otto... And there was quite a to-do in the stadium, when the actors suddenly noticed the famous Frau Meinhold in our box. From then on they played only to us.

RHON What were they playing?

PAUL I'm sorry, I wasn't paying much attention to the play.

RHON And these are the people one pours out one's life's blood for!

PAUL (*to Rhon*) Ah, isn't that your dear wife? Excuse me, gentlemen.
  (*Goes over to Frau Rhon and Gustl, who are sitting at a table*)
      Rhon joins them.
      Friedrich, Aigner.
      Friedrich lights a cigarette and sits down.

AIGNER I had no idea my erstwhile family spent so much time at your villa?

FRIEDRICH Yes, we see each other occasionally. Your former spouse has become particularly friendly with my wife. And Otto and I sometimes play a round of tennis. He plays extremely well. Altogether—you may be congratulated on your son. A great future is predicted for him. He is apparently quite a favourite with his superiors. Perhaps he will become the future Admiral of Austria.

AIGNER You are talking about a young man who is a stranger to me.

FRIEDRICH Tell me though, Aigner, do you really not have the slightest yearning to see him again?

AIGNER See him again? At most one might say, get to know him. Because the midshipman of today and the boy I kissed goodbye some twenty years ago no longer have anything in common, either outwardly or inwardly.

FRIEDRICH So, no yearning to see him again—but what about interest in getting to know him—? Now would be a splendid opportunity. I believe you have business in Vienna shortly—?

AIGNER Yes, I have to see the minister. As you know, we want to build a railway. A direct line up here via Atzwang Völs. You must admit there's room to build another three hotels here.

FRIEDRICH I'll make you a proposal, Aigner. Why not stay with us in Baden? Our villa has more than enough room. There's a pleasant guest room. Very cosy in fact. It's only occasionally visited by the ghosts of dear departed friends who once spent the night there. That wouldn't bother you, would it?

AIGNER No, I have no objections to the ghosts of the deceased. But living ghosts I find more disturbing.

FRIEDRICH You know, Aigner, it would be damned good fun actually, getting you and your son acquainted. It could be so congenially arranged—in our garden, us all playing tennis, you suddenly appearing... the distinguished stranger...

AIGNER Thank you, my dear Hofreiter.—I won't say I would try to avoid a chance encounter, but—as to an arranged meeting,—that would smack unpleasantly of sentimentality.

FRIEDRICH (*casually*) Why is that...?

AIGNER You also forget I'd have to meet my former spouse on the occasion—and I would prefer to avoid that.

FRIEDRICH Whatever you think best.

> *Pause.*

AIGNER Strange coincidences do sometimes happen though...

FRIEDRICH How do you mean?

AIGNER Curious how it was just today... that you started talking to me about my son... right after your descent...

FRIEDRICH It simply happened that way... If Paul Kreindl had not begun...

AIGNER Do you know when I undertook the first ascent of the mountain you've just come down from?—It was very shortly after I had... separated from my wife.

FRIEDRICH Are you suggesting—some connection?

AIGNER Up to a point... I don't want to imply that I was actively seeking death—that could have been more easily accomplished— but at the time I didn't feel I had very much to live for. Perhaps too, I wanted to provoke God's judgement in some way.

FRIEDRICH Look, if every man in that predicament were to go mountain climbing... the situation in the Dolomites would present a ridiculous spectacle. After all, your conduct was no worse than that of many others.

AIGNER It always depends on how the other party reacts with a thing like that... My wife did love me very much.

FRIEDRICH That ought to be one more reason why you should not remain unreconciled.

AIGNER Possibly. But I too loved her dearly. That's the problem!— Boundlessly... more than anyone before or... well, we won't go into that. Otherwise things could certainly have been patched up. But it was precisely the fact that I loved her so much—and yet was capable of betraying her... that made her so furious not only with me but with the entire world. Now there was no longer any certainty on earth... any possibility of trust, if you see what I'm saying, Hofreiter—?—It wasn't so much that it had happened that drove her from me, but that it should have been possible at all.

And I couldn't help but understand. I could even have predicted it.

FRIEDRICH Well, then I have to ask, why...

AIGNER Why did I betray her—?... You may well ask. Hasn't it struck you yet, what complicated creatures we human beings are deep down? There is room for so many conflicting things in us at once—! Love and deceit... faithfulness and infidelity... reverence for one woman and desire for another or for several others. We try to create order within ourselves as best we can, but that order is merely something artificially imposed... The natural state... is chaos. Yes— my good Hofreiter, the soul... is a vast domain, as a poet* once expressed it... Or perhaps it was a hotel director.

FRIEDRICH The hotel director is not far off the mark... certainly. (*Pause*) So basically, the only calamity was that your wife found out. Otherwise you would perhaps be the happiest of married couples to this day.

AIGNER A calamity—indeed...!—

FRIEDRICH How did she find out about it then?

AIGNER ... How? In the simplest way in the world... I confessed...

FRIEDRICH What—? You told her—?

AIGNER Yes. I felt I owed it to her—precisely because I worshipped her. To her and to myself. I would have felt rather a coward if I had kept quiet about it. One shouldn't make things too easy for oneself. Wouldn't you agree...?

FRIEDRICH That was a fairly lofty notion, certainly—if it wasn't merely a form of affectation. Or refinement... Or complacency...

AIGNER Or all of them together, which would also be quite possible. Because the soul—and so on.

FRIEDRICH And despite your phenomenal integrity—and despite all her love, your wife could not bring herself to—

AIGNER For God's sake don't say 'forgive'. Words like that simply don't apply in this case. Nor was there ever any grand scene between us, or anything like that. It was simply all over, my good Hofreiter, finished irretrievably... We both felt so at once. It had to be the end.

FRIEDRICH Had to—?

AIGNER Yes. Well, better let the—living rest. The dead usually look after that without assistance.

FRAU WAHL (*comes down from upstairs*) Ah, there he is—!

FRIEDRICH Hello, Mama Wahl.

FRAU WAHL I shall never speak to you again, Friedrich. What if she had fallen? What would you say then? Could you ever have looked me in the eye again? I'm also finished with Doctor Mauer. Where is he anyway? It's all quite monstrous, I could take the pair of you and...

FRIEDRICH But Mama Wahl, Erna would have gone up without us.

FRAU WAHL You should have tied her down.

FRIEDRICH She was tied, Mama Wahl. So were we all. To the same rope.

FRAU WAHL Give a fool enough rope, I say.

ERNA (*enters in a white summer dress*) Good evening, everyone.

AIGNER Erna, how radiant you look. (*He takes her by both hands and kisses her forehead*) With your permission.

FRIEDRICH Like the older Liszt greeting his young piano pupils.

ERNA (*kisses Aigner's hand*) Or like a very young piano pupil greeting Liszt when in his prime.

AIGNER My dear Erna...

FRAU WAHL And now this on top of everything.

ERNA It was the most beautiful moment I have experienced in my life, Herr von Aigner.

AIGNER Yes of course, up there!... And yet I hope Erna, you will experience more beautiful ones still.

ERNA I think that's very unlikely. Perhaps one might experience life as equally beautiful again. But the sense of at the same time being utterly indifferent to death surely comes only on such rare occasions. And that... is something truly wonderful!... (*Meanwhile the post has arrived. Rosenstock sorts the letters, hotel guests appear, receive their correspondence, etc.*)

PAUL Allow me, Fräulein Erna, too to lay my admiration at your feet.

ERNA Hello, Paul, how are you?

PAUL Well, I'll be damned—pardon me... is nobody here surprised to see me?

FRIEDRICH (*sitting down*) Well, Paul, it's even more surprising that any of us are here at all.

> Aigner stands a little apart with a beautiful Frenchwoman.

RHON (*to Frau Wahl*) You see, Frau Wahl, that's the one for tomorrow. He's stocking up...

ERNA (*to Frau Wahl, who has just received her mail from Rosenstock*) Well, Mama...?

FRAU WAHL From home. Ah, here's a card from your wife. (*To Friedrich*) She sends you her greetings, Friedrich.

FRIEDRICH Does she say—she's coming?

ROSENSTOCK There are some letters here for you as well, Herr Hofreiter.

FRIEDRICH (*stands up*) Really? Ah, here's one from Genia too.

Gustl presses letters to his forehead.

FRAU RHON What are you doing?

GUSTL I don't bother to read letters any more. I simply place them on my forehead and can tell what's in them.

FRAU WAHL (*to Friedrich*) Will she be coming?

FRIEDRICH No, she says Percy has postponed his return, he's been invited to stay with friends in Richmond and will be there another week. The young rascal,—so he has friends in Richmond already.

RHON (*sits and reads his correspondence*) Ha...

FRAU RHON What is it?

RHON It's unbelievable. These questionnaires!—I must say, people are becoming more and more inquisitive. Once they were content to ask whether one preferred eating macaroni to peach compote, or whether Wagner should be abridged or performed in full. But the things they want to know about one now... Listen to this a moment, Hofreiter.

Friedrich sits at the neighbouring table and looks through his mail.

RHON Here's a woman's magazine asking: (*a*) at what age one first experienced the joys of love, (*b*) whether one has ever felt any perverted inclinations.

AIGNER (*to Hofreiter*) I've just received an enquiry about whether the lake is suitable for swimming.

RHON When the water's five degrees... brr!—

AIGNER Now if that could be developed—it would mean the end of Switzerland...

RHON Look, I have an idea. You'd have to... let me in on the profits of course. You've got enormous water power here, with all those waterfalls cascading down the mountains... so what if you were to have your lake electrically heated?

Aigner laughs.

RHON You laugh... of course! But if I knew anything about technical matters—I would build the plant for you myself... I can see it all so clearly in my mind's eye! I just lack the manual skills. If I had those too, I don't think I'd ever have touched a pen.

FRIEDRICH I often wonder whether it isn't usually some inner deficiency in writers... that makes them become writers—?

RHON How do you mean—?

FRIEDRICH I imagine many writers are born criminals—only without the necessary courage—or libertines, who shy away from the expense...

RHON And shall I tell you what light bulb manufacturers are usually, Herr Hofreiter?... Just light bulb manufacturers—that's all.

FRIEDRICH If only that were true...

> *A bell-boy brings Friedrich a letter.*
> *Friedrich opens it, smiles and bites his lip.*
> *Erna registers this.*

FRAU WAHL Well, I must go and change, adieu little poet's wife, adieu great poet.

> *Gustl opening one of his letters.*

FRAU RHON But you're opening it.

GUSTL That's just to check. Sometimes people write the wrong thing, you see.

> *Frau Rhon and Gustl withdraw then exeunt. Aigner moves across*
> *to Rosenstock, then exit. Rhon also withdraws. The lobby becomes*
> *almost empty.*

ERNA (*looking over Friedrich's shoulder*) Love letters?

FRIEDRICH Guess from who? From Mauer...

ERNA Oh...

FRIEDRICH He's just received an urgent telegram from Vienna. Had to leave at once... Has already left in fact... I'm to pass on his regards to everyone.

ERNA I was expecting something like that.

FRIEDRICH So was I. First his high spirits over supper in the hut last night! And then his moodiness during our climb. On the walk back he didn't say a word... Well, Erna, one shouldn't embrace in an open meadow fifty yards from a hut with twenty windows.

ERNA Do you think he saw us?

FRIEDRICH Probably.

ERNA And do you think he would not have left, if that hadn't happened in the meadow? Then you are mistaken. We'd only have had to look at one another and he'd have noticed, just like all the others...

FRIEDRICH What are the others supposed to notice?

ERNA How things are between us.

FRIEDRICH But Erna, how can people...

ERNA Perhaps there's a sort of aura round our heads.

> *Friedrich laughs*

ERNA Yes, it must be something like that. I've often thought so.
Otherwise how does everyone know these things at once...

FRIEDRICH I should have left, Erna.

ERNA Now that would have been clever!!

FRIEDRICH You shouldn't be such a flirt, Erna.

ERNA I'm really not, you know.

FRIEDRICH What are you, then?

ERNA I am the way I am.

FRIEDRICH There you have the advantage over me. I'm no longer the
man I was. I've been mad ever since that kiss yesterday, mad I tell
you. Come closer, Erna. (*Takes her hand*) Sit down here opposite
me.

ERNA How can you be so crude...!

FRIEDRICH Erna, I didn't sleep a wink last night.

ERNA I'm sorry to hear it. I slept wonderfully.

FRIEDRICH It usually happens to me anyway, in that stuffy hut.

ERNA You should have done what I did. I took my rug out into the
meadow—our meadow, and lay down in the open.

FRIEDRICH Didn't you freeze?

ERNA No. I fetched your coat from the dining room and covered
myself with that.

FRIEDRICH So you're using witches' arts as well? Your spell would
work even without them, Erna.

ERNA So I had a wonderful sleep under the stars from ten till three,
and only then returned to the room and fat Frau Rhon.

FRIEDRICH Erna, Erna! I am capable of doing something insanely
stupid. I suddenly understand all the nonsense I once made fun of.
I understand promenading and serenading under windows.
(*Gestures*) I understand how one can draw a knife and attack a rival,
or leap into the abyss from unrequited love.

ERNA Why do you talk of unrequited love?

FRIEDRICH (*seriously*) Why should I delude myself, Erna! Our entire
outing yesterday... the moment on the peak, the squeezing hands,
the illusion of togetherness, the overwhelming sense of happiness,
was nothing more than a kind of euphoria,—of mountain intoxication. At least in your case. The effect of the three thousand metre
altitude, the rarefied air, the danger. But my personal role in your
whole mood was minimal.

ERNA Why do you say that? I've loved you since I was seven years old.
Admittedly with interruptions. But lately it has become much
worse again. I'm serious. Especially over the last two days—up

there—and now!... Ah God, Friedrich, how I long to run my fingers through your hair.

FRIEDRICH Watch what you're doing there. That really isn't necessary. Listen, Erna—I want to ask you something.

ERNA Go on then, ask.

FRIEDRICH Well—What would you say to... Listen to me carefully!— I'm now completely rational again. Well Erna, you know about— my marriage, I don't have to tell you any more on that score. I was largely to blame of course. Anyway—we are not really that compatible, Genia and I. Especially since that strange business over Korsakov I told you about... Ah God, why am I beating about the bush like this. I want to get a divorce from Genia... and to marry you, Erna.

> *Erna laughs.*

FRIEDRICH But why...?

ERNA Because earlier you said you were capable of doing something insanely stupid.

FRIEDRICH It might not be so stupid, if one accepted it for what it is. I know, Erna, that you won't love me eternally.

ERNA But you will me, I suppose!!

FRIEDRICH More likely... Besides, what is eternity! Next year one climbs another peak, and one's sense of communing with eternity is over. Or else it starts in earnest. But I won't get onto that! All I know with absolute certainty is that I can't exist without you. I'm going to die of yearning for you, I won't be able to think, or work or settle to anything sensible at all, until you... until I hold you in my arms, Erna.

ERNA Why didn't you pick up your coat last night?...

FRIEDRICH I beg you, Erna, don't play games with me. I am being honest enough with you. Just say no, and there the matter will end. I can still catch up with Mauer. I've no wish to be made ridiculous. Will you be my wife?

ERNA Wife?—No.

FRIEDRICH Very well.

ERNA Later perhaps.

FRIEDRICH Later—?

ERNA Finish reading your mail.

FRIEDRICH What for? The factory can go to blazes, for all I care. Everything can go to blazes. What's that supposed to mean: later! Life isn't all that long. I can't agree to a reprieve. A kiss like yesterday's commits you. Either to an immediate parting or to an unconditional yes. I cannot wait. I won't. Say no, and I shall leave today.

ERNA I'm not playing games with you. I know what our kiss commits me to.

FRIEDRICH Erna...

ERNA Surely you've always known that I belong to you?

FRIEDRICH Erna... Erna!

> *A gong sounds.*
> *The tourist who fell asleep at the beginning of the act wakes from a dream, gets up, shouts, positively screams and rushes about the stage, eventually making an exit.*
> *Frau Wahl comes down stairs.*

AIGNER (*joins her*) Ah, now that's a buckle I've not seen before! Charming...

FRIEDRICH Well, we've chatted the time away very pleasantly. Now I don't even have time to change.

FRAU WAHL You are handsome enough as you are. Where is Doctor Mauer, by the way?

FRIEDRICH That reminds me, he sends his kind regards; he suddenly received a telegram and had to leave.

FRAU WAHL Doctor Mauer a telegram? That is very... You are not trying to tell me something, are you? He's had a fall!... He's dead!

FRIEDRICH Now listen, Mama Wahl, do you really think we'd be sitting at our ease here if...

FRAU WAHL Well, one never knows with you people.

FRIEDRICH At least I would have worn black gloves.

SERKNITZ (*enters in tails and a white tie, goes across to Aigner*) Your humble servant, Herr Director. My laundry was returned, and I took the liberty of donning a few glad rags in keeping with the high tone of your hotel.

AIGNER You look positively seductive, Herr von Serknitz.

> *Serknitz goes into the dining room.*
> *Frau Wahl and Aigner follow.*
> *Frau Rhon and Gustl, Rhon, Meyer and various others come down the steps and head for the dining room.*
> *Erna and Friedrich together.*

FRIEDRICH (*aloud*) Come along, Erna. (*Softly*) Remember what you said just now?

ERNA Yes.

FRIEDRICH Then it will be our nuptial dinner they serve up to us in there today.

ERNA And nobody, thank God, will drink a toast to us.

FRIEDRICH And you'll be mine.

ERNA Yes.

FRIEDRICH Erna, consider very carefully what you're saying... If your door is locked tonight, I shall beat it down and that'll be the end of both of us.

ERNA Of course it won't be the end of us.

FRIEDRICH Erna...!

ERNA And I expect there will be even more beautiful moments than on the Aignerturm.

FRIEDRICH Erna...

ERNA (*in a tone of complete sincerity*) I love you!—(*They go into the dining room*)

      Curtain.

Act Four

Setting as in Act Two.—Summer afternoon.
Under the walnut tree. Frau Natter's two children, a nine-year-old girl and a seven-year-old boy, with their English governess who is showing them pictures in a book.
Emerging gradually from the house come Genia, Natter, Frau Wahl, Demeter Stanzides, Gustl, Paul, Erna, Otto and Frau Adele Natter.

NATTER The dinner in honour of our worthy host's return was excellent. Just a pity he wasn't there himself.

GENIA He must have been held up at the factory.

NATTER No wonder, after being away three weeks.

FRAU WAHL Didn't you ring him at the office, Genia?

GENIA I didn't think there was any need to, because after his telegram from Innsbruck yesterday I was sure he would be here before mid-day. (*She is now over with the children*) D'you like the pictures, children?...

CHILDREN Oh yes.

GENIA You must ask your Mama to bring you again next Sunday; Percy is sure to be here by then.

GUSTL Well children, I'm going to show you a marvellous game, which good Hindu children play beside the Ganges. Now pay attention... Oh, Fräulein, could you hand me your sunshade a moment. Thank you. Now we're going to draw three concentric circles in the sand, the outer circle one metre in diameter, the middle one three-quarters—the inner one half. (*To the others who are standing by laughing—Frau Wahl, Paul, Adele and Genia*) Believe it or not, Hindu children can do this with mathematical precision to within a millimetre. Now pay attention. Next we draw a line at a tangent to the outer circle, and a second line at right angles to the first and at a tangent to the middle circle. Then we draw a third line parallel to the first and at a tangent to the inner circle. That way of course, we form segments. Now in the outer-most segment to the east we place— (*He takes a little compass from his waistcoat pocket, and addresses the others who again laugh*) I always carry this with me. I can't understand how any self-respecting person can do without a compass. So the east is over here. In the outermost segment we put a little tortoise... in the one over to the west a scorpion, with its sting already drawn of course... So what shall we put here in Europe instead of a scorpion? (*The seven-year-old boy starts to cry*)

ADELE That's enough now, Gustl! (*In English*) Miss... will you— (*Switching to German*) oh, never mind! Would you mind taking the children to the meadow, Miss, there's more room to play there... (*To the children*) There nobody will tell you horrid stories about scorpions and tangents.

> *Exeunt the children and their governess.*
> *Demeter Stanzides has taken a seat on the little bench next to the entrance and picked up a paper lying there. Positioning of the cast from left to right: Stanzides on the bench to the left. Near him Frau Wahl and Otto. Then Paul and Erna. On the far right Gustl, Adele and Genia.*

STANZIDES Listen, listen! (*He reads*) 'According to a report in from the Lake Völs Hotel, a young lady from Vienna, Fräulein Erna Wahl, accompanied by two Viennese tourists, the manufacturer Hofreiter and the well-known physician Doctor Mauer, has scaled the Aignerturm, a notoriously dangerous peak...'

ERNA Come, Paul, let's have a game of tennis.

PAUL Most willingly. (*To Adele*) Frau Adele? Herr Otto?

ADELE I don't play straight after a meal.

OTTO I'd just like to have a cigarette, if you don't mind.

PAUL Very well. It looks like singles for today then. A singles tournament. Let's hope Herr Hofreiter gets back in time to play. We must finalize the ranking today as well...!

> *Exit with Erna.*

FRAU WAHL How does it go on?

STANZIDES (*continues reading*) 'A notoriously dangerous peak in the south-western Dolomites. Seven years ago on this same peak a young physician, Doctor Bernhaupt, fell to his...'

FRAU WAHL You see, Frau Genia, that's the kind of mountain they dragged my Erna up. I've never been so angry in my life as with that Doctor Mauer and your husband.

GUSTL In sheer terror of Mama, the two gentlemen packed up and left immediately.

GENIA (*smiling, with a glance at Erna*) Yes, a guilty conscience has made Friedrich quite restless, it seems. I've been receiving a card from somewhere different every day, Caprile, Pordoi and God only knows where else.

FRAU WAHL (*has picked up the paper and is leafing through it*) What paper is this anyway?

NATTER But surely, Frau Wahl, you're now quite proud of Fraulein Erna's fame...

FRAU WAHL Proud—me?

GENIA (*has come over to about centre stage, where Frau Wahl is standing*) What paper is it? I don't recognize it at all... how did it get here?

FRAU WAHL There's something underlined in red here.

STANZIDES Better not read what's been underlined in red in a rag like that.

FRAU WAHL That's very strange.

ADELE What is?

GUSTL What is?

GENIA What is? (*Spoken simultaneously*)

FRAU WAHL (*reads*) 'For some days a curious rumour has persisted in Vienna's social circles, which—with the usual disclaimers of course—we here report. It concerns the suicide of a world-famous pianist who created a sensation at the beginning of the summer, but then became shrouded in a darkness which even the popular phrase sudden mental derangement isn't quite sufficient to dispel. The aforementioned rumour claims that an American duel* was the cause of this suicide, and that the outcome of this duel was decided not, as normally, by a white and black ball, but by two whites and a red.'—Two whites and a red,—whatever can that mean?

Awkward pause.

GENIA (*calmly*) It was my husband who lost the game of billiards with Korsakov they are referring to. So if... there had been an American duel... Friedrich would have had to shoot himself—wouldn't he? (*Pause*)

STANZIDES It's incredible how one is virtually defenceless against such infamy. Especially as no names are given.

NATTER They will certainly be on their guard.

FRAU WAHL (*finally understands*) Ah, the game of billiards... of course, Frau Genia, you told us all about it. Your husband sent the cigars round to Korsakov's hotel the next morning... now I remember! I might have to be a witness in court!

GUSTL Mama, you won't need to be a witness. No one pays any attention to this sort of thing.

Adele and Stanzides are already on their way over to the tennis court and gradually disappear from the scene.

FRAU WAHL That really is... How does something like that get into the papers...? And why should Friedrich and Korsakov be...

> *Frau Wahl, Gustl, followed shortly by Natter, also move off towards the tennis court.*
> *Otto and Genia remain behind alone.*
> *Otto, Genia.*

GENIA Do you believe it?

OTTO That nonsensical duelling story? You can't be serious!

GENIA I mean, that the story did not get started without good reason—!... In a word, that I was—also Korsakov's mistress.

OTTO No. I don't believe it.

GENIA Why shouldn't you believe it... Because I deny it? That's no proof. If I were in your position... I'd believe it. (*Starts to go to the tennis court*)

OTTO I don't believe it, Genia. I swear, I don't believe a word of it. What's the point in even talking about it. Please don't go! Please!— Who knows whether we'll get another moment to ourselves. I have to go into town first thing tomorrow. I still have a host of things to do there... signing out... shopping... and I'm leaving for Pola by the night train.

GENIA (*gazes at him*) Tomorrow already...

OTTO How can I get news to you?

GENIA You can simply write to me. My letters are never opened. And if you want to be especially careful, write to me—as you are speaking to me now—as to a good friend.

OTTO That's asking a bit much. I don't think I could manage it.

GENIA There's one other alternative.—Not to write, not to write at all.

OTTO Genia...

GENIA Wouldn't that be wisest? We'll never see each other again anyway.

OTTO Genia! In two years I'll be back.

GENIA In two years!

OTTO If only you would trust me, Genia. I could be back even earlier. Much earlier. There are other opportunities open to me... You know that... I needn't go at all, Genia.

GENIA You must. Or rather, you ought to, that's a stronger command.

OTTO How am I to live—without you!

GENIA You will manage. It's been beautiful. Let us be content with that. Good luck on the journey, Otto, and good luck in your future life.

> *Pause.*

OTTO What will you do when I'm gone?

GENIA I don't know. For the moment at least, I don't know. What did we know a few weeks, or days ago!... One drifts. One drifts on and on, who knows where to.

OTTO How can you... Oh, I understand! You're talking like this now to make parting easier for me. Genia... don't you remember, Genia...

GENIA I remember. O yes, I remember well enough. (*Bitterly*) But forgetting starts in the same way.

OTTO Do you enjoy giving me pain?

GENIA Why do you think me better than I am? I'm no better than anybody else. Can't you see that? I lie and I'm a hypocrite. I put on this act in front of everyone,—in front of Herr Natter and Frau Wahl... in front of your mother no less than my own chambermaid. I play the respectable woman—and then at night I leave the window open for my lover. I write and tell my son to stay on with his friends,—this to my beloved son... just so that he doesn't interfere with my affair,—and then I write and tell my husband how Percy really wants to spend more time in Richmond, just so that he himself will stay away a little longer. And if he comes home today and shakes hands with you, I shall stand by, smile and no doubt exult over my own cunning. Do you find all this so very attractive? Do you think—I'm a woman one can trust—? Believe me, Otto, I am just like all the rest.

OTTO You're not like the rest at all. Nobody could blame you. You were free. You did not owe it to him to be faithful. No one would think the less of you.

GENIA No one...

OTTO No one——I'm aware what's going through your mind. No one. Not even my mother, were she to suspect.

GENIA So why didn't she come today?

OTTO Because she doesn't like large gatherings. That's the only reason. She doesn't suspect a thing. She was here only yesterday. Why would she have stayed away specifically today?

GENIA That's what I'm trying to tell you. She thought Friedrich would be back by now. And she'd have found it painful to see you, her son... she couldn't bear to see the three of us together... the husband... the wife... and the lover—that's what she was afraid of. And so she didn't come. Oh, I understand her. How well I understand her.

FRIEDRICH (*appears on the balcony and speaks at once*) Greetings, everybody.

>*Genia and Otto are almost under the balcony by the end of their conversation.*

GENIA (*unperturbed*) Friedrich!

OTTO Good day, Herr Hofreiter.

FRIEDRICH Good to see you, Otto.

GENIA (*airily*) How long have you been back?

FRIEDRICH I got in ten minutes ago. (*He shouts a greeting across to the tennis court, where they have noticed him*) Hello everyone, good evening—(*To Genia*) I've just been changing quickly. (*To Otto*) I'm glad I am in time to catch you. I was afraid you'd be back in Pola by now... or even on the seven seas.

OTTO I'm leaving tomorrow, Herr Hofreiter.

FRIEDRICH So... tomorrow...—? Well, I'll be down in a minute.

>*Disappears from the balcony.*
>*Otto and Genia cross the stage. What follows is spoken very rapidly.*

OTTO You can't stay here.

GENIA Be sensible, Otto.

OTTO Now I'm sure of it. You are not made to lie. You would give yourself away. Or even openly confess!

GENIA That's conceivable.

OTTO (*with sudden resolution*) So let me speak to him.

GENIA Don't be ridiculous!

OTTO Yes! It's really the only option. You feel the same way yourself, anything else would be unworthy, contemptible—

GENIA I'll tell him as soon as you've gone. Tomorrow. Perhaps even today...

OTTO And what will happen then?

GENIA Nothing, probably. And you must never come here again, never. Promise me... never... not even two years from now... never...

OTTO (*with dawning understanding*) You love him—you still love him, don't you!—You're slipping, slipping back to him

>*Enter Frau Wahl, Natter, Stanzides and Gustl from the tennis court. Erna and Paul play on.*

FRIEDRICH (*appears dressed for tennis*) Hello, Genia (*kisses her on the brow. He also greets the others. To Frau Wahl who refuses to shake hands*) Well, Mama Wahl, still angry with me?

FRAU WAHL I refuse to speak to you. I refuse to speak to Doctor Mauer as well.

FRIEDRICH Time will tell.

GENIA He hasn't put in an appearance at all so far.

FRIEDRICH Really?—He will be here today I hope, I wrote to him. There's no stopping Paul and Erna over there of course.

GENIA Tell me, though, when did you actually arrive back in Vienna?

FRIEDRICH Yesterday evening. Yes.—I would very much have liked to be out here for the meal, but unfortunately it was out of the question.

GENIA We had a formal dinner in your honour.

GUSTL The food was superb.

FRIEDRICH Really...? Perhaps, Genia, you would at least be good enough to have them bring me some black coffee. (*He sits down under the walnut tree and lights a cigarette*)

NATTER Weren't you away longer than intended, my dear Hofreiter?

FRIEDRICH Yes. (*Gives him a sharp look*) Yes. Aren't those your children, frolicking about in the meadow out there?

ADELE I thought Percy would be here by now. (*Stanzides and Frau Wahl have meanwhile moved further back*)

FRIEDRICH It's about time he finally arrived. Been getting himself invited to English country houses... the scamp!

GENIA I think he and my sister, Mary... may even surprise us today... because there has been no news from them for three days now.

> *Erna and Paul from the tennis court.*

PAUL Good evening, Herr Hofreiter.

ERNA Good evening, Friedrich. (*They shake hands*)

FRIEDRICH So, how is everything?

PAUL Well, Fräulein Erna has beaten me yet again.

FRIEDRICH So was the rest of the time up at Lake Völs enjoyable enough?—

ERNA Yes, just imagine, very enjoyable indeed, even without you. By the way, it wasn't very nice of you to disappear suddenly like that. Oh yes, thank you for the cards... you seem to have had quite a few more pleasant outings.

FRIEDRICH Your triumph was announced in the paper today, Erna.

FRAU WAHL We've already seen it.

FRIEDRICH Really, you've already—So that paper has reached here already?—an interesting paper—don't you think? (*Pause. The others' embarrassment amuses him*) It was splendid on the Aignerturm, by the way. Which reminds me, Otto. Where is he...? (*Otto is standing to one side with Frau Wahl*) I have greetings to pass on to you, well, not greetings exactly. I talked to your father, you see.

OTTO Your wife told me about it.

FRIEDRICH A pity you are leaving tomorrow. Your father is planning to come to Vienna in the next few days.

OTTO As you know, Herr Hofreiter, there has never been any relationship between my father and myself.

FRIEDRICH One could still develop. Should develop even. It doesn't seem quite right... your sailing off to sea for so long... without having seen your father... don't you think?

OTTO Yes, you may well be right—but it's now too late.

PAUL (*who has been standing with Erna and Frau Wahl, approaches*) Well, Midshipman, are you ready for our game? (*To Friedrich*) So far today, all our matches have been singles. I hope we can include you too, Herr Hofreiter. Herr Otto is leaving tomorrow, and we need to finalize the ranking for the tournament.

FRIEDRICH But of course. I'm at your disposal. Don't let me hold you two up.—I'll just finish my coffee.

> *Herr Natter, Stanzides, Genia and Gustl have already left a bit earlier—after Friedrich's first few words to Otto about Aigner—and Paul, Adele and Otto now follow.*
> *Erna, Friedrich.*
> *Erna has remained behind his chair.*

FRIEDRICH Oh Erna... (*still seated*)

ERNA I'm so happy you're back.

FRIEDRICH Seriously? (*He kisses her hand over the arm rest*) So am I.

ERNA And now tell me quickly the real reason why you left.

FRIEDRICH What's the matter with you, Erna. I've already told you. You were forewarned. If I'd stayed on, in a few days, my God—the very same day, the whole hotel would have known about us. That's just the way things are. Remember... The aura round our heads. We have certainly earned it.

ERNA So what, if they had seen it!

FRIEDRICH Look, my love... One should never let the world know about such things. The less so, the more one despises it. The world just doesn't understand. Or does so after its fashion—which is worse! You should be thankful I haven't 'compromised' you. Later you would have resented me for it.

ERNA Later?... I see!... Friedrich, I don't intend to marry.

FRIEDRICH Don't talk about the future, dearest. One should not try to make predictions, either for oneself or others. Not even a few minutes ahead! Believe me.

ERNA And do you suppose that if I were to fall in love with someone else after you—I could keep quiet about...

FRIEDRICH Of course you could. And you'd be right. That's all we deserve anyway, I can assure you...

ERNA 'We'... There are indeed—better men than you.

FRIEDRICH Do you think so? (*Stands up*)

ERNA What's the matter? Why are you so distracted? Why do you keep looking at the door? Are you expecting someone?

FRIEDRICH Yes, Doctor Mauer.

ERNA Doctor Mauer? What do you want from him?

FRIEDRICH It's a business matter.

ERNA Mauer isn't a lawyer...

FRIEDRICH No, he's a friend.

ERNA Do you think he still is?

FRIEDRICH Yes. Such things never depend on... what sort of adventures one might have together. Disillusionments would not be painful if inner bonds were simply severed by them. But being able to depend on one another absolutely... now that... Eternal love and eternal friendship are all there is. And Mauer is and remains my only friend. That is understood... Even if he were to shoot me one day, that won't change.

ERNA What do you have to discuss with him that's so important?

FRIEDRICH It's about my trip to America.

ERNA So you're going?

FRIEDRICH Yes... And then there are other things to see to— unfinished business, which only Mauer can assist me with.

ERNA Unfinished business...?

FRIEDRICH My God, woman! A wife could not be more inquisitive. Anyway, they are all very tedious matters.

ERNA Yet they seem to be making you extremely nervous.

FRIEDRICH Is that how I seem? Not a bit of it, just a little fatigued.

ERNA How come? You didn't travel overnight, did you?

FRIEDRICH No, but I didn't sleep much either. I went window promenading.

ERNA Last night?

FRIEDRICH Yes, last night. Why are you surprised? I told you on a certain memorable evening... that I suddenly understood all these things—promenading under windows, serenading—manslaughter... suicide——

ERNA I don't understand. Whose window were you... promenading under...

FRIEDRICH Why, yours of course.

ERNA Mine? What sort of...

FRIEDRICH Don't you believe me? Well, listen! Yesterday evening I drove all the way back out to you again. Shortly after arriving in Vienna. It was almost midnight by the time I found myself under your window. Your light was still burning. I watched your shadow gliding past behind the curtains. If your room had been on the ground floor... who knows.

ERNA You were outside my window?!—And then?

FRIEDRICH Then I went away again. I had seen your shadow, had been near you. That's what I'd been longing for.

ERNA You'd been... Friedrich...! And where did you go then?

FRIEDRICH Back to Vienna. My car was waiting for me in the church square. You see, I had things to do in the office at eight o'clock this morning.

ERNA You were outside my window... Friedrich!

FRIEDRICH Why would I tell you something like that, if it weren't true... what would you like me to swear by? By the holy waters of Lake Völs?

ERNA You were outside my window!... My lover!

FRIEDRICH Quiet, quiet. (*He goes over to the door of the house*)

MAUER (*comes out of the house*) Hello, Friedrich. Good day, Fräulein Erna.

ERNA (*calmly*) Good day, Doctor.

MAUER (*with no embarrassment*) So, Fräulein Erna, you got back some time ago?

ERNA Just two days ago... (*To Friedrich*) You were wanting to talk to the Doctor. Goodbye. (*Exit to the tennis court*)

    Mauer, Friedrich.

MAUER I got your letter and so here I am.

FRIEDRICH Thank you again for coming. I hope I haven't kept you away from anything important.

MAUER You said you wanted to consult me. I assume you're not feeling well.

FRIEDRICH (*looks at him*) I see! No, I've asked you to call as a friend.

MAUER As a friend, I see... Well, I'm here.

FRIEDRICH It's about a stupid rumour you may have heard or read about already.

MAUER Which rumour?

FRIEDRICH That Korsakov...

MAUER Well?

FRIEDRICH That Korsakov died as the victim of an American duel.

MAUER Ah.

FRIEDRICH Did you read about it?

MAUER To tell the truth, I heard about it.

FRIEDRICH Well, what I wanted to ask you was: what should I do?

MAUER What should you do? But you have proof in your hands to the contrary. Korsakov's letter to your wife...

FRIEDRICH What use is that? I can't very well... that would be absurd...

MAUER Well, then... simply don't worry about it. The rumour will vanish as it came. It is unlikely sensible people would believe that of you.

FRIEDRICH Even so—something will stick. And someone must have been the first to spread this infamy. If one could find some way to corner him.

MAUER It will scarcely be possible to track the man down.

FRIEDRICH I've traced him already. It's Natter.

MAUER What makes you think so?

FRIEDRICH It's his revenge... you see, all along he...

MAUER (quickly) ... knew?

FRIEDRICH Yes.—There are altogether far fewer deceived husbands than their wives—and sometimes even the lovers—would like to believe.

MAUER Have you any proof that he started this rumour?

FRIEDRICH Proof, no.

MAUER Then you can do nothing.

FRIEDRICH I could confront him.

MAUER He will of course deny it.

FRIEDRICH Give him a hiding, then.

MAUER That wouldn't improve matters.

FRIEDRICH It might improve my mood.

MAUER That would be rather a roundabout way of achieving it.

FRIEDRICH I don't agree. A good mood is the most important thing on earth.

MAUER Well, I rest my case. I can't give you any more advice, with the best will in the world.—So, now I would like to say good evening to your wife, and then be on my way.

FRIEDRICH Mauer... you're not angry with me, are you?

MAUER Angry with you? No. But my urge to stay is weak.

FRIEDRICH I say, Mauer... You know I left Lake Völs shortly after you did?

MAUER 'Shortly after' is a good one.

FRIEDRICH Almost immediately!... the very next day!... And do you know why? I simply took flight.

MAUER Ah!—

FRIEDRICH Yes, from myself. Because I freely admit that I was very much in love with Erna.

MAUER You don't have to account for yourself to me.

FRIEDRICH Of course not. Nor am I trying to. I just don't see why your false suspicions should make me...

MAUER Whatever I may have suspected, justly or unjustly, as far as I'm concerned the matter's closed.—May I now go and bid your wife good evening?

FRIEDRICH You may do so later. For the moment you will be good enough to stay. We have to talk things out. I assure you you're mistaken. Yes, I did kiss her. Once... I don't deny it. An embrace like that out of doors, in fine weather, at an altitude of two thousand metres, doesn't mean a thing. I call it... mountain intoxication...

MAUER Well... if that's all you call it... everything's all right then.

FRIEDRICH Do you imagine there are many unkissed girls left these days? Such things have been known to happen even on the plains. But to imagine oneself too good for any of them... if you don't mind my saying so, is sheer megalomania.

MAUER You enjoy lying, don't you?

FRIEDRICH Sometimes, yes. But this time I'm not lying. And now I'll tell you something else. Even if things had gone any further... than that kiss...

MAUER I didn't ask you. And frankly, at the moment I don't basically care how far things may have gone between you.

FRIEDRICH Anyway, my dear Mauer, you are quite mistaken about that.

MAUER Ah...

FRIEDRICH You might have been better off if she had in fact become my mistress. Then it would be over and done with... You would be safer, so to speak.

MAUER You are beginning to amuse me.

FRIEDRICH I'm glad to hear it. After all, that's the most important thing in any conversation. Whether one gets to hear the truth, of course, one never knows.

MAUER I would hear it from Erna herself.

FRIEDRICH You think so?

MAUER Lying is the one thing I don't think she is capable of.

FRIEDRICH You may be right. And that's what counts in the end. I think it's altogether too one-sided to judge women purely in erotic terms. We keep on forgetting that, even when a woman does have lovers, there are a great many hours in her life when she has other things to think about besides love. She reads books, plays music, organizes charitable societies, cooks, brings up her children,—she may even be an excellent wife and mother. A hundred times more worthy in fact—than a so-called respectable woman. Think of Adele Natter.

MAUER I hope you haven't asked me here to air your philosophical opinions.

FRIEDRICH No, things have just turned out this way. But since we are already on the subject, I'd like to ask you if anything about my wife's affair with the midshipman has come to your ears?

MAUER (*surprised*) Your wife's affair with... Not a word... How should it... I've not been here for three weeks.

FRIEDRICH Well then, you're hearing the news from me. So, what do you say?

MAUER Perhaps it isn't true. And if it were...

FRIEDRICH You wish it on me with all your heart. I know. All I would say is that your malicious relish is totally unfounded. Because it presupposes that I find the whole business hurtful, or at the very least annoying. And that is absolutely not the case. On the contrary. I find it more of an inner liberation. I no longer go around the house feeling guilty. I can breathe again. It's almost as though she had done penance for Korsakov's death, and indeed in a thoroughly rational and painless way. I begin to feel closer to her as a human being again. We again so to speak—inhabit the same planet.

MAUER You are very calm and collected. My compliments. Obviously you don't believe it. Because one can never be absolutely certain about a thing like that.

FRIEDRICH Ah, but sometimes one can. If, for example, one sees the lover climbing out of one's wife's window at half past one in the morning.

MAUER What?

FRIEDRICH Well, what do you say to that? At half past one last night I saw Herr Otto von Aigner, midshipman in his Majesty's navy, climbing out of the window of Genia, lawful wedded wife of Friedrich Hofreiter, factory owner. Herewith legally confirmed by oath!

MAUER Half past one last night?

FRIEDRICH I was already out here last night, you see.

MAUER Really—? And where were you until half past one, if I may ask.

FRIEDRICH Haha, I get the impression you're thinking of Erna again. Well, to put your mind at rest, I caught the last train out from Vienna; I then walked up from the station as I sometimes do, and entered the garden from the meadow through the little gate. Then to my surprise I heard voices. I crept closer and saw a man and a woman sitting here under the tree. Genia and Otto. Here in the garden at midnight. I couldn't of course make out what they were saying. I remained at a discreet distance and after a few minutes the two of them got up and disappeared into the house. I quickly left the garden, again through the back gate, went right round the villa and placed myself so that I was bound to see if anyone came out of the front door. No one came out. Half an hour passed and still no one. The lights in the house went out. I quickly went back round the fence into the meadow again, where I could keep an eye on Genia's bedroom window. The light was out. It was a beautiful night and I stretched out on the meadow in the shadow of the trees beside the fence. And I waited. I waited until half past one. At half past one the window opened and a man climbed out but disappeared from view for a while in the darkness of the garden. Then I heard the garden gate open and almost immediately the lean figure of Midshipman Otto von Aigner swept straight past me.

MAUER I see. And what did you do then?

FRIEDRICH I stretched out on the meadow.

MAUER You were already lying there.

FRIEDRICH Quite right. But I stretched out more comfortably than I was before, because I no longer had to keep watch. And I slept like a log until seven in the morning. It is really splendid, sleeping out of doors on beautiful summer nights. Somebody was raving about it to me recently.

MAUER I hope you are not thinking of taking him or Genia to task over this. The only thing you can and should do now,—is to end things cleanly.

FRIEDRICH Who said anything about ending things?

MAUER But it's self-evident. It could all be done now without attracting too much notice. All you need to do is leave for America a little earlier than you intended.

FRIEDRICH But Genia is coming to America with me.

MAUER Really—?

FRIEDRICH Yes.

MAUER (*shrugging his shoulders*) You'll permit me to regard this provisionally as the final evidence of your confidence in me. Now...

NATTER (*enters*) Oh, good evening, Doctor Mauer, how are you? My dear Hofreiter, I just wanted to ask you, since we can't stay much longer...

MAUER I'll just go and bid your wife good evening...

FRIEDRICH She'll be delighted.

> *Mauer moves off toward the tennis court.*
> *Friedrich, Natter*

NATTER I wanted to ask you, my dear Hofreiter, whether I might have a talk with you in the office tomorrow. There's a lot I need to fill you in on. The consortium has been in touch again. They are offering...

FRIEDRICH Let's leave business till tomorrow, Herr Natter.

NATTER As you wish.

FRIEDRICH Today we'll have a chat.

NATTER With pleasure.

FRIEDRICH Tell me, Natter, what do you think of Demeter Stanzides?

NATTER Stanzides—a very agreeable fellow. A little sentimental for a lieutenant of hussars. But in general a nice enough chap.

FRIEDRICH Does he have debts?

NATTER Not that I know of.

FRIEDRICH Doesn't he mistreat his subordinates?

NATTER I know nothing about that.

FRIEDRICH Have you heard that he's a card-sharp?

NATTER Do you really believe that, Hofreiter?

FRIEDRICH No. I just want to make it easier for you to invent something about him for later, after the affair between him and your wife is over.

> *They stand face to face.*

NATTER I'm glad you don't take me for a fool, Hofreiter.

FRIEDRICH No, for a...

NATTER I caution you against calling me a blackguard. It would rather inconvenience me to have to resolve the matter with a game of billiards.

FRIEDRICH Perhaps by other means then.

NATTER If I had wanted to do that... I had a golden opportunity not too long ago.

FRIEDRICH Why didn't you take it? One doesn't overnight become a... I know full well that as a young man you staked your precious life for less.

NATTER For less? For other things.

FRIEDRICH If you care that much—why stay with your wife?

NATTER Let me explain then. Because for me existence without Adele would be completely meaningless. You see, I am hopelessly in love with her. It does happen, Hofreiter. There is no cure for it. You've no idea the things I've tried, to be rid of her internally—! To no avail... All to no avail... I love her... in spite of everything—! Monstrous, what?—But that's the way it is.

FRIEDRICH And you take your revenge on me by inventing monstrous rumours?

NATTER Perhaps by spreading the truth.

FRIEDRICH Good God, do you really believe?... I was involved in... an American duel...

NATTER Prove the contrary to me.

FRIEDRICH I certainly could do so... I know the reason Korsakov committed suicide. I know that... Oh, where am I going like this? Justifying myself to you, you...

NATTER Be careful.

FRIEDRICH I swear you are mistaken. I swear by...

NATTER By your wife's virtue, perhaps?

FRIEDRICH You... (*rushes at him*)

NATTER (*grips his arm*) Calm down, no scenes. I don't propose to brawl with you. But one more word and...

FRIEDRICH Am I then defenceless against you of all men?

NATTER That's the way things are sometimes.

FRIEDRICH Yes... but against a...

NATTER Against someone who sees life as vastly amusing... my dear Hofreiter—and that's all.

PAUL (*from the tennis court*) My apologies for interrupting. Herr Hofreiter,—your game with Midshipman Otto is coming up next.

FRIEDRICH Yes... yes... I'm ready—Ranking the players is now an urgent matter... I know...

NATTER Of course, don't let me stop you. (*In an undertone*) One might even say, a matter of life and death!

FRIEDRICH Possibly.

> *Mauer and Genia come from further back.*

MAUER (*taking leave*) Well, my dear friend.

FRIEDRICH No, I can't let you go yet. You must detain him, Genia— using all your powers of seduction.

Friedrich, Paul and Natter move off towards the tennis court.

GENIA I'm afraid my powers may not succeed.

MAUER I'm sorry but I really must go, Frau Genia.

GENIA And presumably we won't see you out here again in the near future...

MAUER Presumably.

GENIA (*she gazes at him*) I am sorry that I too have lost a friend. Even though I am truly blameless, at least towards you. Why don't you answer me, Doctor? I don't want to force myself into your confidence, especially since I can easily imagine what is driving you away.

MAUER This time I don't need to compliment you on your astuteness. And now, Frau Genia, perhaps you'll permit me to leave.

GENIA It's not for me to permit you or forbid you anything. Especially when you address me as... Frau Genia. Goodbye, dear Doctor.— And—and allow me to give you one more word of advice for the road!—Don't take it all too much to heart. It would be ridiculous if you, a person familiar with the most serious side of life, were to take such games and high jinks seriously. The affairs of love are no more than that, Doctor, believe me. And once one has realized it, they are fun to watch—and to take part in.

MAUER Once one has realized...

GENIA You will do in due course, dear friend. All those stupid serious words running through your mind, one day you will blow them into the air like bubbles. And then you will see how light they really are. They will float away... all of them... and vanish, all those stupid serious words...

MAUER Perhaps there's really only one serious word in the world— and it's called a lie.

GENIA A lie? Does such a thing exist in games? There it's called jest or cunning.

MAUER A game—?! If only it were so!... Believe me, Genia, I wouldn't have the least objection to a world where love was truly just a delightful game... But one... played honestly, if you please! Honestly to the point of orgies if need be... That I could endorse. But I find this mingling of reserve and impudence, of cowardly jealousy and pretended indifference—of mad passion and empty lust such as I see here everywhere—both saddening and gruesome—... The freedom so much vaunted here lacks the strength of its own convictions. That's why the carefree mask it tries to assume does not succeed... why it grimaces... where it intended to laugh.

GENIA You are unjust, Doctor. We all try to do what we can. It doesn't
happen overnight of course. But we have the best of intentions.
Haven't you noticed? Adele Natter, for example, brings her children over to our house, I chat away with Erna, as if Lake Völs were
the fountain of innocence, Friedrich plays his round of tennis with
Midshipman von Aigner...

MAUER Why shouldn't he?

GENIA Oh, Doctor!...

MAUER Yes, I know... about that too...

GENIA Who told you?

MAUER Who—? Beware, Genia. It was Friedrich himself.
    The tennis match has ended. The players gradually return.

GENIA Friedrich...?! Of course he suspects. I could see it at once from
the way he looked at me... when he hailed us from the balcony. But
why do you warn me to 'beware!'—? He won't hold it against me.
Otto might kill himself as well—like the other one. And after all,
one mustn't hound a young man to death over a trivial thing like
that. Friedrich will be pleased with me. Tomorrow, once... my lover
has left... I myself will tell him the whole story.

MAUER That won't be necessary. He not only suspects, he knows... He
himself saw the midshipman last night... at half past one...
    Genia starts, but quickly controls herself.
    Paul, Gustl, Erna, Stanzides, Adele, Frau Wahl, Natter, Otto
    and Friedrich return from the tennis court.

GENIA Well, who won?

PAUL There's life in the old guard yet. Herr Hofreiter did, nine games
to eight.

STANZIDES Pity you weren't watching, Frau Genia. It was a splendid
match.

FRIEDRICH So, Mauer, you stayed on after all. That's very nice of
you!

PAUL And now there's the match between Fräulein Erna and Herr
Hofreiter.

ERNA It's too dark already, we'll have to postpone it till tomorrow.
And we'll send the midshipman the results of the tournament by
telegraph.

OTTO Well, I'm afraid I must bid you all goodbye now. (*He begins
saying his goodbyes*)

FRIEDRICH (*follows him with his gaze*) Pity we can't play another
round tomorrow, Otto!—I wasn't really satisfied with my victory
today.

PAUL Why not? Herr Otto played superbly, and you, Herr Hofreiter, were even more impressive.

FRIEDRICH I don't know about that. You weren't really in top form, Otto. Your stroke was not quite what I've come to expect from you. Such a distracted, indecisive, timorous stroke... Parting mood probably.

OTTO Embarrassment perhaps, in the face of such a strong, relaxed opponent. Well, when I come again in three years' time, my return game ought to give you greater satisfaction, Herr Hofreiter.

FRIEDRICH Yes, if only one could be sure we'll meet again!... I never talk about things that far ahead... three years!... think of all the things that could happen in the meantime. One can't always keep control of everything. There are events against which all foresight may be of little avail... and all caution.

NATTER Just the qualities that are not regarded as the midshipman's strong points.

OTTO I fear so myself, Herr Natter.

FRIEDRICH You can't tell yourself, Otto, whether or not you are naturally cautious... In a profession as much concerned with discipline and bearing as yours, one has so to speak little opportunity to get to know oneself. Wouldn't you agree?

MAUER That's enough psychology for this time of night, I would have thought. (*To Otto*) Perhaps we can leave together.

FRIEDRICH (*disregarding this completely*) I've no doubt of course that you'd be prepared at any time to lay down your life for Emperor and country, as well as for much slighter things, but then external compulsion plays a considerable part in that. Deep down Otto, at the very bottom of your soul, you are a coward.

    Pregnant pause.

OTTO I don't think I've quite understood you, have I?

FRIEDRICH I don't know what you may or may not have understood. In any case, I shall repeat: you are a coward.

    Otto takes a step towards him.
    Friedrich quickly moves towards him too.

OTTO You will hear from me.

FRIEDRICH I hope so, (*in an undertone*) very shortly. In the park an hour from now...

    Otto exit.
    Paul says something softly to Gustl, and the two of them follow Otto.
    Erna stands motionless.

Genia motionless.

Frau Wahl looks about restlessly, turns to Adele.

NATTER We won't intrude on you further.

FRIEDRICH Oh no, not at all—quite the contrary. (*Aside to Mauer*) I hope I can count on you.

MAUER No. I'm not getting involved in this.

FRIEDRICH As a doctor, Mauer. You can't refuse me that, it's your duty.

MAUER (*shrugs his shoulders*) Very well.

FRIEDRICH Thank you. My dear Stanzides.

STANZIDES I am at your disposal.

FRIEDRICH Thank you. Natter, could I have a word? (*Draws Natter forward*) I think we're agreed in our outlook on life, are we not? A sick joke.

NATTER I have always said so.

FRIEDRICH This latest farce would have an added piquancy for me— if you would consent to be my second.

NATTER It would be a pleasure. The midshipman can't be a bad shot.

GENIA (*with sudden resolve going over to Friedrich*) Friedrich...

FRIEDRICH Later.

GENIA Now.

FRIEDRICH (*to the others*) If you will excuse us. (*Comes forward with her*)
        Frau Wahl goes across to Erna, tries to get her to leave.
        Erna motions her away, stands against the wall of the house.
        Frau Wahl turns to Adele, who is sitting under the walnut tree and watching her husband.
        Natter and Stanzides move towards the back.
        Mauer stands alone.

FRIEDRICH (*to Genia*) Well?

GENIA What are you thinking of? How can you allow yourself to...

FRIEDRICH Well, don't be alarmed, I won't hurt him too much, probably not at all.

GENIA So why? If you cared for me in the least... if it were hate... anger... jealousy... love...

FRIEDRICH Ah well, I certainly feel damned little of any of that. But one doesn't like to be the stooge.
        Turns away from her, follows Natter and Stanzides.
        Genia stands in the foreground motionless.
        Erna stands against the wall of the house. The two women's eyes meet.
        Curtain.

Act Five

*Room in the villa adjoining the veranda familiar from Act One.
Light and friendly. A large glass door stands open leading onto
the veranda. Cupboards to the right and left of the glass door. In
the middle a large table covered with a tablecloth, on it
newspapers, books.—Armchairs. On the wall to the left a
fireplace, in front of which are a little table, chairs etc. Pictures on
the walls. On the right a second door. A grandfather clock in the
foreground on the left. To the right of the fireplace, a stand with a
few books.*

*Genia enters from the right in a morning dress. Very pale and
agitated. Goes to the veranda door, steps out onto the veranda,
comes in again, sits down at the large table, picks up one of the
newspapers lying there, looks through it, then gazes straight
ahead.*

*Erna without a hat, in a summer dress, rushes in from the
veranda.*

GENIA (*rises, quickly in control*) Erna... what is it?

ERNA Aren't they back yet? Is there still no news?

GENIA How should there be any news? Come to your senses, Erna. It
can't possibly take place—before this afternoon. Probably not until
tomorrow morning. At the moment they will still be holding
preliminary discussions.

ERNA (*looks at her*) Yes, of course. Forgive my asking further questions. I know I've no right to do so, but under the circumstances...

GENIA You have as much right to tremble for somebody as I have.

ERNA I'm not trembling, Frau Genia. That is not the way I am. I only
wanted to ask if you've already seen your dear husband today?

GENIA My 'dear husband' went into town last night. To sort out
various things with his lawyer. Well, that's customary, even if it's
quite superfluous. He has to make arrangements. Even burn a few
letters and papers perhaps. In short, behave as if it were an enormously important matter, even though it's just a ridiculous comedy
of vanity and honour, as we all know.

ERNA I'm not convinced of that, Frau Genia.

GENIA I am. Come, Erna, let's go into the garden, it's such a lovely
day. We can talk there. You haven't yet told me anything about your
trip. You had an interesting time... at Lake Völs...

ERNA Can you really be joking at a time like this, Genia?

GENIA I'm not joking. Ah, I am very far from that... You love my 'dear
husband' very much, don't you—?! Well, it's hardly surprising.
One's first lover—well, that at least is an experience. Or does even
that no longer mean anything these days? Yes, you must enlighten
me on that score, Erna.—I don't seem to be able to find my bear-
ings any more. Life has become so much easier lately. When I was
your age, one still took certain things immensely seriously.
Little more than ten years have passed since then, but I have the
impression that the world has altered a great deal.

>   *The chambermaid enters from the right with a telegram. Goes out
>   again at once.*

GENIA (*opens it hastily*) It's from my sister, Mary. She and Percy are
arriving today at noon. Here. (*She hands Erna the telegram*) It will
be a happy reunion. But shall we go into the garden, Erna? Or
perhaps we could go for a little drive? It's such a nice day. The air
will do you good. You're looking pale... Perhaps you didn't sleep
too well.

ERNA No, I was awake. And at five this morning I saw my brother
leave. Any minute now we may hear how it all ended. Even now as
we've been talking, it may well have been over long ago.

GENIA Erna—I told you, Friedrich went into town, to see his lawyer...
probably.

ERNA He didn't go to see his lawyer. I know that. I talked to my
brother as he was leaving the house. Everything had already been
agreed last night. The duel took place at eight this morning. I
assume—not too far from here. Probably in the woods near Heiligenkreuz. And now it's all... over.

GENIA So then it's over... And there's now no changing anything? In
the woods near Heiligenkreuz, you think?—So now they'll all be
sitting under the shady trees in the monastery garden, celebrating
their reconciliation... The seconds will have ordered breakfast in
advance. People are soon reconciled when they were never really
angry. What do you think, Erna, could they be drinking to our
health? Why not? After all, life is altogether so amusing. Perhaps
they will turn up here, arm in arm. Yes... We ought to walk out and
meet them.

ERNA I would like to go home... Perhaps my brother's back already...

GENIA Very well—you go home then, Erna... I shall wait here...

>   *Erna appears to listen to a noise outside.*

GENIA What's the matter—Yes, I can hear footsteps.

ERNA (*going to the veranda door*) It's Frau Meinhold.

GENIA (*starts*) What...?

ERNA She seems very calm. She can't have heard.

GENIA What can she want so early...

ERNA She obviously knows nothing. She's walking slowly enough and her features seem quite placid. If she had the least suspicion, she wouldn't look like that. How should she know anyway? Pull yourself together, Frau Genia!

FRAU MEINHOLD (*enters*) Good morning.

ERNA Good morning, Frau Meinhold.

GENIA Is that you, Frau Meinhold? Well now... (*she gets up*)

ERNA Goodbye!

FRAU MEINHOLD Are you leaving already? I hope I'm not driving you away?

ERNA Not at all, Frau Meinhold. I was on my way out. Adieu, Frau Genia. (*Exit*)

GENIA (*with immense self-control*) I'm so pleased to see you again, Frau Meinhold. I was very sorry you weren't here yesterday.

FRAU MEINHOLD You did have rather a large party and I don't enjoy things then. But today I'm here all the earlier, as you see, Frau Genia.

GENIA It's not really all that early. (*Looking at the hall clock*) Quite right, it's only ten o'clock! I thought it must be almost noon. Friedrich went into town some time ago. You knew, didn't you, Frau Meinhold, that he got back yesterday.

FRAU MEINHOLD Of course I knew. (*Smiling*) Otto passed on your husband's greetings yesterday evening.

GENIA I see.—Your son is leaving today, I believe?

FRAU MEINHOLD My son has already left in fact. He took the last train into town last night. And this evening he's off to Pola.

GENIA This evening already!? Ah!

FRAU MEINHOLD Am I really the first you've heard that from?

GENIA Oh, I knew already. Just that I thought he was intending to devote today entirely to his mother.

FRAU MEINHOLD He has a great many things to see to in town today. So we said goodbye last night... It's better that way.

GENIA I'm sure.

FRAU MEINHOLD You can imagine, Frau Genia, how I felt this morning, when I found myself alone in my arbour at breakfast. Now my little house suddenly seems much emptier... than I've been used to recently. I've been quite spoiled of late—in spite of everything.

And the thought that this time he'll be going for so long and so far away, makes the house seem even emptier and sadder. So I decided to go out...

GENIA I understand.

FRAU MEINHOLD Not that I set out with the intention of disturbing you so early, Frau Genia. Not at all. I just wanted a walk... a lonely walk through the woods. And yet here I am. God knows how it's happened. Something must have driven me here. (*Looks at her for some time*)

GENIA (*answers her gaze*) Thank you.

FRAU MEINHOLD No need to thank me. You see, I've been torn between being very angry with you and—feeling well disposed towards you. And when I left home I had by no means made up my mind. Because these last few days—I can tell you this, Genia, now that he has left—I have sometimes felt quite frightened...

GENIA Frightened—?

FRAU MEINHOLD I know my son... And I could tell how much he has been suffering lately. It is just not in his nature... to cope with disingenuous relationships. I was... afraid for him. You have meant so much to him, Genia! More than his profession, or his future, or me, more than his own life. Oh God, the things I have been afraid might happen. And yet I said nothing. I could not but remain silent. Could not but understand the situation even. I saw it all coming, from the first day Otto set foot inside your house. Yet for all my anguish, fear, and jealousy, I could not help understanding. You were so alone, Genia, and so cruelly wronged... for years on end! Even if a more ignoble person than Otto had come along—I could not have blamed you. And now—with him gone, all my anguish and jealousy have vanished and I simply ask myself: how is she going to bear it? She—who after all did love him!

GENIA Frau Meinhold, I'm truly not worthy of such sympathy.—I shall try to forget him. And I shall succeed. I'm sure of that,—just as sure as I am that he'll succeed as well. I am determined to forget him. Why do you look at me like that, Frau Meinhold? Don't you believe me? You needn't worry. We have made no secret arrangements. I promise you... We won't even be writing to each other. That has been agreed.

FRAU MEINHOLD You are a good person, Genia.

GENIA I am just... clever, Frau Meinhold. Just clever... (*suddenly she starts sobbing violently. Sinks down with her head on the table*)

FRAU MEINHOLD Genia, Genia. (*She strokes her hair*) Don't cry,

Genia! It's small comfort, I know,—but we will bear his absence together... You see, I made the right choice in deciding... not to hate you. There, there, child,—calm yourself. We will be friends, Genia. It's the best we can do. Genia... Genia!

GENIA Frau Meinhold... (*she takes her hand, as if to kiss it*)

FRAU MEINHOLD Must you call me that? I am after all his mother.

GENIA (*shakes her head wildly*) No, no, no, I can't go on...

FRAU MEINHOLD (*Looks at her for some time*) I'd better leave you alone now... Farewell then. But when you are tired of being alone,—come and see me. You will always find me ready to receive you. Goodbye, Genia.—

FRIEDRICH (*comes in from the terrace. Addresses Frau Meinhold in his humorously malicious way, which now gives him a mask-like appearance*) Good morning, Frau Meinhold. (*Hesitating almost imperceptibly, he takes her hand*) How are you?

FRAU MEINHOLD Thank you. Back from town so early?

FRIEDRICH From town? No. I'm about to go in now. I've just had my morning walk. A... glorious day...

FRAU MEINHOLD And did you have a pleasant journey?

FRIEDRICH Yes, very pleasant. Very pleasant. I feel quite refreshed. Good health, interesting people, what more could one ask.

FRAU MEINHOLD Which reminds me, I'm supposed to pass on greetings to you.

FRIEDRICH To me?

FRAU MEINHOLD You may be a little surprised. From Herr von Aigner.

FRIEDRICH From your husband?

FRAU MEINHOLD Yes, this morning. A letter from him arrived before I left the house, the first in years. He'll be here himself in a few days. A conference with the minister, apparently.

FRIEDRICH Yes, of course. About the new railway. It will make a tremendous difference. Besides, your husband is also hoping to be minister one day. A remarkable man in every respect, a very remarkable man. He has a great future.

FRAU MEINHOLD Do you really believe that?

FRIEDRICH Why not?

FRAU MEINHOLD In the letter he also talks about his poor health...

FRIEDRICH Poor health!... He can't go mountain-climbing any more, certainly, but becoming a minister is less strenuous. And losing one's grip is less dangerous. Besides, he's not really ill at all. He is the epitome of life. He will outlive us all. Pardon, I can only speak

for myself of course, indeed all of us can only speak for ourselves...
(*Laughs*) A very interesting person... we talked a lot together...
during the few days... I like him.

FRAU MEINHOLD He seems to have become quite fond of you as well.
Yes, it is a curious letter. Almost moving. And a little affected. He
won't outgrow that now.

FRIEDRICH No, hardly...

FRAU MEINHOLD Well, goodbye then.

FRIEDRICH Goodbye, Frau Meinhold, and if your husband does
come, our house is naturally... Les amis de nos amis... and all that...
Adieu, Frau Meinhold.

> *Genia accompanies her a few steps.*

FRAU MEINHOLD Don't come out, don't come out, my dear Frau
Genia. Goodbye. (*Exit*)

> *Genia quickly comes back.*
> *Genia, Friedrich.*
> *Friedrich has been standing motionless.*

GENIA Well... Everything... alright—?

FRIEDRICH (*looks at her*) Well... !—

GENIA Is he wounded?! Friedrich!...

FRIEDRICH He is dead!

GENIA Friedrich, don't go too far! This is no time for jokes.

FRIEDRICH He is dead. I cannot say it any other way.

GENIA Friedrich, Friedrich... (*going up to him, seizes him by the shoulders*) You killed him, Friedrich... And—shook his mother's hand.

FRIEDRICH (*shrugs*) I had no idea she would be... here with you. What
was I supposed to do?

GENIA Dead... dead! (*Suddenly turning on him*) Murderer!

FRIEDRICH I'm no murderer, it was an honest fight.

GENIA But why...

FRIEDRICH Why—? Obviously... because I wanted to.

GENIA It's not true! Don't make yourself more dreadful than you are.
You didn't mean to. It was a hideous coincidence!... You didn't
mean to... it's not true...

FRIEDRICH At that moment, with him standing there opposite me, it
was true.

GENIA Gruesome man! And then you shook his mother's hand. You
didn't even hate him, yet you killed him. Villain, conceited, gruesome villain.

FRIEDRICH It's not that simple. You can't see inside me, after all.
Nobody can. I feel sorry for poor Frau Meinhold. And for the

decent, ageing Herr von Aigner too. But I cannot help them. Nor you either. Nor him. Nor myself. It had to be.

GENIA Had to?—

FRIEDRICH When I saw him standing opposite me with his insolent young gaze, I knew immediately... it was either him or me.

GENIA You are lying, he would not have... not him...

FRIEDRICH You're wrong. It was a matter of life and death. He wanted it as much as me. I saw it in his eyes as much as he in mine. Him... or me...

> Erna and Mauer come from the garden.
> Erna stops at the door.
> Mauer hastens to Genia, presses her hand.

FRIEDRICH Ah, Mauer, you here already?

MAUER There was nothing more I could do.

GENIA Where is his body?

MAUER On the way.

GENIA Where to?

MAUER To his mother's house.

GENIA Does she know? Who is going to...?

MAUER No one has plucked up the courage to so far.

GENIA I shall tell her. It's my duty. I must go to her.

FRIEDRICH Genia... wait a minute. When you get back, I'm not likely to be here. I can't expect you to shake hands, but—let us say goodbye.

GENIA (*remembering*) Percy is arriving. In an hour.

FRIEDRICH Percy? I shall wait and see him... Then... there will be the usual... well...

GENIA What do you intend to do?

FRIEDRICH Go into town. It will probably be better if I give myself up. Nothing's going to happen to me. All I did was safeguard my honour. Perhaps they will let me out on bail... though they could suspect I might try to flee the country.

GENIA How can you even think of that! With him lying there dead—!

FRIEDRICH Yes, he certainly has it easier than me. For him everything has been resolved. Whereas I—I am still here on earth. And I intend to go on living... One has to make a choice. One way—or the other.

GENIA (*stares at him*) I must go... (*prepares to leave*)

MAUER Frau Genia... you shouldn't go all that way alone. Allow me to escort you.

GENIA (*nods*) Thank you. Let us hurry.

Mauer and Genia exeunt.
Erna, Friedrich.
Friedrich continues to stand rigidly as before.

ERNA (*by the door, motionless*) What will you do?

FRIEDRICH Whatever the outcome, whether I am sentenced or acquitted, I shall of course leave town... leave this part of the world entirely.

ERNA And—wherever you decide to go, Friedrich,—I shall follow you.

FRIEDRICH Thank you, but I can't accept that.

ERNA Friedrich, we belong to one another, I feel it more strongly now than ever.

FRIEDRICH You're mistaken. At the moment, you're swayed by the impression this whole affair has made on you. You are probably even impressed that I... but that's all an illusion. Everything's an illusion. I'm really going to snap one of these days. It's all over between us, Erna. You are twenty, you don't belong to me.

ERNA (*still on the same spot*) You are younger than any of them.

FRIEDRICH Quiet. I know what youth is. An hour ago I saw it gleaming and laughing at me out of an insolent cold eye. I know what youth is right enough.—And, one can't of course pursue every... stay where you are, enjoy yourself and...

ERNA (*listens*) A motor car.

FRIEDRICH (*remains motionless*) Percy.

ERNA (*now drawing a little closer to him*) Friedrich, believe me, I love you, I belong to you.

FRIEDRICH I belong to no one in the world. No one. Nor do I want to...

CHILD'S VOICE IN THE GARDEN Mother! Father!

FRIEDRICH Percy. (*He suppresses a sob*) Yes, Percy. I'm coming. Here I am. (*Hastens out onto the veranda*)

Erna remains standing.
Curtain.

PROFESSOR BERNHARDI
A Comedy in Five Acts

CAST

DR BERNHARDI, *Professor of Internal Medicine, Director of the Elisabethinum*

Also at the Elisabethinum:
DR EBENWALD, *Professor of Surgery, Assistant Director*
DR CYPRIAN, *Professor of Neurology*
DR PFLUGFELDER, *Professor of Gynaecology*
DR TUGENDVETTER, *Professor of Dermatology*
DR LÖWENSTEIN, *Lecturer in Paediatrics*
DR SCHREIMANN,* *Lecturer in Laryngology*
DR ADLER, *Lecturer in Anatomical Pathology*
DR OSCAR BERNHARDI, *Bernhardi's Assistant*
DR KURT PFLUGFELDER, *Bernhardi's Assistant*
DR WENGER, *Tugendvetter's Assistant*
HOCHROITZPOINTNER, *Final year Medical Student*
LUDMILLA, *Nurse*

Not at the Elisabethinum:
PROFESSOR FLINT, *Minister of Education*
COUNCILLOR WINKLER, *in the Ministry of Education*
FRANZ REDER, *Parish Priest at the Church of Saint Florian*
DR GOLDENTHAL, *Council for the Defence*
DR FEUERMANN, *General Practitioner in Oberhollabrunn*
KULKA, *Journalist*
A SERVANT *employed by Bernhardi*
A SERVANT *in the Elisabethinum*
A SERVANT *in the Ministry of Education*

Vienna around 1900

Act One

A moderate-sized anteroom, which leads into a sick ward. On the right a door into the corridor. Doors at the back into the sick ward. A fairly wide window on the left. In the centre more to the left a longish table, on which is a thick registration book, as well as files containing case histories, some official documents and various papers. A coat-stand next to the entrance. An iron stove in the corner on the right. By the window a stand with broad shelves; on the top shelf a rack holding test tubes, next to which are various medicine bottles. On the lower shelves books and magazines. Closed cupboards on each side of the central door. A white coat, an overcoat and a hat are hanging on the coat-stand. Above the stand is a fairly old photograph depicting the professorial collegiate body. Assorted chairs as required.

Nurse Ludmilla, about twenty-eight, pale, quite pretty, with large rather watery eyes, is busy at the stand. Out of the sick ward comes Hochroitzpointner, a pale young man of twenty-five, stout and of medium height, with a small moustache, duelling scar, pince-nez, hair very spruce.

HOCHROITZPOINTNER Isn't the Professor here yet? They're taking their time down there today. (*At the table, opening one of the files*) This is the third autopsy in a week. Rather a lot for a ward of twenty beds. And tomorrow we'll probably have yet another one.

NURSE You think so, Doctor? The girl with septicaemia?

HOCHROITZPOINTNER Yes. By the way, has the report on her been done yet?

NURSE Of course, Doctor.

HOCHROITZPOINTNER There was nothing one could prove of course. But it undoubtedly resulted from an illegal operation. Sadly, Nurse, these things happen out there in the world. (*He notices an opened packet lying on the table*) Ah, so those are the invitation cards to the faculty ball. (*Reads*) Under the patronage of Princess Stixenstein. Well, Nurse, will you be coming too?

NURSE (*smiling*) I don't think so, Doctor.

HOCHROITZPOINTNER Are you forbidden to go dancing?

NURSE Not at all, Doctor. We're a lay order, you know. We're free to do anything.

HOCHROITZPOINTNER (*giving her an arch look*) Really, anything at all?

NURSE But dancing wouldn't be quite proper. Besides, it's not the sort of thing one has on one's mind much in our profession.

HOCHROITZPOINTNER Why ever not? What are we medics supposed to say in that case? Look at Doctor Adler, for example. He's an anatomical pathologist and yet he's very sociable. As for me, I am nowhere in a better mood then in the dissecting lab.

> *Doctor Oscar Bernhardi from right, aged twenty-five, quite elegant, with an obliging but rather hesitant manner. Hochroitzpointner, Nurse.*

OSCAR Good morning.

HOCHROITZPOINTNER AND NURSE Good morning, Doctor.

OSCAR My father will be here shortly.

HOCHROITZPOINTNER Have you just come from the dissecting lab, Doctor? What's the verdict, if one may ask?

OSCAR The tumour was localized in the kidney and hadn't spread at all.

HOCHROITZPOINTNER So it might still have been possible to operate?

OSCAR Well, it might.

HOCHROITZPOINTNER If Professor Ebenwald had been of the same opinion—

OSCAR —we'd have had the autopsy a week earlier. (*At the table*) Ah, so those are the invitation cards to our ball. What's the point of sending them to people...?

HOCHROITZPOINTNER This year, the Elisabethinum's ball is expected to be one of the finest of the carnival season. It's already in the papers. You, Doctor, have already dedicated a waltz to the committee, I gather.

OSCAR (*deprecatingly*) Oh that—(*indicating the sick ward*) Anything happening in there?

HOCHROITZPOINTNER The girl with septicaemia will soon be out of her misery.

OSCAR Ah well... (*regretfully*) There was nothing much to be done there.

HOCHROITZPOINTNER I have given her a camphor injection.

OSCAR Yes, we know all the ins and outs of prolonging life.

> *From right Professor Bernhardi, over fifty, full greying beard, medium length straight hair, in demeanour more a man of the world than a scholar. Doctor Kurt Pflugfelder, his assistant, twenty-seven, moustache, pince-nez, lively but also by nature a*

little stern. Hochroitzpointner, Nurse, Oscar. Greetings all round.

BERNHARDI (*still at the door*) Oh, thank you—

The nurse takes his coat, which he was wearing round his shoulders, and hangs it on a hook.

KURT Well, Professor, I'm sorry to have to say that Doctor Adler would have been better pleased if Professor Ebenwald's diagnosis had been correct.

BERNHARDI (*smiling*) But my dear Doctor Pflugfelder! You scent betrayal everywhere. Where will your suspicions end?

HOCHROITZPOINTNER Good morning, Professor.

BERNHARDI Good morning.

HOCHROITZPOINTNER I've just heard from your son that we've been proved right.

BERNHARDI Yes, my dear colleague. But we've also been proved wrong, haven't we? Or don't you audit Professor Ebenwald's lectures any more?

OSCAR Hochroitzpointner audits lectures in practically every department.

BERNHARDI Then you must have built up quite a range of loyalties.

Hochroitzpointner becomes tight-lipped.

BERNHARDI (*in a friendly tone, putting his hand lightly on the other man's shoulder*) Well, so any new developments?

HOCHROITZPOINTNER The septicaemia case is in a bad way.

BERNHARDI So the poor girl is still alive?

KURT They could have kept her over in Gynaecology.

OSCAR They had no free bed two days ago.

HOCHROITZPOINTNER What do we report as the actual cause of death?

OSCAR Well, septicaemia of course.

HOCHROITZPOINTNER And the cause of the septicaemia? Because it was probably the result of an illegal operation—

BERNHARDI (*who has meanwhile been at the table signing various documents placed before him by the nurse*) We could never prove that. There was no evidence of internal injury. The authorities have been notified and as far as we're concerned, there the matter ends. And as for the poor girl in there... it ended quite some time ago. (*He gets up and prepares to inspect the sick ward*)

Professor Ebenwald enters, a very tall thin man of about forty, overcoat around his shoulders, short full beard, glasses, talks openly with a sometimes exaggerated Austrian accent.

Hochroitzpointner, nurse, Professor Bernhardi, Kurt.

EBENWALD Good morning. I wondered whether the Director—Ah, there you are, Professor.

BERNHARDI Good day, my dear colleague.

EBENWALD Could you spare me a minute?

BERNHARDI Now?

EBENWALD (*drawing closer to him*) If at all possible. Well, it's about the new headship of Tugendvetter's department.

BERNHARDI Is that really so urgent? Could you see me in my office in say half an hour perhaps?

EBENWALD Unfortunately I'm lecturing then, Professor.

BERNHARDI (*after pausing to consider*) Well, if you wouldn't mind waiting, my dear colleague, I shall be finished in there quite soon.

EBENWALD Not at all.

BERNHARDI (*to Oscar*) Have you given Hochroitzpointner the autopsy report yet?

OSCAR Ah, of course. (*Takes it out of his pocket*) Perhaps you wouldn't mind filing it at once.

HOCHROITZPOINTNER Certainly.

> *Bernhardi, Oscar, Kurt, nurse go into the sick ward. Ebenwald, Hochroitzpointner.*
> *Hochroitzpointner sits down and prepares to write.*
> *Ebenwald has gone over to the window, looks down, wipes his glasses.*

HOCHROITZPOINTNER (*solicitously*) Won't you sit down, Professor.

EBENWALD Don't let me interrupt you, Hochroitzpointner. How is everything, by the way?

HOCHROITZPOINTNER Kind of you to ask, Professor. You know how things are just a few weeks away from finals.

EBENWALD Well, you should be all right—after all that hard work.

HOCHROITZPOINTNER Yes, I feel fairly confident about the practical side, Professor, but then there's all that tedious theory.

EBENWALD Ah yes. Well, that was never my strong point either. (*Coming closer to him*) If it's any comfort to you, I failed physiology completely, in my time. And as you see, it hasn't done my career all that much harm.

> *Hochroitzpointner, who has resumed his seat, laughs happily.*

EBENWALD (*looking over Hochroitzpointner's shoulder*) Autopsy report?

HOCHROITZPOINTNER Indeed, Professor.

EBENWALD Rejoicing in Israel*—what?

HOCHROITZPOINTNER (*cautiously*) How do you mean, Professor?

EBENWALD Well, at the Bernhardi department's little triumph.

HOCHROITZPOINTNER Ah, you mean that the tumour turned out to be localized, Professor.

EBENWALD And had started in the kidney.

HOCHROITZPOINTNER In fact, that wasn't established with absolute certainty, it was more of a guess, if I may say so.

EBENWALD My dear Hochroitzpointner, a guess—! How can you possibly—! That's called intuition! Diagnostic acumen!

HOCHROITZPOINTNER And it would certainly no longer have been operable.

EBENWALD Out of the question, I agree. They may be able to afford such experiments over in the hospital, but we here in a relatively young and, as one might say, private institute—You know, in some cases it's always the interns who are in favour of operating, while in others it's we who are in too much of a hurry to do so for their liking.—But carry on with what you're writing.

    Hochroitzpointner starts writing again.

EBENWALD By the way, forgive my interrupting you again, but you do still audit lectures in Tugendvetter's department, don't you?

HOCHROITZPOINTNER I do indeed, Professor.

EBENWALD I just wanted to ask, in confidence of course, how you find Doctor Wenger as a lecturer?

HOCHROITZPOINTNER Doctor Wenger?

EBENWALD Well, he stands in for the old man when he receives an urgent call to join the hunt or visit a sick prince.*

HOCHROITZPOINTNER Yes certainly, then Doctor Wenger gives the lecture.

EBENWALD Well then, how does he lecture?

HOCHROITZPOINTNER (*cautiously*) Quite well, actually.

EBENWALD I see.

HOCHROITZPOINTNER He's perhaps a little too—too learned. But his delivery is lively. Admittedly—but perhaps I shouldn't be commenting on a future head of department—

EBENWALD How do you mean, head of department? That has by no means been decided yet. There are other candidates around. And besides, this is a private conversation. We might be chatting in the Riedhof.* So, tell me more. What have you against Doctor Wenger? The voice of the people is the voice of God.

HOCHROITZPOINTNER Well, it's not so much his lecturing as his whole manner. You see, Professor, he is by nature a little overbearing.

EBENWALD Aha. What you are referring to, my dear colleague, is probably what my cousin in parliament recently so aptly termed Yiddish of the soul.

HOCHROITZPOINTNER Ah, I like that. Yiddish of the soul. (*Emboldened*) But he is insufferable sometimes.

EBENWALD Well, that can't be helped. We're already living in an empire riddled with dialects.

Bernhardi, Oscar, Kurt and the nurse enter from the ward.

BERNHARDI Well, dear colleague, here I am.

The nurse presents him with a sheet to sign.

BERNHARDI What is it? Something else? Oh yes. Excuse me one more second, my dear colleague. (*As he signs*) Life never ceases to amaze one.—(*To Ebenwald*) We have a septicaemia case in there. An eighteen-year-old girl. Completely conscious. Wants to get up and walk about, thinks she is in perfect health. Yet her pulse is too faint to monitor. It could all be over in an hour.

EBENWALD (*in a professional tone*) We often see that.

HOCHROITZPOINTNER (*solicitously*) Perhaps I should give her another camphor injection?

BERNHARDI (*looking at him calmly*) You could have saved yourself the trouble of the last one. (*Reassuring him*) Well perhaps, anyway you probably induced the happiest moments of her life. Of course, I know that wasn't your intention either.

HOCHROITZPOINTNER (*irritably*) Well why not, Director, after all one is not a butcher.

BERNHARDI I don't recall reproaching you with anything of the kind.

Hochroitzpointner and Ebenwald exchange looks.

BERNHARDI (*to the nurse*) Has she any relatives?

NURSE No one has been to see her the entire three days she's been here.

BERNHARDI Not even her lover?

KURT He'll be watching his step.

OSCAR She didn't even name him. Who knows if she ever knew his name.

BERNHARDI And to think such things used to be called the joys of love. (*To Ebenwald*) Well, my dear colleague, I'm finally at your disposal.

OSCAR Excuse me, Papa, will you be coming by the ward again afterwards? Because she's been asking for you repeatedly.

BERNHARDI Yes, I'll look in again.

> *Kurt has gone over to the stand and is busying himself with two test tubes.*
>
> *Oscar joins him, they talk together and shortly return to the ward.*

NURSE (*to Hochroitzpointner*) I'll go over now and fetch the priest.

HOCHROITZPOINTNER Yes, if you would. Even if you're too late when you get back, it won't be a disaster.

> *Nurse exit.*
>
> *Hochroitzpointner takes some case histories out of a file and withdraws into the ward.*
>
> *Ebenwald, Bernhardi.*

EBENWALD (*who by now has become very impatient*) Well, here's the situation, Director. I received a letter from Professor Hell in Graz, to the effect that he would consider accepting a nomination as Tugendvetter's successor.

BERNHARDI He would consider accepting.

EBENWALD That's right, Director.

BERNHARDI Did anyone ask him?

EBENWALD I took the liberty—as an old friend and fellow student.

BERNHARDI But I take it you wrote to him in a private capacity?

EBENWALD Of course, Director. Seeing that no decision has been reached so far. Still, I considered myself justified, especially as I happen to know that Professor Tugendvetter is also sympathetic to Hell's candidacy.

BERNHARDI (*a little sharply*) Professor Tugendvetter doesn't take up his new appointment at the hospital until the beginning of the summer semester. So this discussion—and also, if I may say so, my dear colleague, your correspondence with Professor Hell, seem to me a little premature. And there is even less reason to be hasty, since Tugendvetter's assistant, Doctor Wenger, has more than once demonstrated his aptitude for the position, at least in an acting capacity.

EBENWALD On that score, I can't help expressing my aversion to acting appointments as a matter of principle.

> *Professor Tugendvetter from right, about fifty, grey hair, mutton chops, with something deliberately humorous and jovial, yet uncertain and approval-seeking in his manner; in general looks less like a scholar than a stockbroker.* Enters wearing his hat, which he only takes off after a few seconds. Ebenwald, Bernhardi.*

TUGENDVETTER Good morning. Hello, Bernhardi. How are you, Ebenwald? I've been looking for you upstairs, Bernhardi.

EBENWALD Perhaps I should leave you to it—

TUGENDVETTER Don't think of it. No secrets here.

BERNHARDI Well, what is it? Was there something you wanted to discuss with me?

TUGENDVETTER The situation is this. His Excellency, the Minister of Education has asked me if I might be able to take over the clinic at once.

EBENWALD At once?

TUGENDVETTER As soon as possible.

BERNHARDI But I thought it had been decided that Brunnleitner would continue to direct the clinic until the beginning of the summer semester.

TUGENDVETTER He has put in for leave. Poor devil, a six per cent blood sugar level, apparently. Last days of Pompeii,* what?
> He has the habit of ending certain sentences, especially quotations, with this mindless interrogatory expletive.

BERNHARDI Where did you hear that? Is it authentic?

TUGENDVETTER Authentic? Flint told me so himself. You see, I was at the ministry yesterday. They are supposed to build me a new wing. I'm going to get it too. He sends his regards, by the way.

BERNHARDI Who sends his regards?

TUGENDVETTER Flint. We talked a lot about you. He thinks very highly of you. He still has fond memories of the time when you were interns together under Rappenweiler. His words. Ipsissima verba.* There's a career for you, what? The first case in living memory, at least in Austria, that a clinical professor has become Minister of Education!

BERNHARDI He was always a good politician, your latest friend Flint.

TUGENDVETTER He is very interested in our, in your, no, still for the moment our institute.

BERNHARDI I'm not unaware of that. Yet once upon a time he was so interested that he was bent on running it into the ground.

TUGENDVETTER That wasn't him. That was the entire college. It was the struggle of the older against the younger generation. And anyway, all that was over long ago. Take my word for it, Bernhardi, he regards the Elisabethinum with a great deal of sympathy.

BERNHARDI Which today we could manage without if necessary, thank God.

TUGENDVETTER As proud as a Spaniard,* what?

BERNHARDI Anyway, at the moment all I'm interested in is your response to his offer.

TUGENDVETTER It's not for me to respond. (*Humorously*) It's up to the Director of the Elisabethinum to decide in this matter. I won't hand in my request to the directorate until you have let me know privately that I have your consent. You'll also require something in writing, you old pedant,* what?

BERNHARDI We won't of course keep you a day longer than you wish to stay. I promise to attend to the matter promptly. Fortunately you have an extremely competent assistant, who will continue to run your department in the same spirit as yourself until further notice.

TUGENDVETTER Our good Wenger, yes. Hard-working young man. But you won't have him there as acting head for long, will you?

EBENWALD I too was just observing that in general I consider provisional appointments an unhealthy business, and took the liberty of mentioning a letter I received from Professor Hell in Graz, who would be prepared—

TUGENDVETTER Really. He has already written to me too.

BERNHARDI Well, well, he seems to be quite a zealous fellow.

TUGENDVETTER (*with a quick look at Ebenwald*) Well, you know, Bernhardi, Hell would be quite a coup for your institute.

BERNHARDI Then he must have come along famously in Graz. While he was in Vienna, he was considered thoroughly incompetent.

TUGENDVETTER By whom?

BERNHARDI You for example. And we all know whom he had to thank for his Graz appointment. A little matter of influence in high places.

EBENWALD Well after all, there's nothing to be ashamed of, if one happens to have cured a prince.

BERNHARDI Nor do I hold it against him. But an entire career should not be based on an isolated incident like that. And as to his scientific achievements—

TUGENDVETTER Excuse me, but I think I may claim to be better informed on that score. He has published several excellent research papers.

BERNHARDI That may well be. But in any case, I infer from all this that you would rather propose Hell as your successor than your pupil and assistant Wenger.

TUGENDVETTER Wenger is too young. I am sure he himself hasn't given it a thought.

BERNHARDI Then he would be wrong. His last paper on serum generated widespread interest.

EBENWALD A sensation, Director. That's not the same thing.

TUGENDVETTER He has talent. There's no denying he has talent. But as far as the reliability of his experiments goes—

EBENWALD (*simply*) Some people regard him as—shall we say a fantasist.

TUGENDVETTER That's going a bit far. Anyway, I can't stop anyone from proposing his own candidacy. Be it Hell or Wenger.

BERNHARDI However, I alert you to the fact that you'll have to decide on one of them.

TUGENDVETTER But surely it doesn't depend on me? After all, I don't nominate my own successor.

BERNHARDI But you will take part in the vote. One would hope that the fate of your former department and our institute will still interest you to that extent.

TUGENDVETTER I should certainly think so. It wouldn't be a bad idea at all. You know, (*to Ebenwald*) we founded the Elisabethinum, Bernhardi, myself and Cyprian. There rode three knights, out through the gate,—what? How long ago was it now?

BERNHARDI Fifteen years, my dear Tugendvetter.

TUGENDVETTER Fifteen years, quite a time. It's not going to be easy for me, by God. Look here, Bernhardi, couldn't things be arranged so that to start with I worked both here and in the general hospital—?

BERNHARDI (*decidedly*) Certainly not. The day you take up your position over there, I shall appoint your assistant as acting head.

EBENWALD Then I would request that deliberations over the new permanent appointment be held in the next few days.

BERNHARDI Why is that, if I may ask? It would almost look as if we wanted to deprive Wenger of the opportunity to prove his teaching abilities for a few months.

EBENWALD I don't believe the Elisabethinum was founded as a school for training young academics in the art of lecturing.

BERNHARDI You may safely leave further arrangements to me, my dear Ebenwald. I'm sure you will admit that in our institute nothing so far has been unnecessarily postponed, nor has anything been irresponsibly rushed into.

EBENWALD I reject the insinuation that I have proposed a rash, or even irresponsibly rash course of action.

BERNHARDI (*smiling*) I shall take note of that.

EBENWALD (*glancing at his watch*) I must be getting back to my department. Gentlemen, I bid you good day.

BERNHARDI Yes, I must be off to the Chancellor's office myself. (*Makes way for Ebenwald*) After you, my dear colleague, your students will be waiting.

TUGENDVETTER It's been a pleasure, what?

EBENWALD (*meeting Adler, a young lecturer, at the door*) Good morning.

> *Doctor Adler enters, small, dark, fresh-looking, eager, bright-eyed, duelling scar, about thirty years old, wearing a white dissecting coat. Bernhardi, Tugendvetter.*

ADLER Good morning, gentlemen.

BERNHARDI What brings you to the land of the living, Doctor Adler?

ADLER I just wanted to check something in the file about that case of yours, Director.

BERNHARDI It's all at your disposal.

ADLER Pity by the way that you weren't downstairs just now, Director. A case from Cyprian's department. Just think, on top of the tertiary syphilis diagnosed earlier, there was an incipient tumour in the cerebrum, which apparently had not caused any symptoms at all.

BERNHARDI If one started worrying that some people never get around to having all their illnesses, as it were, one might have doubts about Providence.

OSCAR (*entering from the ward, to Tugendvetter*) Good morning, Professor.

TUGENDVETTER Hello, Oscar. I've heard already: a musician on the side. A dedication waltz called 'Rapid Pulses'.

OSCAR Please, Professor—

BERNHARDI What, you've been composing again without even mentioning it to me? (*Pulls his ear in jest*) Well, are you coming?

OSCAR Yes, I have to go to the laboratory.

TUGENDVETTER Fathers and sons—what?

> *Tugendvetter, Bernhardi and Oscar exeunt. Hochroitzpointner now enters from the ward. Adler, Hochroitzpointner.*

HOCHROITZPOINTNER Good morning, Doctor Adler.

ADLER Hello, my dear colleague. I wonder if I might have another look at that case history.

HOCHROITZPOINTNER Certainly.

> *He takes the sheet out of a folder.*

ADLER Thank you, my dear Doctor Hochroitz—what was it?—

HOCHROITZPOINTNER Hochroitzpointner.

ADLER (*seats himself at the table*) That's quite a name you have.

HOCHROITZPOINTNER Not exactly beautiful?

ADLER (*looking over the case history*) But rather splendid. One immediately thinks of mountain peaks and hikes across glaciers. You're from the Tyrol, aren't you?

HOCHROITZPOINTNER Indeed. From Imst.

ADLER Ah, from Imst. As a student I once did a wonderful walk which started out from there. Up the Wetterfernkogel.

HOCHROITZPOINTNER They built a hut up there last year.

ADLER They are putting huts up everywhere nowadays. (*Again looking over the case history*) No albumen all that time?

HOCHROITZPOINTNER None at all. Tests were done daily.

KURT (*has come out of the ward*) In the last few days albumen has in fact shown up. In significant amounts even.

HOCHROITZPOINTNER Yes, in the last three days, admittedly.

ADLER Aha, there's a note about it here.

HOCHROITZPOINTNER Of course, it's all in there.

ADLER (*to Kurt*) And how is your good father? He never shows his face among us down there. (*Looking at the case history*) So he was only with you for a week?

HOCHROITZPOINTNER Yes, before that he was under Professor Ebenwald. But since it was an inoperable case—

ADLER They can say what they like, but as a diagnostician your boss is first rate.

KURT (*smiling*) Well, what do they say then?

ADLER Why do you ask?

KURT Because you just said: they can say what they like.

ADLER (*almost sweetly*) Why are you being so hard on me, Doctor Pflugfelder? All I meant was that your department's main strength lies in diagnosis rather than in therapy. There, in my humble opinion, you do too damn much experimenting.

KURT But what else are we supposed to do with our in-patients, Doctor? One has to try out new methods when the old ones no longer work.

ADLER And tomorrow the new ones are already out of date. There's nothing you can do about that of course, I've been through it all as well. But it is depressing sometimes, that one is groping in the dark so much. That was why I escaped into anatomical pathology. There one is as it were the auditor in chief.

KURT Excuse me, Doctor, but there is still one Being above you.

ADLER But He has no time to bother about us. He is too busy with a higher faculty. (*Consulting the case history*) Radiotherapy as well? But do you really believe that in cases like this—

KURT We feel it is our duty to try everything, Doctor. Especially where there is nothing to lose. It's neither a gimmick nor a public relations exercise, as is claimed in some quarters, and one shouldn't blame the Professor for it.

ADLER Who is blaming him? Not me, certainly.

KURT Not you, I know, Doctor. But some people do.

ADLER Well, everyone has his detractors.

KURT And enviers.

ADLER Of course. Anyone in fact who works hard and achieves something. The more honour, the more enmity. Bernhardi can't complain. A practice in the highest circles and influence in others which fortunately carry rather more weight—Professor, Director of the Elisabethinum—

KURT Well, who else deserved it if not him? He certainly fought tooth and nail for the Elisabethinum.

ADLER Of course, of course. I am the last person to want to belittle his achievements. Especially since he has attained such eminence in the current social climate.—I have some right to speak about that, since I've never made any secret of my Jewish origins, even though on my mother's side I come from an old-established, middle-class Viennese family. I even had occasion to bleed for my gentile side during my student years.

KURT That's well known, Doctor.

ADLER But I'm pleased that even you are prepared to do our Director the justice he deserves.

KURT Why should that please you particularly, Doctor?

ADLER You were a member of a German nationalist fraternity, weren't you?

KURT And an anti-Semite. Certainly, Doctor. Indeed I still am, generally speaking. Except that I have since become anti-Aryan as well. To me, human beings are altogether a fairly inadequate lot, and one takes comfort in the few exceptions one encounters now and then.

> *Professor Cyprian from right. A small older man with long, still almost blond hair, a rather slow, chanting way of talking, who unconsciously adopts a lecturing manner, speaking as if to an auditorium. Adler, Kurt, Hochroitzpointner.*

CYPRIAN Good day to you, gentlemen. (*Reciprocal greetings*) Is Doctor Adler here by any chance? Ah yes, there you are. I've been looking for you downstairs. May I depend upon it, Doctor Adler, that today's cranium won't go missing again, unlike that of the paralytic the other day?

ADLER The orderly has his instructions, Professor—

CYPRIAN The orderly is nowhere to be found. Probably in the pub again. You may find yourselves faced with the situation I ran into in Prague when working under Heschel.* There too we had an alcoholic employed as an orderly in the pathology department. The fellow gradually drank all the alcohol intended for our preparations.

ADLER Well, Professor, so far ours has restricted himself to ham rolls.

CYPRIAN Anyway, I would like, if I may, to come down this evening. When would you be there?

ADLER At present I normally work until about midnight.

CYPRIAN I see, then I'll come after ten.

> *Bernhardi and Oscar enter from right.*

BERNHARDI Good morning. How are you, Cyprian? Are you looking for me, by the way?

CYPRIAN Actually, I had something to discuss with Doctor Adler. But I am very pleased that I've run into you. Because I wanted to ask you when you might have time to come to the Ministry of Education with me?

BERNHARDI So what's up?

> *They stand apart together. Oscar goes into the ward at once. The other gentlemen continue talking to one side.*

CYPRIAN Nothing in particular. But I think we ought to strike while the iron's hot.

BERNHARDI I really don't understand.

CYPRIAN Now is a propitious moment to press the cause of our institute. Having a doctor, a clinical professor, at the helm is a situation we must take advantage of.

BERNHARDI You all seem to be placing remarkably high hopes in Flint.

CYPRIAN With good reason. I foresaw he would have a brilliant career when we were working in the laboratory together under Brücke,* almost thirty years ago. He is a genius at administration. I have already drafted a memorandum to him. What we are requesting is first and foremost government sponsorship, so that we will no longer need to depend entirely on all those rather undignified private appeals. Furthermore—

BERNHARDI How forgetful you all are. Flint is our bitterest opponent.

CYPRIAN But for goodness sake, all that is over and done with. Today he is very sympathetically disposed toward the Elisabethinum. Councillor Winkler told me as much again yesterday. Quite spontaneously.

BERNHARDI Well.—

OSCAR (*entering from the ward, hastily to Bernhardi*) Excuse me, Papa, but if you want to be in time to speak to her—

BERNHARDI I'm sorry, my dear Cyprian. Perhaps you wouldn't mind waiting five minutes. (*Exit*)

OSCAR (*to Cyprian*) The woman's dying, Professor.
> *Follows his father into the ward.*
> *Hochroitzpointner, Kurt, Adler, Cyprian.*

KURT (*casually*) Septicaemia. A young girl. Abortion.

HOCHROITZPOINTNER (*to Adler*) For tomorrow, Doctor.

CYPRIAN (*in his monotonous way*) When I was still an intern under Skoda,* we had a department head who shall be nameless, nomina sunt odiosa,* and who would ask us to summon him to terminal cases as frequently as possible. Apparently he intended to write a psychological study of people in their dying hour. I remember remarking at the time to Bernitzer, a fellow intern, that there was something fishy about it. Our head wasn't remotely interested in psychology. Well now, imagine, one day he suddenly disappeared. He was a married man with three children. The following night an old tramp was discovered stabbed to death in some out-of-the-way street. Well, you will have guessed the point by now, gentlemen. It turned out that our head and the vagrant who'd been stabbed were one and the same person. He had been living a double life for years. By day he was a busy doctor, at night he was a frequenter of various disreputable haunts, a pimp.—
> *The priest enters, a young man of twenty-eight, with lively intelligent features. The sacristan with him remains standing by the door. Hochroitzpointner, Kurt, Adler, Cyprian.*

ADLER (*solicitously*) Nice to see you, Father.

PRIEST Good day, gentlemen. I hope I've not arrived too late.

KURT No, Father. The Professor is with the patient at this moment. (*He introduces himself*) Doctor Pflugfelder, intern.

PRIEST So there's still some hope then?

OSCAR (*comes out of the ward*) Good day, Father.

KURT I'm afraid, Father, it is a completely hopeless case.

OSCAR This way, Father—

PRIEST Perhaps I'll wait until the Professor's left the patient.

The sacristan withdraws, the door closes. Hochroitzpointner draws up a chair for the priest. At first he does not sit down.

CYPRIAN Ah well, Father, if only we just had to attend the ones we can still help. Sometimes we can offer little more than consolation.

KURT And lies.

PRIEST (*sits down*) That's rather a harsh word, Doctor.

KURT I'm sorry, Father, it was intended for medical ears only. But sometimes that's the hardest and noblest part of our profession.

> *Bernhardi appears at the door, the priest rises. Hochroitzpointner, Adler, Kurt, Cyprian, Oscar, priest, Bernhardi. The nurse comes out of the ward after Bernhardi.*

BERNHARDI (*a little disconcerted*) Oh, Father.

PRIEST We are relieving one another, Professor. (*He holds out his hand*) I hope I shall still find the patient conscious?

BERNHARDI Yes. One might even say, in a heightened state of consciousness. (*Principally to the others*) Complete euphoria has set in. (*By way of explaining to the priest*) She feels on top of the world, so to speak.

PRIEST Well, that's surely a good sign. Who knows!—On the street the other day, I was delighted to meet a young man alive and well, who only a few weeks ago was resigned to death and had received extreme unction from me.

ADLER And who knows, Father, you might have been the one who restored his strength and courage to live.

BERNHARDI (*to Adler*) I think his Reverence has misunderstood me. (*To the priest*) What I meant was that the patient is completely unaware of her true plight. She is beyond hope, yet she believes she is cured.

PRIEST Is that so.

BERNHARDI So you see, Father, it's almost a matter of ensuring that your sudden appearance,—

PRIEST (*very gently*) Have no fear for your patient, Professor. I do not come to pronounce sentence of death.

BERNHARDI Naturally, but even so—

PRIEST Perhaps one could prepare the patient.

> *The nurse, unnoticed by Bernhardi, responds to an almost imperceptible look from the priest, and returns to the ward.*

BERNHARDI But that would not improve matters. As I've already explained, Father, the patient is completely unaware of the situation. And your visit is the last thing she's expecting. Indeed she is under the illusion that in the next few hours someone dear to her will call for her and carry her off—into life and happiness. Father, I don't believe you would be doing a good deed, or even I might add one pleasing to God, if you were to waken her from this last dream.

PRIEST (*after a brief hesitation, more decisively*) Is there any possibility, Professor, that my appearance might adversely affect the course of her—

BERNHARDI (*breaking in quickly*) It's quite possible it would hasten her end, perhaps only by minutes, but even so—

PRIEST (*more eagerly*) Once again: is there any possibility she might still be cured? Would my appearance pose a threat in that sense? In which case I would of course be ready to withdraw at once.

    Adler nods approvingly.

BERNHARDI She can't be saved, there's no doubt about that.

PRIEST In that case, Professor, I see absolutely no reason—

BERNHARDI I'm sorry, Father, but for the present I am still officiating here in my capacity as a doctor. And one of my duties, when it is outside my power to do more, is to ensure that as far as possible my patients are allowed to die happily.

    Cyprian shows slight signs of impatience and disapproval

PRIEST Die happily. We probably mean quite different things by that, Professor. And from what the nurse has given me to understand, your patient is more urgently in need of absolution than most.

BERNHARDI (*with an ironic smile*) Aren't we all sinners, Father?

PRIEST That's not the point, Professor. You can't be sure that in the depths of her soul, which only God is privy to, she isn't feeling some last-minute impulse to unburden herself through confession of her sins.

BERNHARDI Must I repeat yet again, Father? The patient doesn't know that she is doomed. She is light-hearted, happy and—quite without remorse.

PRIEST In that case my burden of guilt would be the heavier, if I were to leave without administering the consolation of our sacred religion to this dying girl.

BERNHARDI Father, God and every judge in the land will absolve you of that guilt. (*Seeing him move*) Be assured of that, Father. For as a doctor I cannot admit you to this patient's bedside.

PRIEST I have been called upon to come here. So I must ask you—

BERNHARDI Not with my authority, Father. And I can only repeat that as a doctor charged with the well-being of his patients until their final hour, I must regretfully forbid you to cross this threshold.

PRIEST (*stepping forward*) You forbid me?

BERNHARDI (*touching him lightly on the shoulder*) Yes, Father.

NURSE (*hurrying out of the ward*) Father—

BERNHARDI You've been in there?

NURSE It will be too late, Father.

> *Kurt quickly enters the ward.*

BERNHARDI (*to the nurse*) Did you tell the patient that his Reverence was here?

NURSE Yes, Director.

BERNHARDI I see. And—now answer me calmly—how did the patient respond? Did she say anything? Tell me. Well?

NURSE She said—

BERNHARDI Well?

NURSE She was rather frightened.

BERNHARDI (*without anger*) Come on, speak up now, what did she say?

NURSE Do I really have to die?

KURT (*coming out of the ward*) It's all over.

> *Short pause.*

BERNHARDI Don't be upset, Father. It is not your fault. You simply wanted to fulfil your duty. So did I. The fact that I did not succeed is upsetting enough.

PRIEST It is not up to you to grant me absolution, Professor. The poor creature in there has passed away in a state of sin, without the consolation of religion. And you are to blame.

BERNHARDI I'm prepared to shoulder it.

PRIEST It remains to be seen whether you will be capable of that, Professor. Good day to you, gentlemen.

> *He departs.*
> *The others stay behind, moved and a little embarrassed.*
> *Bernhardi looks at each of them in turn.*

BERNHARDI Tomorrow morning then, my dear Doctor Adler, at the post-mortem.

CYPRIAN (*to Bernhardi without the others hearing*) That was not right.

BERNHARDI What do you mean, not right?

CYPRIAN And besides it remains an isolated case. You won't change the general situation in the least.

BERNHARDI The general situation? That was never my intention.

ADLER I'd be less than candid, Director, if I didn't tell you that I cannot in all loyalty—formally side with you in this matter.

BERNHARDI And I owe it to you, my good Doctor, to assure you that I never expected it would be otherwise.

  Cyprian and Adler exeunt.
  Oscar bites his lip.

BERNHARDI Ah well, my son, let's hope it won't do too much harm to your career.

OSCAR How can you say that, Papa.

BERNHARDI (*takes him by the head, tenderly*) Come now, I didn't mean to offend you.

NURSE Professor, I thought—

BERNHARDI What did you think? Ah well, what's the use, it's all over now.

NURSE But you see, Director, it's always so—and then (*indicating Hochroitzpointner*) Doctor—

HOCHROITZPOINTNER Well, naturally I did not forbid her to, Director.

BERNHARDI That goes without saying, Doctor Hochroitzpointner. You're probably auditing in church as well, what?

HOCHROITZPOINTNER We live in a Christian country, Director.

BERNHARDI Yes. (*Looks at him for some time*) May the Lord forgive them—for they know damn well what they do.*

  Exit with Kurt and Oscar.
  Hochroitzpointner, Nurse.

HOCHROITZPOINTNER My dear girl, why on earth did you go and apologize like that? You were only doing your duty. But what's the matter—now you're crying—as long as you don't throw a fit on me again.

NURSE (*sobbing*) But the Director was so angry.

HOCHROITZPOINTNER And what if he was. He won't be Director for very much longer. This will ruin his career.

  Curtain.

Act Two

Professor Bernhardi's consulting room. To the right is the main entrance, to the left, a door into the adjoining room. A medicine cabinet on the left, bookshelves partly draped in green take up the whole of the back wall. On the stove in the corner on the left is a bust of Aesculapius.* A desk and chair. A little table next to the desk. Near the desk facing the audience a divan. Photographs of scholars on the walls.

Dr Oscar Bernhardi, seated at the desk, makes a note in a medical record book, then rings. A servant enters.

OSCAR Is there anyone still waiting?

SERVANT No, Doctor.

OSCAR Then I'll be off. If Papa comes back—(*A bell rings outside*) Oh, see who it is, will you.

    Servant exit.

    Oscar closes the record book, tidies the desk.

    Servant enters with a visitor's card.

OSCAR Does he want to speak to me?

SERVANT At first the gentleman asked if the Professor was at home. But—

OSCAR But he doesn't mind making do with me—well then, show him in.

    Servant exit.

    Oscar, Dr Feuermann, a short, dark-bearded, nervous young man with glasses. Hat in hand, overcoat, gloves.

    Oscar advances to meet him.

FEUERMANN I don't know if you will still remember me—

OSCAR My dear Feuermann, still remember you! (*Holds out his hand*)

FEUERMANN Well, it has been eight years—

OSCAR Yes, how time flies. Won't you have a seat? So you wanted a word with Papa?

FEUERMANN As a matter of fact—

OSCAR I've taken over his consultancy for the day, he's been called away to see Prince Constantine in Baden.*

FEUERMANN Yes, your Papa has certainly built up a fine practice. (*He takes a seat*)

OSCAR Well, and how are you? You haven't I take it come here as a patient.—Where are you practising, by the way?

FEUERMANN In Oberhollabrunn.*

OSCAR Yes, of course. So what brings you here? Opening a sana-
torium perhaps, or doing a stint as a doctor in some spa? Or are you
planning to turn Oberhollabrunn into a health resort?

FEUERMANN Nothing like that actually. It's a frightful business.
Haven't you heard yet?

> *Oscar makes a gesture of denial.*

FEUERMANN I've already written to your Papa about it.

OSCAR He receives so many letters.

FEUERMANN But if you were to put in a word for me as well—

OSCAR So what's it all about?

FEUERMANN You know me, Bernhardi. We were students together
and you know I've always been industrious and conscientious. An
accident like that can happen to anyone who is obliged to go into
practice straight from university. Not everyone has things as easy as
you, for instance.

BERNHARDI Well, being the son of a famous father has its drawbacks
too.

FEUERMANN I'm sorry, I didn't mean it quite like that. But it's really
invaluable to be able to continue training in the hospital, and take
courses from the breast of one's alma mater—

OSCAR (*a little impatiently*) So what has happened then?

FEUERMANN I've been charged with medical negligence. I might even
lose my licence. An error of professional judgement, they claim.
Mind you, I won't say that I'm entirely blameless. If I'd had one to
two more years in the obstetrics clinic, the woman would probably
have pulled through. But you have to imagine conditions in that
outpost. No assistance, no proper antiseptics. Ah, what do any of
you know about it here in town. No one gives me credit for the
many lives I've saved. A single bit of bad luck and one might as well
put a bullet through one's head.

OSCAR But Feuermann, you shouldn't immediately assume the
worst—you've not even been convicted yet. The experts are also
going to have a say.

FEUERMANN Yes, the experts. Well, that's exactly why I wanted to see
your Papa.—He knows me too and might even remember something about me, as I once took a short course on heart diseases from
him—

OSCAR Well that—

FEUERMANN He's sure to be on good terms with Professor Filitz,
head of the Elisabethinum's gynaecology department, and Filitz

has been proposed as the expert witness. So I wanted to ask your Papa if he might have a word with Professor Filitz—Oh, I don't want any special treatment, but—

OSCAR Yes of course, my dear Feuermann, though whether an endorsement from my father would help in this case—You see, he's by no means on such good terms with Filitz as you seem to assume.

FEUERMANN But your father is Director of the Elisabethinum—

OSCAR Well yes, but the situation here is not so simple. It's a long story. And anyway, out in Oberhollabrunn it might be hard to appreciate the niceties. A host of trends and counter-trends and undercurrents are entailed—So whether any intervention from Papa might not have precisely the opposite effect—

FEUERMANN Perhaps if he could intercede for me some other way! Your father writes so brilliantly. His articles on the rights of doctors always hit the nail on the head. It would just be a matter of putting my particular case in some more general perspective. Of drawing attention to the root cause of the evil. To the unfortunate material circumstances of young doctors, to the difficulties of country practice, to the animosities, the rivalries and so forth.—Ah, now that really would be a topic for your father,—and I could provide him with plenty of material.

The servant enters with a visiting card.

OSCAR Oh, Fil—(*he gets up*) I'm afraid you'll have to excuse me, Feuermann.—Show him in.

Servant exit.

FEUERMANN Didn't you just say Filitz?

OSCAR Well, I—

FEUERMANN Yes, I believe you did.

OSCAR Surely you don't propose to—If I could perhaps ask you to come through here—

FEUERMANN Oh no. You can't expect me to do that. This is a sign from heaven.

Filitz enters. A handsome blond man of forty, wearing a pince-nez. Oscar, Feuermann.

FILITZ Good day, my dear colleague.

FEUERMANN Would you be good enough to introduce me to the Professor, my dear friend?

OSCAR (*smiling awkwardly*) The Professor probably wishes to see me about—

FEUERMANN (*introduces himself*) Doctor Feuermann. You see, I take it as a sign from heaven, Professor, that at this very moment you should—that I should have the good fortune to—I am a doctor practising in Oberhollabrunn—Doctor Feuermann. A complaint has been lodged against me.

FILITZ Ah yes. I remember now. (*Agreeably*) You hastened somebody's demise,—a teacher's wife—

FEUERMANN (*appalled*) You've been misinformed, Professor. If you'd just look—if you would be good enough to look into the case in detail—It was a string of unfortunate accidents.

FILITZ Yes, that's always the way. But then such accidents would not occur, if young people didn't rush into practice without proper training. They pass a few exams by the skin of their teeth and think God will assist them from there on. But sometimes He doesn't help, and perhaps He has His own cogent reasons.

FEUERMANN Professor, if you don't mind my saying so—I passed all my examinations with distinction, even in obstetrics. And I had to go into practice because otherwise I would have starved. And as to this poor woman's bleeding to death after giving birth, I make so bold as to assert that it could have happened even under a professor.

FILITZ There are all sorts of professors.

FEUERMANN But if it had been a professor, he would not have been indicted, and—and it would have been considered God's inscrutable decree.

FILITZ You think so, do you. I see. (*Moves in front of him and looks him in the eye*) No doubt you are another of those young men who believe they owe it to their scientific dignity to play the atheist?—

FEUERMANN Oh, Professor, to me it's really—

FILITZ Just as you please, Doctor. But I assure you, faith and science are perfectly compatible. I would even venture to say that science without faith will always be a fairly precarious affair, because it lacks the moral basis, the ethical dimension.

FEUERMANN I'm sure you're right, Professor. But getting back to what I was saying, could I ask—

FILITZ There is no shortage of examples to show where nihilistic arrogance leads. And I hope it is not your ambition, Doctor Feuerstein*—

FEUERMANN (*shyly*) Feuermann—

FILITZ —to dismay the contemporary world by providing yet another instance. By the way, I have your file at home. Perhaps you would come round tomorrow morning at eight, and we could discuss the matter further.

FEUERMANN (*almost intoxicated by this new turn of events*) Do I have your permission then, Professor? Oh, I am eternally grateful to you. I'll take the liberty of calling with the relevant material— You see, my very existence is at stake. I have a wife and two children. I would have no option but to kill myself.

FILITZ I would appreciate it, Doctor, if you'd refrain from such sentimental claptrap. If you really have nothing to reproach yourself with, such antics are unnecessary, at least with me.

OSCAR Forgive me if I don't see you out, my dear Feuermann.

FEUERMANN Oh, I'm more than grateful. (*Exit*)

OSCAR I'd like to apologize on his behalf for his rather tactless remarks, Professor. Understandably, he was a little distraught.

FILITZ A fellow student?

OSCAR Indeed, Professor. And a very industrious and conscientious student, I might add. I happen to know that for the first few years he had to live on fifteen or so guilders a month, which he earned by giving lectures.

FILITZ That proves nothing either way, my dear colleague. My father was a millionaire, and I too have turned out reasonably competent. Anyway. Your Papa is away on a trip, I gather?

OSCAR Not on a trip, Professor, he's only in Baden seeing Prince Constantine.

FILITZ Ah.

OSCAR In fact, he intended to be back in time for his consulting hours.

FILITZ (*looking at his watch*) Well, unfortunately I can't wait much longer. Perhaps you would be good enough to inform your Papa— and this ought to interest you too—that my wife was not received by Princess Stixenstein today.

OSCAR (*not quite understanding*) I see. Perhaps the Princess was not at home?

FILITZ My dear colleague, my wife as president of the commemoration ball committee was invited to call on Princess Stixenstein,— their patron and the wife of the president of the board of trustees—today at one o'clock. I think the fact speaks volumes.

> *As is his wont, he again looks Oscar in the eye.*
> *Oscar a little embarrassed.*
> *Servant with visiting card.*

OSCAR Excuse me, Professor. It's Professor Löwenstein.

FILITZ Don't let me hold you up. In any case I was just about to—

OSCAR (*to the servant*) Show him in.

> *Filitz appears to be getting ready to depart.*

Löwenstein enters. About forty, middle height, somewhat brusque in manner, small eyes which he sometimes opens wide. Glasses. He likes to stand opposite the person he is talking to, with his left shoulder drooping and his knee bent slightly, and occasionally runs his fingers through his hair. Filitz, Oscar.

LÖWENSTEIN Good day. Oh, Professor Filitz. You're not going already? Do stay a moment. This business will interest you. Here, Oscar, read this. (*He hands him a letter*) Apologies, Professor Filitz, he has to read it first as a member of the ball committee. Princess Stixenstein has resigned as patron of the ball.

OSCAR (*having rapidly scanned the letter, hands it to Professor Filitz*) Without offering any explanation?

LÖWENSTEIN She did not consider that necessary.

FILITZ Especially when the reasons are so patently obvious to everyone.

OSCAR So has—this affair become that public already? Within a week?

LÖWENSTEIN My dear Oscar, I never doubted that it would. The way the scene was reported to me, I said at once it would provide a feast for certain people and be inflated out of all proportion.

FILITZ Excuse me, Doctor Löwenstein, but nothing has been inflated here, nor does the incident, which speaks for itself, require any inflating.—But I would prefer to express my views on the matter in person to my friend Bernhardi.

OSCAR I need scarcely observe, Professor, that I am entirely on my father's side in this whole matter.

FILITZ Naturally, naturally, that is no more than your duty.

OSCAR It is also my conviction, Professor.

LÖWENSTEIN As indeed it is mine, Professor. And I strongly maintain that only malice could contrive to turn as innocuous an incident as this into anything resembling a scandal. Furthermore, to be absolutely frank, no one would ever attempt to do so, if Bernhardi didn't happen to be a Jew.

FILITZ There you go again with your idée fixe. Now I am anti-Semitic too, I suppose? I who always have at least one Jewish assistant? There is no anti-Semitism against decent Jews.

LÖWENSTEIN Come now, what I am claiming is—

FILITZ If a Christian had behaved as Bernhardi did, it would have created just as much of a scandal. You know that full well, my dear Löwenstein.

LÖWENSTEIN All right. Possibly. But then thousands would have been prepared to rally behind a Christian, who as it is won't take a stand and may even side against him.

FILITZ Who?

LÖWENSTEIN The German Nationalists, and of course the Jews—I mean the sort who never pass up an opportunity to ingratiate themselves with the prevailing powers.

FILITZ Forgive my saying so, Löwenstein, but all that borders on the paranoiac. And I might add that it's precisely people like you, Löwenstein, absurdly suspecting anti-Semitism everywhere, who bear the main responsibility for the regrettable way differences are being emphasized. It would be infinitely preferable—

Bernhardi enters. Filitz, Löwenstein, Oscar.

BERNHARDI (*evidently in a good mood, with his faintly ironic smile, exchanges greetings and shakes hands*) Ah, gentlemen. What's the latest? Are we broke? Or has someone donated us a million?

OSCAR (*handing him the letter*) The Princess has resigned as patron of our ball.

BERNHARDI (*glancing over the letter*) Well, we'll just have to look around for another patron. (*Jestingly to Oscar*) Or are you going to resign as president too, my son?

OSCAR (*a little insulted*) Papa.—

LÖWENSTEIN My dear Bernhardi, your son has just formally declared himself completely on your side.

BERNHARDI (*affectionately stroking Oscar's hair*) But of course he is. I hope you won't take that amiss now, Oscar. And as for you, Löwenstein, I don't even have to ask. But whatever's the matter, Filitz? From your face one would think we really had gone broke.

OSCAR Well, I must be going now. (*Smiling*) You see, there's a meeting of the commemoration ball committee at six. Good day, Professor, good day, Doctor. (*He shakes hands with both of them*) Oh, by the way, Papa, Doctor Feuermann was here. Apparently he wrote to you.

BERNHARDI Ah yes.

FILITZ Don't worry about that Feuerstein fellow. If it's remotely possible, I'll get him off the hook, (*with a look of triumph at Löwenstein*) even though he is a Jew.

OSCAR I honestly believe, Professor, that he's by no means an unworthy—

FILITZ No doubt, no doubt. Good day, my dear colleague.

Oscar exit.

Filitz, Löwenstein, Bernhardi.

BERNHARDI   Was it specifically about this Feuermann that you—

FILITZ   Oh no. I just happened to meet him here. I came to inform you that today at lunchtime my wife was not received by Princess Stixenstein.

BERNHARDI   Well?

FILITZ   Was not received! The Princess not only resigned as patron, she was also not at home to my wife.

BERNHARDI   Really, and you've come to see me about that?

FILITZ   Don't pretend to be innocent, my dear Bernhardi! You know perfectly well that all this, however insignificant in itself, is symptomatic of the way a little incident not unbeknown to you is regarded in influential higher circles.

BERNHARDI (*very genially*)   I in turn might be able to come up with quite different symptoms from perhaps even higher circles. I've just returned from Prince Constantine, who of course has also heard the story, and who appears to regard it in quite a different light from your illustrious Princess Stixenstein.

FILITZ   Please, Bernhardi, spare me your Prince Constantine. For him, being a liberal is a sport, like shooting pigeons for other members of his caste.

BERNHARDI   Nevertheless—

FILITZ   And as far as I'm concerned, Prince Constantine's opinions on this issue are of no interest whatsoever. I choose to take a very different view of the effect of your conduct in the matter we're discussing.

BERNHARDI   I see. Did your good wife send you here to reprimand me?

FILITZ (*very irritably*)   I have absolutely no right to do so, and it is also far from my intention.—In short, I am here to ask what you propose to do to obtain satisfaction for the insult to my wife.

BERNHARDI (*really astounded*)   Ah. Well now! You can't seriously mean—

> *Cyprian enters. Filitz, Löwenstein, Bernhardi.*

CYPRIAN   Good evening gentlemen. My apologies for this unannounced intrusion... But I can well imagine— (*shakes hands with everyone*)

BERNHARDI   Have you also come about Princess Stixenstein's resignation as patron of our ball?

CYPRIAN   That ball committee business is of secondary importance.

FILITZ (*looking at his watch*)   Unfortunately I'm out of time. You'll forgive me, Cyprian. May I repeat my question, Bernhardi, as to how you propose to obtain satisfaction (*with a glance at Cyprian*) for my wife's not having been received by Princess Stixenstein.

> *Löwenstein looks at Cyprian.*

BERNHARDI (*very calmly*) Tell your good wife, my dear Filitz, that I consider her too intelligent to assume she would for a moment be vexed at being excluded from the salon of so illustrious a goose.

FILITZ It is clear from your answer that there is no point in continuing this conversation. It's been a pleasure, gentlemen. (*Exit in haste*)

> *Löwenstein, Bernhardi, Cyprian.*

CYPRIAN You should not have said that, Bernhardi.

LÖWENSTEIN Why shouldn't he have?

CYPRIAN Apart from the fact that one should avoid annoying certain people, in any case he is simply wrong. The Princess is anything but a goose. She is in fact a very clever woman.

BERNHARDI Clever? Babette Stixenstein?

LÖWENSTEIN She's narrow-minded, petty and a bigot.

CYPRIAN There are certain things that the Princess should not even think about, otherwise she would degrade herself just as much as you would, were you to fail to think about them. It's in the nature of things that we should understand these people without their understanding us at all. Besides, this is really only the beginning. Obviously the Prince will draw his own conclusions too,—that means the board of trustees will probably all resign.

LÖWENSTEIN That would be outrageous.

BERNHARDI (*who has been pacing up and down, halts in front of Cyprian*) Excuse me, Cyprian. The board of trustees consists of Prince Constantine, Bishop Liebenberg, Prince Stixenstein, Veith the bank director and Councillor Winkler. And I can guarantee you that, apart from Stixenstein—

CYPRIAN Better not guarantee anything.

BERNHARDI I spoke to the Prince an hour ago.

CYPRIAN Did he express his appreciation?

BERNHARDI He was graciousness itself. And his summoning me today is also telling, because there was nothing wrong with him at all, and he clearly just wanted to talk the matter over with me.

CYPRIAN Did he begin with that?

BERNHARDI Of course.

LÖWENSTEIN What did he say?

BERNHARDI (*smiling, a little flattered*) That a few hundred years ago I would probably have been burned at the stake.

CYPRIAN And you took that to imply agreement?

BERNHARDI You haven't heard what he said next: 'I probably would too.'

LÖWENSTEIN Aha!

CYPRIAN Which doesn't prevent him attending mass regularly, or voting in the Upper House against reforming the marriage laws.

BERNHARD Yes, people have their official obligations.

CYPRIAN And did you happen to ask the Prince what the other members of the board think about the whole business?

BERNHARDI Without my asking, the Prince mentioned something the bishop said.

LÖWENSTEIN Well?

BERNHARDI 'I like the man.'

LÖWENSTEIN You like the bishop?

BERNHARDI No, he likes me.

CYPRIAN Yes, I've heard that remark as well, only with me they didn't miss out the second half.

BERNHARDI The second half?

CYPRIAN In full, the bishop's comment was: 'I like Bernhardi well enough, but he will regret this.'

BERNHARDI And who gave you this information?

CYPRIAN Councillor Winkler, whose office I've just come from, and who also intimated that the board of trustees is intending to resign.

BERNHARDI Come now! The Councillor is on the board himself, and he surely won't leave us in the lurch.

CYPRIAN He won't have any alternative. He can't stay on as the only board member, if all the others go.

BERNHARDI Why not? If he's the man we've always taken him to be.—

LÖWENSTEIN But consider, a councillor—

CYPRIAN What would be gained if he alone were to stand up for you? Can you expect him, for your sake, to—

BERNHARDI You know full well this business is not about me.

CYPRIAN Quite right, it's not about you. You say so yourself. It's about the institute. About our institute. And if the board of trustees goes, we are finished.

BERNHARDI Come, come!

LÖWENSTEIN How do you mean? Neither your Prince Constantine nor his Worship have ever been distinguished for their bounteous generosity.

CYPRIAN But I could name you a dozen Jews, who only donate

anything because a prince and a bishop are on the board. And if we get no more money, we might as well shut up shop.

BERNHARDI And all this is supposed to happen just because I fulfilled my duty as a doctor.—

LÖWENSTEIN It's outrageous, simply outrageous. Well, what if our institute does collapse. We will found another better one, without any Filitzes and Ebenwalds and board members. Ah Bernhardi, the number of times I have warned you about these men. You and your blind trust in people. Perhaps now you will be more circumspect.

CYPRIAN (*who has been trying in vain to calm him down*) Would you mind letting others have a say as well. For the moment the institute still exists. And for the moment we even have a board of trustees still. So far it has not resigned. And it should be possible to find some means of preventing such an awkward situation ever arising.

BERNHARDI What means?

CYPRIAN The Councillor himself, who you won't deny is an intelligent, enlightened man and well disposed towards you, is also of the opinion—

BERNHARDI What opinion? Could you make yourself a little clearer, Cyprian.

CYPRIAN That you wouldn't be conceding anything, Bernhardi, if in some appropriate form you were to—

LÖWENSTEIN (*interrupting*) You want him to apologize?

CYPRIAN Who said anything about an apology. Of course he shouldn't do penance in a hair shirt at the church door. Of course he shouldn't retract anything or swear to some dogma or other. (*To Bernhardi*) All you would need to do is express your regret—

BERNHARDI I have nothing to regret.

LÖWENSTEIN Quite the contrary.

CYPRIAN All right, not your regret. We won't quarrel over words. But you can still declare, without making the slightest concession, that it was far from your intention to offend anyone's religious sensibilities. And it's perfectly true you didn't mean to.

BERNHARDI But people know that.

CYPRIAN As if that were the issue. You always talk as if you were dealing exclusively with honest people. Of course people know that, and those who want to catch one out know it best of all. Nevertheless I can foresee, and there are signs of it already, that they will try to make you out to be a conscious subverter of religion, and will charge you with having treated a holy sacrament contemptuously.

BERNHARDI Hardly!

CYPRIAN Depend upon it. And no one, absolutely no one, will be willing to stand up for you.

BERNHARDI No one?—

CYPRIAN You will have to endure the malicious cries of your born and new-found enemies, and put up with the embarrassed silence or muttered misgivings of those who are indifferent and even of your friends. And of course you won't escape the reproach that you of all people should have been wary of such imprudence, since you lack the prerequisites for a true understanding of the essential nature of the Catholic sacraments.

BERNHARDI Yes, but tell me—

CYPRIAN I've heard all of this already. From well-wishers, my dear fellow, from so-called enlightened people. So that gives you an idea of what to expect from the rest.

LÖWENSTEIN And thanks to that rabble—

CYPRIAN Spare me your interminable moral indignation. Yes, human beings are a rabble—but we have to take that into account. And— Bernhardi, since it's neither your intention nor your business to have dealings with the rabble, and you won't change people or situations by simply being stiff-necked, I again urge you to do your utmost to allay the looming storm, and for the moment to provide some such explanation as I suggested earlier. The opportunity is there. Tomorrow we have a meeting to discuss Tugendvetter's replacement.

BERNHARDI Precisely, precisely. It would be much more to the point to talk about that, rather than about this whole damned—

CYPRIAN I think so too. You don't have to betray your convictions, Bernhardi. As I said before: a simple explanation would suffice.

BERNHARDI And do you believe this will—

LÖWENSTEIN You're not really going to do that, are you, Bernhardi? If you do, I'll take it all upon myself, I'll take up the cause. As if I myself had told the priest—

CYPRIAN Don't let this hothead get you all worked up, Bernhardi. Just think it over. Would you hesitate over so small a sacrifice of your vanity, even for a moment, if for example the future of your son Oscar were involved? And a project like the Elisabethinum is arguably—almost as important as a child. After all, it's principally your work, even though I have laboured at your side. Just think of the attacks you've defended it against, of how you've worked for it, fought for it.

BERNHARDI (*continuing to pace about*) That is true enough, certainly. They really were years of struggle, especially the first few. It was no mean feat, I must admit, managing to—

CYPRIAN And now we've brought the institute this far, is it really to be jeopardized, perhaps even destroyed over a bagatelle like this? You have better things to do than expend your energies in a fruitless and rather absurd wrangle. You are a doctor. And a human life saved is worth more than a banner held aloft.

LÖWENSTEIN Sophistry!

CYPRIAN We are at a turning point. You have only to act, Bernhardi, and our institute will go on to have a brilliant future.

Bernhardi stands still in astonishment.

CYPRIAN But you've not yet heard the most important thing. I've also had a chance to talk to Flint.

BERNHARDI You mean you've discussed this business with him—?

CYPRIAN No, not a word about this. I deliberately avoided it, and so did he. I went to see him about the criminal anthropology exhibition scheduled for this autumn. But we naturally got around to discussing the Elisabethinum, and I can assure you, Bernhardi, he has decidedly altered his attitude towards us.

LÖWENSTEIN Flint is a place-seeker, a gossip.

CYPRIAN He has his faults, we all know that, but he's a brilliant administrator, he has great schemes for the future, and is planning reforms in many areas, especially medical training and basic hygiene; and to accomplish all this—these are his own words—he needs human beings, not bureaucrats. Human beings like you and me—

BERNHARDI Really?—So he needs human beings, does he.—Perhaps he even believed it himself while he was telling you.

CYPRIAN Yes, he kindles easily, we know that. But it's just a matter of keeping his enthusiasm warm. Then a great deal can be achieved through him. And he really values you, Bernhardi. He was positively moved when he talked about your time together as interns under Rappenweiler. He is genuinely sorry you have grown apart, and hopes—these are his own words—that now in the prime of life you will see more of one another. What conceivable reason could he have for saying a thing like that, if he weren't sincere?

BERNHARDI Sincere—at the time. I know him. If you'd stayed quarter of an hour longer, he'd have been imagining he used to be my best friend. He was just as sincere about the Elisabethinum ten years ago, if you remember, calling it a breeding ground for infection in the middle of town, and us—a dubious clique of overly ambitious academics.

CYPRIAN He's older now, and more mature. Today he appreciates the significance of the Elisabethinum, and we might have a friend in him. Believe me, Bernhardi.

BERNHARDI (*after a short pause*) Well, in any case, we will have to have another meeting today, over the new appointment.

CYPRIAN Yes, of course. I will phone Tugendvetter too.

LÖWENSTEIN He isn't coming.

BERNHARDI Well, if everyone's amenable, let's meet in the Riedhof at half past nine, and we can also discuss what form this so-called explanation—

LÖWENSTEIN Bernhardi—

BERNHARDI I really have no desire to play the hero at any price. I have proved repeatedly that in serious matters I'm the man to push through what I want done. So it should be possible to find a satisfactory form—

CYPRIAN I'm not worried about the form. I'm sure you'll find the right thing to say in your inimitable ironic style, but make sure you keep it light. Perhaps if you were to smile, they won't feel they have to report back to the Princess.

LÖWENSTEIN You're brave men, I don't think.

CYPRIAN Calm down, Löwenstein, you're only a kibitzer who doesn't care how high the stakes go.

LÖWENSTEIN I'm no kibitzer, I'm a bird that flies with its own wings.

CYPRIAN Well, goodbye Bernhardi, see you at half past nine. And you'll bring along a draft.

BERNHARDI Yes, one that doesn't offend your religious sensibilities either, Löwenstein.

LÖWENSTEIN That's what I like to hear.

Bernhardi shakes hands with both of them, and they depart.

Bernhardi now alone paces to and fro a few times, then looks at his watch, shakes his head, takes out a notebook and looks something up, then puts it away again with a gesture as if to say: that can wait. Then he sits down at the desk, takes a piece of paper out of a folder and begins to write, earnestly at first, then with an ironic smile on his lips, continuing to write until the servant comes in.

Servant hands him a card.

BERNHARDI (*disconcerted, hesitant—then*) Show him in.

Ebenwald enters. Bernhardi.

EBENWALD Good evening.

BERNHARDI (*advancing towards him and shaking hands*) Good evening, my dear colleague, to what do I owe the pleasure?

EBENWALD If you don't mind, Director, I'd like to dispense with preliminaries and come straight to the point—

BERNHARDI But of course,—shall we sit down? (*Invites him to take a seat*)

> Ebenwald sits down in the armchair beside the desk.
> Bernhardi sits at his desk.

EBENWALD You see, Director, I consider it my duty to inform you that a move is being launched against you, that is, against our institute.

BERNHARDI So that's it? Well, I believe I may reassure you, my dear colleague, that the whole business will be smoothed over.

EBENWALD Which business, if I may ask?

BERNHARDI Surely you're referring to the mooted resignation of the board of trustees?

EBENWALD So the board of trustees is proposing to resign? Well, I must say, that's a bit—but this is the first I've heard of it, Director. I've come about something else entirely. I gather from certain parliamentary circles that a question will be tabled shortly about a matter which won't be entirely unfamiliar to you.

BERNHARDI Oh—! Well, let's assume that tabling of this question will also not proceed.

EBENWALD With all due respect, Director, I don't know how you intend to persuade those who—regrettably if not altogether surprisingly—are against us in this sorry business, to adopt a more favourable position toward us; but I am afraid I can't be as sanguine as you, Director, that the danger of this question being raised in Parliament can be so readily diverted from your, that is, from our head.

BERNHARDI We shall just have to wait and see.

EBENWALD That's one way of looking at it. However, it's not just you that is involved, Director, but our entire institute.

BERNHARDI I'm aware of that.

EBENWALD And so it would be advisable in any case to consider some means of preventing the question being tabled.

BERNHARDI I don't imagine that would be all that easy. Those concerned will undoubtedly be pursuing the matter out of conviction,—in the name of the religion I have insulted. And what on earth could induce right-minded men to desist from a purpose they regard as both necessary and just?

EBENWALD What might induce these people to desist? Well, if they were made to understand that no offence was entailed, or at least not to the degree they originally assumed, if they were persuaded that there had never been any intention to, how shall I put it—make an anti-Catholic point—

BERNHARDI Do people really have to be told that?

EBENWALD No, not told, because telling is easily done. One would have to prove it.

BERNHARDI This is getting more interesting. How do you envisage going about proving such a thing, my dear colleague?

EBENWALD What if one were confronted with a concrete case, from which the consequences I indicated would follow more or less unambiguously.

BERNHARDI (*impatiently*) But one would have to deliberately concoct such a case.

EBENWALD It wouldn't be necessary. There is a case already to hand.

BERNHARDI How do you mean?

EBENWALD Tomorrow, Director, the new headship of Tugendvetter's department is to be decided.

BERNHARDI Ah!

EBENWALD (*coolly*) Just so. There are two candidates competing.

BERNHARDI (*very distinctly*) One who deserves the position, and one who does not deserve it. I don't know any other distinction that should be taken into account.

EBENWALD But surely it's conceivable that both candidates deserve it; besides, I don't know whether you have kept up in dermatology sufficiently, Director, to be so confident in this case—

BERNHARDI I have of course familiarized myself with the work of both candidates over the last few weeks. It's simply ridiculous— and you know this as well as I do, my dear colleague—, to mention these two candidates in the same breath. Doctor Hell has written up a few case histories, in rather doubtful German I might add, whereas Wenger's articles are quite exceptional, even pioneering.

EBENWALD (*very calmly*) On the other hand there are those who take the view that Hell's case histories are excellent and immensely useful to the general practitioner, whereas Wenger's articles may be full of ideas, but cannot in the opinion of the experts be regarded as particularly reliable. And as far as his character goes, his overbearing and unpleasant personality arouses little sympathy, even among his friends. And in my opinion, for a doctor, especially the head of a department, this should—

BERNHARDI (*more and more impatiently*) This discussion seems to me pointless. It's not up to me but to the plenary board to decide.

EBENWALD But in the event of a draw, Director, you have the deciding vote. And a draw is confidently predicted.

BERNHARDI How come?

EBENWALD Well, those voting for Wenger will be: Cyprian, Löwenstein, Adler and of course that tried and true old liberal, Pflugfelder.

BERNHARDI And Tugendvetter.

EBENWALD You don't believe that yourself, Director.

BERNHARDI Has he promised you already?

EBENWALD That would not prove anything. But you know as well as I do that he won't be supporting Wenger. And the fact that Wenger's own teacher can deny him his vote, ought to give you pause as well, Director—

BERNHARDI (*pacing to and fro in his usual way*) Professor Ebenwald, you know very well why Tugendvetter is against his student. Simply because he's afraid of losing out to him in his private practice. Furthermore, you are as aware as the rest of us that Tugendvetter's more recent articles are not his work, but Wenger's.

EBENWALD Are you prepared to say that to Tugendvetter personally, Director?

BERNHARDI Let me worry about that, Professor, I have always been accustomed to telling people to their face what I think. So now let met put it to you, Professor, that the only reason you're canvassing for Hell at all is because—he's not a Jew.

EBENWALD (*very quietly*) I could with equal justice reply, Director, that your position in support of Wenger—

BERNHARDI You forget that three years ago it was you I voted for, Professor Ebenwald.

EBENWALD But only by overcoming your scruples, isn't that so? And that's exactly how I feel about Wenger, Director. And that's why I won't vote for him. One always lives to regret a thing like that. And even if I had a higher opinion of Wenger, Director, in a corporate enterprise it's not just an individual's talent that counts—

BERNHARDI But his character.

EBENWALD I was going to say, the corporate ethos. And here we are back to square one in our discussion. It is really terrible how with us in Austria appointments always come down to politics. But sooner or later one has to reconcile oneself to that. Look here, Director, if Hell were an idiot, of course I wouldn't vote for him or expect you to do so. But when all is said and done, he makes people every bit as healthy as does Wenger. And if you also consider, Director, that a firm commitment in this matter on your part might possibly avert all the unpleasant consequences which that other business threatens to—of course I can't give any guarantees. It's really only a hunch.

BERNHARDI Ah!

EBENWALD That goes without saying. But in any case, Director, it would be well worth considering the matter in a dispassionate moment, sine ira et studio,* as they say. Then we could talk about it again before the meeting tomorrow.

BERNHARDI That would be quite unnecessary.

EBENWALD Whatever you think best, Director. But if you don't mind my saying so, you should not allow a false sense of pride to—all this is of course in strict confidence between us—

BERNHARDI I have no reason to invoke your own discretion, Professor. Tell the gentlemen who sent you,—

EBENWALD Oho!

BERNHARDI That I never get involved in deals of this kind and—

EBENWALD Pardon me, but I was not sent by anyone; so I am not in a position to see to any orders you might wish to place. My visit, Director, was strictly unofficial. Please remember that. I came neither as a messenger nor on my own behalf, since I'm not in the least disposed to share responsibility for your behaviour toward the priest, but solely in your own and the institute's best interests. You have scorned the proffered hand of friendship—

BERNHARDI And you depart an enemy. I prefer it this way. It is the more honourable course.

EBENWALD As you please, Director.—I shall see myself out.

BERNHARDI Good evening.

Accompanies him to the door, Ebenwald exit. Alone, Bernhardi paces up and down a few times, picks up the sheet on which he had earlier begun to write, reads it through, then tears it up. Looks at his watch again, and gets ready to leave. The servant enters.

BERNHARDI What is it?

Servant hands him a card.

BERNHARDI What? In person? I mean, is his Excellency here himself?

SERVANT Indeed, Professor.

BERNHARDI Show him in.

Servant exit. Shortly thereafter Flint enters.

> *Bernhardi, Flint, tall, slim, over fifty, short-cropped hair, tidy mutton chops, a not entirely unintended diplomatic air, very affable and often genuinely warm.*

BERNHARDI (*still at the door*) Your Excellency? (*With his lightly ironic smile*)

FLINT (*shaking hands with him*) It's been some time since we saw each other, Bernhardi.

BERNHARDI Quite recently, actually—at the Medical Association.

FLINT I mean in private like this.

BERNHARDI Well yes, that's true.—Won't you have a seat?

FLINT Thank you. (*He sits down. Bernhardi follows suit. In a deliberately light tone*) Are you surprised to see me here?

BERNHARDI I am—agreeably surprised, and must not forgo the opportunity of congratulating you on your recent appointment to high office.

FLINT High office! You know very well I don't think of my new post like that. Nevertheless, I accept your congratulations with particular complacency. Of course, I haven't come simply to cash in on your congratulations personally, as you can well imagine.

BERNHARDI Of course not.

FLINT (*launching forth*) Well, my dear Bernhardi, I've no need to tell you that I don't intend to use my portfolio as a pillow, and am determined to utilize my possibly brief time in the position to carry out various reforms that, as you may remember, have been dear to my heart since my youth. Reforms in the area of medical training, basic hygiene, general education, and so on. Of course the people the government places at my disposal, though worthy enough, are parochial and routine-bound in their outlook and not up to the task at all. What I need to some degree is a staff—a volunteer staff naturally—of unprejudiced and independent-minded men. There is no shortage of hard-working administrators in Austria, and particularly with us at the Ministry of Education; but what I need to carry out my plans is real human beings. And I've come to ask you, my dear Bernhardi, whether I can count on you.

BERNHARDI (*after a slight hesitation*) Perhaps you would be good enough to formulate things a little more precisely.

FLINT More precisely still?—hmm—Well, I was certainly prepared to find you a bit difficult.

BERNHARDI No, not at all. I only want you to explain things more specifically. Before you do so I cannot of course—I need to know in what area you might need my cooperation. (*With his ironic smile*) In

that of medical training, or basic hygiene, or general education—
have I forgotten anything?

FLINT You haven't changed a bit. But for that very reason, I have high
hopes of you. Perhaps we still have something in common,
although I really don't know—

BERNHARDI (*seriously*) I'll tell you what we have in common, Flint;
our youthful friendship and—whatever subsequently became of it.

FLINT (*warmly*) Well, what did become of it, Bernhardi? We drifted
apart a little in the course of time. That was due to circumstances,
perhaps even to the laws governing our personal development to
some extent.

BERNHARDI My sentiments exactly.

FLINT You are not vindictive, are you, Bernhardi?

BERNHARDI I also have a good memory.

FLINT That can be a fault too, Bernhardi, if it interferes with one's
clear grasp of present circumstances. Actually, I thought we'd buried the hatchet long ago and forgotten all those years of fighting.

BERNHARDI Fighting? That is quite a noble word for a not particularly noble business.

FLINT Bernhardi!

BERNHARDI Well, my dear fellow, it was hardly pretty! And I would
feel I was betraying my own past, if I were to let it pass so lightly.
(*He has stood up*) When I think of the weapons you used to attack us
in those days, you and your establishment professors; the tactics
you deployed to try and undermine our fledgling enterprise! The
lengths you went to to discredit us in the public eye, the way you
suspected and persecuted us. We were founding an institute which
took money away from general practitioners. We were infecting the
town, we were trying to establish a second medical faculty—

FLINT (*interrupting him*) My dear Bernhardi, all these reproaches
could still in a sense be made today, were it not that the good you
are doing on the scientific and humanitarian front has compensated
for the less positive sides of your endeavour. We have recognized
that, I myself especially, Bernhardi, and for that reason alone we
have altered our attitude towards you. Believe me, today the Elisabethinum has no warmer supporter than myself—indeed personal
motives never influenced me in my attitude towards you, only my
conviction that I—

BERNHARDI Yes, in the growing bitterness of battle one can always
persuade oneself of that. One's convictions!

FLINT Excuse me, Bernhardi. We all have our faults. You no doubt as much as I. But if there is one thing I can claim, it's that I have never once spoken or acted against my own convictions.

BERNHARDI Are you quite sure of that?

FLINT Bernhardi!

BERNHARDI Think carefully for a minute.

FLINT (*a little uncertain*) I may have acted in error during my life as we all do, but against my convictions—Never!—

BERNHARDI Now I seem to remember a case in which you acted very prudently against your own convictions.

FLINT I really must—

BERNHARDI And your action at the time even resulted in the death of someone.

FLINT That's a bit strong. I must insist that you—

BERNHARDI By all means. (*He paces to and fro in the room a few times, stops suddenly, then with animation*) We were interns under Rappenweiler at the time. There was a young man in the clinic, I can still see him, even remember his name, one Engelbert Wagner, a filing clerk, whom we all, including our head, had incorrectly diagnosed. When it came to the post-mortem, it turned out that a different (antisyphilitic) treatment might have saved the patient. And as we were standing around and the case became clear, you whispered: I knew it all along. Do you remember? You knew what was wrong with him, you had made the right diagnosis—

FLINT I was the only one.

BERNHARDI Yes, the only one. But you carefully avoided mentioning it while the patient was alive. And why you did so is a question you yourself must answer. It can hardly have been out of conviction.

FLINT Confound it, you have a very good memory. I remember the case too, and it's true that even though I considered a different treatment more promising, essential even, I kept it to myself. And I admit I only remained silent so as not to hurt Rappenweiler's feelings, since as you know he didn't like being upstaged by his assistants. So perhaps you are right to reproach me with having sacrificed a human life. But as to the deeper motivation you ascribe to me, you are quite mistaken. This one sacrifice was necessary, Bernhardi, for the sake of the hundreds of lives who would later put their trust in my professional skills. At the time I could not yet completely dispense with Rappenweiler's patronage, and there was an immediate prospect of a professorship in Prague.

BERNHARDI Do you think Rappenweiler would have dropped you, if you—

FLINT It's very likely. You overestimate human nature, Bernhardi. You've no idea how petty people can be. It would not of course have cost me my career, but it would still have meant delays. And I was keen to get ahead and find the necessary outlet for my talents, which even you will not deny. That, my dear Bernhardi, is why I let filing clerk Engelbert Wagner die, and I can't honestly say that I regret it. It's of little consequence, my dear Bernhardi, whether one acts correctly, or if you prefer, according to one's convictions, in some paltry individual case, it's more a question of remaining true to the immanent idea of one's own life. It's interesting you should conjure poor Wagner up out of his grave in this discussion, because now I see in a flash the essential difference between us, as well as— this may surprise you, Bernhardi—the extent to which we complement each other. You are what is called a decent human being, Bernhardi, more so perhaps than me. Or at least you are more sentimental. But whether you would be able to achieve more for the good of some larger entity, seems to me extremely questionable. What you lack, Bernhardi, is an eye for the essential, and without that all truth to one's convictions is mere self-righteousness. What matters is not being right in an individual case but being effective in the larger context. And to give up the opportunity for such effective action for the sake of some petty sense of having done the right thing in some trivial case, seems to me not only small-minded but in a higher sense immoral. Yes, my dear Bernhardi. Positively immoral.

BERNHARDI (*reflecting*) If I interpret the drift of your remarks correctly, you now apparently have something quite specific in mind.

FLINT Yes, it has as it were intruded itself on my field of vision as I've been speaking.

BERNHARDI And haven't we also not entirely unexpectedly come closer to the actual purpose of your visit?

FLINT Not the actual purpose, but still, not wholly unrelated to it.

BERNHARDI And so that's the reason you've gone to the trouble of—

FLINT That too. Because the matter we both now have in mind is bound, I can confidently predict, to create much wider ripples. You never imagined that of course. As is your likeable but at times exasperating way, in the doubtless high-minded excitement of the moment you neglected to look ahead a little. And so when you confronted his Reverence, you forgot one little thing, that we happen to live in a Christian country—I don't know what there is to smile about in that.

BERNHARDI You will again be surprised how good my memory is. I seem to remember an article you intended to write as a young man. It was to have been titled: 'Places of Worship—Places of Healing.'

FLINT Hmm!

BERNHARDI What you wanted to propose was that more hospitals should be built, rather than so many churches.

FLINT Ah well, one of those articles I intended to write and never got around to.

BERNHARDI And never will.

FLINT Not that one, certainly. Today I understand that places of worship and places of healing can coexist quite well, and that some suffering is cured in the places of worship which we in the hospitals, my dear Bernhardi, are for the moment powerless to treat. But we don't want to get sidetracked into political discussions, do we?

BERNHARDI Particularly as I could hardly keep up with you there.

FLINT Well yes, that's probably true. So we had better confine ourselves to the specific case.

BERNHARDI Yes, why don't we do that. I am curious to hear what sort of proposal his Excellency the Minister for Education and Culture has to put to me.

FLINT Proposal? I don't have a specific proposal. But I won't conceal that the mood towards you everywhere, even in circles where you'd least expect it, is thoroughly unfavourable, and for your own sake and that of your institute, I wish the whole affair could be swept from the face of the earth.

BERNHARDI I wish it could too.

FLINT What?

BERNHARDI I have more important things to do than continuing to bother with this business.

FLINT Are you serious?

BERNHARDI How can you doubt it? In fact less than an hour ago I consulted Cyprian and Löwenstein about an explanation that would satisfy the allegedly injured parties.

FLINT That would—that would of course be excellent. But I'm afraid under the present circumstances it wouldn't quite get us off the hook.

BERNHARDI How come? What should I do then?

FLINT Perhaps if you were to—to my mind you wouldn't be conceding anything, especially since to my knowledge no official denunciation has been issued, if you were to pay a personal visit to the priest and—

BERNHARDI What?

FLINT It would make a very favourable impression. Since after all you were, shall we say, so imprudent as to prevent his Reverence, to some extent by force—

BERNHARDI By force?

FLINT That's too strong a word of course. But even so, you did— from what they say at least—

BERNHARDI What do they say?

FLINT —Show him the door a little roughly.

BERNHARDI That's a lie. Surely you believe me—

FLINT So you didn't throw him out?

BERNHARDI I hardly touched him. Anyone who talks about the use of force is a deliberate liar. Oh, I know well enough who these people are. But they won't succeed in—I myself will—

FLINT Calm down, Bernhardi. Nothing has been lodged officially. If you've made up your mind to submit an explanation already, it would be simplest if you took the opportunity to mention explicitly that all those rumours—

BERNHARDI I'm sorry, my dear Flint, but you are under a misapprehension. I did indeed have an explanation in mind, which I intended in the first instance to put forward at tomorrow's meeting, but circumstances have since arisen, which make my submitting any such explanation quite out of the question.

FLINT What's all this now? What circumstances?

BERNHARDI Compelling ones, believe me.

FLINT Hmm. And you can't disclose anything specific? I would be extremely interested—

BERNHARDI (*again smiling*) Tell me, my dear Flint, have you really just come to help me out of an embarrassing predicament?

FLINT If I didn't care how this matter might affect you—and your institute, I frankly wouldn't bother with it any further. Certainly you have behaved so inappropriately that, if I didn't feel sorry for you and your institute, I would have few qualms about leaving you to stew in your own juice.

BERNHARDI In short, just for my sake you want—me to spare you the trouble of having to answer a question in Parliament.

FLINT Certainly. There isn't much to be salvaged from the situation. As things stand, you have not behaved with absolute decorum toward the priest. And as an honest man I would at least be obliged to concede that, even if I might be prepared to vouch for the purity of your intentions, for your importance as a man of science—

BERNHARDI My dear Flint, you have no idea how much you over-estimate your influence.

FLINT Hmm—

BERNHARDI You evidently imagine that it's still up to you to prevent such a question being tabled.

FLINT It's up to you, I can assure you.

BERNHARDI That's very true. You don't know how right you are. Entirely up to me in fact. Half an hour ago it was within my power to deflect any danger of a question being tabled from both our heads.

FLINT Within your—

BERNHARDI Yes, nothing could have been simpler. As you know, we have to appoint a new head to Tugendvetter's department. We are having a meeting tomorrow. If I had been prepared to commit myself to voting for Hell and not for Wenger in the event of a split vote, everything would have been fine.

FLINT Commit yourself? How do you mean? To whom?

BERNHARDI Ebenwald was here just now. That was the commission he came to deliver.

FLINT Hmm. Are you sure?—

BERNHARDI Or at least I had the distinct impression that Ebenwald was fully authorized to conclude the deal, even though he denied it. Perhaps I was only supposed to fall for it, and the question would have been tabled in Parliament anyway, even if I had voted for Hell.

FLINT (*pacing to and fro*) Our friend Ebenwald is on good terms with his cousin, Ebenwald, the member of parliament. He is a leader of the clerical faction, and if he were against it, tabulation of the question would certainly lapse. I think in this case Ebenwald was as you might say acting with honourable intent. So how did you react to his proposition?

BERNHARDI Flint!

FLINT All right, so you consider Wenger the more substantial dermatologist.

BERNHARDI But you do too. You know as well as I do that Hell is a nonentity. And even if the two of them had been of equal standing, Ebenwald's unreasonable request would have made it impossible for me to vote for anyone but Wenger.

FLINT Yes, Ebenwald certainly didn't use much cunning.

BERNHARDI Cunning—?! Is that all you can say? You seem more than a little complacent, my dear Flint.

FLINT Bernhardi, my dear fellow, politics—

BERNHARDI What concern of mine is politics?

FLINT Politics concerns us all.

BERNHARDI And so you think that because such infamous dealings are a daily occurrence in your so-called politics, I should resign myself with a smile and consider this contemptible deal in any case?

FLINT It's possible the problem may never even arise, that there will be no split vote and either Hell or Wenger will be elected without your intervention.

BERNHARDI My dear Flint, the situation won't be made that easy for you.

FLINT For me? I think—

BERNHARDI (*warmly*) Flint, even though you may be a government minister today, you are also after all a doctor, a man of science, a man of truth. How did you put it earlier yourself? What counts is having an eye for the essential. What is essential here? Don't you see? It's that the ablest man get the department headship, to ensure that he be given the opportunity to accomplish something substantial for science and the sick. That's what counts, isn't it? That is what's essential. Not that you or I be spared the inconvenience of an awkward question being tabled in Parliament, a satisfactory answer to which always can be found if necessary.

FLINT Hmm. I certainly would not be at a loss for an answer.

BERNHARDI That's what I thought.

FLINT Tell me, Bernhardi, would you be prepared to put it all in writing—I mean, could you not write me a letter presenting this whole affair briefly and succinctly, so that if need be—

BERNHARDI If need be?

FLINT Anyway, I would like to have it to hand in black and white. Perhaps it wouldn't even be necessary to read the letter out. One could answer fairly guardedly at first, I mean, when they put the question. And then, if they didn't let up, one could come out with your letter. (*Makes a gesture as though producing the letter from his breast pocket*)

BERNHARDI There your parliamentary experience will doubtless show you the right procedure.

FLINT Experience? More intuition, at the moment. But I don't think it would ever come to that—I mean, to reading out your letter. From my very first words, from the cadence of my voice, they would be aware I had something up my sleeve. Everyone would notice. Then I'd have them, Bernhardi, as soon as I began to speak, I'd have them. Just as I used to rivet my students at the clinic, I'd hold the attention of the floor. When there was a debate recently about an amendment to the education bill, I only joined in very casually, but you can scarcely imagine the breathless silence in the House, Bernhardi. I must honestly admit I didn't say anything very special. But I had their ear at once. And that's what counts. They listen to me. And once one is really listening to someone, it's harder to believe he can be entirely wrong.

BERNHARDI Certainly.

FLINT And at the risk of your putting it down to vanity, Bernhardi, I'm almost beginning to wish they would table that question after all.

BERNHARDI Flint!

FLINT Because given an opportunity like this, one could go into things more generally. In this specific case, for instance, I see a symbol of our entire political predicament.

BERNHARDI And so it is.

FLINT That's always the way it is with me,—even in response to apparently quite meaningless specific cases. For me each of them somehow becomes a symbol. That must be why I am cut out for a political career.

BERNHARDI Undoubtedly.

FLINT And that's why I think one could use this opportunity to go into things more generally.

BERNHARDI Aha, places of worship—places of healing.

FLINT You may smile.—Unfortunately it's not in my nature to take such matters lightly.

BERNHARDI Yes, my dear Flint, after all you've just said, one almost has the impression you might be disposed to side with me in this affair.

FLINT It would not require all that much brilliance, I admit. I was initially reluctant,—because I still find your conduct toward the priest indecorous.—But this Ebenwald deal puts a completely new complexion on the matter. It's important of course that for now all this remains a secret between you and me. I mean, don't breathe a word about this Ebenwald business, even to your friends. Because if people get wind of what I have in mind, they might think twice and forgo the parliamentary question. You of course will retain a copy of the letter, but its contents will remain secret until the moment when I put it on the table in the House.

He gestures without exaggerating.

BERNHARDI Of course I am delighted that you're so—however—I'd like to give you one more thing to think about. The faction you would be confronting is extremely powerful and extremely ruthless,—so the question arises, whether you would be able to govern without them.

FLINT One would have to put it to the test.

BERNHARDI Nevertheless, if you value your office more than—

FLINT Than you—

BERNHARDI Than the truth,—which is the only thing that counts, then you'd better stay away from the whole business and not stand up for me.

FLINT For you? I'm not doing it for you at all. But for the truth, the cause.

BERNHARDI And are you really now convinced, Flint, that this trivial affair is worth the candle?

FLINT This trivial affair? Bernhardi! Do you still not see that things of much higher import are at stake here than might at first appear? That in a sense we are dealing with the eternal struggle between light and darkness—But that sounds like empty rhetoric.

BERNHARDI At any rate a struggle, my dear Flint, whose outcome these days is quite uncertain, and which all your ministerial glory may not be—

FLINT Let me worry about that. Come when it may, I can imagine no more beautiful death than in a just cause and—on behalf of someone who—you might as well admit it—just an hour ago was still my enemy.

BERNHARDI I was not your enemy. And in any case I shall be more than willing to recant, if I have done you an injustice. But I will tell you one thing, Flint, even if the whole business does not turn out to your advantage, I shall not have qualms of conscience. You know where justice lies in this case, and I decline in advance to admire you for doing your duty when duty calls.

FLINT Nor would I expect you to, Bernhardi. (*They shake hands*) Farewell. (*As lightly as possible*) I was on the look-out for a real human being, and now I've found one. Goodbye!

BERNHARDI Goodbye, Flint! (*Hesitating*) Thank you.

FLINT Oh! Never do that either. Our mutual liking should have a firmer basis.

    Exit.

BERNHARDI (*stands there a while reflecting*) Well, we'll see.

    Curtain.

Act Three

*Boardroom in the Elisabethinum. Furnished in the usual way.
Long green table in the middle, cupboards, two windows in the
centre at the back. Photographs of famous physicians, a portrait
of Empress Elisabeth* over the entrance door on the left. It is
evening, artificial lighting. Chandelier with large green shade. To
begin with, not all the flames have been turned up high. On the
right against the wall a small table.*

*Hochroitzpointner, seated over a large ledger, copying from
another piece of paper.*

*Doctor Schreimann enters. He is tall, bald, with a military
moustache, a duelling scar on his brow and wearing glasses.
Remarkably deep, frank German voice,* distinctly Austrian
dialect, with occasional Jewish inflexions coming through
suddenly.*

HOCHROITZPOINTNER (*leaps to his feet*) Good morning, Maj—good
morning, Doctor Schreimann.

SCHREIMANN Hello, Hochroitzpointner. Get any sleep after the ball?

HOCHROITZPOINTNER I didn't even go to bed, Sir. It wasn't worth
it.

SCHREIMANN (*since Hochroitzpointner is still standing to attention*) At
ease, at ease, man.

HOCHROITZPOINTNER (*standing more comfortably*) I was dancing
until seven, by eight I was in the department for internal medicine,
by ten in the department of surgery, by twelve—

SCHREIMANN (*interrupting him, sits down at the table*) Enough, I know
you get around. So you've been making a fair copy of the minutes
from the meeting?

HOCHROITZPOINTNER I couldn't get to it earlier unfortunately, Sir.

SCHREIMANN Don't worry, it isn't your duty after all. Allow me as
secretary to thank you. Were you able to make everything out
clearly? (*Going over to him, reading in the ledger, mumbling the
vote*)—four votes for Professor Hell from Graz, four for Doctor
S. Wenger*—(*turning to Hochroitzpointner*) Samuel—

HOCHROITZPOINTNER But that's not normally spelt out in full.

SCHREIMANN I'd like to know why not. My grandfather for instance
was called Samuel and he always spelt it out in full, and I am called
Siegfried* and always spell it out in full as well.

HOCHROITZPOINTNER (*stupidly*) Yes, Major.

SCHREIMANN But I'm no longer your regimental doctor. (*He reads on*) The Director made use of his statutory right to a deciding vote in the event of a draw, and voted in favour of Doctor Wenger, who accordingly was formally elected head of the department of dermatology and syphilis. (*Short pause*) Well, are you happy with your new head?

HOCHROITZPOINTNER (*involuntarily clicking his heels*) Certainly.

SCHREIMANN (*laughing and putting his hand on his shoulder*) What are you doing there, Hochroitzpointner? You're no longer a military cadet under my command, you know.

HOCHROITZPOINTNER Unfortunately not, Sir. Those were good times.

SCHREIMANN Yes, we were younger then. But tell me, Hochroitzpointner, since we've touched on the subject, when do you intend to sit for your finals?

    Ebenwald enters. Schreimann, Hochroitzpointner.

EBENWALD Yes, I'm always asking him the same question.

HOCHROITZPOINTNER Good evening, Professor.

EBENWALD Hello, Schreimann.

SCHREIMANN Good evening.

EBENWALD You know, Hochroitzpointner, sometime soon you really should take leave from your various departments and cram. Just cram for a few weeks and get it over with. What are you doing here in the boardroom, incidentally?

SCHREIMANN He was good enough to make a fair copy of the minutes for me.

EBENWALD That on top of everything else. What would the Elisabethinum do without Hochroitzpointner!—And at the ball yesterday you were the first to dance, I hear?

HOCHROITZPOINTNER (*stupidly*) First and last to dance, Professor.

SCHREIMANN And then he didn't even go to bed.

EBENWALD Ah well, young people!—How was the ball anyway?

HOCHROITZPOINTNER Absolutely packed. Very lively.

EBENWALD (*to Hochroitzpointner*) Do you know where you were dancing last night, Hochroitzpointner? On a volcano.

HOCHROITZPOINTNER It was pretty hot, Professor.

EBENWALD (*laughing*) Ha! Well then, take some leave, sit your exams and no more dancing on volcanoes! Not even an extinct one. Good evening to you. (*Shakes hands in parting*)

    Schreimann does the same.

Hochroitzpointner again clicks his heels.

EBENWALD Like a lieutenant!—

SCHREIMANN That's what I just told him.

Hochroitzpointner exit.

Schreimann, Ebenwald.

EBENWALD So, his Excellency from the Ministry of Education was there too?

SCHREIMANN Yes, in fact he stayed on to talk to Bernhardi for at least half an hour.

EBENWALD That's rather strange.

SCHREIMANN Hardly, during a ball.

EBENWALD But he must know that the board of trustees has resigned.

SCHREIMANN That may well be, but there was a board member at the ball even so.

EBENWALD Who?

SCHREIMANN Councillor Winkler.

EBENWALD He is such a rebel though.

SCHREIMANN Besides, the whole business is not official yet.

EBENWALD It's as good as official. Anyway, the meeting to discuss their resignation has been scheduled for today. I say—(*hesitating*) can I depend on you, Schreimann?

SCHREIMANN (*airily*) If you don't mind my saying so, I find that rather a strange question.

EBENWALD Come off it, we're not students any more.

SCHREIMANN You can always depend on me as long as I agree with you. And as that is fortunately normally the case—

EBENWALD But perhaps there might also be questions where you would have reservations about going along with me.

SCHREIMANN As I've already told you, my dear Ebenwald, in my view this whole affair should not be treated from some religious or denominational point of view, but as a question of tact. In other words, even if I were a Jewish nationalist, in this case I would side against Bernhardi. But quite apart from that, allow me to remind you that I am a German, just like you. And I can assure you, it takes more courage these days for someone of my ethnic origins to declare himself a German and a Christian, than to remain what one was when one came into the world. As a Zionist I would have had an easier time of it.

EBENWALD Very probably. You'd have been sure of a professorship in Jerusalem.

SCHREIMANN A poor joke.

EBENWALD Well, Schreimann, you know how I feel about you, but at the same time you have to understand that we live in such confused times—and such a confused country—

SCHREIMANN I hope you're not going to tell me about your anonymous letters again.

EBENWALD Ah, you remember then? By the way, they were not anonymous at all. They were all signed in full by old friends from my student days. Of course they were surprised that I had taken you under my wing. Don't forget, my dear Schreimann, at university and later as an alumnus I was a leading member of one of the strictest German nationalist fraternities. And you know what that means: 'Watch on the Rhine'*—Bismarck oaks*—Waidhofen resolution*—no satisfaction given to Jews, not even people of Jewish descent—

SCHREIMANN Sometimes it happened anyway, despite all your strict observance. I received this scar while I was still a Jew.

EBENWALD Well, didn't I say we live in a confused country? Today you are prouder of your Jewish scar than of your entire German heritage.

Professor Pflugfelder enters. Schreimann, Ebenwald.

PFLUGFELDER (*sixty-five, learned countenance, glasses*) Good evening, gentlemen. Have you heard? The board of trustees has resigned!

EBENWALD That's why we are here, Professor.

PFLUGFELDER Well, what do you say to it?

EBENWALD You seem surprised. Most people were expecting it.

PFLUGFELDER Surprised? Not a bit. You know, I've long given up being surprised by anything. But not being disgusted, I'm afraid. I've had a belly full of that.

SCHREIMANN What, disgust?

PFLUGFELDER Surely you'll admit, gentlemen, this witch-hunt against Bernhardi is totally unjustified.

EBENWALD I don't know anything about a witch-hunt.

PFLUGFELDER Ah! So you don't know anything about it? I see, I see.—And you don't know that your cousin, Ottokar Ebenwald, is the ringleader either, I suppose?

EBENWALD I really must ask you—

PFLUGFELDER But I don't of course wish to identify you with your cousin. You may quite justifiably deny that you espouse a common cause. Because it now transpires that your cousin, after his glorious beginnings as a German nationalist, is devoting himself exclusively to the interests of the clerical faction. And you are no clericalist,

Ebenwald. You are German, an old German student. And what are the German virtues, Ebenwald? Courage, loyalty, determination. Have I forgotten any? Never mind. Those will do for the moment. And so I hope today we can agree to make solemn reparation to our good Bernhardi.

EBENWALD Reparation? Whatever for? What has happened to him? So far nothing beyond the resignation of the board, which means we might as well close down, because now we don't know where the money's going to come from. Whether that's an appropriate pretext for an ovation in praise of the Director, after he has landed us in this predicament through sheer tactlessness—

PFLUGFELDER I see—oh well. You are what you are, Ebenwald. Nor would I let myself be operated on by anybody else. At least you know what you're doing there. What about you, Schreimann. Don't you have anything to say? Are you also against Bernhardi? Also appalled that he should have begged the priest to allow a poor sick child to die in peace?—Understandable enough. We must spare such new-found religious sensibilities at all cost.

EBENWALD (*calmly*) Don't let him bait you, Schreimann.

SCHREIMANN (*very calmly*) As I explained to our colleague Ebenwald a little earlier, Professor, it is not my religious sentiments but my sense of good form that has been offended. I don't consider a sick ward an appropriate place to engage in politics.

PFLUGFELDER Politics! Bernhardi engaged in politics! You can't persuade me you believe that yourself. That's really—

Filitz enters. Schreimann, Ebenwald, Pflugfelder. Greetings.

FILITZ Good evening, gentlemen. I shall tell you at once what I propose to do. You may take it as you wish. I propose to follow the sound example of the board and to resign.

EBENWALD What?

PFLUGFELDER Huh!

FILITZ I don't see what other proper course of action one can take, unless one is prepared to endorse the conduct of our good Director, which I won't go into further, and—

EBENWALD If I may say so, Professor, I don't agree with you at all. There is surely some other way of demonstrating that we have no intention of endorsing our Director's conduct. We cannot simply leave the institute to its fate, especially now. We must try instead to persuade the board to withdraw its resignation.

FILITZ That will never happen, as long as Bernhardi remains at the helm.

SCHREIMANN Exactly,—as long as he remains at the helm.

FILITZ As long as—

PFLUGFELDER So it's come to this already, gentlemen! This really is—

Adler enters. Pflugfelder, Ebenwald, Schreimann, Filitz.

ADLER Good evening, gentlemen, have you read the latest?

EBENWALD What is it?

ADLER The question tabled in Parliament.

SCHREIMANN About the Bernhardi affair?

ADLER It's in the evening paper.

EBENWALD (*rings*) We haven't read anything about it. (*To Filitz*) I thought it was supposed to be tomorrow.

SCHREIMANN We medical practitioners don't have time to sit in coffee houses all afternoon.

Servant enters.

EBENWALD Would you mind going over to the kiosk for the paper.

FILITZ Bring three.

SCHREIMANN Six.

EBENWALD (*to the servant*) Get a dozen while you're at it. But hurry.

Servant exit.

SCHREIMANN (*to Adler*) Is the wording of the question fairly harsh?

PFLUGFELDER Does anyone here already know the wording?

Dr Wenger enters. Pflugfelder, Filitz, Adler, Schreimann, Ebenwald.

WENGER (*a short man, oppressed and uncertain though sometimes overly loud and assertive, wearing glasses*) Good evening, gentlemen.

SCHREIMANN Let's have a look, Doctor Wenger. (*Takes the paper out of Wenger's pocket*) He's got a copy.

WENGER I must say, Doctor!

EBENWALD Good of you to bring it with you right away.

WENGER Bring what with me? Oh, I see. Is that the custom here, to have your faculty Benjamin* bring the evening paper to committee meetings?

EBENWALD (*scrutinizing the paper*) Here it is!

The others, apart from Adler and Wenger, try to get a look at the paper over Ebenwald's shoulder.

ADLER (*to Wenger*) What do you think of that?

WENGER Well, what am I supposed to think? I don't understand politics. And anyway I wasn't there.

SCHREIMANN (*to Ebenwald*) None of us is going to see anything like this—Read it out.

EBENWALD Very well, gentlemen, the wording is as follows: 'The undersigned consider it their duty—'

PFLUGFELDER You've got a frog in your throat already. Let Professor Filitz read! He's rhetorical and sonorous and his tone carries conviction.

EBENWALD I've plenty of that, but perhaps Professor Filitz is the better reader. Here you are.

FILITZ (*reads*) 'The undersigned consider it their duty to bring to the government's notice the following incident, which took place on 4 February in the Elisabethinum'—and so on, and so forth. 'The Reverend Franz Reder, parish priest at the church of St Florian, was summoned by Nurse Ludmilla to the deathbed of Philomena Beier, spinster, to administer the holy sacrament of Extreme Unction. In the ante-room outside the ward, Father Reder found several doctors gathered, among them Professor Bernhardi, head of the department concerned and director of the institute, who roughly requested that Father Reder desist from his intended ministrations, on the grounds that the excitement might be detrimental to the health of the dying woman.'

PFLUGFELDER No, no!

THE OTHERS Quiet!

FILITZ (*reads on*) 'Professor Bernhardi, who subscribes to the Mosaic confession, was then given to understand by Father Reder that he had come to fulfil a sacred duty, which in this case was all the more urgent because the sick woman had succumbed to the effects of an illegal operation, for which she had only herself to blame; whereupon Professor Bernhardi contemptuously asserted his proprietorial rights in hospital premises built and maintained of course with money donated by noble patrons. When Father Reder declined further discussion and tried to enter the ward, Professor Bernhardi blocked his way, and just as Father Reder grasped the door-handle, determined to enter the ward and carry out his sacred duty, Professor Bernhardi gave him a shove—'

ADLER Absolutely untrue!

PFLUGFELDER Infamous!

SCHREIMANN Were you there?

FILITZ As if the shove were what's at issue.

EBENWALD But there are witnesses.

PFLUGFELDER I know your witnesses.

ADLER I was there too.

PFLUGFELDER But you haven't been interrogated.

WENGER Interrogated?

PFLUGFELDER By a certain commission. I suppose you don't know anything about the commission either, Professor Ebenwald?

SCHREIMANN Read on!

FILITZ (*reads*) 'During this scene in the ante-room the patient died, without having received the comfort of religion which, as Nurse Ludmilla has testified, she had urgently requested. In drawing attention to this incident, we would like to ask the government, and in particular his Excellency the Minister for Education and Culture, how he proposes to make reparation for the outrage this incident has caused to the religious; what measures his Excellency proposes to take to prevent a repetition of such shocking incidents; and finally, whether in view of this incident it does not seem to his Excellency appropriate that from now on, no one should be considered for public employment who by reason of ethnic origin, education and character is unlikely to show the necessary understanding for the religious sensibilities of the indigenous Christian population.' Signed... (*A stir*)

EBENWALD Now we're in a pretty pickle.

WENGER Why we? Not a word is said against the institute.

SCHREIMANN Quite right!

EBENWALD Well done, Wenger!

WENGER (*encouraged*) The Elisabethinum remains pure and unsullied.

PFLUGFELDER And the Director?

WENGER So does he, of course, if he succeeds—which I don't for a moment doubt—in refuting the allegations in the question to Parliament.

PFLUGFELDER Allegations?—You call those allegations?—But my dear colleague, this question to Parliament,—does one really have to point this out—, is no more than a political manoeuvre by the combined clerical and anti-Semitic factions.

FILITZ Nonsense!

EBENWALD Listen to the old forty-eighter!*

WENGER I'm sorry, but as far as I'm concerned, there are no religious or national differences. I am a man of science. I deplore—

SCHREIMANN So do we all deplore!

> *Bernhardi and Cyprian enter. Adler, Schreimann, Ebenwald, Pflugfelder, Wenger.*

BERNHARDI (*very expansive, his mode of speaking a little more humorous and ironically inflected than usual, but with a touch of embarrassment.*

He takes the evening papers from the servant, who opens the door for him) Good evening, gentlemen. Here, help yourselves. I apologize for being a little late, but I trust in the interim you have found plenty to amuse you.

> *Greetings all round; Bernhardi immediately takes his place at the head of the table, the others gradually take their seats, some smoke.*

BERNHARDI I declare the meeting open. Before I proceed to today's agenda, I should like in the name of the Elisabethinum to extend a warm welcome to our new member, who is today attending a meeting of our faculty for the first time, and as it happens an unscheduled one. Let me also express the hope that Doctor Wenger will feel at home in our midst, and continue in his new more responsible position to demonstrate his devotion to duty, to nourish his talent and develop into the ornament of our institution that every one of us here present represents. (*The joke falls flat*) Doctor Wenger, in the name of all of us, I again bid you a very warm welcome.

WENGER Mr Chairman, my esteemed colleagues! It would be immodest of me to take up your valuable time with a lengthy speech—so I will confine myself to extending my sincerest thanks to you all for the great honour—(*Disquiet*)

SCHREIMANN (*rises*) Since it's already quite late, I propose that our esteemed colleague postpone his doubtless pithy thank-you speech to the next meeting, so that we may proceed at once to today's agenda.

THE OTHERS Agreed! Hear, hear!

> *Schreimann shakes hands with Wenger, some follow his example.*

BERNHARDI Gentlemen, I've taken the liberty of calling an unscheduled meeting, and must apologize at once for holding it at such a late hour, which gives me all the more reason to express my satisfaction that everyone has managed to attend.

ADLER Löwenstein is absent.

BERNHARDI He will still come, I hope.—I see in this fresh evidence of your keen, not to say loyal, interest in our institute, and of the firm collegial bonds that we have formed, despite our occasional differences which after all can never be completely avoided in any larger corporate body, the less so the more distinguished are its members. (*Disquiet*) But it has been amply demonstrated that we are of one mind on all substantive issues, and this will I hope continue to be so in future, to the satisfaction of our true sponsors and the frustration of our enemies! For enemies we also have. Gentlemen, I don't think I need fear you will reproach me with keeping you on tenterhooks. You all know why I have called this meeting. Nevertheless it is my duty to read you a letter delivered to me by registered mail this morning.

FILITZ Quiet!

BERNHARDI (*reads*) 'Dear—' etc. etc. 'I have the honour of informing you that the members of the board of trustees—' etc. etc.—'have reached the unanimous decision to resign their honorary positions. In bringing this decision to your attention as Director, I would request that you kindly convey this information to the honourable members of the executive and teaching staff. I remain yours faithfully—' etc. etc.—'Councillor Winkler, Secretary.'

 Ebenwald stoops over the letter.

BERNHARDI Read for yourselves, gentlemen. (*The letter circulates. Bernhardi smiles*) You will I hope convince yourselves that I haven't withheld one word of this interesting document from you. The board has resigned and logically enough the agenda for today reads: position of the executive and faculty on this issue. Professor Ebenwald wishes to address the meeting, I believe.

EBENWALD I would like to ask the Director whether he knows the reason for the board's resignation, a question which seems all the more appropriate since the board itself is so conspicuously silent on the matter.

PFLUGFELDER (*nettled*) Eh!

BERNHARDI I could respond by asking whether Professor Ebenwald or anybody else is not acquainted with the reason. But as we all have other things to do outside this meeting—

CYPRIAN Quite right!

BERNHARDI —and the proceedings shouldn't be prolonged unnecessarily, I shall answer Deputy Director Ebenwald's question briefly. Yes, I am well aware of the reason. They have resigned over the incident described in the so-called letter to Parliament you've all just read, with varying degrees of satisfaction.

SCHREIMANN That letter has no business in the paper.

BERNHARDI Quite right. In my view, it has no business even in Parliament—

PFLUGFELDER Well said.

BERNHARDI Because, gentlemen, that letter distorts an incident for which I bear full responsibility and which many of you here witnessed, in the interests of a particular faction—

FILITZ Of which faction?

PFLUGFELDER The anti-Semitic-clerical joint faction—

FILITZ Nonsense!

BERNHARDI Of a particular faction which none of us has any doubt exists, however mixed our feelings may be about it—

PFLUGFELDER Well said!

BERNHARDI —and distorts it for factional purposes. Furthermore, I am not here to justify myself to anyone, I appear before you as Director of this institution, to ask you how we are to react to the board's resignation. Professor Cyprian has the floor.

CYPRIAN (*beginning in his monotonous way*) A few years ago, I happened to be on vacation in Holland, and was standing in the art gallery—(*Disquiet*) What's the matter, gentlemen?

SCHREIMANN Since time is getting on, I would like to urge Professor Cyprian not to tell us any anecdotes today, but to come to the point at once if possible.

CYPRIAN It wasn't going to be an anecdote, it would have been in a profound sense—But as you wish, gentlemen. Well, the board has resigned. We all know the reason, or rather the pretext. We all know that, when he denied the priest access to the ward, Bernhardi was acting solely in the execution of his duty as a doctor. In that situation, we would all have behaved in exactly the same way.

FILITZ Oho!

EBENWALD And yet you've never behaved like that yourself.

SCHREIMANN Nor has Bernhardi, as far as we know.

FILITZ Very true.

CYPRIAN If we haven't done so, gentlemen, it's only because the situation Professor Bernhardi found himself in seldom arises in quite such a clear-cut way. Nobody would want to deny that countless believers—and doubters for that matter—, when faced with death, have found peace and strength in the last rites and the consoling words of kindly priests; nor has a doctor ever denied a priest access who has been requested by a dying person or his relatives.

FILITZ Quite rightly so!

CYPRIAN But the appearance of a priest at a sickbed against the will of the person dying, or the scruples of the person responsible for him in his final hour, can only be described as an unwarranted intrusion of ecclesiastical—concern; and resisting it may in certain cases not only be permissible, but become a duty. And such, gentlemen, is the case before us. So I repeat: I'm convinced that every one of us would have acted as Bernhardi did—you too, Professor Ebenwald—you too, Professor Filitz.—

FILITZ Not at all!

CYPRIAN Or to be more precise: we would have been bound at least to act like that, if we had given in to our primary impulse as doctors. Only a secondary assessment of the possible wider repercussions would have prompted us to allow the priest to enter. Bernhardi's error, if we even want to call it that, consisted solely in the fact that he didn't consider these repercussions, that he followed his instinct as a doctor and a human being, which as doctors and human beings we can only condone; so that only one answer to the board's letter seems appropriate, namely that we unanimously declare our complete confidence in our director, Professor Bernhardi.

PFLUGFELDER Bravo!

> *Adler nods, though a little uncertainly.*
> *Wenger looks at Adler, then at the others.*

BERNHARDI Deputy Director Ebenwald has the floor.

EBENWALD Gentlemen, let us not delude ourselves, the resignation of the board of trustees under present circumstances is just about the worst possible thing that could happen to our institute. I do not hesitate to call it a catastrophe. Yes, gentlemen, a catastrophe. I shall not go into whether the board was justified in resigning in a moral sense. We are not here to deal with religious questions, as Professor Cyprian seemed to find necessary,—to criticize Prince Constantine or his Excellency or bank director Veith and so on; we are simply faced with the fact that the sponsors of our institute, to whom we are materially and intellectually beholden, and on whose continued support we are dependent, (*interjections*)—yes we are, gentlemen—that these sponsors have turned their back on us; and we are faced with the further indisputable fact that our esteemed director, Professor Bernhardi, bears the sole responsibility for this misfortune.

BERNHARDI And bear it I do.

EBENWALD So to my mind, it would be acting not only with extreme ingratitude towards the board, but also quite indefensibly towards the institute if, at a moment when the Director has brought us, albeit without malicious intent but nevertheless extremely thoughtlessly, to the very brink of disaster, we were to come out in support of his behaviour. Therefore, unlike Professor Cyprian, I am not only against a vote of confidence in Professor Bernhardi, but would propose that we formulate a suitable expression of our regret for the incident, and emphasize our disapproval of the Director's conduct towards his Reverence in the strongest possible terms. (*He shouts down the rising disquiet*) I further propose that the resolution be brought to the attention of the board in an appropriate way, and that they be requested to withdraw their resignation on this basis. (*Commotion*)

BERNHARDI Gentlemen! (*Continued disquiet. He starts again*) Gentlemen!—To forestall any misunderstanding I would like to point out at once, that the more predictable your no confidence votes, the less I am affected by them, but that I am also in the fortunate position of being able to dispense with official votes of confidence. Nevertheless, to save you from taking steps you might regret later, I would like to disclose that in the foreseeable future we will probably no longer need a board of trustees. We are already fairly sure of a sizeable government grant for the immediate future, and more significantly in the longer term, the authorities are seriously considering nationalizing our institute, as his Excellency intimated to me again yesterday.

EBENWALD Ballroom gossip.

CYPRIAN (*stands up*) I ought to mention that a few days ago his Excellency told me the same thing—

FILITZ None of this is relevant.

SCHREIMANN Don't count your chickens!

EBENWALD A subsidy now, after this scandal!

FILITZ After a question to Parliament! (*Commotion*)

BERNARDI (*loudly*) Gentlemen, you are forgetting that this question to Parliament has to be answered. Doubts about how the answer may be received in Parliament should not concern us, or rather would imply a lack of confidence in the Minister of Education, who should be well briefed on events leading up to this parliamentary letter.

FILITZ Let's hope not one-sidedly so.

SCHREIMANN The question to Parliament is not at issue in this meeting.

FILITZ Quite right. A motion is before us.

SCHREIMANN Put it to the vote!

CYPRIAN (*to Bernhardi, in an undertone*) Yes, let's vote on it first.

BERNHARDI Gentlemen! Two motions are before us. One from Professor Ebenwald which reads—

 Löwenstein, the others.

LÖWENSTEIN Gentlemen, I've just come from Parliament. (*Stir*) The letter has been responded to.

EBENWALD Could we take the vote please, Mr Chairman.

CYPRIAN We've moved on from all that parliamentary palaver, gentlemen. What we all want to know now is—

SCHREIMANN (*who has noticed Löwenstein's distraught look*) I think I am expressing the sentiments of everybody present in asking the Director to interrupt the official meeting for a few minutes, to give our colleague Doctor Löwenstein a chance to tell us more about the reply to the question tabled in Parliament.

BERNHARDI Is everyone agreed? Then I shall briefly suspend the meeting. (*Humorously*) Löwenstein, you have the floor.

LÖWENSTEIN They are—going to conduct an inquiry into you for causing a religious disturbance. (*Appropriate commotion*)

PFLUGFELDER I don't believe it!

CYPRIAN Löwenstein!

SCHREIMANN Oh!

ADLER Religious disturbance?

CYPRIAN Tell us more.

EBENWALD Perhaps our colleague Doctor Löwenstein would be kind enough to provide us with more information.

Bernhardi stands motionless.

LÖWENSTEIN What more information do you want? They are going to set up this inquiry. It's despicable. You have achieved your purpose.

FILITZ No invective, my dear Löwenstein.

CYPRIAN Well, get on with it!

LÖWENSTEIN What more can I tell you, gentlemen? You will read the details in tomorrow morning's paper. The most telling part of the whole speech came at the end, as I've told you already. The fact that at the beginning his Excellency was evidently driving at something completely different is really beside the point.

CYPRIAN What was he driving at?

SCHREIMANN My dear Löwenstein, do your best to explain to us in context—

LÖWENSTEIN Well, gentlemen, at the beginning, it seemed certain that those who tabled the question were in for a humiliating defeat. The Minister spoke of the great merits of our Director, and specifically emphasized that there could have been no question of any deliberate provocation on his part, that Professor Bernhardi was not remotely interested in political manoeuvring, and that there was no case for filling public positions on any other basis than probity and merit. By this stage there were already interjections: 'Yes, if only that were true!' and 'Judaization of the University!' and the like. Then the Minister somehow lost sight of his topic and became confused and irritable, or so it seemed at least. Somehow he got onto the need for religious education, and the possibility of reconciling the progress of science with a Christian outlook, and then as I've already intimated he suddenly ended—I am convinced to his own surprise—, by announcing that he would sound his opposite number in the Ministry of Justice, (*scornfully*) about whether he could see any grounds for initiating proceedings against Professor Bernhardi for causing a religious disturbance, in order to ensure—this was the gist—that the individual case censured by the signatories would be cleared up in a manner free from prejudice and equally acceptable to all parties in the House and the populace at large.

PFLUGFELDER It stinks!

FILITZ Oho!

CYPRIAN And how did the House respond?

LÖWENSTEIN A good deal of clapping, no rebuttals so far as I know.—The speaker was congratulated.

ADLER It's not possible that you misheard, is it, Löwenstein?

LÖWENSTEIN You don't have to believe me.

CYPRIAN Anyway, it basically doesn't have anything to do with us.

FILITZ Well now!

EBENWALD I think we might resume the meeting.

BERNHARDI (*pulling himself together*) I believe I'm expressing the sentiments of all those present in extending our thanks to Doctor Löwenstein for his report. I would ask you all, gentlemen, to settle down, and after that brief interruption hereby reopen the meeting. Gentlemen, as you rightly observed earlier, the question to Parliament is not at issue here, nor is the Minister's reply; two motions are before us.

EBENWALD I withdraw my motion.

A stir. Adler explains the situation to Löwenstein in a whisper.

EBENWALD Or rather, I would like it subsumed under another motion which, in view of the situation created by the Minister's reply, seems to be called for in the interests of our institute.

CYPRIAN The Minister's reply is not the business of this meeting.

PFLUGFELDER His reply has absolutely nothing to do with us.

EBENWALD My motion is: that our esteemed Director be suspended from his duties as head of the Elisabethinum, until such time as the legal inquiry being conducted against him has been concluded. (*Great commotion*)

PFLUGFELDER Shame on you, Ebenwald!

CYPRIAN You don't even know yet whether the charge is going to be upheld.

LÖWENSTEIN Outrageous!

CYPRIAN Even if you withdraw your motion, mine still stands, namely that we express our complete confidence in our Director—

PFLUGFELDER (*interrupts*) What do the question to Parliament and the Minister's reply have to do with us? It's a purely external matter.

EBENWALD (*bellowing*) Remember, we risk making ourselves ridiculous in the eyes of the whole world if we continue deliberating and deciding here—in view of the likelihood that at the very next opportunity a higher authority will annul all our resolutions.

CYPRIAN I'm sorry, Ebenwald, but that is absolute nonsense.

ADLER Who has the right to annul our resolutions anyway?

LÖWENSTEIN Professor Bernhardi is and remains Director of the Elisabethinum. No one can depose him.

FILITZ As far as I'm concerned, even today he is no longer so.

CYPRIAN (*to Bernhardi*) Put my motion to the vote. (*A stir*)

BERNHARDI As a point of order, I shall—(*Disquiet*)

ADLER (*very excited*) Gentlemen, allow me just a few words. If the inquiry proposed by the Minister for Education and Culture leads to a hearing, it will not be possible to dispense with my testimony, as I was present at the incident. And not only I but all those here present know that the account of it given by the authors of the question tabled in Parliament was not wholly in accordance with the truth. But precisely because in my heart of hearts I am convinced of Professor Bernhardi's innocence, indeed can testify to it—

BERNHARDI Thank you.

ADLER —precisely for this reason I welcome—and we should all, regardless of any party line, welcome the fact that—

SCHREIMANN There is no party line!

ADLER —the whole affair will be cleared up in full view of the public by means of a proper inquiry. And we should also avoid giving the wrong impression, as though by prematurely taking sides here, before the conclusion of the judicial inquiry, we were trying to anticipate the final outcome, which of course can only be favourable to Professor Bernhardi. If then I support the motion of Deputy Director Ebenwald to suspend the Director—

    A stir.

FILITZ Bravo!

ADLER —I would ask you all, and above all our esteemed Professor Bernhardi, to regard this as proof of my confidence in him—and of my conviction that he will be completely exonerated by the inquiry.

CYPRIAN But Doctor Adler, this way you are conceding there is some justification for undertaking the inquiry in the first place.

FILITZ Who doesn't concede that?

LÖWENSTEIN On the basis of a denunciation like that—

FILITZ That remains to be seen.

PFLUGFELDER Ministerial toadying! He's crawling to the clericals!

LÖWENSTEIN Nor is it the first time!

CYPRIAN (*to Bernhardi*) Put my motion to the vote!

BERNHARDI Gentlemen! (*Disquiet*)

SCHREIMANN Can this be called a meeting any longer? It's a coffee house without a billiard table!

FILITZ Professor Ebenwald's motion is the more inclusive, it must be voted on first.

BERNHARDI Gentlemen! I have a question to put to Deputy Director Ebenwald.

SCHREIMANN What's all this?

FILITZ According to the rules of procedure, that is not admissible.

PFLUGFELDER Childish parliamentary games!

BERNHARDI It will be up to Professor Ebenwald whether he decides to answer my question or not.

EBENWALD Ask away.

BERNHARDI I would like to ask you, Professor Ebenwald, whether you are aware that I could have prevented the question, the Minister's response to which has occasioned the motion calling for my suspension, from being submitted to Parliament at all?

SCHREIMANN Don't answer!

BERNHARDI If you are a man, Professor Ebenwald, you will answer. (*Stir*)

EBENWALD Gentlemen, Professor Bernhardi's question comes as no surprise to me. I have in fact been expecting it throughout this extraordinary meeting. But you will not hold it against me if, in view of the curious tone the Director is pleased to adopt towards me, I abstain from answering him directly, and instead give you all some insight into what lies behind the Director's somewhat insinuating question. (*Disquiet, tension*) Well then, gentlemen, shortly after the incident that has put our institute into such an unpleasant situation, I made a point of calling on the Director, to express my concern that Parliament might well take the opportunity to intervene in the case in a way which would be detrimental to the interests of our institute. As you know, our institute has always had its enemies, and today it has more than some of you may be aware. For there are still those among you, gentlemen, who seem unable to come to terms with historical and demographic trends, and in public institutions one has to take account of them, whether or not one regards them as justified from a philosophical perspective. Many people do not consider it right that in an institute whose trustees include a prince and a bishop, and where statistically eighty-five per cent of the patients are Catholic, the majority of the doctors treating them should belong to a different faith. The fact is that this creates bad blood in certain circles.

LÖWENSTEIN But eighty per cent of the money we get also comes from those of a different faith.

EBENWALD That is a subsidiary matter, the patients are the main issue.—Well then, as you know, the question arose as to who should get Professor Tugendvetter's department. Professor Hell from Graz or Doctor Wenger. I may speak about it now, despite the presence of our worthy colleague, since he knows it all already. Hell is above all a hard-working practical physician, whereas our colleague Doctor Wenger's work has been principally in theoretical areas, and naturally he has not yet had as much practical experience as Hell, though that will come in time. Well now, gentlemen, imagine that a good friend comes to see one—

PFLUGFELDER Or a cousin—

EBENWALD —it could have been a cousin—and says to one: you know it's going to stick out like a sore thumb if you appoint a Jew to the Elisabethinum again, especially after that embarrassing incident the whole of Vienna is already talking about. And you may well find Parliament descending on you. Yes, gentlemen, do you find it so reprehensible that one should then go to the Director as I did, and say to him, we'd better take Hell, who is after all no fool, to avoid any possible unpleasantness.

WENGER Quite right! (*Amusement*)

EBENWALD You hear that! Perhaps I should have gone to Doctor Wenger instead, and asked him to withdraw his application. But I don't like hole and corner tactics. And so I went straight to the

Director. So that is the point of Professor Bernhardi's question, which no doubt was intended to sting me to the quick. And it's true that we might perhaps have been spared the question to Parliament, if Hell instead of Wenger were sitting here today. I won't say it would have been too pretty, but all this need never have arisen. And now we're in hot water. Dixi,* I have done.

PFLUGFELDER Bravo, Bernhardi!

BERNHARDI Gentlemen, Professor Ebenwald has followed the example of some distinguished models by providing a rhetorical answer to my question, rather than a factual one. But each of you will be able to make up your own mind about this business. To defend myself by saying that I did not agree to the deal proposed to me—

SCHREIMANN Oho!

BERNHARDI I may allow myself to call it a deal with at least as much justification as my conduct towards the priest has been called a religious disturbance.

PFLUGFELDER Well said.

BERNHARDI Nevertheless, I must admit to being at fault,—at fault in not having done my level best as Director to stop the question to Parliament being tabled, which seems designed to tarnish the reputation of the institute among hypocrites and fools. And to take the appropriate action myself, as well as to prevent further delays, I hereby resign as Director of the institute!

   Great commotion.

CYPRIAN What are you thinking of!

LÖWENSTEIN You mustn't do that!

PFLUGFELDER It has to be put to the vote.

BERNHARDI What for? Professor Ebenwald, Professor Filitz, and Doctors Schreimann and Adler are in favour of my suspension—

LÖWENSTEIN That's only four.

BERNHARDI And I prefer to spare Doctor Wenger any inner conflict. He might vote for me out of gratitude for my deciding in his favour recently, and I don't wish to be indebted to any such motive for what is no longer the unequivocal honour of continuing to serve as your Director.

SCHREIMANN Oho!

FILITZ That's going too far!

CYPRIAN But what are you going to do about it?

PFLUGFELDER This is your fault, Adler.

LÖWENSTEIN It must be put to the vote.

PFLUGFELDER It would be deserting the flag!

BERNHARDI Deserting?

CYPRIAN You ought to wait for the vote.

LÖWENSTEIN Let's vote!

BERNHARDI No, I won't allow a vote, I will not submit to judgement.

FILITZ Especially as it has been passed already.

SCHREIMANN Has Professor Bernhardi resigned the directorship or not?

BERNHARDI Yes.

SCHREIMANN In that case according to the statutes, as Deputy Director Professor Ebenwald has to take over leadership of the institute, and more immediately the chairing of this meeting.

LÖWENSTEIN Outrageous!

PFLUGFELDER Do we have to put up with this?

CYPRIAN Bernhardi! Bernhardi!

EBENWALD As Professor Bernhardi has regrettably resigned from the position of director, under paragraph 7 of our statutes I hereby assume leadership of the Elisabethinum and the chairmanship of the present meeting. I would ask you, gentlemen, for the same confidence you so generously bestowed on the outgoing Director, and hope to prove worthy of it too. And now, gentlemen, Professor Filitz has the floor.

LÖWENSTEIN Infamous!

PFLUGFELDER You are not the director, Professor Ebenwald, not yet! (*Disquiet*)

FILITZ We are now confronted with the question of who should take over as head of Professor Bernhardi's department.

CYPRIAN What are you talking about?

BERNHARDI Gentlemen, I may no longer be Director, but I am a member of the institute like the rest of you, and head of my department.

ADLER That goes without saying.

WENGER Certainly.

CYPRIAN There can be absolutely no discussion about that.

SCHREIMANN It would undoubtedly lead to unpleasantness, if the suspended director of the institute—

LÖWENSTEIN He is not suspended.

CYPRIAN He resigned from leadership of the institute.

FILITZ Not quite voluntarily.

PFLUGFELDER He flung it in your faces!

EBENWALD Quiet, quiet, gentlemen!

BERNHARDI (*who has now completely lost his composure*) No one of course has the right to remove me from the headship of my department, but I am taking leave until my case has been resolved.

CYPRIAN What did you say?

BERNHARDI —taking leave—

EBENWALD It is granted.

BERNHARDI Thank you! And in my absence, I entrust the interim direction of my department to my former assistants, Doctors Kurt Pflugfelder and Oscar Bernhardi.

EBENWALD I see no objection.

BERNHARDI And now, gentlemen, I am going on leave and have the honour of bidding you good evening.

LÖWENSTEIN Likewise.

> *Cyprian takes his hat.*

BERNHARDI That's just what these gentlemen want. Please, both of you, stay!

PFLUGFELDER It's above all you who must stay!

BERNHARDI Here?

ADLER (*to Bernhardi*) Professor, I should be distressed if you were to misinterpret my conduct. I would like here and now, before all those present, to express my profound respect for you.

BERNHARDI Very kind of you. He who is not for me is against me.* Good evening, gentlemen. (*Exit*)

PFLUGFELDER (*speaks amid growing disquiet, which he frequently has to shout against*) Are you going to let him go, gentlemen? I beg you one last time to come to your senses. You shouldn't let Bernhardi go. Put all personal animosities aside. Pardon me too, if I was too forceful earlier. Cast your minds back, think how this whole regrettable business started,—and you must come to your senses. A poor wretch lies dying in hospital, a mere child who has paid dearly for her morsel of youth and happiness and, if you will, sin—paid with mortal anxiety, pain and indeed her life. In her final hour she becomes euphoric. She feels elated, she is happy once again, she is unaware of the approach of death. She believes she is recovering! She dreams of her lover returning to fetch her away, lead her out of those halls of misery and suffering, back into life and happiness. It was perhaps the most beautiful moment of her life, her final dream. And Bernhardi didn't want to have her wakened from this dream to face the terrible reality. This is the crime he has committed! This and nothing more. He begged the priest to let the poor girl quietly drift off into the hereafter. Begged him. You all know this. Even if he had been less polite, anyone would have forgiven him. What monstrous mendacity is required to see the case in any other way than in purely human terms. Show me the man whose religious sensibilities would have been genuinely offended by Bernhardi's conduct. And if he exists, who else is to blame other than those who have spread a maliciously distorted version of the case. Who else, gentlemen, other than precisely those who had an interest in seeing people's religious sensibilities offended, who have an interest in the existence of those prepared to offend such sensibilities? And if there were no ambition, no parliamentary factionalism, no human baseness—in a word, no politics, would it ever have been possible to inflate this incident into a scandalous affair? Well, gentlemen, it has happened because rogues, careerists and simpletons exist. But surely we have no wish to belong to any of these categories, gentlemen. What blindness is driving us, you as doctors, people accustomed to standing beside deathbeds, we who have been granted insight into real misery, into the essence of things behind appearances. What blindness is driving you to collaborate in this miserable charade, to act out this absurd parody of parliamentary procedure, with arguments pro and con, with motions and hole and corner intrigues, with sly looks at one another, with skulduggery and two-faced gossip—to persist in averting your gaze from the heart of the matter, and out of small-minded concern for daily politics to abandon a man who has done no more than what seemed to him self-evident! For I am far from praising him and holding him up to be a hero, just because he is a man. And all I ask of you, gentlemen, is that you too show yourselves worthy of this modest accolade, that you simply consider today's resolutions and decisions null and void, and beg Professor Bernhardi to resume his office, which could have no better, no worthier representative than him. Recall him, gentlemen, I entreat you to recall him.

EBENWALD May I ask whether Professor Pflugfelder has come to the end of his performance? Apparently so. In that case, gentlemen, let us move on to the agenda.

PFLUGFELDER Gentlemen, I take my leave.

CYPRIAN Adieu!

LÖWENSTEIN There is no longer a quorum, gentlemen.

SCHREIMANN We won't let the institute down.

FILITZ We'll take responsibility for passing our resolutions without you.

PFLUGFELDER (*opening the door*) Ah, that's good timing! Doctor Hochroitzpointner, step inside.

LÖWENSTEIN Congratulations, Deputy Director!

PFLUGFELDER So now you are all assembled, gentlemen, I trust you will enjoy yourselves!

Cyprian, Pflugfelder, Löwenstein exeunt.

EBENWALD Was there something you wanted, Doctor Hochroitzpointner?

HOCHROITZPOINTNER Oh! (*He stands by the door*)

EBENWALD Close the door, would you! (*This is done*) The meeting continues, gentlemen.

Curtain.

Act Four

Sitting room in Bernhardi's apartment. Door at the back. Door to the right.

Pflugfelder, followed by Löwenstein from right.

LÖWENSTEIN (*still behind the scene*) Professor Pflugfelder!
Enters.

PFLUGFELDER Ah, Löwenstein!—But you're quite out of breath.

LÖWENSTEIN I've been running after you all down the street. (*Questioning*) So what's the news—?

PFLUGFELDER Weren't you in court?

LÖWENSTEIN I was called away just as they were considering the verdict. How long—?

PFLUGFELDER Two months.

LÖWENSTEIN Two months, in spite of the priest's testimony? Surely not?

PFLUGFELDER That testimony! The only one who benefited was the priest himself. Bernhardi didn't gain anything at all from it.

LÖWENSTEIN That's a bit—How did it benefit the priest—?

PFLUGFELDER But didn't you listen to the prosecution's plea?

LÖWENSTEIN Only the beginning. I'm afraid I was called away four times today during the proceedings. Usually one waits for days before a patient takes it into his head to—

PFLUGFELDER Come now, no need to reproach yourself—

LÖWENSTEIN So what were you saying about the prosecution?

PFLUGFELDER Well, when the priest conceded that he had not been pushed but only touched lightly on the shoulder, this gave the prosecution the pretext to praise his Reverence as a model of forbearance, and then to sing the praises of the entire priesthood, which would hardly have collapsed without them.

LÖWENSTEIN In other words, Bernhardi was in fact condemned solely on the strength of the testimony of that hysterical nurse, Ludmilla, and that young hopeful, Hochroitzpointner? Because all the other testimonies exonerated him completely. I must apologize at once to Adler. He has behaved splendidly. And Cyprian too. To say nothing of your son!

Cyprian enters. Löwenstein, Pflugfelder. Greetings.

PFLUGFELDER What's happened to Bernhardi?

LÖWENSTEIN Could they have taken him into custody already?

CYPRIAN He's probably coming over with Doctor Goldenthal.

PFLUGFELDER Really? So Goldenthal is bringing him along?

CYPRIAN (*displeased*) We can scarcely dispense with our defence counsel at today's meeting.

PFLUGFELDER We should have dispensed with him from the beginning.

LÖWENSTEIN Very true.

CYPRIAN What have you against him? He spoke superbly. Not very cogently perhaps, but—

PFLUGFELDER One certainly couldn't claim that.

LÖWENSTEIN He's been baptized! His wife even wears a cross. He's sending his son to be educated in Kalksburg!* Now they belong to the right set.

CYPRIAN You and your idée fixe, you really get on one's nerves sometimes.

LÖWENSTEIN Well, I'm no ostrich any more than I'm a kibitzer. Doctor Goldenthal is one of those who are always afraid one might suspect—With a different lawyer, things would have turned out differently.

PFLUGFELDER How?

CYPRIAN We mustn't reproach Bernhardi after the event, my friends, particularly today. But even his most ardent admirers couldn't claim he behaved especially prudently.

LÖWENSTEIN How so? I thought he behaved admirably. The way he remained calm during that craven scoundrel Hochroitzpointner's testimony—

CYPRIAN You call that remaining calm? It was obstinacy.

LÖWENSTEIN Obstinacy? How do you mean, obstinacy?

PFLUGFELDER (*to Cyprian*) He probably wasn't there when Bernhardi asked for Ebenwald to be subpoenaed.

LÖWENSTEIN Ah!

CYPRIAN Didn't you know that?—He also wanted Flint, the Minister of Education, to be summoned.

LÖWENSTEIN Splendid!

CYPRIAN It was anything but splendid. What have Flint and Ebenwald to do with the court case?

LÖWENSTEIN Well, listen to that—

CYPRIAN Absolutely nothing. It almost looked like sensation-mongering.

PFLUGFELDER Well now—

CYPRIAN If one were really determined to get to the bottom of things, think of the people one would have had to haul before the court today! It would have been an illustrious company, I can tell you.

LÖWENSTEIN The more's the pity!

> *Kurt enters.*

PFLUGFELDER Kurt!

> *Goes up to him and embraces him.*

LÖWENSTEIN (*to Cyprian*) What's this touching little family scene about?

CYPRIAN Don't you know? Kurt called Hochroitzpointner a liar in court.

LÖWENSTEIN What—

CYPRIAN And was fined two hundred crowns for his pains.

LÖWENSTEIN My dear Doctor Pflugfelder, allow me to give you a kiss too.

KURT Very kind of you, Doctor, I'll consider it bestowed already.

LÖWENSTEIN Then at least let me contribute the two hundred crowns.

PFLUGFELDER We'll take care of that. (*To Kurt*) But I must tell you, Kurt, if you take it into your head to fight a duel with this fellow—

KURT Just let him try and challenge me. I'll bring the whole thing up before a court of honour. And then we'll see—

LÖWENSTEIN He'll be on his guard.

KURT I'm afraid you're right. But either way, the Hochroitzpointner affair is not closed yet, even if that may be so with the Bernhardi case.

CYPRIAN Which we certainly hope it isn't.

LÖWENSTEIN What do you have in mind, Doctor Kurt?

> *Doctor Goldenthal, a portly man of forty-five with greying curly hair, dark mutton chops, dignified, a little unctuous and nasal, enters. Cyprian, Pflugfelder, Löwenstein, Kurt.*

GOLDENTHAL Good evening, gentlemen.

CYPRIAN Where is Bernhardi?

GOLDENTHAL I advised the Professor to leave the courthouse by a side door.

LÖWENSTEIN To avoid the ovation awaiting him?

GOLDENTHAL Patience, gentlemen, that may happen yet.

CYPRIAN Well—

GOLDENTHAL Because even if we didn't win the battle this time—

LÖWENSTEIN One certainly couldn't claim that.

GOLDENTHAL It was nevertheless an honourable defeat.

PFLUGFELDER At least for those who are not behind bars.

GOLDENTHAL (*laughs*) Are you referring to your defence counsel, Professor? Well, that is one of the few injustices of life I've never yet felt the need to do anything about. (*In a different tone*) But now, gentlemen, let's discuss things seriously for a moment. It's perhaps just as well that Professor Bernhardi has not arrived yet. Because I wanted to urge you to give me your full support at the next hearing.

CYPRIAN In what sense?

GOLDENTHAL Our esteemed Professor Bernhardi is—how shall I put it—a little self-willed. Unfortunately it came out again during today's proceedings. All that about subpoenaing the Minister of Education and his obstinate silence afterwards—it didn't make a good impression!—Well, we'll say no more about it.—But now Professor Bernhardi seems to want to continue playing the injured party, and intends to dispense with due legal process even before judgement has been handed down—and that—

CYPRIAN I foresaw something of the kind.

LÖWENSTEIN And you want to try and get the verdict quashed, is that it, Doctor Goldenthal?

GOLDENTHAL Of course.

LÖWENSTEIN It would be pointless.

PFLUGFELDER I know what we should do now. We should appeal to the public.

GOLDENTHAL Forgive me, Professor, but this trial has not been taking place behind closed doors.

PFLUGFELDER We should address the public, that's what I mean. The idiocy was, keeping our mouths shut as long as this. Look at the opposition! The clerical papers have been agitating for all they are worth. They were the ones who succeeded in getting Bernhardi immediately arraigned not for a misdemeanour but for a crime, and thus having him brought before a jury. They didn't even wait for the proceedings to end before writing about the affair, as our liberal papers evidently deemed necessary.

LÖWENSTEIN They're more restrained.

PFLUGFELDER One's inclined to call it something less flattering at times. But things have turned out unfortunately, as they so often do in this world. What the unscrupulousness and hatred of one's enemies didn't quite accomplish has been seen to by the laxness and cowardice of one's so-called friends.

CYPRIAN Do you really want to appeal to the public? Our ordinary people? The jury today should serve you as a representative example.

PFLUGFELDER Perhaps today we didn't find the right words to sway them.

GOLDENTHAL Oh!

PFLUGFELDER Call me a fool if you like, but I believe in the basic sense of justice of minds not warped by legal training, and in the sound good sense of ordinary people.

LÖWENSTEIN Pflugfelder is right! We must call mass meetings and inform people about the Bernhardi case.

CYPRIAN Mass meetings to discuss the Bernhardi case will probably not be allowed.

PFLUGFELDER There will be other opportunities. Provincial government elections are just around the corner.

CYPRIAN Are you a candidate, by any chance?

PFLUGFELDER No, but I shall be speaking. And I won't be neglecting the Bernhardi case—

CYPRIAN What can you say? You'll be obliged to state the obvious.

PFLUGFELDER I have no objection. If the opposition has the cheek to deny the obvious, we have no alternative but to proclaim it to the world. The fear that snobs might take the opportunity to denounce us as mere phrase-mongers should not lead us to surrender the field to lies and paradoxes.

LÖWENSTEIN And we should seriously consider whether it might not be in the interests of the cause for Bernhardi to serve his two months in jail in any case.

Laughter.

PFLUGFELDER That would certainly highlight the infamous way he has been treated.

Bernhardi and Oscar enter. Pflugfelder, Cyprian, Kurt, Löwenstein, Goldenthal.

BERNHARDI (*very cheerful, as he has just heard the others laughing*) A merry company, I see.* Pray count me in. Sorry to have kept you waiting. (*They shake hands*)

CYPRIAN So, did you manage to escape the ovations?

BERNHARDI Not altogether. There were several gentlemen at the side door—waiting just in case, and they certainly gave me an appropriate reception.

LÖWENSTEIN What, did they unharness your horses?

BERNHARDI They were shouting: Down with the Jews! Down with the freemasons!

LÖWENSTEIN Did you hear that!

BERNHARDI You'll give me the pleasure of staying to supper, I hope, gentlemen. Could you look into it, Oscar, and see if we have enough provisions. You see, my housekeeper has given notice. Her father confessor told her she couldn't possibly remain in a house like this without grave peril to her soul!—It will of course be a little frugal, as befits the table of a budding convict. Oscar! I do believe the lad has tears in his eyes. (*More softly*) Don't let's get sentimental.

OSCAR I'm just so angry. (*Exit, then returns shortly*)
    Adler enters.

BERNHARDI Welcome, Doctor Adler. A sinner who repenteth is more pleasing to my sight than ten who are righteous.*

ADLER (*lightly*) I was never a sinner, Professor. I emphasize again that this trial seemed to me necessary from the very beginning. Admittedly I could not foresee that Hochroitzpointner would receive more credence in court than Professor Cyprian and me.

CYPRIAN We can't complain. The priest himself fared no better.

GOLDENTHAL Indeed, gentlemen. The priest himself!—It was certainly a remarkable, and in a sense even perhaps a historic moment, when Father Reder gave his testimony and—admittedly only when prompted by my questioning—expressed his conviction that Professor Bernhardi had never intended any hostile demonstration against the Catholic Church. It's a measure of how powerful certain trends must be in our society today, if even the priest's testimony was unable to assist our cause.

BERNHARDI If Father Reder had suspected as much, he no doubt would have testified otherwise.

GOLDENTHAL Oh Professor! How can you assume a servant of the Church would ever knowingly tell a lie.

PFLUGFELDER They say it has been known to happen.

ADLER I think, Professor, you are doing the priest an injustice. One could tell from his words, indeed from his whole attitude, that he almost had a liking for you. He's no ordinary person. Even in the ward at the time, I had that impression.

BERNHARDI Liking. That's something I believe in only when it's combined with a willingness to risk having to prove it.

GOLDENTHAL I doubt whether Father Reder's testimony today will be especially to his advantage in his career. Let us hope moreover that he will be called upon to give evidence again;—and then perhaps, Professor, after you have received justice, you will also judge more fairly.

BERNHARDI I've already told you, Doctor Goldenthal, I propose to forgo due legal process. Today's trial was a farce. I have no intention of appearing before those people or their likes again. Besides, Doctor, you know as well as I do, it would be completely pointless.

GOLDENTHAL I beg your pardon!—how the higher courts might decide is impossible to—

PFLUGFELDER The higher they are, the worse they get.

GOLDENTHAL Gentlemen, it will not have escaped you either that just in the last few months certain shifts in the political constellation have been building up.

LÖWENSTEIN I haven't noticed anything. It gets worse and worse.

GOLDENTHAL Forgive me, but I feel a breath of freedom beginning to sweep through our fatherland,—and a new trial might well take place beneath less oppressive skies.

BERNHARDI And what would be the utmost I could hope for? An acquittal. I'm no longer satisfied with that. If all I receive is justice, I will still be far from even with Flint, Ebenwald and company.

GOLDENTHAL My dear Professor, as I've already told you, there is no such thing as legal evidence when it comes to the kind of thing you're accusing these gentlemen of.

BERNHARDI They will believe me—even without legal evidence.

GOLDENTHAL But it is quite impossible to mount a legal case against these people at all.

BERNHARDI That's precisely why I intend to forgo any further legal assistance with my case.

GOLDENTHAL It is my duty, Professor, to warn you against being overhasty. And I do so here in front of witnesses. I fully understand that the injustice done to you really makes your blood boil. But down the path you seem to be considering, there will only be more court cases—

CYPRIAN And more convictions probably.

BERNHARDI People will know where the truth lies, just as they know today.

PFLUGFELDER Whatever your intentions, you may count on me.

LÖWENSTEIN And on me too. And I maintain that the whole system must be targeted.

PFLUGFELDER Flint should be ousted, and to hell with him.

GOLDENTHAL Gentlemen, please!

LÖWENSTEIN Yes, this Flint in whom you all placed such high hopes, and who has now become merely the stooge of the clericalists. This so-called man of science, under whom the clergy have become more insolent than ever. If things go on as they are, he will deliver the entire school system into the hands of the sable brethren, this Minister of Hypocrisy and Culture.

GOLDENTHAL Pardon me, but it's a well-known fact that undeniably liberal journalists are always in and out of the Ministry of Education. And as regards certain measures taken by the Minister which you are evidently alluding to, gentlemen, I have to say, at the risk of incurring your displeasure, that I don't find them so totally objectionable.

PFLUGFELDER What, you're in favour of making confession compulsory for school children? You're in favour of founding a Catholic university, Doctor?

GOLDENTHAL I don't mean to say I would permit my sons to study there.

LÖWENSTEIN Why not, Doctor? Getting in should be a piece of cake from Kalksburg.

GOLDENTHAL Kalksburg, gentlemen, is one of the most outstanding schools in Austria. And I would point out that among the clergy too, however much maligned in some quarters, there are men of intellectual distinction, indeed brave and high-minded men, as was revealed again today. And my principle, even in the most embattled cases, has always been to respect the convictions of the opposition.

LÖWENSTEIN The convictions of Minister Flint!

GOLDENTHAL He defends everyone's convictions, and that is his duty on the particular watch allotted him by Providence. Believe me, gentlemen, there are some things one should not meddle with—nor should one let others meddle with them.

PFLUGFELDER Why not, if I may ask? The world has only advanced at all because someone had the courage to meddle with things which others, in whose interest it was to do so, insisted for hundreds of years should not be meddled with.

GOLDENTHAL Couched in such general terms, your ingenious assertion would scarcely be easy to substantiate; and in any case it can have no bearing on our affair, since reforming the world was the last thing our esteemed friend Professor Bernhardi had in mind, as he will no doubt readily concede.

LÖWENSTEIN Perhaps one day he will turn out to have done exactly that.

BERNHARDI Oh! Oh! Don't get carried away!

PFLUGFELDER The way things are today, this issue can only be considered in a wider context. After all, your opponents made the first move in this regard. And the prosecution certainly didn't hesitate to do so. Could you have failed to notice that, Doctor?

GOLDENTHAL I could not follow the prosecuting counsel into that territory. My task is not to engage in politics but to defend my clients.

PFLUGFELDER If only you'd fulfilled that task at least.

BERNHARDI Look, Pflugfelder, I will not permit—

GOLDENTHAL Oh, let him have his say, Professor, this is beginning to interest me—So in your view I did not defend my client?

PFLUGFELDER In my humble opinion—no. Because to listen to you, Dr Goldenthal, anyone would have believed the religious sensibilities of the entire Catholic world, from his Holiness the Pope down to the remotest village pietist, had been deeply offended by Bernhardi's conduct to the priest. And instead of explaining that any doctor must have acted as Bernhardi did, and that only a rogue or a nincompoop would dispute this, you insisted on excusing as an act of thoughtlessness what had merely been his duty as a doctor. You treated the idiots on the jury, who were bent on finding Bernhardi guilty from the outset, as if they were the most learned pates in the empire—and the judges, who had as it were brought Bernhardi's prison sentence all ready in their briefcase, as if they were models of acuity and fairness. You even handled that clod Hochroitzpointner and the nurse Ludmilla with kid gloves, and actually gave credence to their false testimony. And you behaved as though deep down you yourself, Doctor Goldenthal, believed in the indispensable power of the sacrament against which Bernhardi is supposed to have offended, and insinuated that he would be wrong not to believe in it himself. First a polite nod to your client, then a kowtow to his enemies—to stupidity, hypocrisy and calumny. If Bernhardi is satisfied with your performance, that's his affair, but I for one, Doctor Goldenthal, cannot compliment you on your defence.

GOLDENTHAL And I, Professor, must applaud you for having devoted your great gifts to medicine and not to law, because with your temperamental disposition and your sense of the dignity of the courtroom, you would certainly have succeeded in making even the most innocent man out to be a criminal.

LÖWENSTEIN You're quite good at that yourself, Doctor, despite your mercifully untemperamental disposition.

BERNHARDI I really think this is enough. I must ask you—

The door into the dining room has meanwhile opened.

GOLDENTHAL (*defensively*) Lucky the man who can claim such friends, Professor. For my part, I'm happy to admit that I am not one of those unscrupulous lawyers who abandon their clients to the mercy of the judges for the sake of a rhetorical effect.—But of course, Professor, I wouldn't think of imposing my services on you further, and leave it to you—

CYPRIAN (*to Pflugfelder*) You see!

BERNHARDI What are you thinking of, Doctor?

PFLUGFELDER If anyone here ought to leave, it should be me of course. I must also apologize, my dear Bernhardi, for having allowed myself to get carried away; though of course I cannot retract anything I've said. Say no more, Bernhardi, I am quite superfluous here.

> *Servant enters and whispers something to Bernhardi.*
> *Bernhardi very disconcerted, hesitates a moment, considers turning to Cyprian, thinks better of it.*
> *Pflugfelder meanwhile has withdrawn.*

BERNHARDI Excuse me, gentlemen, it's a visitor I can't possibly refuse. I hope we won't be long.—Please start the meal without me. Oscar, if you'd be so good—

CYPRIAN (*to Bernhardi*) What's up?

BERNHARDI Later, later.

> *Oscar, Kurt, Löwenstein, Adler, Cyprian and Goldenthal go into the dining room.*
> *Servant exit.*
> *Bernhardi draws the curtain across the dining room.*
> *Priest enters. Bernhardi and the priest.*

BERNHARDI (*receiving him at the door*) Do come in—

PRIEST Good evening, Professor.

BERNHARDI A condolence visit, Father?

PRIEST Not exactly. But I felt an urgent need to talk to you this evening.

BERNHARDI I'm at your disposal, Father.

> *Offers him a chair, both sit down.*

PRIEST Although the outcome of the trial didn't favour you, Professor, it should be clear that I am not to blame for your conviction.

BERNHARDI If I were to thank you for telling the truth under oath, Father, I would be afraid I might insult you. So—

PRIEST (*already a little vexed*) I haven't come to receive your thanks, Professor, although I did not confine myself to answering the questions, which as a witness was all I was duty-bound to do. For if you will kindly recall, when asked by your counsel, I unhesitatingly expressed my conviction that your behaviour toward me outside the ward was not prompted by any hostility toward the Catholic Church.

BERNHARDI No doubt you went well beyond the call of duty in doing so, Father, but perhaps the effect of your testimony will have been its own reward.

PRIEST Whether that effect will be to my advantage outside the court-room, Professor, is another matter. But as you can probably imagine, I haven't come to repeat my court testimony to you in private. What prompted me to call on you so late was that I have a—larger confession to make.

BERNHARDI A larger confession?

PRIEST Yes. In court I said I didn't believe you acted out of deliberate hostility to me or—to what I represent. But now I find myself obliged to admit, Professor, that in the specific instance we're concerned with, you acted quite properly in your capacity as a doctor, that you could not have acted otherwise within your sphere of duty, any more than I could within mine.

BERNHARDI Have I understood correctly? Are you admitting that my conduct was entirely—that I could not have acted otherwise?

PRIEST That as a doctor you could not have acted otherwise.

BERNHARDI (*after a pause*) If that is your opinion, Father, then I am bound to say that a better time for this admission, indeed the only appropriate one, would have been a few hours ago in court.

PRIEST I need hardly assure you that it wasn't lack of courage that sealed my lips. Otherwise would I be here, Professor?

BERNHARDI So what—

PRIEST I will tell you, Professor. What made me refrain from speak-ing out in court was the dawning realization, aided by divine illumination, that one more word and I would have done irrepar-able harm to something truly sacred, something which I perhaps hold sacred above all else.

BERNHARDI I cannot imagine how, for so courageous a man as your-self, Father, there could be anything more sacred than the truth.

PRIEST What? Nothing more sacred, Professor, than the petty truth about that specific case, which I'm supposed to have vouched for all along. You yourself won't want to claim that surely. If I'd not only admitted publicly that you had good intentions—which went fur-ther than many right-minded people would forgive me for—but had conceded your right to turn me away from a dying woman, a

Christian and a sinner, the enemies of our Holy Church would have exploited such a declaration beyond anything I could have answered for. Because, as I'm sure you are aware, Professor, not all our enemies are honourable. And the petty truth that I might have spoken would thus have become in a higher sense a lie. And what would have been the result? I would then have been regarded not merely as overly indulgent but as an apostate, a traitor in the eyes of those to whom I am accountable and owe allegiance—and in the eyes of God himself. That is why I did not speak out.

BERNHARDI Then why, Father, do you do so now?

PRIEST Because the moment that illumination came to me, I vowed I would confess to you, as perhaps the only person I owed it to, what the public would have misunderstood and misrepresented.

BERNHARDI Thank you, Father. And may I hope that you never find yourself in the position of having to testify publicly to something where more might be at stake than—my insignificant fate. Because you might again experience what to me seem highly personal deliberations as divine illumination, and so an even higher truth might come to grief than the one you believe you represent and must protect.

PRIEST I cannot acknowledge a truth higher than my Church, Professor. And the highest law of my Church is integration and obedience. For if I were cast out of the fellowship whose influence radiates such blessings through the world, then unlike men in a secular profession such as yourself, Professor, I would lose any chance of being spiritually effective and thus the entire purpose of my existence.

BERNHARDI I thought there have been priests, Father, the purpose of whose existence only began when they severed all ties of fellowship, and disregarding hardship and danger, proclaimed what they considered to be just and true.

PRIEST If I belonged among them, Professor—

BERNHARDI Well?

PRIEST —then surely God would have allowed me to declare in court what you have just learned between these four walls.

BERNHARDI So it was God who sealed your lips there. And now God has sent you to me, so you can admit to me in private what you were forbidden to declare in court. One feels bound to say, your God seems to arrange things very conveniently for you.

PRIEST (*rising*) I'm sorry, Professor, but I have nothing to add to my confession, which strangely you seem to interpret as an admission that I have done you an injustice. It was never my intention to enter into a discussion with you of things we scarcely could agree about.

BERNHARDI So that's how you slam the door in my face, is it, Father—? Well, I certainly don't find it acceptable as proof that you are on the inside and I on the outside. So I can only regret, Father, that you have put yourself to the trouble of coming over here in vain.

PRIEST (*with a touch of irony*) In vain?

BERNHARDI Because I am unable to absolve you as fully as you perhaps might have expected after so unusual a step.

PRIEST Absolution? That's certainly not what I was after, Professor. Peace of mind perhaps. And that I have achieved, more fully than I might have hoped. Because now, Professor, I am beginning to see the whole matter in a new light. I'm beginning to realize that I was quite wrong about the true reason for my coming here, for my being sent here.

BERNHARDI Oh!

PRIEST It was not to confess to you, as I thought at first, but to free myself from a doubt. From a doubt, Professor, which I myself wasn't conscious of as such when I entered this room. But now it has been dispelled, clarity pervades my soul, and I regret to say, Professor, that I must retract what I admitted earlier.

BERHARDI Retract it? But I've already heard it, Father.

PRIEST It's no longer valid. Because now, Professor, I know you were not right to turn me away from the bedside of that dying woman.

BERNHARDI Ah!

PRIEST Not you! Others in the same situation might have been. But you are not among them. I understand this now. You are at best deceiving yourself, if you imagine it was medical attentiveness or human compassion that prompted you to refuse me access to her deathbed. Your compassion and attentiveness were merely pretexts; not entirely conscious perhaps, but no more than pretexts nonetheless.

BERNHARDI Pretexts! All of a sudden, Father, you no longer recognize what a moment ago you openly admitted to me, that I was charged with a responsibility—as indeed were you!?

PRIEST I don't deny that. All I dispute is whether it was out of this sense of responsibility that you refused to admit me to her. The true reason for your attitude towards me lay not in your sense of responsibility, nor in some noble impulse of the moment, as you perhaps imagine and even I almost believed, but much deeper, at

the very root of your being. Yes, Professor, the real reason was,—
how shall I put it—, your antipathy towards me—an ungovernable
antipathy—or rather animosity—

BERNHARDI Animosity—?

PRIEST —towards what this cassock signifies for you—and men like
you. Oh, you've given me proof enough of how things stand in the
course of this discussion. And now I realize that from first to last
your whole attitude, your every word, has resonated with that
deep invincible animosity which men of your sort simply cannot
overcome for men like me.

BERNHARDI Animosity! You keep repeating the word. And supposing
it were so! Don't you think that after all I've been through in the
last few weeks, the whole witch-hunt against me, that you yourself
consider dishonest and undignified, I might in retrospect be justified to some degree in feeling what you term animosity, even if I
hadn't done so earlier. And I won't deny that despite my innate and
sometimes annoying disposition to want justice, in the last few
weeks I have felt more than a little such—animosity stirring in
me—not so much toward you personally, Father—as toward the—
society that has closed ranks around you. But I swear to you,
Father, that at that moment when I denied you access to the sick
ward, there wasn't a trace of animosity in me. I faced you in as
much purity of heart in my capacity as a doctor—as ever a man of
your calling administered the sacrament at the altar. With no less
purity of heart than you faced me—you who had come to administer the last rites to my patient. You knew that when you first
entered my room. You admitted as much to me. You ought not
suddenly to repudiate this acknowledgement,—because you feel—
as I also feel—and perhaps have never felt more strongly than at
this moment, that something divides us,—which even in more
amicable circumstances it would be hard to delude ourselves did
not exist.

PRIEST You say you have never felt it more strongly than at this
moment?

BERNHARDI Yes,—at this moment, as I stand facing one of the most
liberal men of your cloth. But it seems to me, Father, that animosity
is much too poor and petty a word for what does, and perhaps
always must divide us. That is something altogether higher—and to
my mind—more hopeless.

PRIEST You may well be right about that, Professor. Hopeless. And so
it will prove to be again—between you and me. Because I have

often had similar discussions into frontier territory with scholars and (*a little scornfully*) enlightened persons from your intellectual sphere; yet the possibility of some accommodation between us never seemed as remote as it does here tonight. Though admittedly this is perhaps the one evening I should have avoided trying to—follow you to those frontiers in a discussion.

BERNHARDI I hope, Father, that you will show me sufficient—respect, not to make shall we say an embittered mood occasioned by my personal experience today responsible for my entire way of—looking at the world.

PRIEST Far from it, Professor—when such an unbridgeable chasm opens up between two men like—you and me, who may well feel no—(*smiling*) animosity towards one another, then there must surely be some deeper reason. To my mind, the reason is that while some accommodation ought to be possible between faith and doubt,—none is possible between humility and,—you won't misunderstand the word if you recall some of your earlier remarks—, between humility and—presumption.

BERNHARDI Presumption—?! And you, Father, though you can think of no more—benign word for what you suspect lies at the bottom of my soul, do you consider yourself free of—animosity towards—men of my sort?

PRIEST (*appears indignant at first, but after collecting himself, with a faint smile*) I know myself to be free of it. My religion, Professor, bids me love those that hate me.

BERNHARDI (*emphatically*) And mine, Father,—or whatever has replaced it in my breast,—bids me understand where I am not understood.

PRIEST I don't doubt your good will. But understanding, Professor, has its limits. Wherever the human intellect holds sway—you'll have doubtless experienced this often enough yourself—, there is error and deception. What does not deceive,— cannot deceive people of my sort,—is—(*hesitates*) I would prefer to choose a word which you won't object to either, Professor, is—inner feeling.

BERNHARDI Let us call it that then, Father. This inner feeling, even though it may infuse my soul from a rather different source, is something I too try to rely on. What alternative—do any of us have perhaps? And if it is not as easy for—people like me as for men of your sort, Father, no doubt God, who—created you so humble and me so presumptuous, this—incomprehensible God will have his reasons.

The priest looks at him for some time; then, with sudden resolution, stretches out his hand towards him.

BERNHARDI (*hesitating, with the trace of a smile*) Across—the abyss, Father?

PRIEST Let us not—look down—for a moment!
They shake hands.

PRIEST Farewell, Professor!—
Exit.

Bernhardi alone, for a while apparently irresolute and lost in thought, his knitted brow clearing however as he makes a gesture of shaking something off, and then draws back the curtain and opens the partition doors. The others are seen at the table, some of them already standing smoking.

CYPRIAN At last!

ADLER We're already on to the cigars.

CYPRIAN (*stepping out of the room and coming up to Bernhardi*) What was the matter? Today—a patient as late as this?

BERNHARDI —That's difficult to answer.

OSCAR (*also coming out of the room*) Several telegrams have come for you, Papa.

BERNHARDI (*opening one*) Ah, how nice.

CYPRIAN Are we allowed to know?

BERNHARDI A former patient assuring me of his sympathy. A poor devil who was laid up for a few weeks in the Elisabethinum.

GOLDENTHAL May I have a look? Florian Ebeseder?

LÖWENSTEIN Ebeseder? Florian? That sounds like a Christian.

PFLUGFELDER (*touching him on the shoulder*) They do exist!

BERNHARDI (*opening another telegram*) Oh God! (*To Cyprian*) Take a look at this.

ADLER Read it, read it out!

CYPRIAN (*reads*) 'We wish to assure the manly warrior in the cause of freedom and enlightenment of our sincere esteem and sympathy, and ask him to believe us when we say that he will always find us on his side in the struggle against clerical obscurantism. Doctor Reiss, Walter König—'

BERNHARDI Names I don't even know.

GOLDENTHAL That is extremely encouraging. We may assume it won't be the last.

BERNHARDI Can't we do anything to stop it?

GOLDENTHAL (*laughing*) What? The very idea that we should—

OSCAR Papa, won't you sit down and have something to eat after all this?

The servant brings a card.

BERNHARDI Who is it now?

OSCAR (*reads*) The Chairman of the Brigittenau Association of Freethinkers.

BERNHARDI Freethinkers from Brigittenau—? I am not at home. Please inform the gentlemen.

GOLDENTHAL But why?

BERNHARDI I'm in prison already—I've been executed. (*Goes into the dining room with the others, all except Goldenthal and Löwenstein*)

Later Doctor Kulka.

GOLDENTHAL (*to the servant, whom he catches at the door*) Tell the gentlemen the Professor is quite exhausted at the moment, but he will be—when was it the Professor has his consulting hours?

SERVANT From two o'clock on.

GOLDENTHAL Well then, the Professor will be delighted to receive them at a quarter to two tomorrow.

Servant exit.

LÖWENSTEIN Delighted? Are you sure about that?

GOLDENTHAL You leave me to look after my client's interests.

Löwenstein with a shrug goes into the dining room.

Servant enters with a card.

GOLDENTHAL (*turns round*) What is it? Let's have a look. Oh!

SERVANT The gentleman won't be put off.

GOLDENTHAL Very well, show him in.

Servant exit.

Goldenthal clears his throat, readies himself.

KULKA (*enters*) Oh, Doctor Goldenthal?—if I'm not mistaken.

GOLDENTHAL That's me. But I think we have met before, Doctor Kulka—you'll have to make do with me today, I'm afraid. The Professor is rather fatigued, as you can imagine—

KULKA Fatigued?—Hmm—I suppose another time would—But I wouldn't like to have to answer to my boss—

GOLDENTHAL You heard now, Doctor Kulka—

KULKA Yes, indeed I heard. And of course I understand, but what good is that to me. If I can't speak to the Professor personally, I'll be the one blamed by my boss.

GOLDENTHAL Perhaps I might be in a position to answer your questions.

KULKA (*hesitating*) If you wouldn't mind—Might I ask, Doctor, whether it's true that Professor Bernhardi does not intend to try and get the verdict quashed?

GOLDENTHAL As a matter of form, we have requested time to consider.

Kulka has taken out a notebook.

GOLDENTHAL (*influenced by this, in a rhetorical tone*) For although it is far from our intention to cast the slightest doubt on the wisdom and legal knowledge of our Austrian judges, or even to distrust the good sense of the citizens of Vienna on the jury, we cannot turn a blind eye to the possibility that the factional bias of a certain paper, which will here be nameless, may have been the basis for a miscarriage of justice and—

Bernhardi enters.

KULKA Oh, Professor.

BERNHARDI What's all this?

GOLDENTHAL I took the liberty, Professor, as you didn't wish to be disturbed,—and believe I have represented your—

BERNHARDI With whom do I have the pleasure?

KULKA Kulka from the 'Latest News'. My boss, who has the honour of being acquainted with you personally, sends his kind regards and—

GOLDENTHAL There are rumours abroad which it would seem best to respond to at once.

KULKA It is said, Professor, that you intend to forgo due process—

GOLDENTHAL I have already informed Doctor Kulka that we have requested time to consider.

BERNHARDI That is correct. (*Gradually, Löwenstein, Cyprian, Adler, Kurt, Oscar come out of the adjoining room*)

KULKA I am very grateful for that information. But now, Professor, I have a special proposition from my boss to put to you. I understand, Professor, that during today's proceedings you requested that the Minister of Education be subpoenaed. It would therefore appear that important aspects of this affair have not been mentioned, or been disallowed during the trial. Now my boss would consider it an honour, Professor, to be able to put the columns of our paper at your disposal—

BERNHARDI (*deprecatingly*) Very kind.

KULKA I am sure you are aware, Professor, that while our paper confidently welcomed his Excellency at the beginning of his term, it has since felt obliged to take a firm stand against some of the Minister's more retrogressive, indeed distinctly reactionary measures, so as to safeguard that moderate ethos which has always seemed to us a precondition for progressive action in the political arena. And so in our fight for freedom and progress we would very much welcome having a man like yourself on our side, whose decorously restrained passion would assure us of an ally—

BERNHARDI Excuse me, I am not your ally.

KULKA But we are yours, Professor.

BERNHARDI That may appear so to you today. But my affair is a purely personal one.

LÖWENSTEIN But—

KULKA Some personal affairs do sometimes carry political seeds within them though. Now yours—

BERNHARDI That is a coincidence I take no responsibility for. I don't belong to any party and don't wish to be claimed by any.

KULKA Professor, you will not be able to avoid—

BERNHARDI I will not be party to it. Whoever campaigns for me does so at his own risk. (*As lightly as ever, and now with his customary ironic smile*) Just as today I was accused of having affronted the Catholic religion, tomorrow I might find myself suspected of being the enemy of another faith, perhaps closer to home in your case. —

KULKA I subscribe to no religion, Professor. That is true of all of us, privately at least. The position of our paper is widely known to be one of absolute freedom of conscience. What was it Frederick the Great* said?—Every man must find salvation in his own way.

BERNHARDI Well then, I would ask you to treat me too according to that principle. Thank your boss for his kind invitation, but it would simply be a misuse of his trust, a sort of false declaration, were I to accept.

KULKA Is that really your last word, Professor?

BERNHARDI My last seldom differs from my first.

KULKA My boss will be very sorry indeed—I really don't know how to—But please, Professor, should you decide after all to express your sentiments about his Excellency in published form, could we at least count on your not giving any other paper—

BERNHARDI You may depend upon it, whatever else I may decide, the last thing I intend to do is to seek support from a newspaper. My kind regards to your boss.

KULKA Thank you, Professor. It's been a pleasure, gentlemen.

> *Exit. Short, uncomfortable pause.*

CYPRIAN Well, that was hardly necessary.

GOLDENTHAL I must say I agree, Professor—

BERNHARDI Do you still not understand, gentlemen, I want absolutely nothing to do with these people, who wish to turn my case into a political affair.

LÖWENSTEIN But it already is one.

GOLDENTHAL Certainly, the way things have developed, you are now in the thick of a political battle. And indeed we ought to welcome it—

BERNHARDI Please, Doctor Goldenthal, don't welcome any such thing! I'm not prepared to fight any political battles. The ridiculous war cries being raised in certain quarters are not going to tempt me to take on a role which does not suit me, and which I have no aptitude for precisely because it would only be a role. And as regards time to consider, Doctor, I hereby request you to consider it as having lapsed.

GOLDENTHAL I don't understand—

BERNHARDI I want to begin my sentence as soon as possible. Probably tomorrow.

CYPRIAN But—

BERNHARDI I want to get the whole business over with. That's all that matters to me now. From the point of view of my work and my profession, the last few months have been as good as wasted. Nothing but meetings and judicial hearings. And what good has come out of it all? The whole affair was unedifying enough as a law case, now it looks like becoming a political football, and from that I must escape, even to prison if need be. I'm in the business of curing people,—or at least trying to persuade them that I can. And I want the opportunity to do that again as soon as practical.

LÖWENSTEIN And your revenge?

BERNHARDI Who said anything about revenge?

LÖWENSTEIN Well, Flint, Ebenwald and so on. Are you going to let these people off so lightly?

BERNHARDI There will be no revenge—more a matter of settling accounts. And it will come to that no doubt. But skirmishing with these people is not going to suddenly become the sole object of my life. I will see to it in passing. But don't worry. I won't be doing them any favours.

CYPRIAN Whether you intend to pursue the matter politically, legally or privately, I still maintain it wasn't necessary to so to speak show Mr Kulka the door.

GOLDENTHAL I too would like to emphasize that the goodwill of the paper Mr Kulka represents—

BERNHARDI (*interrupting him*) My dear Doctor Goldenthal, one has
to take one's enemies as they come; my friends I can choose for
myself—fortunately—
        Curtain.

Act Five

A Council room in the Ministry. Appropriately furnished, quite comfortable

Councillor Winkler, about forty-five, but looks younger, slim, fresh-faced, small moustache, short blond hair flecked with grey, sparkling blue eyes, alone, busy with files. As the curtain rises, he gets up and puts the files away in a cupboard. Telephone rings.

COUNCILLOR (*returning to the table, speaks into the telephone*) This is the Imperial Ministry of Education and Culture—No, Councillor Winkler. Oh, Professor Ebenwald.—He's not here yet.—Perhaps in half an hour or so.—His Excellency certainly won't be leaving for Parliament before half past one.—Well, unfortunately I'm not in a position to give you any information on that score, at least not over the telephone.—It will be a pleasure. Goodbye, Professor. (*Rings off; resumes what he was doing*)

    Office servant enters, bringing the post and a visitor's card.

COUNCILLOR Doctor Kulka?

SERVANT But he wants to speak to his Excellency personally.

COUNCILLOR He should come again later.

SERVANT There were two gentlemen from the papers here earlier as well. They said they'd come back later.

COUNCILLOR Very well, you've no need to show any of the people from the press into my office. They all want to see his Excellency personally.

    Servant exit.
    Telephone rings again.

COUNCILLOR This is the Imperial Ministry of Education and Culture—Yes, Councillor Winkler.—Of course, I should have recognized the voice. How are you, dear lady.—This evening?—Yes, I'd love to if I can manage it.—I have no comment at all on the elections.—No.—Because I don't approve of beautiful women getting involved in politics.—None of them understands politics.—You'll have to wait at least twenty years for that, dear lady.—Goodbye then. Kind regards to your husband. (*Rings off*)

    Servant with a card.

COUNCILLOR Yet another one? Ah, Doctor Feuermann.—Very well, show him in.

    Servant exit.

Doctor Feuermann enters

COUNCILLOR Good day, Doctor. To what do we owe the pleasure?

FEUERMANN I've come about a very serious matter, Councillor.

COUNCILLOR Oh, Doctor, not another mishap, I hope, after the good citizens of Oberhollabrunn have shown such good sense in—

FEUERMANN That's true, Councillor, they have exonerated me. But what good is that? I never see a patient. If I stay on as a district doctor in Oberhollabrunn, I will simply starve. So I am taking the liberty of applying for transfer and—(*telephone rings*)

COUNCILLOR Excuse me, Doctor. (*Into the telephone*) Yes, Councillor Winkler.—Oh, hello Sir. Who? What? (*Astounded*) I don't believe it!—Are you serious? Nurse Ludmilla? Now that would be a remarkable coincidence.—Well, because he's being released today.—Professor Bernhardi, of course.—Yes, today.—You'll come yourself?—yes.—How can you think that!—Of course I won't say anything to his Excellency for now, if you so wish.—Goodbye, Undersecretary!—(*Rings off.—Very agitated at first, then to Feuermann*) You were saying.

FEUERMANN And I especially wanted to ask for your support, Councillor,—you who have always—

Flint enters. Feuermann, Councillor.

FLINT Good day, Councillor. (*Notices Feuermann*) Ah—

FEUERMANN (*bowing deeply*) Excellency, my name is Doctor Feuermann.

FLINT Ah, of course.—I've already—from the 'Monday' weekly ———

COUNCILLOR (*in an undertone*) Not a journalist, your Excellency—Doctor Feuermann from Oberhollabrunn.

FLINT Ah yes,—Doctor Feuermann.

COUNCILLOR (*as before*) Who was accused of so-called medical negligence and cleared.

FLINT Yes, I remember. Professor Filitz submitted an illuminating report. Ten votes to two,—

FEUERMANN Nine to—

The Councillor signals disapproval.

FLINT I congratulate you, my dear Doctor Feuermann.

FEUERMANN I am deeply touched, Excellency, that you should consider my trivial case all that—

FLINT To me there are no trivial cases. Someone in my position cannot allow there to be any. In a higher sense, everything is equally important. (*He glances at the Councillor, seeking applause*) And perhaps it may give you some satisfaction to learn that radical reforms to the medical curriculum are being considered, in no small measure due to the impression made by your 'trivial' affair. Let us hope it will be possible to implement them as recommended. Generally speaking, if one didn't always have to ask Parliament beforehand—(*with a glance at the Councillor*) how easy governing would be.

COUNCILLOR Or at least, much quicker, and that is after all the main thing.

FEUERMANN I took the liberty, your Excellency—

COUNCILLOR I assume you've set out everything in your application, Doctor.

FEUERMANN I also just wanted to mention—

COUNCILLOR You've no doubt put that in there too—

FEUERMANN Certainly.

COUNCILLOR Well, give it to me, Doctor, and it will be attended to as soon as possible. Good day to you, Doctor.

FLINT (*who has meanwhile been given several newspapers by the servant*) Goodbye, Doctor. (*Shakes hands with him*)

> *Feuermann exit.*
> *Flint, Councillor.*

FLINT (*looking over a paper*) What does he want, actually?

COUNCILLOR He's requesting a transfer, your Excellency. The poor devil is being boycotted in Oberhollabrunn, of course, despite having been cleared.—

FLINT Well, you probably wouldn't want to be treated by him either.

COUNCILLOR Certainly not, if I were about to have a child.

FLINT (*throwing the paper aside irritably*) What else is new?

COUNCILLOR Professor Ebenwald telephoned. He will be dropping in during the course of the morning.

FLINT What, again? But he was only here two days ago.

COUNCILLOR They are in urgent need of money at the Elisabethinum. They are up to their ears in debt.

FLINT But surely the board of trustees withdrew its resignation after Bernhardi was removed.

COUNCILLOR Yes, it all goes to show that the only person who stirred things up a little was Bernhardi. Since then, they've all been asleep. Myself included.

FLINT They must receive a subsidy. I did promise Bernhardi at the time.

COUNCILLOR We're hugely over-committed this time round, your

Excellency, we won't be able to squeeze more than three thousand for them out of our allocation. The Minister of Finance is annoyed enough with us already. I'm not even sure yet whether we will get the money for the physiology institute extension. And that is after all more—

FLINT If we don't get it through the budget committee—along with a few other things, then I shall request a separate allocation from Parliament.

COUNCILLOR Oh!

FLINT They won't be able to refuse me. The Liberals and Social Democrats can hardly do so, they would be cutting their own throats if they were suddenly to demand that the government exercise restraint when it comes to building scientific institutes. And as far as the members of the Christian Social Party go, surely I have the right not to expect any trouble there. Don't you agree?

COUNCILLOR They certainly have every reason to be grateful to your Excellency.

FLINT Hardly a clinching argument, though, Councillor. It's not gratitude that counts in public life but correct bookkeeping. One must await the balance sheet.—By the way, I must also congratulate you on yesterday's provincial elections. Ten new Social Democrat representatives, who would have anticipated that?

COUNCILLOR Once the parliamentary elections are over, Excellency, I shall be in a position to accept your congratulations.

FLINT The parliamentary election results should be completely different. Besides, even yesterday the margins were not all that wide. So don't count your chickens before they've hatched, my worthy Mr Anarchist.

COUNCILLOR Your Excellency seems ready to promote me very quickly. Just now you honoured me with the title of a Social Democrat.

FLINT Not that much of a difference.

COUNCILLOR I mustn't omit to congratulate you on your speech yesterday, Excellency.

FLINT Speech?—Nonsense, a few impromptu words. But they were certainly effective.

COUNCILLOR It's being discussed everywhere. (*Indicating the papers*)

FLINT Anyway, Councillor, your joining the chorus of congratulations attests to your commendable objectivity. You were the one I was positively anxious about.

COUNCILLOR You are too flattering, Excellency.

FLINT It seemed improbable at first, that you of all people, Councillor, should be in favour of increasing the hours of religious instruction.

COUNCILLOR And what about you, Excellency?

FLINT My dear Councillor, my personal views on this and other issues would require a chapter in itself. Glibly trotting out one's views is the mark of the dilettante in politics. On the other hand, the heart-felt tone of conviction can easily ring hollow. What works best in politics is the gentle art of counterpoint.

COUNCILLOR Until someone comes along, your Excellency, who can whistle a new tune.

FLINT Very clever. But to descend from our musical analogies into the real world, do you honestly believe, Councillor, that the people are ready, or ever will be ready to cope with life without religion?

COUNCILLOR What I understand by religion, your Excellency, can be more readily learned anywhere other than during what is commonly called religious instruction.

FLINT Come now, my dear Councillor, are you an anarchist or not?

COUNCILLOR Well, Excellency,—as a civil servant one only has one choice apparently—between being an anarchist or a fool—

FLINT (laughing) Well now, surely you would acknowledge a few steps in between. But believe me, my dear Councillor, anarchism is an unfruitful state of mind. I went through a similar phase myself once. I got over it. Now my philosophy of life, my dear Councillor, could be summed up in a word: work, achievement! In the face of this imperious demand, everything else recedes into the background. And since as you know I have a host of projects which can't do without the cooperation of Parliament, I am obliged as they say to make concessions. Anarchists too have to make concessions, my dear Councillor, otherwise you could never have become a councillor. (More seriously) But you are mistaken if you believe making concessions is always an easy matter. Or perhaps, Councillor, you think throwing my old friend Bernhardi to the wolves didn't involve any personal sacrifice on my part? And yet it was essential. One day the ins and outs of it all will emerge more clearly. It is all on record. And should the time come when I decide to shake certain people from my coat-tails, well, I won't say any more,—but people will realize that I am not the Minister for Education and Concordat,* as some smart alec reporter was pleased to describe me in his so-called editorial today.

COUNCILLOR Ah!

FLINT A man after your own heart, what? And yet it isn't even his idea. The phrase was coined by honest Pflugfelder, who launched it recently at one of those totally superfluous voters' assemblies, where he couldn't resist bringing up the Bernhardi affair. Frankly, my dear Councillor, I think government forces have failed to act with appropriate rigour at some of these assemblies.

COUNCILLOR But Excellency, the assembly which Pflugfelder addressed was actually dispersed, so what more could one ask.

FLINT But at what stage? Only after Pflugfelder had attacked the archbishop for transferring the priest who spoke up for Bernhardi to somewhere near the Polish border.

COUNCILLOR Yes, of course archbishops enjoy greater government protection than do ministers.

FLINT Bernhardi affair indeed! People don't seem able to let the matter rest. An absolutely perfidious article appeared again in 'Labour' recently—your favourite paper, Councillor.

COUNCILLOR It wasn't badly written. But I don't have a favourite paper. I am against all newspapers.

FLINT I'm beginning to be that way myself! And now the liberal papers, having so far shown restraint, are starting to portray Bernhardi as a martyr, a political victim of clerical intrigue, a sort of medical Dreyfus.* Have you read the article in today's 'Latest News'? A formal salute to celebrate his release from prison. That's really a bit much.

COUNCILLOR At least Bernhardi is innocent on that score.

FLINT Not altogether. He's clearly enjoying his celebrity. You also know of course that only three weeks into his sentence he was encouraged to submit a plea for clemency to his Majesty, which probably would not have been refused, since you were the one who kindly undertook that little mission.

COUNCILLOR As your Excellency knows, I did go and have a talk to him. But I was actually quite pleased when he wouldn't hear of asking for clemency.

FLINT Well, it would be unfortunate if he allowed friends to embroil him further in an affair in which he must always draw the shorter straw. Because I am not at all disposed—and the Minister of Justice, whom I spoke to yesterday, is completely in agreement—to continue turning a blind eye to certain practices. We have a case, and are determined if necessary to take legal action, whatever the consequences might be. And if that did become necessary, I would be sorry for Bernhardi's sake. Because however unwisely he has behaved so far, and however much anguish he has caused me here—(*indicating his heart*) I still feel a certain fondness for him. One never quite gets rid of that sort of thing, apparently.

COUNCILLOR Yes, youthful friendship—

FLINT That's it, certainly. But men in my position need to be completely free of such sentimental bonds. After all, what has the fact that we were interns under Rappenweiler fifty years ago got to do with the whole business? Or that we walked in the gardens of the hospital together and confided our future plans to one another? In our position, one should have no memories and possibly no heart; we might have to step over corpses, Councillor—there's no denying that.

> *Servant enters, bringing a card.*

COUNCILLOR Professor Ebenwald.

FLINT Show him in.

> *Servant exit.*

FLINT How much did you say we could request for the Elisabethinum?

COUNCILLOR Three thousand.—

> *Ebenwald enters.*
> *Ebenwald, Flint, Councillor.*
> *Ebenwald bows.*

FLINT Good morning, my dear Professor, or Director rather.

EBENWALD Not yet, Excellency, only acting. It is by no means impossible that Professor Bernhardi will be reinstated in the next few days. After all, he has only been suspended.

COUNCILLOR There might be a hitch over his reinstatement. For as things stand at the moment, Bernhardi is neither a professor nor a doctor.

EBENWALD Well, there is little doubt that he will be indulgently treated as regards the legal consequences of his conviction. Thanks to the efforts of a few friends and of a certain newspaper, the public mood seems to be swinging. Your Excellency will probably also have heard that he has just been released from prison and escorted home in triumph.

FLINT What?

EBENWALD Yes, my students told me.

FLINT In triumph, what does that mean?

EBENWALD Well, apparently a number of students greeted him with cheers outside the prison gates.

FLINT The only thing missing now is a torchlight procession.

COUNCILLOR Perhaps your Excellency would like me to order—

EBENWALD If I might be permitted to observe, I think it very probable these demonstrations have something to do with the results of yesterday's elections.

FLINT Do you think so? It's quite possible. Well, there you are you see, Councillor, one should never underestimate such things. Not that I wish to attribute any special importance to this demonstration. They were probably Zionists.

EBENWALD But now they are also beginning to gain power here.

FLINT Oh well.—(*changing the subject*) You've come about the question of a subsidy, my dear Professor?

EBENWALD Indeed, your Excellency.

FLINT We will only be able to put a portion of the sum you've been expecting at your disposal. But at the same time, I am in a position to inform you that nationalization of your institute is being seriously considered.

EBENWALD Your Excellency knows as well as I do, how long the road is regrettably between serious consideration and decisive action.

FLINT Very true, my dear Professor. But you mustn't forget that here we have to deal not just with the Elisabethinum, and not just with the Faculty of Medicine, but with the whole vast field of Education and Concor—Education and Culture.

EBENWALD And we at the Elisabethinum have dared to hope that, since your Excellency started out in our profession and has graced our faculty as an academic teacher, you might foster the very branch of medical education that was so sorely neglected under the previous minister.

FLINT (*to the Councillor*) This man knows how to exploit my weaknesses. My dear Professor, I have not forgotten that I am a doctor and a teacher. The fact is, one can give up being anything else, but being a doctor—never. And I'll tell you something else, Professor,—but don't disclose it, because it would be used in Parliament against me,—I sometimes have a sort of nostalgia for the laboratory and sick-ward. It is more tranquil and attractive work, believe you me. And when one achieves something, it gets noticed. An occupation like ours, that of a politician I mean, where results sometimes only become apparent to later generations—

Servant again brings in a card.

COUNCILLOR Professor Tugendvetter.

FLINT I'll let you see to him, Councillor. This way, Professor—

Flint, Ebenwald and Servant exeunt.

Tugendvetter, Councillor.

TUGENDVETTER Good morning, Councillor. I won't keep you long. When accompanied by lively conversation, work flows merrily along*—what? Well then, you'll permit me to enquire again how that little business of mine is coming on.

COUNCILLOR Very propitiously, Professor.

TUGENDVETTER I need hardly tell you, Councillor, titles don't mean much to me personally. But you know what women are, Councillor.—

COUNCILLOR How would I know that, Professor?

TUGENDVETTER Ah yes. I am lonely, but not alone*—what? Well, we are in private here. You see, my wife is driving herself mad over this councillor title business. She simply can't wait any longer. So if it were possible to arrange the nomination before the first of June— that is my wife's birthday, you see. I would like to present her with my Councillor's title as a birthday present.

COUNCILLOR Certainly a practical and inexpensive birthday gift.

TUGENDVETTER So if you were able to do anything to speed things up, Councillor—

COUNCILLOR (*in the officious language of bureaucracy*) The Minister of Education is unfortunately not in a position to take personal relationships, in particular the domestic circumstances of the Professor, into special consideration when bestowing titles, in as much as this has not been warranted by any special provision.

Servant brings a card.

COUNCILLOR (*astonished*) Ah.

SERVANT The gentleman wishes to speak to his Excellency personally.

COUNCILLOR There will certainly be no objection, but I would very much appreciate welcoming the Professor in my office beforehand.

TUGENDVETTER I must be going.

COUNCILLOR It's an old acquaintance of yours.

Bernhardi enters. Servant exit.

Councillor, Tugendvetter, Bernhardi.

Tugendvetter rather taken aback.

BERNHARDI Oh, you are not alone, Councillor.

TUGENDVETTER Bernhardi!

COUNCILLOR (*shaking him warmly by the hand*) I am very pleased to see you again, Professor.

BERNHARDI Very good to see you too.

TUGENDVETTER Greetings, Bernhardi. (*Holds out his hand*)

BERNHARDI (*takes it coolly*) Isn't his Excellency available yet?

COUNCILLOR He will not be long. Won't you have a seat, Professor?

TUGENDVETTER My dear fellow—you look splendid. I—I—well do you know, I had totally forgotten,—how long have you been—

COUNCILLOR (to Bernhardi) I have yet to congratulate you on the ovations you received this morning.

TUGENDVETTER Ova—

BERNHARDI Ah, you've heard already. But ovation is surely rather an inflated term.

COUNCILLOR There is even talk of a torchlight procession past your window,—of serenading by the Brigittenau Association of Freethinkers.

TUGENDVETTER Do you know, my dear Bernhardi, I had totally forgotten that your prison sentence ends today. Incredible how quickly two months pass.

BERNHARDI Especially in the open air.

TUGENDVETTER But you really look quite radiant. Isn't that true, Councillor? He couldn't look better if he'd been on the Riviera. Positively invigorated.

COUNCILLOR If you felt equal to a little blasphemy, Professor, I could guarantee you an equally cheap holiday.

TUGENDVETTER (laughing) Very kind of you.

BERNHARDI Actually, I did not have too bad a time of it at all. There was an angel watching over me: the guilty conscience of the people who put me behind bars.

TUGENDVETTER I am pleased to have this opportunity to tell you that my sympathies have been unwaveringly on your side in this affair.

BERNHARDI So you've now found an opportunity at last? I'm pleased to hear it.

TUGENDVETTER I hope you've never doubted that I—

BERNHARDI Would it be possible to let his Excellency know I'm here? The matter is quite urgent.

COUNCILLOR I'm sure his Excellency won't be very long now.

TUGENDVETTER Do you know what I heard recently? That you intend to write a history of the entire affair.

BERNHARDI So, that's what they say?

COUNCILLOR It would make an interesting book. You have had an opportunity to study your fellow human beings.

BERNHARDI In fact, Councillor, one found one knew most of it already. And perhaps it's not surprising that people behave shabbily toward those they dislike, or to gain some personal advantage. But one type has always remained something of a riddle to me—

TUGENDVETTER Namely?

BERNHARDI The sort who are one might say disinterestedly malicious. People who behave maliciously without its being in the least to their advantage, merely for the joy of it.

Flint and Ebenwald enter.

Tugendvetter, Councillor, Bernhardi, Flint, Ebenwald.

FLINT (*quickly adjusting*) Oh Bernhardi!

EBENWALD (*also adjusting*) Good day, Professor.

BERNHARDI Good day. You're doubtless here on behalf of the Elisabethinum, Professor?

EBENWALD Indeed.

FLINT It is about that subsidy.—

BERNHARDI I always believed the interests of my project would be in good hands—during my absence.

EBENWALD Thank you for the kind acknowledgement, Professor.

FLINT (*to Bernhardi*) You wanted to speak to me, Bernhardi?

BERNHARDI I won't take up too much of your time.

COUNCILLOR (*to Ebenwald and Tugendvetter*) Perhaps you gentlemen would like to come this way.—(*Exit with the other two*)

Bernhardi, Flint.

FLINT (*taking the plunge*) I would like to take this opportunity, my dear Bernhardi, to congratulate you on your release from prison. Unfortunately in my official position I wasn't able to find an appropriate way to let you know how painfully surprised I was at the outcome of your trial;—but now that the affair has been resolved, I shall be all the more pleased to be of service in whatever way I can.

BERNHARDI That is very good of you, my dear Flint. As a matter of fact, I have come to ask a favour.

FLINT I'm listening.

BERNHARDI The situation is this: Prince Constantine is seriously ill and has sent for me.

FLINT Really?—But I didn't know—

BERNHARDI Sent for me as a doctor. He wants me to resume responsibility for treating him.

FLINT Well then, what's preventing you?

BERNHARDI What is preventing me? I don't want to find myself guilty of another offence.

FLINT An offence?

BERNHARDI Of course you know. If I were to resume treatment of Prince Constantine, I would be practising without a licence.

Because I allowed myself to get carried away and offend against religion, I have been deprived of my medical degree, and with it the right to practise as a doctor. And so I've taken the liberty of coming personally to hand you my petition for clemency as regards the legal consequences of my conviction. I have come to you, my old friend, because as has become evident from other cases, you are in a position to exert some influence on the decisions of the Minister of Justice; and I would also ask you as far as practical to expedite the matter, so that if my petition should be granted, the Prince will not be kept waiting too long.

FLINT I see, I see. You've come to make fun of me.

BERNHARDI In what way? I am simply going by the book. I have absolutely no desire to do time again, even though I was relatively well treated. So, if you would be good enough—(*hands him the petition*)

FLINT Granted. I'll take the responsibility. Now there's no reason why you should not respond to Prince Constantine's call at once. I give you my word, you will not have to face any consequences of a criminally indictable nature. Is that good enough?

BERNHARDI It ought to be good enough this time, since keeping your word should not in this case entail any unpleasantness for you.

FLINT Bernhardi!

BERNHARDI Excellency?

FLINT (*quickly recovering*) You can't say that I don't know you now, Bernhardi! Didn't I sense immediately that you hadn't come on Prince Constantine's behalf? Well, so be it. Let's talk about the matter you allude to. I wasn't going to let it pass in any case. So you accuse me of breaking my word?

BERNHARDI I do indeed, my dear Flint.

FLINT And do you want to know my answer? Well then, I never broke my word to you. I never promised you anything more than to intercede on your behalf. And there was no better way I could have done it than by striving for and enforcing procedural clarity as regards your case. Furthermore: supposing I had 'broken my word', as you call it, it would be stupid to reproach me because, even if I'd kept my word you were already doomed. A private complaint had already been lodged against you, and the inquiry into your conduct could no longer be prevented. If only you could finally grasp that in political life there is something higher than keeping one's word, as you call it. And that is: keeping one's goal in mind, not letting oneself be distracted from one's task. Never have

I felt this more deeply than at that memorable moment when, just as I was on the point of championing your cause, I sensed all the displeasure, mistrust and bitterness of Parliament bearing down upon me, and yet through a lucky turn of phrase was able to assuage the gathering storm.

BERNHARDI 'Turn' sounds like the operative word.

FLINT My excellent Bernhardi, the only choice I had, as I recognized at the time in a flash, was either to plunge into the abyss with you, and so to commit a crime against myself, my mission, and the state needing my services, or—to sacrifice a person who in any case was doomed; but then to be in a position to build new scientific institutes, to redesign the curriculum of various faculties in ways more in keeping with the modern spirit, to raise the people's health and to carry through reforms in numerous areas of our intellectual life, or at least to prepare the way for them, for all of which, as you yourself will one day admit, two months of not especially onerous incarceration ought not to be too high a price to pay. Because I hope you don't imagine your martyrdom has particularly impressed me. Now if it had been in the cause of something great—an idea, the fatherland, your faith—that you'd put up with these indignities, which anyway have since been compensated for by various small triumphs, then I might have felt some respect for you. But as it is I can see nothing in your whole behaviour,—as an old friend I may say this to you—but a tragicomedy of stubbornness, and furthermore I doubt you would have acted with the same resolve if people in Austria today were still burned at the stake.

Bernhardi looks at him for a while, then begins to clap.

FLINT What's got into you?

BERNHARDI I thought you might miss it.

FLINT Have you no better answer than that rather feeble joke?

BERNHARDI You know as well as I do what answer to expect; and besides—as an old friend I may say this to you—I'm sure you'd put it much more eloquently than I could. So what would be the sense in answering you in private?

FLINT I see. That's it. Well, don't imagine that the Ministry is unaware of your intentions. But I can't help asking myself what prompted you under the circumstances to do me the honour of a personal visit? Because it wasn't on Prince Constantine's behalf—

BERNHARDI Perhaps I was a little too inquisitive, my dear fellow. It's perfectly understandable that I should be interested in what you had to say about your behaviour towards me. And this conversation between his Excellency and the released convict could provide a very effective final chapter to a book I have in mind, if writing it were worth the trouble.

FLINT Oh, I hope you won't be deterred. It could even double as your candidature speech.

BERNHARDI Candidature?

FLINT Oh, I'm sure it's only a matter of days before they offer you the nomination.

BERNHARDI My dear Flint, I shall continue to leave politics entirely to you.

FLINT Politics! Politics! If only you would all stop bothering me about it. To hell with all your politics. I accepted the portfolio because I knew there's no one else who can do what needs to be done in Austria today. But even if I am perhaps destined to usher in a new epoch, these few ministerial years—or maybe months—will remain no more than an episode in my existence. I have always known that and feel it more strongly by the day. I am a doctor, a teacher, I yearn for patients, students.—

The Councillor enters. Flint, Bernhardi.

COUNCILLOR I do apologize for interrupting, Excellency,—but I've just received an important memorandum from the Ministry of Justice,—and since it bears on the Professor's case—

BERNHARDI On mine?

COUNCILLOR Yes. Apparently Nurse Ludmilla, the crown witness in your case, has submitted a statement accusing herself of having given false testimony during your trial.

BERNHARDI Accusing herself—

FLINT What's all this about ———

COUNCILLOR Undersecretary Bermann from the Ministry of Justice will be here shortly, to give you a more detailed report in person. As to the facts, there can be no room for doubt. The nurse's statement has been tabled.

FLINT Tabled?

COUNCILLOR And you of course, Professor, will immediately ask for the case to be reopened.

BERNHARDI Reopened?

COUNCILLOR Of course.

BERNHARDI I have no intention of doing so.

FLINT Ah!

BERNHARDI What would be the point? Am I to go through the whole dishonest charade again? Now in an entirely different light? All reasonable people know that I was innocent, and no one is going to restore those two lost months to me.

FLINT Those two months! Those two months again! As though that were the point. Higher values are at stake here, Bernhardi. You have no sense of justice.

BERNHARDI Evidently.

FLINT Do you have any further information, Councillor?

COUNCILLOR Not much. The strangest thing about the case, according to the Undersecretary over the phone, is that Nurse Ludmilla, as she herself attests in her own statement, first admitted her false testimony in the confessional, and it was her father confessor who enjoined her to make whatever amends she could for so grave a sin.

FLINT Her father confessor?

COUNCILLOR Evidently he had no idea what it was all about.

FLINT How so? How do you know all this?

BERNHARDI So now I'm supposed to appear in court again? Well, I'm ready, and I shall file a complaint testifying that Sister Ludmilla is profoundly hysterical and of unsound mind.

FLINT That would be just like you.

BERNHARDI What good would it do me, if this person were retroactively locked up.——

COUNCILLOR But that could still happen to someone else involved in the case. There's a gentleman by the name of Hochroitzpointner, for whom things may go badly, especially as fate is threatening him from another quarter too.

BERNHARDI In this case fate must surely be called Kurt Pflugfelder?

COUNCILLOR I believe so.

FLINT You are remarkably well informed, Councillor.

COUNCILLOR My duty, Excellency.

BERNHARDI That wretched fellow is really not worth wasting time over. How our good Kurt, who has better things to do, can be bothered—

FLINT (who has been pacing to and fro) In the confessional.—That will certainly leave some good people flabbergasted. Perhaps it will transpire that these Catholic customs may sometimes even benefit those who belong to other faiths.

BERNHARDI I for one am willing to forgo such benefits. I want to be left in peace!

COUNCILLOR One can't assume, Professor, that further developments in the case will entirely depend on you. Things will take their course, even without you.

BERNHARDI They will have no choice.

FLINT Allow me to point out, Bernhardi, that it is not simply a matter of your convenience in this case. And it would make rather an odd impression if, now that you've been shown the correct course you should take to obtain justice, you were to embark on a different and perhaps less worthy one, allowing yourself to become involved with all sorts of undesirables, reporters and the like—

BERNHARDI I don't intend to embark on any path at all. I've had enough. For me this whole affair is closed.

FLINT Come, come.

BERNHARDI Completely closed.

FLINT Why so sudden? I seem to remember some talk about your wanting to write a pamphlet, or even a book about the case. Wasn't that the story, Councillor—

BERNHARDI I now see that it is no longer necessary.—And if it should come to a second trial, they already have my statement from the first one, I have nothing more to add. I will forgo subpoenaing the Minister.

FLINT I see. But you won't be able to do very much about it, if I should decide that the right thing to do is to appear in court. People will understand, even you, Bernhardi, will eventually have to understand, that from the outset all my actions have tended toward generating greater clarity. The first trial was a necessary evil;—how else could we have reached the second, which will at last bring total clarity. So it might be as well not to light one's powder too soon, my dear Bernhardi. (*Points to his breast pocket*)

BERNHARDI What's that?

FLINT A letter, my dear fellow. A particular letter, which may yet serve its purpose in the battle that lies ahead. Your letter!

BERNHARDI Ah, my letter. I thought perhaps it might have been— your article.

FLINT What article—

BERNHARDI You know, the famous one from your days as an intern— 'Places of Worship—Places of Healing'—

FLINT I see—

Councillor a questioning expression.

FLINT Yes, my dear Councillor, an article from my—revolutionary days. If it's of any interest, I'd be happy to dig it out for you sometime and—

BERNHARDI What, it actually exists?

FLINT (*putting his hand to his brow*) Amazing how memory can play tricks on one,—of course, I never actually got round to writing it,—but who knows, perhaps I shall shortly be able to—recite it.

SERVANT (*enters*) Undersecretary Bermann would like to speak to his Excellency personally—

FLINT Ah! (*To Bernhardi*) Would you be kind enough to wait a while?

BERNHARDI Well, Prince Constantine—

FLINT Has waited two months for you already. The extra half hour shouldn't make much difference. Don't let him go, Councillor. We might need to draw up a joint plan of attack. So, Bernhardi, I hope I can ask you this small favour. (*Exit, followed by the servant*)
      Councillor, Bernhardi.

COUNCILLOR You've been called in by Prince Constantine, Professor? What, today already? That's just like him!

BERNHARDI I'll go out there and see if he can dispense with my professional services for the time being. Rather than face what now seems to be brewing, I shall take flight.

COUNCILLOR I fear you might be absent longer than would be congenial to your numerous patients. Because the whole affair is just beginning, Professor,—and it could last quite some time!

BERNHARDI Well, what am I supposed to do?

COUNCILLOR You'll get used to it. You'll even be proud of it in time.

BERNHARDI Proud? Me? You can't imagine, Councillor, how ridiculous I feel. Especially this morning,—that reception at the prison gates! And then that article in the 'Latest News'—, have you read it? I felt truly ashamed,—and all my various plans seem to have dissolved in this tepid feeling of becoming ridiculous.

COUNCILLOR Plans—? Ah, you mean—your book.

BERNHARDI Not specifically.—Though much the same thing happened to me over that, at an earlier stage in the proceedings. When I set about writing it in the quiet retirement of my cell, I was still quite furious, but as work proceeded that feeling slowly evaporated. What had started as an indictment of Flint and company, gradually became,—I scarcely know how myself—, perhaps as I reflected on a particular experience—, something more like a philosophical tract.

COUNCILLOR Your publisher will hardly be pleased about that.

BERNHARDI The issue was no longer Austrian politics, or for that matter politics at all, rather I suddenly seemed to be dealing with wider ethical matters, with responsibility and revelation and ultimately the question of free will.—

COUNCILLOR Yes, it always comes back to that eventually, once one starts delving into the root cause of things. But it's better to apply the brakes a little earlier, otherwise one discovers some fine day that one is beginning to understand and forgive everything,—and once one is no longer allowed to love and hate,—then where's the spice in life?

BERNHARDI One just has to go on loving and hating, my dear Councillor! But anyway, as you can imagine, there was not much room left in my book for his Excellency, Minister Flint. And then I decided, if he wasn't going to read what I harboured in my heart against him, at least he was going to have to listen to it.

COUNCILLOR And so that is why we have had the pleasure?

BERNHARDI Yes, I was determined to tell him to his face—well, you can imagine more or less what. Even this morning, when I woke up in prison for the very last time, this was still my firm intention. But then came the ovation and the editorial, and letters I found awaiting me at home, and all I could think of was how to confront my old friend again as soon as possible, while I could still muster enough seriousness of purpose to have our final reckoning. But when I finally found myself before him, the last trace of malice in me vanished. You should have heard him—! It was impossible to be angry with him. I almost believe I never have been.

COUNCILLOR The Minister has always been very fond of you as well, I can assure you!

BERNHARDI And now, what with this business over Nurse Ludmilla—and a retrial in prospect, well, you can understand, Councillor, that if I'm ever to recover my self-respect and find my feet again, I must escape this clamour which is breaking out around me, simply—because people are gradually realizing that I was right.

COUNCILLOR But Professor, what do you expect? No one has ever become popular by being right. That only happens when it suits some political party for one to be right. And anyway, Professor, that's just a delusion of yours.

BERNHARDI What, Councillor? Delusion that I—Did I understand correctly?

COUNCILLOR I believe so.

BERNHARDI Do you really think so, Councillor—? Perhaps you'd be good enough to explain. Should I in your opinion have allowed the priest to—

COUNCILLOR With the greatest respect, of course you should,

Professor! Because in all probability you were never born to be a reformer.

BERNHARDI Reformer—? Might I ask—

COUNCILLOR Any more than I was.—That may well be because inwardly we do not feel prepared to go to any lengths—and ultimately to risk our lives for our convictions. And that's why it's best, indeed only decent, for people like us not to get involved in such—affairs.—

BERNHARDI But—

COUNCILLOR Nothing ever comes of it. What would you have achieved ultimately, Professor, if you had spared that poor woman on her deathbed one last fright?—That seems to me just like trying to solve the social problem by giving some poor devil a present of a villa.

BERNHARDI What you forget like everyone else, my dear Councillor, is that I never had the faintest intention of trying to solve questions. I simply did what I held to be right in a specific case.

COUNCILLOR And that was where you went wrong. If one forever went round doing right, or rather, if in the morning one began by doing right, without giving it a further thought, and went on doing right throughout the day, one would undoubtedly be in prison by supper-time.

BERNHARDI And shall I tell you something, Councillor? In my situation, you would have acted just the same.

COUNCILLOR Possibly.—In which case I would have been—forgive me, Professor—just as much an ass as you.

    Curtain.

EXPLANATORY NOTES

FLIRTATIONS

2 *MIZI*: pet form of 'Marie'.

12 *Orpheum*: a music-hall, founded in 1868, in the Wasagasse in the Ninth District of Vienna.

16 *Double Eagle*: a military march composed in the 1880s by Josef Franz Wagner (1856–1908).

25 *Lehner Garden*: a park in the Fifteenth District, west of the Josefstadt (Eighth District) where the Weirings live.

33 *Kahlenberg*: a wooded hill, part of the Vienna Woods, on the north-west side of Vienna.

34 *Schiller*: Friedrich Schiller (1759–1805), whose dramas are not only classics but a standard part of the school curriculum.

Hauff: Wilhelm Hauff (1802–27), a late-Romantic writer of fairy-tales.

A Book for Everyone: an illustrated annual.

ROUND DANCE

51 *Augarten Bridge*: a bridge over the Danube Canal, north of the centre of Vienna.

53 *Prater*: a public park north-east of the centre of Vienna, with many restaurants and bars; the part called the Wurstelprater, frequented by the lower classes, had dance-halls and popular theatres.

Swoboda's: a dance-hall in the Prater.

65 *Odilon*: the actress Helene Odilon (1864–1939), whom Schnitzler knew personally; references in his diary suggest her sexual fascination.

Stendhal: this anecdote, from the section of *De l'amour* (1822) by Stendhal (pseudonym of Henri Beyle, 1783–1842) dealing with 'fiascos', runs: 'I knew a handsome lieutenant of Hussars, twenty-three years old, who, from excess of love, as I understand the matter, could do no more than kiss her and weep for joy throughout the first three nights he spent with a mistress whom he had adored for six months and who had treated him very harshly while she grieved over another lover killed in the war' (*Love*, trans. Gilbert and Suzanne Sale (London, 1957), 180). Since in Stendhal only the man weeps, the Young Wife is right to be sceptical of the Young Master's version.

74 *venture forth into the hostile world*: quotation from the very popular poem by Schiller, 'Das Lied von der Glocke' ('The Song of the Bell', 1800).

75 *Riedhof*: restaurant in the Eighth District, well known for its *chambres particulières* or *chambres séparées* where illicit couples could spend the evening privately.

84 *Weidling*: a village in the Vienna Woods.

88 *Cavalleria Rusticana*: opera (1890) by Pietro Mascagni (1863–1945).

99 *puszta*: the Hungarian plain.

Steinamanger: German name for Szombathely, town in western Hungary.

THE GREEN COCKATOO

111 *Palais Royal*: a place of public entertainment, where political agitators met during the French Revolution.

Camille Desmoulins: a French Revolutionary leader and journalist (1760–94).

112 *Cerutti*: a prominent Revolutionary journalist.

141 *Delaunay*: governor of the Bastille, killed when it was taken by a mass attack on 14 July 1789.

THE LAST MASKS

147 *I mean to take a long sleep soon*: quotation from Schiller's play *Wallenstein's Death* (1800), uttered by Wallenstein, with unwitting dramatic irony, shortly before his assassination.

Olmütz: important provincial town, now Olomouc in the Czech Republic.

149 *And so farewell, thou silent house!*: first line of a well-known song in the Viennese popular comedy *Der Alpenkönig und der Menschenfeind* (*The Spirit of the Alps and the Misanthropist*, 1828) by Ferdinand Raimund (1790–1836).

158 *Abbazia*: holiday resort on the Adriatic; now Opatija in Croatia.

159 *Concordia*: a society for writers and journalists.

COUNTESS MIZZI

165 *Mauer and Rodaun*: areas on the south-western side of Vienna, now in the Twenty-Third District.

168 *Meyerhofgasse*: in the Fourth District.

170 *Ursulines*: an order of nuns founded in 1535 by St Angela of Merici to educate young girls.

172 *Krems*: a town up the Danube from Vienna.

173 *Wiesinger-Florian*: Olga Wisinger-Florian (1844–1926), a painter of flowers and landscapes.

185 *Ottakring*: a working-class district of Vienna.

THE VAST DOMAIN

196 *naval midshipman*: it must be remembered that the Austro-Hungarian Empire included a long stretch of coast on the Adriatic and had a large navy, with its main base at Pola (now Pula).

Demeter Stanzides: this character appears also in Schnitzler's novel *The Road to the Open* (1908), as 'the perfect embodiment of world-weary acquiescence in social convention' (Martin Swales, *Arthur Schnitzler: A Critical Study* (Oxford, 1971), 34).

Baden: a town some 15 kilometres from Vienna, whose warm springs have made it a popular spa.

Lake Völs: Völs is the name of two villages, one just north of Atzwang on the road between the present Chiusa and Bolzano in the Italian Alps (formerly Klausen and Bozen in the Austrian South Tyrol), and the other higher up, south-west of Siusi (formerly Seis); the hotel is by a lake at the higher village, providing a base for climbers.

200 *Imperial*: famous hotel on the Kärntner Ring in Vienna.

205 *North German Lloyd*: Norddeutscher Lloyd, a steamship line.

206 *freedom fighters*: the original is 'Irredentisten', i.e. irredentists who wish the Italian-speaking South Tyrol to be transferred from Austria to Italy.

208 *Proudhon*: Pierre Joseph Proudhon (1809–65), French socialist thinker.

221 *Toblach*: in Tyrol; the Falzarego Pass leads from Cortina di Ampezzo to Caprile.

235 *Heiligenkreuz*: village near Baden with a fine Romanesque church.

238 *Halle*: university town in Thuringia; Rosenstock shares the widespread Austrian antipathy to people from northern Germany.

239 *Semmering Hotel*: a famous hotel at an altitude of 1,000 metres where the road and railway south from Vienna cross the mountains leading into Styria.

241 *swift is Death's approach to man*: from Schiller's *Wilhelm Tell* (1804), end of Act IV.

243 *Lord Chamberlain*: a confused reference to Joseph Chamberlain (1836–1914), British statesman.

Bülow: Bernhard von Bülow (1849–1929), Chancellor of Germany from 1900 to 1909.

253 *poet*: most likely the early Greek philosopher Heraclitus, one of whose fragments runs: 'You would not find out the boundaries of [the] soul,

even by travelling along every path: so deep a measure does it have' (*The Presocratic Philosophers*, ed. G. S. Kirk, J. E. Raven, and M. Schofield, 2nd edn. (Cambridge, 1983), 203).

263 *American duel*: determined not by weapons but by drawing lots; the loser was obliged to commit suicide. Friedrich is supposed to have rigged the duel.

PROFESSOR BERNHARDI

290 *Dr Schreimann*: since 'Schrei' means 'scream', making him a throat specialist is a little joke.

295 *Rejoicing in Israel*: when alone with Hochroitzpointner, Ebenwald makes no secret of his anti-Semitism.

    sick prince: the original ('zu einem ang'steckten Fürsten') implies that Bernhardi treats noblemen who have caught venereal infections.

    Riedhof: see note to p. 75.

297 *stockbroker*: in making Tugendvetter, who is obviously not a Jew, look like a financier, Schnitzler is working against anti-Semitic stereotypes.

298 *Last Days of Pompeii*: novel (1834) by Edward Bulwer Lytton (1803–73).

    Ipsissima verba: his very words.

    as proud as a Spaniard: Tugendvetter, who constantly uses stale quotations, is here slightly misquoting from Schiller's *Don Carlos* (1787), Act III, scene 10.

299 *You'll also require . . . pedant*: quoted from Goethe's *Faust Part One*, line 1716.

304 *Heschel*: Richard Heschel (1824–81), professor of pathological anatomy at the Vienna Medical School from 1875 until his death.

    Brücke: Ernst Brücke (1819–92), a distinguished scientist, trained in Berlin, who was professor of physiology in Vienna from 1849 to 1890; his pupils included Freud.

305 *Skoda*: Joseph Skoda (1805–81), professor of internal medicine at Vienna from 1847 on.

    nomina sunt odiosa: names are hateful, i.e. don't let's mention the name.

309 *you know damn well what you do*: one of Bernhardi's numerous allusions to the New Testament, parodying Luke 23: 34: 'And Jesus said, Father, forgive them; for they know not what they do.'

310 *Aesculapius*: Greek god of medicine.

    Baden: the resort near Vienna where much of *The Vast Domain* is set, and where the Prince is no doubt taking the waters.

311 *Oberhollabrunn*: small town in Lower Austria, north of Vienna.

313 *Feuerstein*: Filitz (deliberately?) substitutes a more obviously Jewish name.

327 *sine ira et studio*: calmly.

338 *Empress Elisabeth*: Elisabeth Amalia Eugenia, Duchess of Bavaria (1837–98), married the young Emperor of Austria, Franz Joseph, in 1853; her marriage was unhappy, two of her children died (one, the Crown Prince Rudolf, by suicide in 1889), and she spent much time travelling. She was stabbed in Geneva by an anarchist. To name the clinic after her is both loyal and unpropitious.

German voice: Schnitzler uses the unusual expression 'Bierdeutsch' ('beer-German'), implying heavy conviviality. The *Jewish inflexions* may be explained by Schnitzler's diary entry on first hearing his voice recorded: 'the decidedly nasal, Jewish character of my voice' (19 March 1907). Cf. Dr Goldenthal's voice, 'a little unctuous and nasal' (p. 363).

S. Wenger: an obviously Jewish name such as Samuel was sometimes hidden by the use of an initial: cf. 'M. Blüthenzweig' in Thomas Mann's story 'Gladius Dei' (1901).

Siegfried: assimilated Jews sometimes adopted such ultra-German, Wagnerian names; cf. the twins Siegmund and Sieglinde in Thomas Mann's story 'The Blood of the Volsungs' (written 1905).

341 *'Watch on the Rhine'*: German patriotic song, composed by Max Schneckenburger (1818–49) in 1840, and increasingly popular during and after the Franco-Prussian War (1870–1).

Bismarck oaks: oaks planted by German patriots in honour of the Chancellor Otto von Bismarck (1815–98), the architect of German unification.

Waidhofen resolution: a resolution agreed in 1896 by German nationalist student societies in Austria that Jews were unworthy to duel with Gentiles. Schnitzler refers to this resolution with great indignation in his memoirs.

343 *Benjamin*: the youngest member (from the youngest of Jacob's twelve sons in the Book of Genesis).

345 *forty-eighter*: someone still loyal to the liberal ideals of the unsuccessful 1848 revolutions.

356 *Dixi*: I have spoken.

358 *He who is not for me is against me*: quoting Matthew 12: 30.

362 *Kalksburg*: a private school run by Jesuits.

365 *A merry company, I see*: a quotation from Schiller's *Wallenstein's Camp* (1800); ironically, the original speaker is a fanatical Capuchin monk.

366 *A sinner . . . righteous*: Luke 15: 7.

379 *Frederick the Great*: (1712–86), King of Prussia 1740–86, made this declaration of religious toleration in a letter of June 1740.

386 *Concordat*: an agreement between the Catholic Church and a civil power; such an agreement, confirming the autonomy of the Church in the Austro-Hungarian Empire, allowing it to supervise all education of Catholic children, declaring Church property inviolable, and forbidding any utterance disparaging of the Church, was signed in 1855, but repudiated in 1870 after the Church adopted the dogma of papal infallibility.

387 *Dreyfus*: Captain Alfred Dreyfus (1859–1935), a Jewish officer on the French General Staff, was charged in 1894 with selling military secrets to Germany, court-martialled, and sent to Devil's Island; although new evidence exonerated him, he was retried, reconvicted, but immediately pardoned; the resulting controversy divided France.

390 *lively conversation... along*: a quotation from Schiller's 'The Song of the Bell'.

I am lonely, but not alone: a quotation from the musical drama *Preciosa* (1821), text by Pius Alexander Wolff, music by Carl Maria von Weber (1786–1826).

The Oxford World's Classics Website

www.worldsclassics.co.uk

- Information about new titles
- Explore the full range of Oxford World's Classics
- Links to other literary sites and the main OUP webpage
- Imaginative competitions, with bookish prizes
- Peruse the Oxford World's Classics Magazine
- Articles by editors
- Extracts from Introductions
- A forum for discussion and feedback on the series
- Special information for teachers and lecturers

www.worldsclassics.co.uk

American Literature

British and Irish Literature

Children's Literature

Classics and Ancient Literature

Colonial Literature

Eastern Literature

European Literature

History

Medieval Literature

Oxford English Drama

Poetry

Philosophy

Politics

Religion

The Oxford Shakespeare

A complete list of Oxford Paperbacks, including Oxford World's Classics, Oxford Shakespeare, Oxford Drama, and Oxford Paperback Reference, is available in the UK from the Academic Division Publicity Department, Oxford University Press, Great Clarendon Street, Oxford OX2 6DP.

In the USA, complete lists are available from the Paperbacks Marketing Manager, Oxford University Press, 198 Madison Avenue, New York, NY 10016.

Oxford Paperbacks are available from all good bookshops. In case of difficulty, customers in the UK can order direct from Oxford University Press Bookshop, Freepost, 116 High Street, Oxford OX1 4BR, enclosing full payment. Please add 10 per cent of published price for postage and packing.